W9-CNQ-763

Taking SIDES

Clashing Views on Controversial Economic Issues

Ninth Edition

Taking

SIDES

Clashing Views on Controversial Economic Issues

Ninth Edition

Edited, Selected, and with Introductions by

Thomas R. Swartz
University of Notre Dame

and

Frank J. Bonello
University of Notre Dame

Dushkin/McGraw-Hill
A Division of The McGraw-Hill Companies

This book is dedicated to the thousands of students who have persevered in the "Bonello/Swartz (B.S.)" introductory economics course sequence at the University of Notre Dame. It is also dedicated to our children and grandchildren. In order of their birth dates they are Mary Elizabeth, Karen Ann, Jennifer Lynne, John Anthony, Anne Marie, Rebecca Jourdan, David Joseph, Stephen Thomas, Chelsea Margaret, Kevin Joseph, Meghan Claire, Maureen Keating, Michael Thomas, Thomas Jourdan, and Amanda Marie.

Photo Acknowledgments

Cover image: © 2000 by PhotoDisc, Inc.

Cover Art Acknowledgment

Charles Vitelli

Library of Congress Cataloging-in-Publication Data

Main entry under title:
    Taking sides: clashing views on controversial economic issues/edited, selected, and with introductions by Thomas R. Swartz and Frank J. Bonello.—9th ed.
    Includes bibliographical references and index.
    1. United States—Economic policy—1971–1981. 2. United States—Economic policy—1981–1993. 3. United States—Economic policy—1993–. I. Swartz, Thomas R., *comp.* II. Bonello, Frank J., *comp.*

338.9'22

0-07-232739-1   ISSN: 1094-7612

Printed on Recycled Paper

PREFACE

Where there is much desire to learn, there of necessity will be much arguing.

—John Milton (1608–1674), English poet and essayist

Presented here are 18 debates on important and compelling economic issues, which are designed to stimulate critical thinking skills and initiate lively and informed discussion. These debates take economic theory and show how it is applied to current, real-world public policy decisions, the outcomes of which will have an immediate and personal impact. How these debates are resolved will affect our taxes, jobs, wages, environment, and so on; in short, they will shape the world in which we live.

It has been our intent throughout each of the nine editions of *Taking Sides: Clashing Views on Controversial Economic Issues* to select issues that reveal something about the nature of economics itself and something about how it relates to current, everyday newspaper headlines and television news stories on public policy issues that deal with economic considerations (and almost all do these days). To assist the reader, we begin each issue with an *issue introduction,* which sets the stage for the debate as it is argued in the "yes" and "no" selections. Each issue concludes with a *postscript* that briefly reviews the arguments and makes some final observations. The introduction and postscript do not preempt what is the reader's own task: to achieve a critical and informed view of the economic issue at stake. Certainly, the reader should not feel confined to adopt one or the other of the positions presented. The views presented should be used as starting points, and the suggestions for further reading that appear in each issue postscript offer additional resources on the topic. Internet site addresses (URLs) have been provided at the beginning of each part, which should also prove useful as resources for further research. At the back of the book is a listing of all the *contributors to this volume,* which provides information on the economists, policymakers, political leaders, and commentators whose views are debated here.

Changes to this edition   This new edition of *Taking Sides* represents a considerable revision to this book. Sixteen of the 36 selections and 7 of the 18 issues are new. Thus, as we enter the twenty-first century, this heavily revised book will help us to understand the implication of a changing set of economic issues that were not part of our world just a few years ago. The new issues are *Is There Discrimination in U.S. Labor Markets?* (Issue 4); *Is the Department of Justice Being Too Hard on Microsoft?* (Issue 5); *Do Private Prisons Pay?* (Issue 7); *Is Deflation Coming?* (Issue 8); *Does the Consumer Price Index Suffer from Quality and New Product Bias?* (Issue 10); *Should Federal Government Budget Surpluses Be Used to Reduce Taxes?* (Issue 11); and *Is Free Trade a Viable Option for the*

New Millennium? (Issue 14). For Issue 18, on the North American Free Trade Agreement, the issue question has been retained but both selections have been replaced to bring a fresh perspective to the debate.

As with all of the previous editions, the issues in the ninth edition can be used in any sequence. Although the general organization of the book loosely parallels the sequence of topics found in a standard introductory economics textbook, you can pick and choose which issues to read first, since they are designed to stand alone. Note that we have retained the modification to Part 3 introduced in the seventh edition. That part, "The World Around Us," allows us to more fully represent the host of problems our society faces in this ever-changing world we live in.

A word to the instructor An *Instructor's Manual With Test Questions* (multiple-choice and essay) is available through the publisher. A general guidebook, *Using Taking Sides in the Classroom,* which discusses methods and techniques for integrating the pro-con approach into any classroom setting, is also available. An online version of *Using Taking Sides in the Classroom* and a correspondence service for *Taking Sides* adopters can be found at http://www.dushkin.com/usingts/. For students, we offer a field guide to analyzing argumentative essays, *Analyzing Controversy: An Introductory Guide,* with exercises and techniques to help them to decipher genuine controversies.

Taking Sides: Clashing Views on Controversial Economic Issues is only one title in the Taking Sides series. If you are interested in seeing the table of contents for any of the other titles, please visit the Taking Sides Web site at http://www.dushkin.com/takingsides/.

Acknowledgments We have received many helpful comments and suggestions from our friends and readers across the United States and Canada. As always, their suggestions were very welcome and have markedly enhanced the quality of this edition of *Taking Sides.* If as you read this book you are reminded of an essay that could be included in a future edition, we hope that you will drop us a note. We very much appreciate your interest and help, and we are always pleased to hear from you.

Our special thanks go to those who responded with suggestions for the ninth edition:

Tony Barret
College of St. Scholastica

Robert Brownlee
Centre College of
 Kentucky

Joan Buccino
Florida Southern College

Glenn Clayman
Columbus State Community
 College

Nirmalendu Debnath
Lane College

Demetrios Giannaros
University of Hartford

Stephen Jones
College of the Ozarks

Nazma Latif-Zaman
Providence College

Brian McKenna
St. Xavier University

Joe Mullin
Columbus State Community
   College

Reuben Slesinger
University of
   Pittsburgh–Pittsburgh

Harlan Smith
University of Minnesota at
   Minneapolis

Kimberly Smith
St. Francis College

Michael H. Truscott
University of Tampa

We also offer our very special thanks to James (Jim) P. Conboy, Jr.—CEO of Conboy Enterprises—who has helped us repeatedly to keep sight of how the "real world" actually works. Additionally, we are most appreciative of the encouragement and the effort that Theodore Knight, list manager of the Taking Sides and Sources series at Dushkin/McGraw-Hill, has expended on our behalf in expediting this edition of Taking Sides. The one soul who has suffered most in the preparation of this manuscript was Cheryl Reed, who had to read and transcript Swartz's tortured handwriting. Finally, we want to thank our graduate assistant here at the University of Notre Dame, Jennifer Kelly. She always maintained a smile even when our requests to run to the library were outrageous.

To all those mentioned above, we owe a huge debt, many thanks, and none of the blame for any shortcomings that remain in this edition of *Taking Sides*.

Thomas R. Swartz
University of Notre Dame

Frank J. Bonello
University of Notre Dame

CONTENTS IN BRIEF

CONTENTS

Professor of economics William A. Darity, Jr., and associate professor of economics Patrick L. Mason assert that the lack of progress made since the mid-1970s toward establishing equality in wages between the races is evidence of persistent discrimination in U.S. labor markets. Professor of economics James J. Heckman argues that markets—driven by the profit motive of employers—will compete away any wage differentials that are not justified by differences in human capital.

Antitrust critic Adam D. Thierer, an Economic Policy Fellow of the Heritage Foundation, charges the U.S. Department of Justice with conducting a vendetta against one of America's most successful companies. Social critic and author Richard Wolffe argues that Microsoft and Bill Gates have "masterminded a conspiracy" to kill off rivals and establish "control over 90 percent of the world's computers."

Physician Paul M. Ellwood, Jr., and editor George D. Lundberg argue that we cannot return to fee-for-service medicine. Professors John H. McArthur and Francis D. Moore warn that managed care will ensure primarily the profitability of the corporation.

Social critic and policy analyst Adrian T. Moore maintains that there is extensive evidence to suggest that private sector prisons provide quality correctional services at a lower cost to taxpayers. Columnist Eric Bates contends that "privatizing prisons is really about privatizing tax dollars [and] about transforming public money into private profits."

Charles W. McMillion, president of MBG Information Services, asserts that a sharp decline in consumer spending is very possible and that this will intensify the deflationary pressures that already exist in the U.S. economy. Professor of economics Martin Feldstein and Kathleen Feldstein, president of Economic Studies, Inc., argue that deflation is unlikely because the forces that have put downward pressure on prices have abated.

Robert M. Ball, former commissioner of Social Security, asserts that Social Security is in good shape financially. Sylvester J. Schieber, a business executive, sees a serious Social Security funding problem.

Economist Michael J. Boskin and his colleagues argue that the Consumer Price Index (CPI) suffers from quality and new product bias, which means that the CPI overstates inflation and increases in the cost of living. Economists Katharine G. Abraham, John S. Greenlees, and Brent R. Moulton argue that the conclusions drawn about the upward bias of the CPI are either based on weak evidence, based on improper inference from the evidence, or based on the identification of problems that have no practical solution.

Political economist Daniel J. Mitchell argues that current and projected federal government budget surpluses should be used for tax cuts because this will promote economic growth and lead to rising living standards. In constructing the U.S. fiscal year 2000 budget, the Office of Management and Budget argues that current and projected surpluses should be used to invest in America's future.

Orthodox neoclassical economist Thomas Rustici asserts that the minimum wage creates unemployment among least-skilled workers. Labor economist Charles Craypo argues that a high minimum wage is good for the economy.

Heritage Foundation senior policy analyst Robert Rector contends that Wisconsin has won more than half the battle against welfare dependence. Economist Michael Wiseman concludes that the governor of Wisconsin has not found the key to welfare savings.

Columnist Robert J. Samuelson charges that critics of free trade ignore economics, which he feels is the one thing that "trade has going for it." Social critic and three-time presidential hopeful Patrick J. Buchanan argues that the purpose of international trade is to benefit American workers, farmers, businessmen, and manufacturers, not mankind in general.

Columnist and social critic William Greider warns that blind acceptance of "free-market doctrine" must inevitably lead to inequality. Gary Burtless, a senior fellow at the Brookings Institution, states that although the wages of less-skilled workers have plunged, this shift is not confined to the traded-goods sector.

Cynthia Pollock Shea, a senior researcher with the Worldwatch Institute, argues that immediate action must be taken to halt emissions of chemicals that deplete the ozone. Professor of economics Lester B. Lave warns that drastic solutions could be harmful or costly.

Alan S. Blinder, a member of the Board of Governors of the Federal Reserve System, maintains that market energy can solve America's environmental problems. Social critic David Moberg argues that public policy and direct government intervention have positive effects on the environment.

Joe Cobb, president of the Trade Policy Institute in Washington, D.C., asserts that the North American Free Trade Agreement (NAFTA) has been a success. Researcher Alan Tonelson negatively assesses NAFTA based on his contentions that the real winners were large U.S. multinational corporations, that median wages in the United States and Mexico have declined, and that the flows of illegal immigrants and drugs into the United States from Mexico are high.

INTRODUCTION

Economics and Economists: The Basis for Controversy

Thomas R. Swartz
Frank J. Bonello

> *I think that Capitalism, wisely managed, can probably be more efficient for attaining economic ends than any alternative system yet in sight, but that in itself it is in many ways extremely objectionable.*
>
> ——Lord John Maynard Keynes, *The End of Laissez-Faire* (1926)

Although more than 70 years have passed since Lord Keynes (1883–1946) penned these lines, many economists still struggle with the basic dilemma he outlined. The paradox rests in the fact that a free-market system is extremely efficient. It is purported to produce more at a lower cost than any other economic system. But in producing this wide array of low-cost goods and services, problems arise. These problems—most notably a lack of economic equity and economic stability—concern some economists.

If the problems raised and analyzed in this book were merely the product of intellectual gymnastics undertaken by eggheaded economists, we could sit back and enjoy these confrontations as theoretical exercises. The essays contained in this book, however, touch each and every one of us in tangible ways. Some focus upon macroeconomic topics, such as the minimum wage and the Federal Reserve's monetary policy. Another set of issues deals with microeconomic topics. We refer to these issues as micro problems not because they are small problems but because they deal with small economic units, such as households, firms, or individual industries. A third set of issues deals with matters that do not fall neatly into the macroeconomic or microeconomic classifications. This set includes three issues relating to the international aspects of economic activity and two involving pollution.

The range of issues and disagreements raises a fundamental question: Why do economists disagree? One explanation is suggested by Lord Keynes's 1926 remark. How various economists will react to the strengths and weaknesses found in an economic system will depend upon how they view the relative importance of efficiency, equity, and stability. These are central terms, and we will define them in detail in the following pages. For now the important point is that some economists may view efficiency as overriding. In other cases, the same economists may be willing to sacrifice the efficiency generated by the market in order to ensure increased economic equity and/or increased economic stability.

Given the extent of conflict, controversy, and diversity, it may appear that economists rarely, if ever, agree on any economic issue. We would be most misleading if we left the reader with this impression. Economists rarely challenge the internal logic of the theoretical models that have been developed and articulated by their colleagues. Rather, they will challenge either the validity of the assumptions used in these models or the value of the ends these models seek to achieve. The challenges typically focus upon such issues as the assumption of functioning, competitive markets, and the desirability of perpetuating the existing distribution of income. In this case, those who support and those who challenge the operation of the market agree on a large number of issues. But they disagree most assuredly on a few issues that have dramatic implications.

This same phenomenon of agreeing more often than disagreeing is also true in the area of economic policy. In this area, where the public is most acutely aware of differences among economists, these differences are not generally over the kinds of changes that will be brought about by a particular policy. The differences more typically concern the timing of the change, the specific characteristics of the policy, and the size of the resulting effect or effects.

ECONOMISTS: WHAT DO THEY REPRESENT?

Newspaper, magazine, and TV commentators all use handy labels to describe certain members of the economics profession. What do the headlines mean when they refer to the Chicago School, the Keynesians, the institutional economists, or the radical economists? What do these individuals stand for? Since we too use our own labels throughout this book, we feel obliged to identify the principal groups, or camps, in our profession. Let us warn you that this can be a misleading venture. Some economists—perhaps most of them —defy classification. They drift from one camp to another, selecting a gem of wisdom here and another there. These are practical men and women who believe that no one camp has all the answers to all the economic problems confronting society.

Recognizing this limitation, four major groups of economists can be identified. These groups are differentiated on the basis of two basic criteria: how they view efficiency relative to equity and stability, and what significance they attach to imperfectly competitive market structures. Before describing various views on these criteria, it is essential to understand the meaning of certain terms to be used in this description.

Efficiency, equity, and stability represent goals for an economic system. An economy is efficient when it produces those goods and services that people want without wasting scarce resources. Equity in an economic sense has several dimensions. It means that income and wealth are distributed according to accepted principles of fairness, that those who are unable to care for themselves receive adequate care, and that mainstream economic activity is open to all persons. Stability is viewed as the absence of sharp ups and downs in business activity, in prices, and in employment. In other words, stability is marked by steady increases in output, little inflation, and low unemployment.

When the term *market structures* is used, it refers to the number of buyers and sellers in the market and the amount of control they exercise over price. At one extreme is a perfectly competitive market where there are so many buyers and sellers that no one has any ability to influence market price. One seller or buyer obviously could have great control over price. This extreme market structure, which we call pure monopoly, and other market structures that result in some control over price are grouped under the broad label of imperfectly competitive markets. With these terms in mind, we can begin to examine the various schools of economic thought.

Free-Market Economists

One of the most visible groups of economists and perhaps the easiest group to identify and classify is the *free-market economists*. These economists believe that the market, operating freely without interferences from government or labor unions, will generate the greatest amount of well-being for the greatest number of people.

Economic efficiency is one of the priorities for free-market economists. In their well-developed models, *consumer sovereignty*—consumer demand for goods and services—guides the system by directly influencing market prices. The distribution of economic resources caused by these market prices not only results in the production of an array of goods and services that are demanded by consumers, but this production is undertaken in the most cost-effective fashion. The free-market economists hold that, at any point, some individuals must earn incomes that are substantially greater than those of other individuals. They contend that these higher incomes are a reward for greater efficiency or productivity and that this reward-induced efficiency will result in rapid economic growth that will benefit all persons in the society. They might also admit that a system driven by these freely operating markets will be subject to occasional bouts of instability (slow growth, inflation, and unemployment). They maintain, however, that government action to eliminate or reduce this periodic instability will only make matters worse. Consequently, government, according to the free-market economist, should play a minor role in the economic affairs of society.

Although the models of free-market economists are dependent upon functioning, competitive markets, the lack of such markets in the real world does not seriously jeopardize their position. First, they assert that large firms are necessary to achieve low per-unit costs; that is, a single large firm may be able to produce a given level of output with fewer scarce resources than a large number of small firms. Second, they suggest that the benefits associated with the free operation of markets are so great compared to government intervention that even a second-best solution of imperfectly competitive markets still yields benefits far in excess of government intervention.

These advocates of the free market have been given various labels over time. The oldest and most persistent label is *classical economists*. This is because the classical economists of the eighteenth century, particularly Adam Smith, were the first to point out the virtues of the market. In *The Wealth of Nations* (1776), Smith captured the essence of the system with the following words:

> Every individual endeavors to employ his capital so that its produce may be of greatest value. He generally neither intends to promote the public interest nor knows how much he is promoting it. He intends only his own security, only his own gain. And he is in this led by an invisible hand to promote an end which was no part of his intention. By pursuing his own interest he frequently promotes that of society more effectively than when he really intends to promote it.

Liberal Economists

Another significant group of economists in the United States can be classified as *liberal economists*. Liberal here refers to the willingness to intervene in the free operation of the market. These economists share with the free-market economists a great respect for the market. The liberal economist, however, does not believe that the explicit and implicit costs of a freely operating market should or can be ignored. Rather, the liberal maintains that the costs of an uncontrolled marketplace are often borne by those in society who are least capable of bearing them: the poor, the elderly, and the infirm. Additionally, liberal economists maintain that the freely operating market sometimes results in economic instability and the resultant bouts of inflation, unemployment, and slow or negative growth.

Consider for a moment the differences between free-market economists and liberal economists at the microeconomic level. Liberal economists take exception to the free market on two grounds. First, these economists find a basic problem with fairness in the marketplace. Since the market is driven by the forces of consumer spending, there are those who through no fault of their own (they may be aged, young, infirm, or physically or mentally handicapped) may not have the wherewithal to participate in the economic system. Second, the unfettered marketplace does not and cannot handle spillover effects, or what are known as externalities. These are the third-party effects that may occur as a result of some action. Will a firm willingly compensate its neighbors for the pollutants it pours into the nearby lake? Will a truck driver willingly drive at the speed limit and in the process reduce the highway accident rate? Liberal economists think not. These economists are therefore willing to have the government intervene in these and other, similar cases.

The liberal economists' role in macroeconomics is more readily apparent. Ever since the failure of free-market economics during the Great Depression of the 1930s, Keynesianism (still another label for liberal economics) has become widely known. In his 1935 book *The General Theory of Employment, Interest, and Money*, Lord John Maynard Keynes laid the basic groundwork for this school of thought. Keynes argued that the history of freely operating market economies was marked by periods of recurring recessions, sometimes very deep recessions, which we call depressions. He maintained that government intervention through its fiscal policy—government tax and spending power —could eliminate, or at least soften these sharp reductions in economic activity and as a result move the economy along a more stable growth path. Thus, for the Keynesians, or liberal economists, one of the extremely objectionable aspects of a free-market economy is its inherent instability.

Liberal economists are also far more concerned about the existence of imperfections in the marketplace than are their free-market counterparts. They reject the notion that imperfect competition is an acceptable substitute for competitive markets. They may agree that the imperfectly competitive firms can achieve some savings because of their large size and efficiency, but they assert that since there is little or no competition the firms are not forced to pass these cost savings on to consumers. Thus, liberal economists, who in some circles are labeled antitrusters, are willing to intervene in the market in two ways: They are prepared to allow some monopolies, such as public utilities, to exist, but they contend that these must be regulated by government. Or they maintain that there is no justification for monopolies, and they are prepared to invoke the powers of antitrust legislation to break up existing monopolies and/or prevent the formation of new ones.

Mainstream Critics and Radical Reform Economists
There are two other groups of economists we must identify. One group can be called *mainstream critics*. Included in this group are individuals like Thorstein Veblen (1857–1929), with his critique of conspicuous consumption, and John Kenneth Galbraith (b. 1908), with his views on industrial structure. One reasonably cohesive subgroup of mainstream critics are the post-Keynesians. They are post-Keynesians because they believe that as the principal economic institutions have changed over time, they have remained closer to the spirit of Keynes than have the liberal economists. As some have suggested, the key aspect of Keynes as far as the post-Keynesians are concerned is his assertion that "expectations of the future are not necessarily certain." On a more practical level post-Keynesians assert, among other things, that the productivity of the economic system is not significantly affected by changes in income distribution, that the system can still be efficient without competitive markets, that conventional fiscal policies cannot control inflation, and that "incomes policies" are the means to an effective and equitable answer to the inflationary dilemma. This characterization of post-Keynesianism is drawn from Alfred S. Eichner's introduction in *A Guide to Post-Keynesian Economics* (M. E. Sharpe, 1978).

The fourth and last group can be called the *radical reform economists*. Many in this group trace their ideas back to the nineteenth-century philosopher-economist Karl Marx and his most impressive work, the three volumes of *Das Kapital*. As with the other three groups of economists, there are subgroups of radical reform economists. One subgroup, which may be labeled contemporary Marxists, is best represented by those who have published their research results over the years in the *Review of Radical Political Economics*. These economists examine issues that have been largely ignored by mainstream economists, such as war, sexism, racism, imperialism, and civil rights. In their analyses of these issues they borrow from and refine the work of Marx. In the process, they emphasize the role of class in shaping society and the role of the economy in determining class structures. Moreover, they see a need to encourage explicitly the development of some form of democratic socialism, for only then will the greatest good for the greatest number be ensured.

In concluding this section, we must warn you to use these labels with extreme care. Our categories are not hard and fast. There is much grayness around the edges and little that is black and white in these classifications. This does not mean, however, that they have no value. It is important to understand the philosophical background of the individual authors. This background does indeed color or shade their work.

SUMMARY

It is clear that there is no shortage of economic problems that demand solutions. At the same time there is no shortage of proposed solutions. In fact, the problem is often one of oversupply. The 19 issues included in this volume will acquaint you—or, more accurately, reacquaint you—with some of these problems. And, of course, there are at least two proposed solutions for each of the problems. Here we hope to provide new insights regarding the alternatives available and the differences and similarities of these alternative remedies.

If this introduction has served its purpose, you will be able to identify common elements in the proposed solutions to the different problems. For example, you will be able to identify the reliance on the forces of the market advocated by free-market economists as the remedy for several economic ills. This introduction should also help you to understand why there are at least two proposed solutions for every economic problem; each group of economists tends to interpret a problem from its own philosophical position and to advance a solution that is grounded in that philosophical framework.

Our intention, of course, is not to connect persons to one philosophic position or another. We hope instead to generate discussion and promote understanding. To do this, not only must each of us see a proposed solution, we must also be aware of the foundation that supports that solution. With greater understanding, meaningful progress in addressing economic problems can be achieved.

On the Internet . . .

The Dismal Scientist
The Dismal Scientist provides free economic data, analysis, and forecasts on a variety of topics. *http://www.dismal.com*

The Economist
The Web edition of *The Economist* is available free to subscribers of the print edition or for an annual fee to those who wish to subscribe online. A selection of articles is available free to those who want to dip into the journal. *http://www.economist.com*

Electronic Policy Network
This site offers timely information and ideas about national policy on economics and politics, welfare and families, education, civic participation, and health policy in the form of a virtual magazine. *http://epn.org*

Resources for Economists on the Internet
This is the table of contents for Resources for Economists on the Internet. This resource of the WWW Virtual Library on Economics is an excellent starting point for any research in economics by academic and practicing economists and anyone interested in economics. It has many Web links. *http://rfe.wustl.edu/sc.html*

Statistical Resources on the Web: Comprehensive Economics
Here is an excellent source of statistics collated from federal bureaus, economic indicators (both historical and current), the Federal Reserve Board, economic sources, federal statistical tables, and a consumer price inflator/deflator, plus many links to other sources. *http://www.lib.umich.edu/libhome/Documents.center/stecon.html*

WebEc: WWW Resources in Economics
This is a complete virtual library of economics facts, figures, and thoughts. *http://netec.wustl.edu/webec.html*

PART 1

Microeconomic Issues

Our lives are profoundly affected by economic decisions made at the microeconomic level. Some important decisions are those regarding profit motives of businesses, gun ownership, city subsidies for sports venues, the health care industry, enforcement of antitrust policies, and the need for more prison space.

■ Are Profits the Only Business of Business?

■ Should We Encourage the Private Ownership of Guns?

■ Should Cities Subsidize Sports and Sports Venues?

■ Is There Discrimination in U.S. Labor Markets?

■ Is the Department of Justice Being Too Hard on Microsoft?

■ Is Managed Competition the Cure for Our Ailing Health Care System?

■ Do Private Prisons Pay?

ISSUE 1

Are Profits the Only Business of Business?

YES: Milton Friedman, from "The Social Responsibility of Business Is to Increase Its Profits," *The New York Times Magazine* (September 13, 1970)

NO: Robert Almeder, from "Morality in the Marketplace," in Milton Snoeyenbos, Robert Almeder, and James Humber, eds., *Business Ethics,* rev. ed. (Prometheus Press, 1998)

ISSUE SUMMARY

YES: Free-market economist Milton Friedman contends that the sole responsibility of business is to increase its profits.

NO: Philosopher Robert Almeder maintains that if capitalism is to survive, it must act in socially responsible ways that go beyond profit making.

Every economic society—whether it is a traditional society in Central Africa, a fossilized planned economy such as Cuba's, or a wealthy capitalist society such as those found in North America, Western Europe, or the Pacific Rim —must address the basic economic problem of resource allocation. These societies must determine *what* goods and services they can and will produce, *how* these goods and services will be produced, and *for whom* these goods and services will be produced.

The *what, how,* and *for whom* questions must be answered because of the problem of scarcity. Even if a given society were indescribably rich, it would still confront the problem of scarcity—in the case of a rich society, "relative scarcity." It might have all the resources it needs to produce all the goods and services it would ever want, but it could not produce all these things simultaneously. Thus, even a very rich society must set priorities and produce first those goods and services with the highest priority and postpone the production of those goods and services with lower priorities. If time is of the essence, this society would determine *how* these goods and services should be produced. And since this wealthy society cannot produce all it wants instantly, it must also determine *for whom* the first bundle of goods and services will be produced.

Few, if any, economic societies are indescribably rich. On the other hand, there are many examples of economic societies that face grinding deprivation daily. In these societies and in all the societies that fall between poverty and great affluence, the *what, how,* and *for whom* questions are immediately apparent. Somehow these questions must be answered.

In some societies, such as the Amish communities of North America, the answers to these questions are found in tradition: Sons and daughters follow in their parents' footsteps. Younger generations produce *what* older generations produced before them. The methods of production—the horsedrawn plow, the hand-held scythe, the use of natural fertilizers—remain unchanged; thus, the *how* question is answered in the same way that the *for whom* question is answered—by following historic patterns. In other societies, such as self-sustaining religious communities, there is a different pattern of responses to these questions. In these communities, the "elder" of the community determines *what* will be produced, *how* it will be produced, and *for whom* it will be produced. If there is a well-defined hierarchical system, it is similar to one of the former stereotypical command economies of Eastern Europe.

Although elements of tradition and command are found in the industrialized societies of Western Europe, North America, and Japan, the basic answers to the three questions of resource allocation in these countries are determined by profit. In these economic societies, *what* will be produced is determined by what will yield the greatest profit. Consumers, in their search for maximum satisfaction, will bid for those goods and services that they want most. This consumer action drives the prices of these goods and services up, which, in turn, increases producers' profits. The higher profits attract new firms into the industry and encourage existing firms to increase their output. Thus, profits are the mechanism that ensures that consumers get what they want. Similarly, the profit-seeking behavior of business firms determines *how* the goods and services that consumers want will be produced. Since firms attempt to maximize their profits, they select those means of production that are economically most efficient. Lastly, the *for whom* question is also linked to profits. Wherever there is a shortage of goods and services, profits will be high. In the producers' attempts to increase their output, they must attract factors of production (land, labor, and capital) away from other economic activities. This bidding increases factor prices or factor incomes and ensures that these factors will be able to buy goods and services in the open marketplace.

Both Milton Friedman and Robert Almeder recognize the merits of a profit-driven economic system. They do not quarrel over the importance of profits. But they do quarrel over whether or not business firms have obligations beyond making profits. Friedman holds that the *only* responsibility of business is to make profits and that anyone who maintains otherwise is "preaching pure and unadulterated socialism." Almeder, who is clearly not a "socialist," contends that business must act in socially responsible ways "if capitalism is to survive."

YES   Milton Friedman

THE SOCIAL RESPONSIBILITY OF
BUSINESS IS TO INCREASE ITS PROFITS

When I hear businessmen speak eloquently about the "social responsibilities of business in a free-enterprise system," I am reminded of the wonderful line about the Frenchman who discovered at the age of 70 that he had been speaking prose all his life. The businessmen believe that they are defending free enterprise when they declaim that business is not concerned "merely" with profit but also with promoting desirable "social ends; that business has a social conscience" and takes seriously its responsibilities for providing employment, eliminating discrimination, avoiding pollution and whatever else may be the catchwords of the contemporary crop of reformers. In fact they are—or would be if they or anyone else took them seriously—preaching pure and unadulterated socialism. Businessmen who talk this way are unwitting puppets of the intellectual forces that have been undermining the basis of a free society these past decades.

The discussions of the "social responsibilities of business" are notable for their analytical looseness and lack of rigor. What does it mean to say that "business" has responsibilities? Only people can have responsibilities. A corporation is an artificial person and in this sense may have artificial responsibilities, but "business" as a whole cannot be said to have responsibilities, even in this vague sense. The first step toward clarity in examining the doctrine of the social responsibility of business is to ask precisely what it implies for whom.

Presumably, the individuals who are to be responsible are businessmen, which means individual proprietors or corporate executives. Most of the discussion of social responsibility is directed at corporations, so in what follows I shall mostly neglect the individual proprietor and speak of corporate executives.

In a free-enterprise, private-property system, a corporate executive is an employee of the owners of the business. He has direct responsibility to his employers. That responsibility is to conduct the business in accordance with their desires, which generally will be to make as much money as possible while conforming to the basic rules of the society, both those embodied in

From Milton Friedman, "The Social Responsibility of Business Is to Increase Its Profits," *The New York Times Magazine* (September 13, 1970). Copyright © 1970 by The New York Times Co. Reprinted by permission.

law and those embodied in ethical custom. Of course, in some cases his employers may have a different objective. A group of persons might establish a corporation for an eleemosynary purpose —for example, a hospital or a school. The manager of such a corporation will not have money profit as his objective but the rendering of certain services.

In either case, the key point is that, in his capacity as a corporate executive, the manager is the agent of the individuals who own the corporation or establish the eleemosynary institution, and his primary responsibility is to them.

Needless to say, this does not mean that it is easy to judge how well he is performing his task. But at least the criterion of performance is straightforward, and the persons among whom a voluntary contractual arrangement exists are clearly defined.

Of course, the corporate executive is also a person in his own right. As a person, he may have many other responsibilities that he recognizes or assumes voluntarily—to his family, his conscience, his feelings of charity, his church, his clubs, his city, his country. He may feel impelled by these responsibilities to devote part of his income to causes he regards as worthy, to refuse to work for particular corporations, even to leave his job, for example, to join his country's armed forces. If we wish, we may refer to some of these responsibilities as "social responsibilities." But in these respects he is acting as a principal, not an agent; he is spending his own money or time or energy, not the money of his employers or the time or energy he has contracted to devote to their purposes. If these are "social responsibilities," they are the social responsibilities of individuals, not of business.

What does it mean to say that the corporate executive has a "social responsibility" in his capacity as businessman? If this statement is not pure rhetoric, it must mean that he is to act in some way that is not in the interest of his employers. For example, that he is to refrain from increasing the price of the product in order to contribute to the social objective of preventing inflation, even though a price increase would be in the best interests of the corporation. Or that he is to make expenditures on reducing pollution beyond the amount that is in the best interests of the corporation or that is required by law in order to contribute to the social objective of improving the environment. Or that, at the expense of corporate profits, he is to hire "hard-core" unemployed instead of better-qualified available workmen to contribute to the social objective of reducing poverty.

In each of these cases, the corporate executive would be spending someone else's money for a general social interest. Insofar as his actions in accord with his "social responsibility" reduce returns to stockholders, he is spending their money. Insofar as his actions raise the price to customers, he is spending the customers' money. Insofar as his actions lower the wages of some employees, he is spending their money.

The stockholders or the customers or the employees could separately spend their own money on the particular action if they wished to do so. The executive is exercising a distinct "social responsibility," rather than serving as an agent of the stockholders or the customers or the employees, only if he spends the money in a different way than they would have spent it.

But if he does this, he is in effect imposing taxes, on the one hand, and deciding how the tax proceeds shall be spent, on the other.

This process raises political questions on two levels: principle and consequences. On the level of political principle, the imposition of taxes and the expenditure of tax proceeds are governmental functions. We have established elaborate constitutional, parliamentary and judicial provisions to control these functions, to assure that taxes are imposed so far as possible in accordance with the preferences and desires of the public—after all, "taxation without representation" was one of the battle cries of the American Revolution. We have a system of checks and balances to separate the legislative function of imposing taxes and enacting expenditures from the executive function of collecting taxes and administering expenditure programs and from the judicial function of mediating disputes and interpreting the law.

Here the businessman—self-selected or appointed directly or indirectly by stockholders—is to be simultaneously legislator, executive and jurist. He is to decide whom to tax by how much and for what purpose, and he is to spend the proceeds—all this guided only by general exhortations from on high to restrain inflation, improve the environment, fight poverty and so on and on.

The whole justification for permitting the corporate executive to be selected by the stockholders is that the executive is an agent serving the interests of his principal. This justification disappears when the corporate executive imposes taxes and spends the proceeds for "social" purposes. He becomes in effect a public employee, a civil servant, even though he remains in name an employee of a private enterprise. On grounds of political principle, it is intolerable that such civil servants—insofar as their actions in the name of social responsibility are real and not just window-dressing—should be selected as they are now. If they are to be civil servants, then they must be selected through a political process. If they are to impose taxes and make expenditures to foster "social" objectives, then political machinery must be set up to guide the assessment of taxes and to determine through a political process the objectives to be served.

This is the basic reason why the doctrine of "social responsibility" involves the acceptance of the socialist view that political mechanisms, not market mechanisms, are the appropriate way to determine the allocation of scarce resources to alternative uses.

On the grounds of consequences, can the corporate executive in fact discharge his alleged "social responsibilities"? On the one hand, suppose he could get away with spending the stockholders' or customers' or employees' money. How is he to know how to spend it? He is told that he must contribute to fighting inflation. How is he to know what action of his will contribute to that end? He is presumably an expert in running his company—in producing a product or selling it or financing it. But nothing about his selection makes him an expert on inflation. Will his holding down the price of his product reduce inflationary pressure? Or, by leaving more spending power in the hands of his customers, simply divert it elsewhere? Or, by forcing him to produce less because of the lower price, will it simply contribute to shortages? Even if he could answer these questions, how much cost is he justified in imposing on his stockholders, customers and employees for this social purpose?

What is the appropriate share and what is the appropriate share of others?

And, whether he wants to or not, can he get away with spending his stockholders', customers' or employees' money? Will not the stockholders fire him? (Either the present ones or those who take over when his actions in the name of social responsibility have reduced the corporation's profits and the price of its stock.) His customers and his employees can desert him for other producers and employers less scrupulous in exercising their social responsibilities.

This facet of "social responsibility" doctrine is brought into sharp relief when the doctrine is used to justify wage restraint by trade unions. The conflict of interest is naked and clear when union officials are asked to subordinate the interest of their members to some more general social purpose. If the union officials try to enforce wage restraint, the consequence is likely to be wildcat strikes, rank-and-file revolts and the emergence of strong competitors for their jobs. We thus have the ironic phenomenon that union leaders—at least in the U.S.—have objected to Government interference with the market far more consistently and courageously than have business leaders.

The difficulty of exercising "social responsibility" illustrates, of course, the great virtue of private competitive enterprise—it forces people to be responsible for their own actions and makes it difficult for them to "exploit" other people for either selfish or unselfish purposes. They can do good—but only at their own expense.

Many a reader who has followed the argument this far may be tempted to remonstrate that it is all well and good to speak of government's having the responsibility to impose taxes and determine expenditures for such "social" purposes as controlling pollution or training the hard-core unemployed, but that the problems are too urgent to wait on the slow course of political processes, that the exercise of social responsibility by businessmen is a quicker and surer way to solve pressing current problems.

Aside from the question of fact—I share Adam Smith's skepticism about the benefits that can be expected from "those who affected to trade for the public good"—this argument must be rejected on grounds of principle. What it amounts to is an assertion that those who favor the taxes and expenditures in question have failed to persuade a majority of their fellow citizens to be of like mind and that they are seeking to attain by undemocratic procedures what they cannot attain by democratic procedures. In a free society, it is hard for "good" people to do "good," but that is a small price to pay for making it hard for "evil" people to do "evil," especially since one man's good is another's evil.

I have, for simplicity, concentrated on the special case of the corporate executive, except only for the brief digression on trade unions. But precisely the same argument applies to the newer phenomenon of calling upon stockholders to require corporations to exercise social responsibility (the recent G.M. crusade, for example). In most of these cases, what is in effect involved is some stockholders trying to get other stockholders (or customers or employees) to contribute against their will to "social" causes favored by the activists. Insofar as they succeed, they are again imposing taxes and spending the proceeds.

The situation of the individual proprietor is somewhat different. If he acts to reduce the returns of his enterprise in order to exercise his "social responsibility," he is spending his own money, not someone else's. If he wishes to spend his money on such purposes, that is his right, and I cannot see that there is any objection to his doing so. In the process, he, too, may impose costs on employees and customers. However, because he is far less likely than a large corporation or union to have monopolistic power, any such side effects will tend to be minor.

Of course, in practice the doctrine of social responsibility is frequently a cloak for actions that are justified on other grounds rather than a reason for those actions.

To illustrate, it may well be in the long-run interest of a corporation that is a major employer in a small community to devote resources to providing amenities to that community or to improving its government. That may make it easier to attract desirable employees, it may reduce the wage bill or lessen losses from pilferage and sabotage or have other worthwhile effects. Or it may be that, given the laws about the deductibility of corporate charitable contributions, the stockholders can contribute more to charities they favor by having the corporation make the gift than by doing it themselves, since they can in that way contribute an amount that would otherwise have been paid as corporate taxes.

In each of these—and many similar—cases, there is a strong temptation to rationalize these actions as an exercise of "social responsibility." In the present climate of opinion, with its widespread aversion to "capitalism," "profits," the "soulless corporation" and so on, this is one way for a corporation to generate goodwill as a by-product of expenditures that are entirely justified in its own self-interest.

It would be inconsistent of me to call on corporate executives to refrain from this hypocritical window-dressing because it harms the foundations of a free society. That would be to call on them to exercise a "social responsibility"! If our institutions, and the attitudes of the public make it in their self-interest to cloak their actions in this way, I cannot summon much indignation to denounce them. At the same time, I can express admiration for those individual proprietors or owners of closely held corporations or stockholders of more broadly held corporations who disdain such tactics as approaching fraud.

Whether blameworthy or not, the use of the cloak of social responsibility, and the nonsense spoken in its name by influential and prestigious businessmen, does clearly harm the foundations of a free society. I have been impressed time and again by the schizophrenic character of many businessmen. They are capable of being extremely far-sighted and clear-headed in matters that are internal to their businesses. They are incredibly short-sighted and muddle-headed in matters that are outside their businesses but affect the possible survival of business in general. This short-sightedness is strikingly exemplified in the calls from many businessmen for wage and price guidelines or controls or incomes policies. There is nothing that could do more in a brief period to destroy a market system and replace it by a centrally controlled system than effective governmental control of prices and wages.

The short-sightedness is also exemplified in speeches by businessmen on social responsibility. This may gain them kudos in the short run. But it helps to strengthen the already too prevalent view that the pursuit of profits is wicked and immoral and must be curbed and controlled by external forces. Once this view is adopted, the external forces that curb the market will not be the social consciences, however highly developed, of the pontificating executives; it will be the iron fist of Government bureaucrats. Here, as with price and wage controls, businessmen seem to me to reveal a suicidal impulse.

The political principle that underlies the market mechanism is unanimity. In an ideal free market resting on private property, no individual can coerce any other, all cooperation is voluntary, all parties to such cooperation benefit or they need not participate. There are no "social" values, no "social" responsibilities in any sense other than the shared values and responsibilities of individuals. Society is a collection of individuals and of the various groups they voluntarily form.

The political principle that underlies the political mechanism is conformity. The individual must serve a more general social interest—whether that be determined by a church or a dictator or a majority. The individual may have a vote and a say in what is to be done, but if he is overruled, he must conform. It is appropriate for some to require others to contribute to a general social purpose whether they wish to or not.

Unfortunately, unanimity is not always feasible. There are some respects in which conformity appears unavoidable, so I do not see how one can avoid the use of the political mechanism altogether.

But the doctrine of "social responsibility" taken seriously would extend the scope of the political mechanism to every human activity. It does not differ in philosophy from the most explicitly collectivist doctrine. It differs only by professing to believe that collectivist ends can be attained without collectivist means. That is why, in my book "Capitalism and Freedom," I have called it a "fundamentally subversive doctrine" in a free society, and have said that in such a society, "there is one and only one social responsibility of business—to use its resources and engage in activities designed to increase its profits so long as it stays within the rules of the game, which is to say, engages in open and free competition without deception or fraud."

NO

Robert Almeder

MORALITY IN THE MARKETPLACE: REFLECTIONS ON THE FRIEDMAN DOCTRINE

INTRODUCTION

In seeking to create a climate more favorable for corporate activity, International Telephone and Telegraph allegedly contributed large sums of money to "destabilize" the duly elected government of Chile. Even though advised by the scientific community that the practice is lethal, major chemical companies reportedly continue to dump large amounts of carcinogens and mutagens into the water supply of various areas and, at the same time, lobby strongly to prevent legislation against such practices. General Motors Corporation, other automobile manufacturers, and Firestone Tire and Rubber Corporation have frequently defended themselves against the charge that they knowingly and willingly marketed a product that, owing to defective design, had been reliably predicted to kill a certain percentage of its users and, moreover, refused to recall promptly the product even when government agencies documented the large incidence of death as a result of the defective product. Finally, people often say that numerous advertising companies happily accept, and earnestly solicit, accounts to advertise cigarettes knowing full well that as a direct result of their advertising activities a certain number of people will die considerably prematurely and painfully. Most recently, of course, American Tobacco Companies have been charged with knowingly marketing a very addictive product known to kill untold numbers in slow, painful and costly deaths while the price of the stock of these companies has made fortunes for the shareholders. We need not concern ourselves with whether these and other similar charges are true because our primary concern here is with what might count as a justification for such corporate conduct were it to occur. There can be no question that such corporate behavior sometimes occurs and is frequently legal, or at least not illegal. The question is whether corporate behavior should be constrained by nonlegal or moral considerations. If so, to what extent and how could it be done? As things presently stand, it seems to be a dogma of contemporary capitalism rapidly emerging throughout the world that the sole responsibility of business is to make as much money as is *legally* possible. But the interesting question is whether this view is rationally defensible.

Sometimes, although not very frequently, corporate executives will admit to the sort of behavior depicted above and then proceed proximately to justify such behavior in the name of their responsibility to the shareholders or owners (if the shareholders are not the owners) to make as much profit as is legally possible. Thereafter, less proximately and more generally, they will proceed to urge the more general utilitarian point that the increase in profit engendered by such corporate behavior begets such an unquestionable overall good for society that the behavior in question is morally acceptable if not quite praiseworthy. More specifically, the justification in question can, and usually does, take two forms.

The first and most common form of justification consists in urging that, as long as one's corporate behavior is not illegal, the behavior will be morally acceptable because the sole purpose of being in business is to make a profit; and the rules of the marketplace are somewhat different from those in other places and must be followed if one is to make a profit. Moreover, proponents of this view hasten to add that, as Adam Smith has claimed, the greatest good for society in the long run is achieved not by corporations seeking to act morally, or with a sense of social responsibility in their pursuit of profit, but rather by each corporation seeking to maximize its own profit, unregulated in that endeavor except by the laws of supply and demand along with whatever other laws are inherent to the competition process. This, they say, is what has made capitalist societies the envy of the world while ideological socialisms sooner of later fail miserably to meet deep human needs. Smith's view, that there is an invisible hand, as it were, directing an economy governed solely by the profit motive to the greatest good for society in the long run,[1] is still the dominant motivation and justification for those who would want an economy unregulated by any moral concern that would, or could, tend to decrease profits for some *alleged* social or moral good.

Milton Friedman, for example, has frequently asserted that the sole moral responsibility of business is to make as much profit as is legally possible; and by that he means to assert that attempts to regulate or restrain the pursuit of profit in accordance with what some people believe to be socially desirable ends are in fact *subversive* of the common good because the greatest good for the greatest number is achieved by an economy maximally competitive and unregulated by moral rules in its pursuit of profit.[2] So, on Friedman's view, the greatest good for society is achieved by corporations acting legally, but with no further regard for what may be morally desirable; and this view begets the paradox that, *in business,* the greatest good for society can be achieved only by acting without regard for morality, at least in so far as moral rules are not reflected in the legal code. Moreover, adoption of this position constitutes a fairly conscious commitment to the view that while one's personal life may well need moral governance beyond the law, when pursuing profit, it is necessary that one's corporate behavior be unregulated by any moral concern other than that of making as much money as is legally possible; curiously enough, it is only in this way that society achieves the greatest good. So viewed, it is not difficult to see how a corporate executive could sincerely and consistently adopt rigorous standards of morality in his or her personal life and yet feel quite comfortable in abandoning those standards in the pursuit of profit. Albert Carr, for example, likens the conduct of business to that of playing poker.[3] As Carr would have it, moral busybodies who insist on corporations acting morally might do just as well to censure a good bluffer in poker for being deceitful. Society, of course, lacking a perspective such as Friedman's and Carr's is only too willing to view such behavior as strongly hypocritical and fostered by an unwholesome avarice.

The second way of justifying, or defending, corporate practices that may appear morally questionable consists in urging that even if corporations were to take seriously the idea of limiting profits because of a desire to be moral or more responsible to social needs, then corporations would be involved in the unwholesome business of selecting and implementing moral values that may not be shared by a large number of people. Besides, there is the overwhelming question of whether there can be any non-questionable moral values or non-controversial list of social priorities for corporations to adopt. After all, if ethical relativism is true, or if ethical nihilism is true (and philosophers can be counted upon to argue agressively for both positions), then it would be fairly silly of corporations to limit profits for what may be a quite dubious reason, namely, for being moral, when there are no clear grounds for doing it, and when

it is not too clear what would count for doing it. In short, business corporations could argue (as Friedman has done)[4] that corporate actions in behalf of society's interests would require of corporations an ability to clearly determine and rank in noncontroversial ways the major needs of society; and it would not appear that this could be done successfully.

Perhaps another, and somewhat easier, way of formulating this second argument consists in urging that because moralists and philosophers generally fail to agree on what are the proper moral rules (if any), as well as on whether we should be moral, it would be imprudent to sacrifice a clear profit for a dubious or controversial moral gain. To authorize such a sacrifice would be to abandon a clear responsibility for one that is unclear or questionable.

If there are any other basic ways of justifying the sort of corporate behavior noted at the outset, I cannot imagine what they might be. So, let us examine these two modes of justification. In doing this, I hope to show that neither argument is sound and, moreover, that corporate behavior of the sort in question is clearly immoral if anything is immoral—and if nothing is immoral, then such corporate behavior is clearly contrary to the long-term interest of a corporation. In the end, we will reflect on ways to prevent such behavior, and on what is philosophically implied by corporate willingness to act in clearly immoral ways.

THE "INVISIBLE HAND"

Essentially, the first argument is that the greatest good for the greatest number will be, and can only be, achieved by corporations acting legally but unregulated by any moral concern in the pursuit of profit.

As we saw earlier, the evidence for this argument rests on a fairly classical and unquestioning acceptance of Adam Smith's view that society achieves a greater good when each person is allowed to pursue her or his own self-interested ends than when each person's pursuit of self-interested ends is regulated in some way or another by moral rules or concern. But I know of no evidence Smith ever offered for this latter claim, although it seems clear that those who adopt it generally do so out of respect for the perceived good that has emerged for various modern societies as a direct result of the free enterprise system and its ability to raise the overall standard of living of all those under it.

However, there is nothing inevitable about the greatest good occurring in an unregulated economy. Indeed, we have good inductive evidence from the age of the Robber Barons that unless the profit motive is regulated in various ways (by statute or otherwise) untold social evil can, and *will*, occur because of the natural tendency of the system to place ever-increasing sums of money in ever-decreasing numbers of hands as a result of the nature of competition unregulated. If all this is so, then so much the worse for all philosophical attempts to justify what would appear to be morally questionable corporate behavior on the grounds that corporate behavior, unregulated by moral concern, is necessarily or even probably productive of the greatest good for the greatest number. Moreover, a rule utilitarian would not be very hard pressed to show the many unsavory implications to society as a whole if society were to take seriously a rule to the effect that, if one acts legally, it is morally permissible to do whatever one wants to do to achieve a profit. We shall discuss some

of those implications of this rule below before drawing a conclusion.

The second argument cited above asserts that even if we were to grant, for the sake of argument, that corporations have social responsibilities beyond that of making as much money as is legally possible for the shareholders, there would be no noncontroversial way for corporations to discover just what these responsibilities are in the order of their importance. Owing to the fact that even distinguished moral philosophers predictably disagree on what one's moral responsibilities are, if any, it would seem irresponsible to limit profits to satisfy dubious moral responsibilities.

For one thing, this argument unduly exaggerates our potential for moral disagreement. Admittedly, there might well be important disagreements among corporations (just as there could be among philosophers) as to a priority ranking of major social needs; but that does not mean that most of us could not, or would not, agree that certain things ought not be done in the name of profit even when there is no law prohibiting such acts. Doubtless, there will always be a few who would do most anything for a profit; but that is hardly a good argument in favor of their having the moral right to do so rather than a good argument showing that they refuse to be moral. In sum, it is difficult to see how this second argument favoring corporate moral nihilism is any better than the general argument for ethical nihilism based on the variability of ethical judgments or practices; and apart from the fact that it tacitly presupposes that morality is a matter of what we all in fact would, or should, accept, the argument is maximally counterintuitive (as I shall show) by way of suggesting that we cannot generally agree that corporations have certain clear social responsibilities to avoid certain practices. Accordingly, I would now like to argue that if anything is immoral, a certain kind of corporate behavior is quite immoral although it may not be illegal.

MURDER FOR PROFIT

Without caring to enter into the reasons for the belief, I assume we all believe that it is wrong to kill an innocent human being for no other reason than that doing so would be more financially rewarding for the killer than if he were to earn his livelihood in some other way. Nor, I assume, should our moral feeling on this matter change depending on the amount of money involved. Killing an innocent baby for fifteen million dollars would not seem to be any less objectionable than killing it for twenty cents. It is possible, however, that a self-professing utilitarian might be tempted to argue that the killing of an innocent baby for fifteen million dollars would not be objectionable if the money were to be given to the poor; under these circumstances, greater good would be achieved by the killing of the innocent baby. But, I submit, if anybody were to argue in this fashion, his argument would be quite deficient because he has not established what he needs to establish to make his argument sound. What he needs is a clear, convincing argument that raising the standard of living of an indefinite number of poor persons by the killing of an innocent person is a greater good for all those affected by the act than if the standard of living were not raised by the killing of an innocent person. This is needed because part of what we mean by having a basic right to life is that a person's life cannot be taken from him or her without a good reason. If our utilitarian cannot provide a convincing justification for his claim that a greater good is served by killing an innocent person in order to raise the standard of living for a large number of poor people, then it is hard to see how he can have the good reason that he needs to deprive an innocent person of his or her life. Now, it seems clear that there will be anything but unanimity in the moral community on the question of whether there is a greater good achieved in raising the standard of living by killing an innocent baby than in leaving the standard of living alone and not killing an innocent baby. Moreover, even if everybody were to agree that the greater good is achieved by the killing of the innocent baby, how could that be shown to be true? How does one compare the moral value of a human life with the moral value of raising the standard of living by the taking of that life? Indeed, the more one thinks about it, the more difficult it is to see just what would count as objective evidence for the claim that the greater good is achieved by the killing of the innocent baby. Accordingly, I can see nothing that would justify the utilitarian who might be tempted to argue that if the sum is large enough, and if the sum were to be used for raising the standard of living for an indefinite number of poor people, then it would be morally acceptable to kill an innocent person for money.

These reflections should not be taken to imply, however, that no utilitarian argument could justify the killing of an innocent person for money. After all, if the sum were large enough to save the lives of a large number of people who would surely die if the innocent baby were not killed, then one would as a rule be justified in killing the innocent baby for the sum in question. But this situation is obviously quite different from the situation in which one would attempt to justify the killing of an innocent person in order to raise the standard of living for an indefinite number of poor people. It makes sense to kill one innocent person in order to save, say, twenty innocent persons; but it makes no sense at all to kill one innocent person to raise the standard of living of an indefinite number of people. In the latter case, but not in the former, a comparison is made between things that are incomparable.

Given these considerations, it is remarkable and somewhat perplexing that certain corporations should seek to defend practices that are in fact instances of killing innocent persons for profit. Take, for example, the corporate practice of dumping known carcinogens into rivers. On Milton Friedman's view, we should not regulate or prevent such companies from dumping their effluents into the environment. Rather we should, if we like, tax the company after the effluents are in the water and then have the tax money used to clean up the environment.[5] For Friedman, and others, the fact that so many people will die as a result of this practice seems to be just part of the cost of doing business and making a profit. If there is any moral difference between such corporate practices and murdering innocent human beings for money, it is hard to see what it is. It is even more difficult to see how anyone could justify the practice and see it as no more than a business practice not to be regulated by moral concern. And there are a host of other corporate activities that are morally equivalent to deliberate killing of innocent persons for money. Such practices number among them contributing funds

to "destabilize" a foreign government, selling cigarettes while knowing that they are highly addictive killers of innocent people, advertising cigarettes, knowingly marketing children's clothing having a known cancer-causing agent, and refusing to recall (for fear of financial loss) goods known to be sufficiently defective to directly maim or kill a certain percentage of their unsuspecting users because of the defect. On this latter item, we are all familiar, for example, with convincingly documented charges that certain prominent automobile and tire manufacturers will knowingly market equipment sufficiently defective to increase the likelihood of death as a direct result of the defect, and yet refuse to recall the product because the cost of recalling and repairing would have a greater adverse impact on profit than if the product were not recalled and the company paid the projected number of predictably successful suits. Of course, if the projected cost of the predictably successful suits were to outweigh the cost of recall and repair, then the product would be recalled and repaired, but not otherwise.

In cases of this sort, the companies involved may admit to having certain marketing problems or a design problem, and they may even admit to having made a mistake; but, interestingly enough, they do not view themselves as immoral or as murderers for keeping their product in the market place when they know people are dying from it, people who would not die if the defect were corrected.

The important point is not whether in fact these practices have occurred in the past, or occur even now; there can be no doubt that such practices have occurred and continue to occur. Rather the point is that when companies act in such ways as a matter of policy, they must either not know what they do is murder (i.e., unjustifiable killing of an innocent person), or knowing that it is murder, seek to justify it in terms of profit. And I have been arguing that it is difficult to see how any corporate manager could fail to see that these policies amount to murder for money, although there may be no civil statute against such corporate behavior. If so, then where such policies exist, we can only assume that they are designed and implemented by corporate managers who either see nothing wrong with murder for money (which is implausible) or recognize that what they do is wrong but simply refuse to act morally because it is more financially rewarding to act immorally.

Of course, it is possible that corporate executives would not recognize such acts as murder. They may, after all, view murder as a legal concept involving one non-corporate person or persons deliberately killing another non-corporate person or persons and prosecutable only under existing criminal statute. If so, it is somewhat understandable how corporate executives might fail, at least psychologically, to see such corporate policies as murder rather than as, say, calculated risks, tradeoffs, or design errors. Still, for all that, the logic of the situation seems clear enough.

CONCLUSION

In addition to the fact that the only two plausible arguments favoring the Friedman doctrine are unsatisfactory, a strong case can be made for the claim that corporations *do* have a clear and noncontroversial moral responsibility not to design or implement, for reasons of profit, policies that they know, or have good reason to believe, will kill or otherwise seriously injure innocent persons affected by those policies. Moreover, we have said nothing about wage discrimination, sexism, discrimination in hiring, price fixing, price gouging, questionable but not unlawful competition, or other similar practices that some will think businesses should avoid by virtue of responsibility to society. My main concern has been to show that because we all agree that murder for money is generally wrong, and since there is no discernible difference between that and certain corporate policies that are not in fact illegal, then these corporate practices are clearly immoral (that is, they ought not to be done) and incapable of being morally justified by appeal to the Friedman doctrine since that doctrine does not admit of adequate evidential support. In itself, it seems sad that this argument needs to be made and, if it were not for what appears to be a fairly strong commitment within the business community to the Friedman doctrine in the name of the unquestionable success of the free enterprise system, the argument would not need to be stated.

The fact that such practices do exist —designed and implemented by corporate managers who, for all intents and purposes appear to be upright members of the moral community—only heightens the need for effective social prevention. Presumably, of course, any company willing to put human lives into the profit and loss column is not likely to respond to moral censure. Accordingly, I submit that perhaps the most effective way to deal with the problem of preventing such corporate behavior would consist in structuring legislation such that senior corporate managers who knowingly concur in practices of the sort listed above can effectively be tried, at their own expense, for murder, rather than censured and fined a sum to be paid out of corporate profits. This may seem a somewhat extreme or unrealistic proposal. However, it seems more unrealistic to think that aggressively competitive corporations will respond to what is morally necessary if failure to do so could be very or even minimally profitable. In short, unless we take strong and appropriate steps to prevent such practices, society will be reinforcing a destructive mode of behavior that is maximally disrespectful of human life, just as society will be reinforcing a value system that so emphasizes monetary gain as a standard of human success that murder for profit could be a corporate policy if the penalty for being caught at it were not too dear.

Fortunately, a number of states in America have enacted legislation that makes corporations subject to the criminal code of that state. This practice began to emerge quite strongly after the famous Pinto case in which an Indiana superior court judge refused to dismiss a homicide indictment against the Ford Motor Company. The company was indicted on charges of reckless homicide stemming from a 1978 accident involving a 1973 Pinto in which three girls died when the car burst into flames after being slammed in the rear. This was the first case in which Ford, or any other automobile manufacturer, had been charged with a criminal offense. The indictment went forward because the state of Indiana adopted in 1977 a criminal code provision permitting corporations to be charged with criminal acts. At the time, incidentally, twenty-two other states had similar codes. At any rate, the judge, in refusing to set aside the indictment, agreed with the prosecutor's argument that the charge was based not on the Pinto design fault, but rather on the fact that Ford

had permitted the car "to remain on Indiana highways knowing full well its defects." The fact that the Ford Motor company was ultimately found innocent of the charges by the jury is incidental to the point that the increasing number of states that allow corporations to fall under the criminal code is an example of social regulation that could have been avoided had corporations and corporate managers not followed so ardently the Friedman doctrine.

In the long run, of course, corporate and individual willingness to do what is clearly immoral for the sake of monetary gain is a patent commitment of a certain view about the nature of human happiness and success, a view that needs to be placed in the balance with Aristotle's reasoned argument and reflections to the effect that money and all that it brings is a means to an end, and not the sort of end in itself that will justify acting immorally to attain it. What that beautiful end is and why being moral allows us to achieve it, may well be the most rewarding and profitable subject a human being can think about. Properly understood and placed in perspective, Aristotle's view on the nature and attainment of human happiness could go a long way toward alleviating the temptation to kill for money.

In the meantime, any ardent supporter of the capitalistic system will want to see the system thrive and flourish; and this it cannot do if it invites and demands government regulation in the name of the public interest. A *strong* ideological commitment to what I have described above as the Friedman doctrine is counterproductive and not in anyone's long-range interest because it is most likely to beget an ever-increasing regulatory climate. The only way to avoid such encroaching regulation is to find ways to move the business community into the long-term view of what is in its interest, and effect ways of both determining and responding to social needs before society moves to regulate business to that end. To so move the business community is to ask business to regulate its own modes of competition in ways that may seem very difficult to achieve. Indeed, if what I have been suggesting is correct, the only kind of enduring capitalism is humane capitalism, one that is at least as socially responsible as society needs. By the same token, contrary to what is sometimes felt in the business community, the Friedman doctrine, ardently adopted for the dubious reasons generally given, will most likely undermine capitalism and motivate an economic socialism by assuring an erosive regulatory climate in a society that expects the business community to be socially responsible in ways that go beyond just making legal profits.

In sum, being socially responsible in ways that go beyond legal profit making is by no means a dubious luxury for the capitalist in today's world. It is a necessity if capitalism is to survive at all; and, presumably, we shall all profit with the survival of a vibrant capitalism. If anything, then, rigid adherence to the Friedman doctrine is not only philosophically unjustified, and unjustifiable, it is also unprofitable in the long run, and therefore, downright subversive of the long-term common good. Unfortunately, taking the long-run view is difficult for everyone. After all, for each of us, tomorrow may not come. But living for today only does not seem to make much sense either, if that deprives us of any reasonable and happy tomorrow. Living for the future may not be the healthiest thing to do; but do it we must, if we have good reason to think that we will have a future. The trick is to provide for the future without living in it, and that just requires being moral.[6]

This paper is a revised and expanded version of "Morality in the Marketplace," which appears in Business Ethics *(revised edition) eds. Milton Snoeyenbos, Robert Almeder and James Humber (Buffalo, N.Y.: Prometheus Press, 1992) 82–90, and, as such, it is a revised and expanded version of an earlier piece "The Ethics of Profit: Reflections on Corporate Responsibility," which originally appeared in* Business and Society *(Winter 1980, 7–15).*

NOTES

1. Adam Smith, *The Wealth of Nations*, ed. Edwin Canaan (New York: Modern Library, 1937), p. 423.

2. See Milton Friedman, "The Social Responsibility of Business Is to Increase Its Profits," in *The New York Times Magazine* (September 13, 1970), pp. 33, 122–126 and "Milton Friedman Responds," in *Business and Society Review* no. 1 (Spring 1972), p. 5ff.

3. Albert Z. Carr, "Is Business Bluffing Ethical?" *Harvard Business Review* (January–February 1968).

4. Milton Friedman in "Milton Friedman Responds," in *Business and Society Review* no. 1 (Spring 1972), p. 10.

5. Ibid

6. I would like to thank J. Humber and M. Snoeyenbos for their comments and criticisms of an earlier draft.

POSTSCRIPT

Are Profits the Only Business of Business?

Friedman dismisses the pleas of those who argue for socially responsible business action on the grounds that these individuals do not understand the role of the corporate executive in modern society. Friedman points out that the executives are responsible to the corporate owners, and if the corporate executives take a "socially responsible" action that reduces the return on the owners' investment, they have spent the owners' money. This, Friedman maintains, violates the very foundation of the American political-economic system: individual freedom. If the corporate executives wish to take socially responsible actions, they should use their own money; they should not prevent the owners from spending their money on whatever social actions they might wish to support.

Almeder argues that some corporate behavior is immoral and that defense of this immoral behavior imposes great costs on society. He likens corporate acts such as advertising cigarettes, marketing automobiles that cannot sustain moderate rear-end collisions, and contributing funds to destabilize foreign governments to murdering innocent children for profit. He argues that society must not condone this behavior but, instead, through federal and state legislation, must continue to impose regulations upon businesses until businesses begin to regulate themselves.

Perhaps no single topic is more fundamental to microeconomics than the issue of profits. Many pages have been written in defense of profits; see, for example, Milton and Rose Friedman's *Free to Choose: A Personal Statement* (Harcourt Brace Jovanovich, 1980). A classic reference is Frank H. Knight's *Risk, Uncertainty, and Profits* (Kelly Press, 1921). Friedrich A. Hayek, the author of many journal articles and books, is a guru for many current free marketers. There are a number of other books and articles, however, that are highly critical of the Friedman-Knight-Hayek position, including Christopher D. Stone's *Where the Law Ends: Social Control of Corporate Behavior* (Harper & Row, 1975). Others who challenge the legitimacy of the notion that markets are morally free zones include Thomas Mulligan, "A Critique of Milton Friedman's Essay 'The Social Responsibility of Business Is to Increase Its Profits,'" *Journal of Business Ethics* (1986); Daniel M. Hausman, "Are Markets Morally Free Zones?" *Philosophy and Public Affairs* (Fall 1989); and Andrew Henley, "Economic Orthodoxy and the Free Market System: A Christian Critique," *International Journal of Social Economics* (vol. 14, no. 10, 1987).

ISSUE 2

Should We Encourage the Private Ownership of Guns?

YES: Daniel D. Polsby, from "The False Promise of Gun Control," *The Atlantic Monthly* (March 1994)

NO: Arthur L. Kellermann et al., from "Gun Ownership as a Risk Factor for Homicide in the Home," *The New England Journal of Medicine* (October 7, 1993)

ISSUE SUMMARY

YES: Law professor Daniel D. Polsby alleges that guns do not increase crime rates or violence in the streets but that the "proliferation of gun-control laws almost certainly does."

NO: Emergency room physician Arthur L. Kellermann and his colleagues argue that gun ownership increases an individual's risk of being murdered rather than providing that person with self-protection.

In 1992 crimes committed with handguns increased by almost 50 percent over the previous five-year annual average. In that year, handguns were used in 931,000 violent crimes. It may be because of statistics such as these that the Brady Bill—federal legislation requiring a five-day waiting period and a background check for individuals wishing to purchase guns—was passed by Congress in November 1993 after numerous attempts to pass gun-control legislation were defeated by the powerful pro-gun lobby during the previous seven years.

The pro-gun interests in the United States are well articulated by the National Rifle Association (NRA) and its members. This organization boasts a membership in excess of 3.3 million, and it claimed liquid assets of more than $90 million in 1990. Throughout its existence, the NRA has effectively blocked nearly every attempt at governmental control over private ownership of guns. Traditionally, the NRA and others have defended their position on the grounds that legislation in this area would violate the "right to bear arms," which they allege is protected by the Second Amendment to the Constitution.

However, in recent years public opinion has increasingly turned against the gun lobby. Also, society has begun to question whether or not the Second Amendment is applicable to private gun ownership. The amendment in full states: "A well regulated Militia, being necessary to the security of a free

State, the right of people to keep and bear Arms, shall not be infringed." Many argue that the NRA's constitutional argument is rendered invalid by the reference to a "well regulated Militia." Most legal scholars maintain that the Supreme Court's 1939 decision in *United States v. Miller* still stands as the appropriate interpretation of the Second Amendment. Here the Court ruled that the intent of the amendment was to ensure a collective right having "some reasonable relationship to the preservation or efficiency of a well-regulated militia." The Court did not rule that individuals have a right to keep and bear arms. Indeed, lower courts have turned to the *Miller* decision to *uphold*, not strike down, gun-control legislation.

The most recent Supreme Court ruling in this area came in 1980, when the Court reaffirmed that attempts to control the use of guns through legislative action "do not trench upon any constitutionally protected liberties." It is noteworthy that both Warren E. Burger, the chief justice at that time, and the current chief justice William H. Rehnquist, both conservatives, joined the majority of the Court in this interpretation.

If there is no constitutional prohibition against gun control, what are the costs and benefits of private ownership of handguns? The NRA has long argued that handguns are necessary for self-protection. The NRA's new advertising slogan, "Refuse to Be a Victim," is directed toward getting that message across to women, who as a group have traditionally been more opposed to gun ownership than men. The arguments of those opposed to gun control go far beyond this, however. This becomes clear in the essay by Daniel D. Polsby that follows. Polsby raises fundamental economic questions about the demand for guns, the sources of the supply of guns, and the elastic characteristics of both supply and demand.

In large measure, the purpose of Polsby's selection is to respond to the medical community, which has challenged the NRA's contention that guns are an important means of self-protection. In this regard, Arthur L. Kellermann and his associates argue in the second selection that guns are more likely to result in injury to a member of a gun-owning household than they are to protect the household from intruders.

YES

Daniel D. Polsby

THE FALSE PROMISE OF GUN CONTROL

During the 1960s and 1970s the robbery rate in the United States increased sixfold, and the murder rate doubled; the rate of handgun ownership nearly doubled in that period as well. Handguns and criminal violence grew together apace, and national opinion leaders did not fall to remark on the coincidence.

It has become a bipartisan article of faith that more handguns cause more violence. Such was the unequivocal conclusion of the National Commission on the Causes and Prevention of Violence in 1969, and such is now the editorial opinion of virtually every influential newspaper and magazine, from *The Washington Post* to *The Economist* to the *Chicago Tribune*. Members of the House and Senate who have not dared to confront the gun lobby concede the connection privately. Even if the National Rifle Association [NRA] can produce blizzards of angry calls and letters to the Capitol virtually overnight, House members one by one have been going public, often after some new firearms atrocity at a fast-food restaurant or the like. And last November they passed the Brady bill.

Alas, however well accepted, the conventional wisdom about guns and violence is mistaken. Guns don't increase national rates of crime and violence —but the continued proliferation of gun-control laws almost certainly does. Current rates of crime and violence are a bit below the peaks of the late 1970s, but because of a slight oncoming bulge in the at-risk population of males aged fifteen to thirty-four, the crime rate will soon worsen. The rising generation of criminals will have no more difficulty than their elders did in obtaining the tools of their trade. Growing violence will lead to calls for laws still more severe. Each fresh round of legislation will be followed by renewed frustration.

Gun-control laws don't work. What is worse, they act perversely. While legitimate users of firearms encounter intense regulation, scrutiny, and bureaucratic control, illicit markets easily adapt to whatever difficulties a free society throws in their way. Also, efforts to curtail the supply of firearms inflict collateral damage on freedom and privacy interests that have long been considered central to American public life. Thanks to the seemingly never-ending war on drugs and long experience attempting to suppress prostitution and pornography, we know a great deal about how illicit markets function and how costly to the public attempts to control them can be. It is essential that we make use of this experience in coming to grips with gun control.

The thousands of gun-control laws in the United States are of two general types. The older kind sought to regulate how, where, and by whom firearms could be carried. More recent laws have sought to make it more costly to buy, sell, or use firearms (or certain classes of firearms, such as assault rifles, Saturday-night specials, and so on) by imposing fees, special taxes, or surtaxes on them. The Brady bill is of both types: it has a background-check provision, and its five-day waiting period amounts to a "time tax" on acquiring handguns. All such laws can be called scarcity-inducing, because they seek to raise the cost of buying firearms, as figured in terms of money, time, nuisance, or stigmatization.

Despite the mounting number of scarcity-inducing laws, no one is very satisfied with them. Hobbyists want to get rid of them, and gun-control proponents don't think they go nearly far enough. Everyone seems to agree that gun-control laws have some effect on the distribution of firearms. But it has not been the dramatic and measurable effect their proponents desired.

Opponents of gun control have traditionally wrapped their arguments in the Second Amendment to the Constitution. Indeed, most modern scholarship affirms that so far as the drafters of the Bill of Rights were concerned the right to bear arms was to be enjoyed by everyone, not just a militia, and that one of the principal justifications for an armed populace was to secure the tranquillity and good order of the community. But most people are not dedicated antiquitarians, and would not be impressed by the argument "I admit that my behavior is very dangerous to public safety, but the Second Amendment says I have a right to do it anyway." That would be a case for repealing the Second Amendment, not respecting it.

FIGHTING THE DEMAND CURVE

Everyone knows that possessing a handgun makes it easier to intimidate, wound, or kill someone. But the implication of this point for social policy has not been so well understood. It is easy to count the bodies of those who have been killed or wounded with guns, but not easy to count the people who have avoided harm because they had access to weapons. Think about uniformed police officers, who carry handguns in plain view not in order to kill people but simply to daunt potential attackers. And it works. Criminals generally do not single out police officers for opportunistic attack. Though officers can expect to draw their guns from time to time, few even in big-city departments will actually fire a shot (except in target practice) in the course of a year. This observation points to an important truth: people who are armed make comparatively unattractive victims. A criminal might not know if any one civilian is armed, but if it becomes known that a large number of civilians do carry weapons, criminals will become warier.

Which weapons laws are the right kinds can be decided only after considering two related questions. First, what is the connection between civilian possession of firearms and social violence? Second, how can we expect gun-control laws to alter people's behavior? Most recent scholarship raises serious questions about the "weapons increase violence" hypothesis. The second question is emphasized here, because it is routinely overlooked and often mocked when noticed; yet it is crucial. Rational gun control requires understanding not only the relationship between weapons and violence but also the relationship between laws and people's behavior. Some things are very hard to accomplish with laws. The purpose of a law and its likely effects are not always the same thing. Many statutes are notorious for the way in which their unintended effects have swamped their intended ones.

In order to predict who will comply with gun-control laws, we should remember that guns are economic goods that are traded in markets. Consumers' interest in them varies. For religious, moral, aesthetic, or practical reasons, some people would refuse to buy firearms at any price. Other people willingly pay very high prices for them.

Handguns, so often the subject of gun-control laws, are desirable for one purpose—to allow a person tactically to dominate a hostile transaction with another person. The value of a weapon to a given person is a function of two factors: how much he or she wants to dominate a confrontation if one occurs, and how likely it is that he or she will actually be in a situation calling for a gun.

Dominating a transaction simply means getting what one wants without being hurt. Where people differ is in how likely it is that they will be involved in a situation in which a gun will be valuable. Someone who *intends* to engage in a transaction involving a gun—a criminal, for example—is obviously in the best possible position to predict that likelihood. Criminals should therefore be will-ing to pay more for a weapon than most other people would. Professors, politicians, and newspaper editors are, as a group, at very low risk of being involved in such transactions, and they thus systematically underrate the value of defensive handguns. (Correlative, perhaps, is their uncritical readiness to accept studies that debunk the utility of firearms for self-defense.) The class of people we wish to deprive of guns, then, is the very class with the most inelastic demand for them —criminals—whereas the people most likely to comply with gun-control laws don't value guns in the first place.

DO GUNS DRIVE UP CRIME RATES?

Which premise is true—that guns increase crime or that the fear of crime causes people to obtain guns? Most of the country's major newspapers apparently take this problem to have been solved by an article published by Arthur Kellermann and several associates in the October 7, 1993, *New England Journal of Medicine*. Kellermann is an emergency-room physician who has published a number of influential papers that he believes discredit the thesis that private ownership of firearms is a useful means of self-protection. (An indication of his wide influence is that within two months the study received almost 100 mentions in publications and broadcast transcripts indexed in the Nexis data base.) For this study Kellermann and his associates identified fifteen behavioral and fifteen environmental variables that applied to a 388-member set of homicide victims, found a "matching" control group of 388 nonhomicide victims, and then ascertained how the two groups differed in gun ownership. In interviews Kellermann made clear his belief that owning a handgun markedly increases a person's risk of being murdered.

But the study does not prove that point at all. Indeed, as Kellermann explicitly conceded in the text of the article, the causal arrow may very well point in the other direction: the threat of being killed may make people more likely to arm themselves. Many people at risk of being killed, especially people involved in the drug trade or other illegal ventures, might well rationally buy a gun as a precaution, and be willing to pay a price driven up by gun-control laws. Crime, after all, is a dangerous business. Peter Reuter and Mark Kleiman, drug-policy researchers, calculated in 1987 that the average crack dealer's risk of being killed was far greater than his risk of being sent to prison. (Their data cannot, however, support the implication that ownership of a firearm causes or exacerbates the risk of being killed.)

Defending the validity of his work, Kellermann has emphasized that the link between lung cancer and smoking was initially established by studies methodologically no different from his. Gary Kleck, a criminology professor at Florida State University, has pointed out the flaw in this comparison. No one ever thought that lung cancer causes smoking, so when the association between the two was established the direction of the causal arrow was not in doubt. Kleck wrote that it is as though Kellermann, trying to discover how diabetics differ from other people, found that they are much more likely to possess insulin than nondiabetics, and concluded that insulin is a risk factor for diabetes.

The New York Times, the *Los Angeles Times, The Washington Post, The Boston Globe,* and the *Chicago Tribune* all gave prominent coverage to Kellermann's study as soon as it appeared, but none saw fit to discuss the study's limitations. A few, in order to introduce a hint of balance, mentioned that the NRA, or some member of its staff, disagreed with the study. But readers had no way of knowing that Kellermann himself had registered a disclaimer in his text. "It is possible," he conceded. "that reverse causation accounted for some of the association we observed between gun ownership and homicide." Indeed, the point is stronger than that: "reverse causation" may account for *most* of the association between gun ownership and homicide. Kellermann's data simply do not allow one to draw any conclusion.

If firearms increased violence and crime, then rates of spousal homicide would have skyrocketed, because the stock of privately owned handguns has increased rapidly since the mid-1960s. But according to an authoritative study of spousal homicide in the *American Journal of Public Health,* by James Mercy and Linda Saltzman, rates of spousal homicide in the years 1976 to 1985 fell. If firearms increased violence and crime, the crime rate should have increased throughout the 1980s, while the national stock of privately owned handguns increased by more than a million units in every year of the decade. It did not. Nor should the rates of violence and crime in Switzerland, New Zealand, and Israel be as low as they are, since the number of firearms per civilian household is comparable to that in the United States. Conversely, gun-controlled Mexico and South Africa should be islands of peace instead of having murder rates more than twice as high as those [in the United States]. The determinants of crime and law-abidingness are, of course, complex matters, which are not fully understood and certainly not explicable in terms of a country's laws. But gun-control enthusiasts, who have made capital out of the low murder rate in England, which is largely disarmed, simply ignore the counterexamples that don't fit their theory.

If firearms increased violence and crime, Florida's murder rate should not have been falling since the introduction, seven years ago, of a law that makes it easier for ordinary citizens to get permits to carry concealed handguns. Yet the murder rate has remained the same or fallen every year since the law was enacted, and it is now lower than the national murder rate (which has been rising). As of last November 183,561 permits had been issued, and only seventeen of the permits had been revoked because the holder was involved in a firearms offense. It would be precipitate to claim that the new law has "caused" the murder rate to subside. Yet here is a situation that doesn't fit the hypothesis that weapons increase violence.

If firearms increased violence and crime, programs of induced scarcity would suppress violence and crime. But —another anomaly—they don't. Why not? A theorem, which we could call the futility theorem, explains why gun-control laws must either be ineffectual or in the long term actually provoke more violence and crime. Any theorem depends on both observable fact and assumption. An assumption that can be made with confidence is that the higher the number of victims a criminal assumes to be armed, the higher will be the risk—the price—of assaulting them. By definition, gun-control laws should make weapons scarcer and thus more expensive. By our prior reasoning about

demand among various types of consumers, after the laws are enacted criminals should be better armed, compared with noncriminals, than they were before. Of course, plenty of noncriminals will remain armed. But even if many noncriminals will pay as high a price as criminals will to obtain firearms, a larger number will not.

Criminals will thus still take the same gamble they already take in assaulting a victim who might or might not be armed. But they may appreciate that the laws have given them a freer field, and that crime still pays—pays even better, in fact, than before. What will happen to the rate of violence? Only a relatively few gun-mediated transactions —currently, five percent of armed robberies committed with firearms—result in someone's actually being shot (the statistics are not broken down into encounters between armed assailants and unarmed victims, and encounters in which both parties are armed). It seems reasonable to fear that if the number of such transactions were to increase because criminals thought they faced fewer deterrents, there would be a corresponding increase in shootings. Conversely, if gun-mediated transactions declined—if criminals initiated fewer of them because they feared encountering an armed victim or an armed good Samaritan—the number of shootings would go down. The magnitude of these effects is, admittedly, uncertain. Yet it is hard to doubt the general tendency of a change in the law that imposes legal burdens on buying guns. The futility theorem suggests that gun-control laws, if effective at all, would unfavorably affect the rate of violent crime.

The futility theorem provides a lens through which to see much of the debate. It is undeniable that gun-control laws work—to an extent. Consider, for example, California's background-check law, which in the past two years has prevented about 12,000 people with a criminal record or a history of mental illness or drug abuse from buying handguns. In the same period Illinois's background-check law prevented the delivery of firearms to more than 2,000 people. Surely some of these people simply turned to an illegal market, but just as surely not all of them did. The laws of large numbers allow us to say that among the foiled thousands, some potential killers were prevented from getting a gun. We do not know whether the number is large or small, but it is implausible to think it is zero. And, as gun-control proponents are inclined to say, "If only one life is saved..."

The hypothesis that firearms increase violence does predict that if we can slow down the diffusion of guns, there will be less violence; one life, or more, *will* be saved. But the futility theorem asks that we look not simply at the gross number of bad actors prevented from getting guns but at the effect the law has on *all* the people who want to buy a gun. Suppose we succeed in piling tax burdens on the acquisition of firearms. We can safely assume that a number of people who might use guns to kill will be sufficiently discouraged not to buy them. But we cannot assume this about people who feel that they must have guns in order to survive financially and physically. A few lives might indeed be saved. But the overall rate of violent crime might not go down at all. And if guns are owned predominantly by people who have good reason to think they will use them, the rate might even go up.

Are there empirical studies that can serve to help us choose between the futility theorem and the hypothesis that guns increase violence? Unfortunately, no: the best studies of the effects of gun-control laws are quite inconclusive. Our statistical tools are too weak to allow us to identify an effect clearly enough to persuade an open-minded skeptic. But it is precisely when we are dealing with undetectable statistical effects that we have to be certain we are using the best models available of human behavior....

ADMINISTERING PROHIBITION

Assume for the sake of argument that to a reasonable degree of criminological certainty, guns are every bit the public-health hazard they are said to be. It follows, and many journalists and a few public officials have already said, that we ought to treat guns the same way we do smallpox viruses or other critical vectors of morbidity and mortality—namely, isolate them from potential hosts and destroy them as speedily as possible. Clearly, firearms have at least one characteristic that distinguishes them from smallpox viruses: nobody wants to keep smallpox viruses in the nightstand drawer. Amazingly enough, gun-control literature seems never to have explored the problem of getting weapons away from people who very much want to keep them in the nightstand drawer.

Our existing gun-control laws are not uniformly permissive, and, indeed, in certain places are tough even by international standards. Advocacy groups seldom stress the considerable differences among American jurisdictions, and media reports regularly assert that firearms are readily available to anybody anywhere in the country. This is not the case. For example, handgun restrictions in Chicago and the District of Columbia are much less flexible than the ones in the United Kingdom. Several hundred thousand British subjects may legally buy and possess sidearms, and anyone who joins a target-shooting club is eligible to do so. But in Chicago and the District of Columbia, excepting peace officers and the like, only grandfathered registrants may legally possess handguns. Of course, tens or hundreds of thousands of people in both those cities—nobody can be sure how many—do in fact possess them illegally.

Although there is, undoubtedly, illegal handgun ownership in the United Kingdom, especially in Northern Ireland (where considerations of personal security and public safety are decidedly unlike those elsewhere in the British Isles), it is probable that Americans and Britons differ in their disposition to obey gun-control laws: there is reputed to be a marked national disparity in compliance behavior. This difference, if it exists, may have something to do with the comparatively marginal value of firearms to British consumers. Even before it had strict firearms regulation, Britain had very low rates of crimes involving guns; British criminals, unlike their American counterparts, prefer burglary (a crime of stealth) to robbery (a crime of intimidation).

Unless people are prepared to surrender their guns voluntarily, how can the U.S. government confiscate an appreciable fraction of our country's nearly 200 million privately owned firearms? We know that it is possible to set up weapons-free zones in certain locations—commercial airports and many courthouses and, lately, some troubled big-city high schools and housing projects. The sacrifices of privacy and convenience, and the costs of paying guards, have been thought worth the (perceived) gain in security. No doubt it would be possible, though it would probably not be easy, to make weapons-free zones of shopping centers, department stores, movie theaters, ball parks. But it is not obvious how one would cordon off the whole of an open society.

Voluntary programs have been ineffectual. From time to time community-action groups or police departments have sponsored "turn in your gun" days, which are nearly always disappointing. Sometimes the government offers to buy guns at some price. This approach has been endorsed by Senator Chafee and the *Los Angeles Times*. Jonathan Alter, of *Newsweek,* has suggested a variation on this theme: youngsters could exchange their guns for a handshake with Michael Jordan or some other sports hero. If the price offered exceeds that at which a gun can be bought on the street, one can expect to see plans of this kind yield some sort of harvest—as indeed they have. But it is implausible that these schemes will actually result in a less-dangerous population. Government programs to buy up surplus cheese cause more cheese to be produced without affecting the availability of cheese to people who want to buy it. So it is with guns. . . .

The solution to the problem of crime lies in improving the chances of young men. Easier said than done, to be sure. No one has yet proposed a convincing program for checking all the dislocating forces that government assistance can set in motion. One relatively straightforward change would be reform of the educational system. Nothing guarantees prudent behavior like a sense of the future, and with average skills in reading, writing, and math, young people can realistically look forward to constructive employment and the straight life that steady work makes possible.

But firearms are nowhere near the root of the problem of violence. As long as people come in unlike sizes, shapes, ages, and temperaments, as long as they diverge in their taste for risk and their willingness and capacity to prey on other people or to defend themselves from predation, and above all as long as some people have little or nothing to lose by spending their lives in crime, dispositions to violence will persist.

This is what makes the case for the right to bear arms, not the Second Amendment. It is foolish to let anything ride on hopes for effective gun control. As long as crime pays as well as it does, we will have plenty of it, and honest folk must choose between being victims and defending themselves.

NO

Arthur L. Kellermann et al.

GUN OWNERSHIP AS A RISK FACTOR FOR HOMICIDE IN THE HOME

Homicide claims the lives of approximately 24,000 Americans each year, making it the 11th leading cause of death among all age groups, the 2nd leading cause of death among all people 15 to 24 years old, and the leading cause of death among male African Americans 15 to 34 years old. Homicide rates declined in the United States during the early 1980s but rebounded thereafter. One category of homicide that is particularly threatening to our sense of safety is homicide in the home.

Unfortunately, the influence of individual and household characteristics on the risk of homicide in the home is poorly understood. Illicit-drug use, alcoholism, and domestic violence are widely believed to increase the risk of homicide, but the relative importance of these factors is unknown. Frequently cited options to improve home security include the installation of electronic security systems, burglar bars, and reinforced security doors. The effectiveness of these protective measures is unclear, however.

Many people also keep firearms (particularly handguns) in the home for personal protection. One recent survey determined that handgun owners are twice as likely as owners of long guns to report "protection from crime" as their single most important reason for keeping a gun in the home. It is possible, however, that the risks of keeping a firearm in the home may outweigh the potential benefits.

To clarify these issues, we conducted a population-based case–control study to determine the strength of the association between a variety of potential risk factors and the incidence of homicide in the home....

RESULTS

Study Population

There were 1860 homicides in the three counties [from which samples were taken] during the study period. Four hundred forty-four (23.9 percent) took place in the home of the victim. After we excluded the younger victim in

From Arthur L. Kellermann, Frederick P. Rivara, Norman B. Rushforth, Joyce G. Banton, Donald T. Reay, Jerry T. Francisco, Ana B. Locci, Janice Prodzinski, Bela B. Hackman, and Grant Somes, "Gun Ownership as a Risk Factor for Homicide in the Home," *The New England Journal of Medicine,* vol. 329, no. 15 (October 7, 1993), pp. 1084–1091. Copyright © 1993 by The Massachusetts Medical Society. Reprinted by permission. References omitted.

19 double deaths, 2 homicides that were not reported to project staff, and 3 late changes to a death certificate, 420 cases (94.6 percent) were available for study.

Reports on the Scene

Most of the homicides occurred inside the victim's home. Eleven percent occurred outside the home but within the immediate property lines. Two hundred sixty-five victims (63.1 percent) were men; 36.9 percent were women. A majority of the homicides (50.9 percent) occurred in the context of a quarrel or a romantic triangle. An additional 4.5 percent of the victims were killed by a family member or an intimate acquaintance as part of a murder–suicide. Thirty-two homicides (7.6 percent) were related to drug dealing, and 92 homicides (21.9 percent) occurred during the commission of another felony, such as a robbery, rape, or burglary. No motive other than homicide could be established in 56 cases (13.3 percent).

The great majority of the victims (76.7 percent) were killed by a relative or someone known to them. Homicides by a stranger accounted for only 15 cases (3.6 percent). The identity of the offender could not be established in 73 cases (17.4 percent). The remaining cases involved other offenders or police acting in the line of duty.

Two hundred nine victims (49.8 percent) died from gunshot wounds. A knife or some other sharp instrument was used to kill 111 victims (26.4 percent). The remaining victims were either bludgeoned (11.7 percent), strangled (6.4 percent), or killed by other means (5.7 percent).

Evidence of forced entry was noted in 59 cases (14.0 percent). Eighteen of these involved an unidentified intruder; six involved strangers. Two involved the police. The rest involved a spouse, family member, or some other person known to the victim.

Attempted resistance was reported in 184 cases (43.8 percent). In 21 of these (5.0 percent) the victim unsuccessfully attempted to use a gun in self-defense. In 56.2 percent of the cases no specific signs of resistance were noted. Fifteen victims (3.6 percent) were killed under legally excusable circumstances. Four were shot by police acting in the line of duty. The rest were killed by another member of the household or a private citizen acting in self-defense.

Comparability of Case Subjects and Controls

... Interviews with a matching control* were obtained for 99.7 percent of the case interviews, yielding 388 matched pairs. Three hundred fifty-seven pairs were matched for all three variables, 27 for two variables, and 4 for a single variable (sex). The demographic characteristics of the victims and controls were similar, except that the case subjects were more likely to have rented their homes (70.4 percent vs. 47.3 percent) and to have lived alone (26.8 percent vs. 11.9 percent). ...

Univariate Analysis

Alcohol was more commonly consumed by one or more members of the households of case subjects than by members of the households of controls. Alcohol was also more commonly consumed by the case subjects themselves than by their matched controls. Case subjects were reported to have manifested behavioral correlates of alcoholism (such as trouble at work due to drinking) much more

---

*[Controls were matched with the case subjects according to sex, race, age, and neighborhood of residence.—Eds.]

often than matched controls. Illicit-drug use (by the case subject or another household member) was also reported more commonly by case households than control households.

Previous episodes of violence were reported more frequently by members of case households. When asked if anyone in the household had ever been hit or hurt in a fight in the home, 31.8 percent of the proxies [who were interviewed as representatives of] the case subjects answered affirmatively, as compared with only 5.7 percent of controls. Physical fights in the home while household members were drinking and fighting severe enough to cause injuries were reported much more commonly by case proxies than controls. One or more members of the case households were also more likely to have been arrested or to have been involved in a physical fight outside the home than members of control households.

Similar percentages of case and control households reported using deadbolt locks, window bars, or metal security doors. The case subjects were slightly less likely than the controls to have lived in a home with a burglar alarm, but they were slightly more likely to have controlled security access. Almost identical percentages of case and control households reported owning a dog.

One or more guns were reportedly kept in 45.4 percent of the homes of the case subjects, as compared with 35.8 percent of the homes of the control subjects.... Shotguns and rifles were kept by similar percentages of households, but the case households were significantly more likely to have a handgun.... Case households were also more likely than control households to contain a gun that was kept loaded or unlocked.

Multivariate Analysis

Six variables were retained in our final conditional logistic-regression model: home rented, case subject or control lived alone, any household member ever hit or hurt in a fight in the home, any household member ever arrested, any household member used illicit drugs, and one or more guns kept in the home. Each of these variables was strongly and independently associated with an increased risk of homicide in the home. No home-security measures retained significance in the final model. After matching for four characteristics and controlling for the effects of five more, we found that the presence of one or more firearms in the home was strongly associated with an increased risk of homicide in the home....

Stratified analyses with our final regression model revealed that the link between guns and homicide in the home was present among women as well as men, blacks as well as whites, and younger as well as older people. Restricting the analysis to pairs with data from case proxies who lived in the home of the victim demonstrated an even stronger association than that noted for the group overall. Gun ownership was most strongly associated with homicide at the hands of a family member or intimate acquaintance.... Guns were not significantly linked to an increased risk of homicide by acquaintances, unidentified intruders, or strangers. We found no evidence of a protective benefit from gun ownership in any subgroup, including one restricted to cases of homicide that followed forced entry into the home and another restricted to cases in which resistance was attempted. Not surprisingly, the link between gun ownership and homicide was due entirely to a strong association between gun ownership and homicide by firearms. Homicide by other means was not significantly linked to the presence or absence of a gun in the home.

Living in a household where someone had previously been hit or hurt in a fight in the home was also strongly and independently associated with homicide, even after we controlled for the effects of gun ownership and the other four variables in our final model.... Previous family violence was linked to an increased risk of homicide among men as well as women, blacks as well as whites, and younger as well as older people. Virtually all of this increased risk was due to a marked association between prior domestic violence and homicide at the hands of a family member or intimate acquaintance....

DISCUSSION

Although firearms are often kept in homes for personal protection, this study shows that the practice is counterproductive. Our data indicate that keeping a gun in the home is independently associated with an increase in the risk of homicide in the home. The use of illicit drugs and a history of physical fights in the home are also important risk factors. Efforts to increase home security have largely focused on preventing unwanted entry, but the greatest threat to the lives of household members appears to come from within.

We restricted our study to homicides that occurred in the home of the victim, because these events can be most plausibly linked to specific individual and household characteristics. If, for example, the ready availability of a gun increases the risk of homicide, this effect should be most noticeable in the immediate environment where the gun is kept.

Although our case definition excluded the rare instances in which a nonresident intruder was killed by a homeowner, our methodology was capable of demonstrating significant protective effects of gun ownership as readily as any evidence of increased risk....

Four limitations warrant comment. First, our study was restricted to homicides occurring in the home of the victim. The dynamics of homicides occurring in other locations (such as bars, retail establishments, or the street) may be quite different. Second, our research was conducted in three urban counties that lack a substantial percentage of Hispanic citizens. Our results may therefore not be generalizable to more rural communities or to Hispanic households. Third, it is possible that reverse causation accounted for some of the association we observed between gun ownership and homicide—i.e., in a limited numbers of cases, people may have acquired a gun in response to a specific threat. If the source of that threat subsequently caused the homicide, the link between guns in the home and homicide may be due at least in part to the failure of these weapons to provide adequate protection from the assailants. Finally, we cannot exclude the possibility that the association we observed is due to a third, unidentified factor. If, for example, people who keep guns in their homes are more psychologically prone to violence than people who do not, this could explain the link between gun ownership and homicide in the home. Although we examined several behavioral markers of violence and aggression and included two in our final logistic-regression model, "psychological confounding" of this sort is difficult to control for. "Psychological autopsies" have been used to control for psychological differences between adolescent victims of suicide and inpatient controls with psychiatric disorders, but we did not believe this approach was practical for a study of homicide victims and neighborhood controls. At any rate, a link between gun ownership and any psychological tendency toward violence or victimization would have to be extremely strong to account for an adjusted odds ratio of 2.7.

Given the univariate association we observed between alcohol and violence, it may seem odd that no alcohol-related variables were included in our final multivariate model. Although consumption of alcoholic beverages and the behavioral correlates of alcoholism were strongly associated with homicide, they were also related to other variables included in our final model. Forcing the variable "case subject or control drinks" into our model did not substantially alter the adjusted odds ratios for the other variables. Furthermore, the adjusted odds ratio for this variable was not significantly greater than 1.

Large amounts of money are spent each year on home-security systems, locks, and other measures intended to improve home security. Unfortunately, our results suggest that these efforts have little effect on the risk of homicide in the home. This finding should come as no surprise, since most homicides in the home involve disputes between family members, intimate acquaintances, friends, or others who have ready access to the home. It is important to realize, however, that these data offer no insight into the effectiveness of home-security measures against other household crimes such as burglary, robbery, or sexual assault. In a 1983 poll, Seattle homeowners feared "having someone break into your home while you are

gone" most and "having someone break into your home while you are at home" 4th on a list of 16 crimes. Although homicide is the most serious of crimes, it occurs far less frequently than other types of household crime. Measures that make a home more difficult to enter are probably more effective against these crimes.

Despite the widely held belief that guns are effective for protection, our results suggest that they actually pose a substantial threat to members of the household. People who keep guns in their homes appear to be at greater risk of homicide in the home than people who do not. Most of this risk is due to a substantially greater risk of homicide at the hands of a family member or intimate acquaintance. We did not find evidence of a protective effect of keeping a gun in the home, even in the small subgroup of cases that involved forced entry.

Saltzman and colleagues recently found that assaults by family members or other intimate acquaintances with a gun are far more likely to end in death than those that involve knives or other weapons. A gun kept in the home is far more likely to be involved in the death of a member of the household than it is to be used to kill in self-defense. Cohort and interrupted time-series studies have demonstrated a strong link between availability of guns and community rates of homicide. Our study confirms this association at the level of individual households.

Previous case–control research has demonstrated a strong association between the ownership of firearms and suicide in the home. Also, unintentional shooting deaths can occur when children play with loaded guns they have found at home. In the light of these observations and our present findings, people should be strongly discouraged from keeping guns in their homes.

The observed association between battering and homicide is also important. In contrast to the money spent on firearms and home security, little has been done to improve society's capacity to respond to the problem of domestic violence. In the absence of effective intervention, battering tends to increase in frequency and severity over time. Our data strongly suggest that the risk of homicide is markedly increased in homes where a person has previously been hit or hurt in a family fight. At the very least, this observation should prompt physicians, social workers, law-enforcement officers, and the courts to work harder to identify and protect victims of battering and other forms of family violence. Early identification and effective intervention may prevent a later homicide.

POSTSCRIPT

Should We Encourage the Private Ownership of Guns?

The real issue here is whether or not the firearms industry should go unregulated. Advocates of regulation note that many consumer goods that appear to be far less dangerous than handguns are regulated. If everyday items such as children's toys, over-the-counter drugs, and small kitchen appliances are regulated, why are handguns left unregulated? Surely, more individuals are maimed and killed each year by handguns than by many of the goods that society now regulates.

The NRA would be quick to point out that regulation of the gun industry is not the answer. Indeed, they might argue that the answer is to deregulate all consumer goods. This is the position taken by Jacob Sullivan, managing editor of *Reason*. In an article in *National Review* (February 7, 1994), Sullivan takes great care to show how ineffective regulation such as the Brady Bill will be. Waiting periods and background checks, he argues, will not stop the Colin Fergusons of the world. (Ferguson shot 23 people, fatally wounding 6 of them, on a New York train running from Manhattan to Hicksville on the Long Island Railroad.) Ironically, according to Sullivan, these gun regulations would not have even stopped John Hinckley, who attempted to assassinate President Ronald Reagan and seriously wounded and permanently handicapped Reagan's press secretary James Brady, for whom the Brady Bill is named.

Polsby and other spokespersons for the NRA's position assert that gun control would disarm the law-abiding citizenry and leave the "bad guys" with a monopoly on guns. Kellermann and others within and outside of the medical field, however, find that the cost paid for gun ownership is too high: There are too many accidental shootings; there are too many successful gun-related suicides; and there are too many friends and family members shot in the heat of passion. For Kellermann, guns are too efficient in killing people.

There has been much written about the firearms industry and gun control, particularly after Congress passed the Brady Bill in November 1993. For background, see Jonathan Alter, "How America's Meanest Lobby Ran Out of Ammo," *Newsweek* (May 16, 1994); Frank Lalli, "The Cost of One Bullet: $2 Million," *Money* (February 1994); and Owen Ullmann and Douglas Harbrecht, "Talk About a Loaded Issue," *Business Week* (March 14, 1994). For a good discussion on the limitations of gun control, see David B. Kopel, "Hold Your Fire: Gun Control Won't Stop Rising Violence," *Policy Review* (Winter 1993). And to hear from another member of the medical community, read the editorial by Jerome P. Kassirer entitled "Guns in the Household," which appeared in the October 7, 1993, issue of *The New England Journal of Medicine* along with the Kellermann article.

Finally, we should call your attention to the struggle by the NRA to gain the support of women. In magazines such as *Women and Guns* (published by the Second Amendment Foundation) and in an ad campaign entitled "Refuse to Be a Victim," which has appeared in women's journals such as *Woman's Day* and *Redbook*, the NRA has urged women to "declare your independence from the tragic fear that has become the shameful plague of our times." For a discussion of this campaign, see Sally Chew, "The NRA Goes Courting," *Lear's* (January 1994).

ISSUE 3

Should Cities Subsidize Sports and Sports Venues?

YES: Thomas V. Chema, from "When Professional Sports Justify the Subsidy: A Reply to Robert Baade," *The Journal of Urban Affairs* (vol. 18, no. 1, 1996)

NO: Robert A. Baade, from "Stadium Subsidies Make Little Economic Sense for Cities: A Rejoinder," *The Journal of Urban Affairs* (vol. 18, no. 1, 1996)

ISSUE SUMMARY

YES: Attorney and economic development expert Thomas V. Chema asserts that a sports venue has both direct and indirect returns to invested dollars.

NO: Economics professor and urban sports facilities consultant Robert A. Baade argues that although one might justify a sports subsidy on the basis of "image" or "enhanced quality of life," one cannot justify spending limited development dollars on the economic returns that come from sports venues.

The cities of Vail, Colorado; Green Bay, Wisconsin; Cooperstown, New York; Indianapolis, Indiana; and Louisville, Kentucky, are all united by a common denominator. Each boasts a well-known sports venue or sporting event. South Bend, Indiana, may be known to most people as the home of the Fighting Irish football team of Notre Dame, but only our family and a few friends know, or for that matter care, that Bonello and Swartz live there too!

Is there an economic value to the city of South Bend that is totally separate and apart from the dollars spent by 90,000 college football fans who will search for the 80,000 tickets that are available six times each fall semester? In broader terms, is there an economic value for the "city fathers and mothers" associated with your ability to correctly connect ski lifts, a football team, a baseball hall of fame, an auto race, and a horse race with their respective cities? This is the essence of this issue. Robert A. Baade argues that too few individuals utilize sports facilities to make them worthy candidates for public investment. Thomas V. Chema disagrees, particularly if the venues are strategically placed within the urban community.

We should first examine the impact of a few sports venues. Perhaps no single sports arena has had a longer, more lasting effect on its urban surroundings than the Coliseum in Rome, Italy. This marvelous, 2,000-year-old structure was home to some of the most gruesome "sports" events in Western history. In spite of its crumbling walls and hundreds of years of physical neglect, it still attracts thousands of visitors daily. In fact, this long-abandoned structure still anchors the economic development of the southeast corner of modern Rome.

Alternatively, consider the impact of the America's Cup challenge match to western Australia. The America's Cup is awarded to the winner of a world-wide sailing competition. Until 1986 the competition was always held off the New England coast because the U.S. team had never lost this international competition. Their first loss came at the hands of the Australians, who then had the right to host the challenge match in Fremantle, western Australia. This small, nineteenth-century port city had fallen into serious economic decline prior to the America's Cup challenge match. Although the Australians lost their treasured cup in 1986, they gained much in return. When the sleek racing ships sailed out of the mouth of the Swan River Bay on their return home, they left behind a transformed city awash with cappuccino shops, boutiques, restaurants, microbreweries, and pricey loft condos.

What part of Fremantle's rehabilitation is the direct result of the two or three dozen challenge teams that had to be housed and wined and dined in the two years leading up to the races? What part can be traced to the positive externalities or spillover effects associated with the presence of wealthy sailing teams and the hangers-on who could afford to go halfway around the world to see a sporting event?

In the following selections, Chema attributes large portions of economic development to the presence of sports teams, while Baade contends that it is necessary to carefully measure the dollar costs of sports enterprises to ensure that they do not result in the diversion of leisure dollars to absentee team owners and players.

YES

Thomas V. Chema

WHEN PROFESSIONAL SPORTS JUSTIFY THE SUBSIDY: A REPLY TO ROBERT BAADE

Since virtually the dawn of recorded history the public has been digging into its collective pockets to subsidize the construction of sports venues. Granted, this has not always been a voluntary effort, but then the niceties of democracy were often lost on pharaohs, kings, emperors, and other potentates. The rationale for the public subsidy has varied over time and geography but, with relatively few exceptions, sports have consistently been subsidized.

Robert A. Baade has made a decade long career (or perhaps crusade) arguing against the subsidy. In his most recent paper, "Professional Sports as Catalysts for Metropolitan Economic Development," he purports to demonstrate, using two economic modeling formulae, that subsidy cannot be justified on the basis of economic development and job growth.

For a host of reasons, I disagree with the ultimate conclusion reached by Professor Baade that "cities should be wary of committing substantial portions of their capital budgets to building stadiums." Before cataloging areas of disagreement, let's accept that it is true that professional sports and sport venues are not a panacea for all urban problems. In fact, like Professor Baade, I believe that they are not necessarily even development tools. Their value as catalysts for economic development (job growth and the creation of wealth) depends upon where they are located and how they are integrated into a metropolitan area's growth strategy.

Cities of the future will be important and successful if they can create a critical mass of opportunities for people to socialize within their borders. Several millennia ago, Plato and Aristotle characterized human beings as social creatures. We want to come together, to interact.

For the past 500 years much of that interaction has taken place in cities as people did business and engaged in commerce. Today, with the information superhighway and advanced communications, we tend to be much more isolated in business transactions. Thus, we continually look for other ways to generate human contact and interaction. Cities which understand that cultural activities, recreations, sports and plain old socializing not only bring people together, but form a solid base for economic growth, will be the cities which prosper. Cleveland, Baltimore, Indianapolis, and Minneapolis are cities which recognize that sports venues and events can fit into an overall vision for strategic growth. They have integrated the facilities into the urban fabric and they are successful.

The key to sports venues being a catalyst for economic development is locating them in an urban setting and integrating them into the existing city infrastructure. It is the spin-off development generated by two million or more people visiting a specific area of a city during a concentrated time frame which is critical. The return on the public investment in a ballpark or arena, in dollar and cents terms as opposed to the intangible entertainment value comes not from the facility itself, but from the jobs created in new restaurants, taverns, retail, hotels, etc., that spring up on the periphery of the sports venue.

In Cleveland, for example, since the opening of Jacob Field, 20 new restaurants employing nearly 900 people have opened within two blocks of second base. There are two new retail establishments on Prospect Avenue where there had been none since World War II. There are six projects to convert vacant upper stories of office and commercial buildings to market rate apartments and condominiums and the Gateway facility is only two years old.

This development is materializing because 5,000,000 visitors are coming to games and entertainment and they are spending their money outside the walls of the sports venues before and after the events. Moreover, they are discovering for the first time in 30 years, that downtown has much to offer. They are coming even when there are no sporting events.

Such success dramatizes the flaw in Professor Baade's past and current analyses and conclusions. Baade has researched essentially nonurban facilities which were not intended to be economic development tools. The multiuse stadiums that proliferated in the late 60s and early 70s were specifically designed to be apart from the city. The design characteristics give the impression more of a fort than a marketplace. Moreover, during the period surveyed most new venues were located in suburban or rural locations. The relatively few urban venues might as well have been in suburbs because they were separated from their host city by a moat of surface parking. These facilities became and continue to be isolated attractions. People drive to them, park on surface lots, enjoy the events in the building, and then go home. This is not bad, but it does not generate economic development spin-off. Contrary to Professor Baade's conclusion, however, it is not the sport activity, but the context which is key.

With the exception of Arlington, Texas, the post-1990 ballparks are in urban settings. They connect with the host city and give people an opportunity to spend money in that host city. Given that opportunity, people accept it and the city benefits. Drawing conclusions about the economic development impact from the last generation of sports facility is questionable at best. Certainly, there is no merit in extrapolating from the flying saucers of Pittsburgh, Cincinnati, Philadelphia, etc., and drawing conclusions as to the public return from investment in today's Camden Yards and Jacobs Field.

Moreover, the economic model proposed by Dr. Baade intuitively raises several questions. First, emphasis is placed on the assumption that most of the money generated by a stadium is "quickly disbursed beyond the stadium's environs." That may well be, but is that not equally true of a steel mill or auto plant? What is the point here, surely not that a business enterprise to be a growth generator must reinvest the income in the immediate surroundings?

Second, the fact that the current generation of public assembly facilities is a self-contained series of profit centers does not mean that spin-off development will not occur. Given the correct location and avoiding surrounding the venue with a sea of surface parking, entertainment related enterprises will spring up and flourish in the shadow of the stadiums. Witness Cleveland and Denver. Even in the dead times these businesses can survive once the public becomes familiar with them. Indeed in the modern facility there will be less true dead time because the facility will strive to maximize its usefulness, drawing people to its restaurants, team shops, etc., even when there is no event.

Third, the analysis totally ignores the fiscal impact sporting events and revenues have on the host public jurisdiction. Assuming the implausible circumstance where no sports-related revenues stay in the metropolis from a private sector perspective, there still would be the impact of tax revenues left behind. Virtually every host city has a wage or income tax, a sales tax, and/or admissions tax. This reality, multimillions of dollars, seems to be ignored by the models proposed by Professor Baade.

Fourth, it is difficult to accept the rather narrow definition of economic development posited in the study. What is the value in measuring the metropolitan growth vis-à-vis other cities? Moreover, it seems clear that the fully loaded cost of a stadium cannot be recovered from the stadium revenue alone. Indeed, that is why a subsidy is needed. The return on the subsidy investment must be judged not only on the revenue potential of the facility (and players) but on the spin-off as well. Of course, the subsidy is not made only because an economic return on investment is expected, but also because of the entertainment value of the sports activity or venue. This is not an exclusive analysis nor is the sale to the public of the subsidy ever exclusively based on the expected economic development return on investment.

Fifth, what is the rationale for measuring capital investment and sports revenue receipts on a per capita basis? I strongly suspect that any other entertainment-related industry would provide similar results to that which Professor Baade shows in his paper. In fact, if this type of analysis were applied to investments in steel mills, computer factories, supermarkets, or most other industries, the relative results would make stadium investments look pretty good. Contrary to the implication, using Professor Baade's Chicago example, the investment of $150 million in a stadium which equates to approximately $54.00 per capita is returned in less than three years based on $22.00 per capita in sports franchise revenue. A three year payback on investment is generally viewed favorably in the private sector. Such a return on a public sector investment that should last at least 40 years ought to be viewed very positively.

Sixth, the low wage, seasonal job argument which is typically made by opponents of sports facility investments is, frankly, offensive. Every community, but particularly major urban centers, need to have a diverse mixture of job types in their economy. Not everyone is a rocket scientist. Not everyone could become one even if there were such jobs available, which clearly there are not. Some members or potential members of the labor force need jobs as ushers, ticket takers, vendors, etc. These jobs are neither demeaning to their holders nor do they cause a city to gain "a comparative advantage is unskilled and seasonal labor." This type of reasoning is the product of effete snobbery.

Seventh, how does one measure the opportunity cost involved in public subsidies of sports? I have yet to see or hear of a single instance where the alternative to building a new stadium, for example, was something other than doing nothing. At least since 1989, there have been no proposals of schools v. stadiums or jails v. arenas! The real issue here is collective public investment or individual private expenditures. Economically, this is true of every public investment and sport is no exception.

Eighth, is it really appropriate to measure the economic contribution of an industry based on the growth of the host city rather than on the industry's contribution to the economy of that city? . . .

Finally, it is not clear what jobs are counted as having been created by professional sports in the Baade analysis. Clearly the team and the stadium direct employees, even including all event-related staff, constitute a small number. Most of the jobs created are not going to show up in SIC 794. This model is of very little utility.

It is appropriate for the public to review its investment in a sports venue as an investment in public infrastructure. Like a road, bridge, or water line, the return on the investment comes indirectly as well as directly. A proper analysis includes a review of the entertainment value of the facility and the spin-off value created by the facility. Similarly, a road is justified by transportation utility and the development that it opens on its periphery.

Just as not every road is equal in its economic impact, not every stadium will generate development that justifies a public subsidy. However, when a city establishes a development strategy that includes sports as part of a critical mass of attractions designed to lure people into the urban core, then a sport team or venue can and will provide significant economic value to the city.

NO

Robert A. Baade

STADIUM SUBSIDIES MAKE LITTLE ECONOMIC SENSE FOR CITIES: A REJOINDER

The thoughtful critiques of my research authored by Messrs. Chema and Rosentraub indicate significant agreement among us about the economic impact that professional sports teams and stadiums have on local and regional economies. The areas of alleged disagreement can be broadly characterized as either technical (those monetary benefits and costs that are generally recognized and quantified) or qualitative. Some of the technical issues can be addressed, perhaps resolved, through a clarification of the methods I employed and their outcomes. Other questions can be resolved only with additional data which will enable evaluation of the urban stadiums constructed after 1990. The purpose of this rejoinder is to help advance the stadium debate by commenting on issues raised by Mr. Chema and Dr. Rosentraub.

Before elaborating on specifics relating to these issues, several matters deserve comment. First, I do not have preconceived notions on whether cities, taken individually or collectively, should subsidize the construction of sports facilities. The persistent and ubiquitous use of an economic/investment rationale for public stadium subsidies, however, compels an evaluation of the economic contribution of commercial sport to metropolitan economies. Stadium subsidies represent a classic public finance issue involving both equity and efficiency questions. My research sounds a cautionary note for governments contemplating subsidies on economic grounds. Specifically, cities should reconsider how the stadium is integrated into the urban economy and/or reconsider using the promise of economic gain as a means of selling the subsidy to a skeptical public.

On a personal note, my research about the economic impact of professional sports teams and stadiums has been inspired by my interest in public finance issues and my lifelong experience with sports. In large part my choice to teach at a liberal arts college was conditioned by my affection for both academics and sport. Lake Forest College gave me an opportunity to coach as well as teach. I raise this point in response to Mr. Chema's reference to my "decade long career (or perhaps crusade) arguing against the subsidy." While he may have mistakenly inferred from my work that I dislike sports, to the contrary, I have valued sports as a participant, coach, educator, and fan.

Given my experience, I may be in a better position than some to evaluate the intangibles so often used in discussing and defending sports. The second point I wish to make is that I have not discussed intangibles in my work except to recognize their potential importance. Because proponents of subsidies rationalize their position first and foremost on economic grounds, it is logical to evaluate first the merits of these arguments. My work focuses exclusively on the economic dimension. If we can resolve the issue as it relates to economics, then it may be necessary to move the stadium subsidy debate to the psychological arena where intangibles are properly the focus.

Third, I have chosen to do retrospective stadium analysis because I recognize that identifying and accurately measuring all the dollar inflows and outflows to an area's economy that are induced by commercial sport is a daunting task. Stadium economic impact studies are prospective in nature and are heavily dependent on the assumptions about the financial inflows and outflows to an area's economy as the consequences of professional sports activities. On a practical level, my approach has been to provide a filter through which the promises of increased economic growth for municipalities through professional sports can be evaluated. In retrospect it would appear that prospective economic impact studies in general have failed to capture all the significant inflows and outflows that are essential for even a ballpark estimate of the economic contribution of professional sports. On the other hand, retrospective analysis is limited by data availability.

In reacting to specific areas of concern, Mr. Chema notes the importance of stadium context. In referring to stadium location he observed: "Their value as catalysts for economic development... depends upon where they are located and how they are integrated into a metropolitan area's growth strategy." In noting the success of urban sports facilities constructed after 1990, he alleged a flaw in my research. "Such success dramatizes the flaw in Professor Baade's past and current analyses and conclusions." In response to this allegation I would refer him to Baade and Dye (1988, pp. 272–273) where we wrote:

> If an urban stadium is being planned, the plan should be expanded to incorporate ancillary development.... A stadium is not usually enough of a significant development to anchor an area's economy alone. Rather, in considering the revitalization of an urban neighborhood, a number of potential economic anchors should be developed simultaneously.... Commercial ventures require traffic. The stadium can provide infusions of people, but residential development incorporated with commercial development will ensure a balanced, nonseasonal clientele for business in the stadium neighborhood.

I have emphasized stadium context in public presentations and in my work with stadium planners and architects. Camden Yards and the Gateway Complex in Cleveland represent important experiments relating to stadium context. Research by a number of social scientists, including my own, has identified a stadium and team novelty effect. All else equal, a stadium and team will attract greater interest in the first few years of their existence. So while there is reason to be encouraged by some aspects of the economic performance of Camden Yards and Gateway (not all the financial news from Gateway is good), I am sure that Mr. Chema recognizes that sound statistical analysis of these two projects requires more than a few observations of economic outcomes. As previously noted, retrospective analysis is limited by data availability.

Furthermore, in evaluating the stadium's economic contribution, a model must be constructed that is capable of separating the stadium from other parts of the development. An integrated development complicates the task for the scholar seeking to determine the stadium's economic contribution separate from other elements of the plan.

Mr. Chema's emphasis on context ignores at least one important contextual point. Many of the stadiums that are currently planned or under construction replace stadiums that have been deemed economically obsolete by a team. Boston, Cincinnati, Milwaukee, Minneapolis, New York, and Seattle currently are in the throes of debates about new stadiums for Major League baseball (MLB). Cincinnati, Minneapolis, and Seattle have facilities that are 25 years old or less. The dome in Minneapolis is 13 years old. This shorter stadium shelf life has important economic implications. One concern is how the new generation of facilities born out of economic imperative will affect the neighborhood's economy.

Mr. Chema opines that "the fact that the current generation of public assembly facilities is a self-contained series of profit centers does not mean that spin-off development will not occur." Given the correct developmental context, that may be true, but many stadiums are being designed with the team's bottom line in mind, often to the detriment of the local economy. When a stadium is moved across the street (Chicago's Comiskey Park comes to mind) in the absence of a broader development plan to explicitly include the neighborhood, many of the economic activities and revenues appropriated by local entrepreneurs are appropriated by the stadium operatives seeking to maximize their share of stadium induced revenues.

In focusing on Cleveland and Camden Yards, Mr. Chema concentrates on the exceptions rather than the rule in stadium planning. The reality is that most stadium deals are signed at the midnight hour by legislators opting to do what is necessary to retain a team rather than formulating a plan that integrates the stadium and team into a broader development package. One could blame legislators alone for myopic stadium legislation, but these outcomes are inspired at least as much by the structure of professional sports leagues which serve their own economic interest by maintaining an excess demand for teams. St. Petersburg, Nashville, and Charlotte do not serve the economic interests of Chicago, Houston, and Milwaukee.

Mr. Chema raised other issues that are more technical in nature. He alleges that my "analysis totally ignores the fiscal impact sporting events and revenues have on the host public jurisdiction." Tax revenues are derived. If the tax base expands, tax revenues increase. Professional sports generate additional tax revenues to the extent that they expand the local economy. If sport is construed as part of the entertainment industry, as no less an authority than Bud Selig, MLB's current commissioner, contends, commercial sport from the perspective of the global economy is arguably a zero-sum game. If all the fans supporting a professional sports team within a city are residents of that city, that team will serve to realign economy activity within the city rather than expanding its tax base. Because taxes are derived, tax revenues do not change in such a situation. Does it matter much to the city whether it derives its revenues from sports entertainment or recreation provided by the local theater?

If we drew an imaginary circle from economic ground zero, the point at which the stadium activity occurs, the larger the circle the smaller the net change in economic activity. This reality should help focus the debate about stadium subsidies for various levels of government. For example, the State of Kentucky on purely economic grounds may not want to use its general funds to build a stadium for Louisville unless it can be demonstrated that either fans will pour across the Indiana, Ohio, West Virginia, and Tennessee borders or that Louisville is in need of urban renewal, a public goods argument that could justify an infusion of state funds. If the stadium replaces leisure and recreational spending in Danville with spending in Louisville, Danville may want to argue against the use of state funds for a stadium in Louisville.

Mr. Chema raised the question "what is the value in measuring the metropolitan growth vis-à-vis other cities?" As Professor Rosentraub has indicated in his critique, commercial sport contributes little in an absolute sense to a metropolitan economy. At present modeling the economies of each city that hosts professional sport is not possible and so an alternative technique must be devised to assess the actual contribution of professional sport relative to the economic promise articulated by boosters. Furthermore, an economist would be remiss if the question of opportunity cost was ignored. Public officials must evaluate the stadium not only on its own merit but relative to alternative uses of those funds. Both issues are considered at length in my paper. An argument can be made that in the municipal auction for professional sports franchises, like the auction for free agent players, the winning bid likely exceeds the team's marginal revenue product. It is likely that the greater the excess demand for professional sports teams, the greater the difference between the team's marginal revenue product and the price the host city pays.

Mr. Chema uses the figures I provided on per capita stadium investments and returns to argue that stadiums provide a good return on investment. The per capita returns were not computed for individual sports, but were calculated for commercial sports in general. For individual cities, I have calculated returns on taxpayer equity on the order of 1–2% for an individual sport and those calculations were based on figures provided from the economic impact studies of subsidy supporters. In football and baseball the trend is decidedly away from multipurpose facilities, a trend that is driven by economic imperatives (individual teams want exclusive control of stadium revenues). By the year 2000, it is not unreasonable to predict that baseball and football will no longer share a single facility in the United States.

With regard to Mr. Chema's claim that "at least since 1989, there have been no proposals of schools v. stadiums", I was puzzled by the use of the word proposals. With all due respect, I would encourage Mr. Chema to listen to the tapes of the 1995 Cincinnati City Council debates on the use of public funds for new stadiums for the NFL Bengals and the MLB Reds.

Mr. Chema understandably found offensive the use of the low wage job creation argument in conjunction with opposition to stadium subsidies. Most of us recognize the need for all types of employment. Rather than construing this argument as the product of "effete snobbery," I would ask him to recognize that some of us are trying to explain why sport might not contribute in absolute dollar terms as much as subsidy proponents suggest. My work should not be construed as a recipe for job creation, but rather as an explanation for why stadium subsidies may not have provided the projected economic boost.

As noted earlier, I argued that a retrospective approach to assessing the economic contribution of a stadium or team is necessary, give the complex manner in which dollar inflows and outflows may be affected. An after-the-fact audit of how a change in the professional sports industry influences a metropolitan economy tacitly includes both direct and indirect effects. Indirect changes include an altered city psyche or vision or a heightened spirit of cooperation. All these indirect changes may, indeed, alter the economic landscape. On page 274 of my 1988 article cited previously, I noted (Baade & Dye, 1988, p. 274):

the most significant contribution of sports is likely to be in the area of intangibles. The image of a city is certainly affected by the presence of professional franchises. Professional sports serve as a focal point for group identification. Sports contests are a part of civic culture. There may well be a willingness of voters to pay taxes to subsidize this kind of activity just like there is for parks and museums.

Professor Rosentraub, in particular, has articulated the less visible ways in which a large public project translates into a more vibrant economy. Without repeating his words, I echo his sentiments.

An after-the-fact audit includes the economic impact of these laudable intangibles and, even then, commercial sport does not emerge as a statistically significant contributor to metropolitan economies. Dr. Rosentraub has emphasized the fact that the professional sports industry is too small to significantly influence a large metropolitan economy. I would only add that it is not only its small size which renders commercial sport relatively unimportant. It is a fact that sports spectating is but one leisure option available to the residents of a large diverse metropolis. Money spent on sports spectating is financed by reduced spending in other recreational venues and that fact contributes to the consistently statistically insignificant results for professional sports my research has yielded using a variety of models.

This fundamental principle is fortified by the fact that the primary beneficiaries of public stadium largesse are owners and players and fans for whom commercial sports produce substantial consumer surplus. For owners and players, particularly those who reside outside the city extending the subsidy, there may be adverse economic effects from diverting leisure dollars from locally owned entertainment centers to absentee owners and players.

In the final analysis I can only repeat what I have said so often. If cities subsidize commercial sports in the quest for an improved image or to enhance the quality of life for its citizens, then taxpayers should be allowed to decide the stadium subsidy issue on these bases. Using economics as a justification for the subsidy is a political expedient, perhaps necessity, but it is inconsonant with the statistical evidence.

REFERENCES

Baade, R. A., & Dye, R. F. (1988). Sports stadiums and area development: a critical review. *Economic Development Quarterly, 2*, 265–275.

POSTSCRIPT

Should Cities Subsidize Sports and Sports Venues?

You probably have been directly or indirectly affected by a sports facility sometime in your life. For many of us this means being part of the crowd that shoulders its way into a baseball park or a basketball arena to watch a favorite team play. For others this means being trapped in a traffic jam as thousands of cars rush home at the end of a football game or the end of a day at the races. Are these modern-day coliseums that dominate the cityscape worth the millions of dollars that taxpayers are asked to pay to support them? Would the community be better advised to spend these dollars attracting industry that supports high-paying jobs or by stabilizing neighborhoods that are in distress?

Chema advocates attracting professional sports teams to cities by offering them substantial subsidies. He argues that Baade has biased his results by focusing his analysis on suburban facilities, which he says are surrounded by "a moat of surface parking." Chema details benefits such as spin-off development, a whole range of taxes, entertainment value, and relative rates of return in other industries. Baade contends that communities should be wary of the many promises made by prospective professional sports franchises. A city should not be intimidated by a team's threat to leave for one that is willing to build a new, more costly facility. Baade argues that most of the dollars generated by sports teams are earned by absentee team owners and players and that most of the new employment associated with operating these facilities are at the minimum wage level.

A surprising amount has been written on this topic. In part this can be traced to the fact that a few conservative journals have been persuaded by Baade's position. For example, look for two essays by Raymond J. Keating: "We Wuz Robbed! The Subsidized Stadium Scam," *Policy Review* (March/April 1977) and "Pitching Socialism: Government-Financed Stadiums Invariably Enrich Owners at Public Expense," *National Review* (April 22, 1996). There is plenty written on the other side as well. See Curt Smith, "Comeback: The Triumphant Return of Old-Style Ball Parks Show That Tradition Can Be Popular," *The American Enterprise* (March/April 1997), and, on a related topic, Joanna Cagau and Neil de Mause, "Buy the Bums Out," *In These Times* (December 9, 1996). Finally, there are many articles that examine the economic impact of the Summer Olympics in Atlanta, Georgia. See for example, Matthew Cooper, "Welcome to the Olympic Village," *The New Republic* (July 15 and 22, 1996).

ISSUE 4

Is There Discrimination in U.S. Labor Markets?

YES: William A. Darity, Jr., and Patrick L. Mason, from "Evidence on Discrimination in Employment: Codes of Color, Codes of Gender," *The Journal of Economic Perspectives* (Spring 1998)

NO: James J. Heckman, from "Detecting Discrimination," *The Journal of Economic Perspectives* (Spring 1998)

ISSUE SUMMARY

YES: Professor of economics William A. Darity, Jr., and associate professor of economics Patrick L. Mason assert that the lack of progress made since the mid-1970s toward establishing equality in wages between the races is evidence of persistent discrimination in U.S. labor markets.

NO: Professor of economics James J. Heckman argues that markets—driven by the profit motive of employers—will compete away any wage differentials that are not justified by differences in human capital.

Forty-five years have passed since Rosa Parks refused to give up her seat on a segregated Montgomery, Alabama, bus. America has had 45 years to finally overcome discrimination, but has it? Have the domestic programs of Presidents John F. Kennedy and Lyndon Johnson that were enacted after those turbulent years following Parks's act of defiance made it possible for African Americans to succeed within the powerful economic engine that drives American society? Or does racism still stain the Declaration of Independence, with its promise of equality for all?

Before we examine the economics of discrimination, perhaps we should look backward to see where America has been, what progress has been made, and what is left—if anything—to accomplish. American history, some say, reveals a world of legalized apartheid where African Americans were denied access to the social, political, and economic institutions that are the mainstays of America. Without this access, millions of American citizens were doomed to live lives on the fringes of the mainstream. Thus, the Kennedy/Johnson programs left one legacy, which few now dispute: These programs effectively dismantled the system of legalized discrimination and, for the first time since the end of slavery, allowed blacks to dream of a better life.

The dream became a reality for many. Consider the success stories that are buried in the poverty statistics that were collected and reported in the

1960s. Poverty scarred the lives of one out of every five Americans in 1959. But poverty was part of the lives of fully one-half of all African American families. Over time fewer and fewer Americans, black and white, suffered the effects of poverty; however, even though the incidence of poverty has been cut in half for black Americans, more than 25 percent of African American families still live in poverty. Even more distressing is the reality that African American children bear the brunt of this economic deprivation. In 1997, 37.2 percent of the "next generation" of African Americans lived in families whose total family income was insufficient to lift them out of poverty. (Note that although black Americans suffer the effects of poverty disproportionately, white-not-Hispanic families are the single largest identifiable group who live in poverty: white-not-Hispanic people make up 46.4 percent of the entire poor population; white-Hispanic, 22.2 percent; and black, 25.6 percent.)

The issue for economists is why so many African Americans have failed to prosper and share in the great prosperity of the 1990s. Few would deny that in part the lack of success for black Americans is directly associated with a lack of "human capital": schooling, work experiences, and occupational choices. The real question, however, is whether differences between blacks and whites in terms of human capital can explain most of the current wage differentials or whether a significant portion of these wage differentials can be traced to labor market discrimination.

In the following selections, William A. Darity, Jr., and Patrick L. Mason argue that a significant part of the reason for black Americans' lack of economic success is discrimination, while James J. Heckman maintains that the issue is all human capital differences.

YES

William A. Darity, Jr., and
Patrick L. Mason

EVIDENCE ON DISCRIMINATION
IN EMPLOYMENT

There is substantial racial and gender disparity in the American economy. As we will demonstrate, discriminatory treatment within the labor market is a major cause of this inequality. The evidence is ubiquitous: careful research studies which estimate wage and employment regressions, help-wanted advertisements, audit and correspondence studies, and discrimination suits which are often reported by the news media. Yet, there appear to have been periods of substantial reductions in economic disparity and discrimination. For example, Donohue and Heckman (1991) provide evidence that racial discrimination declined during the interval 1965–1975. Gottschalk (1997) has produced statistical estimates that indicate that discrimination against black males dropped most sharply between 1965 and 1975, and that discrimination against women declined during the interval 1973–1994. But some unanswered questions remain. Why did the movement toward racial equality stagnate after the mid–1970s? What factors are most responsible for the remaining gender inequality? What is the role of the competitive process in elimination or reproduction of discrimination in employment?

The Civil Rights Act of 1964 is the signal event associated with abrupt changes in the black-white earnings differential (Bound and Freeman, 1989; Card and Krueger, 1992; Donohue and Heckman, 1991; Freeman, 1973). Along with other important pieces of federal legislation, the Civil Rights Act also played a major role in reducing discrimination against women (Leonard, 1989). Prior to passage of the federal civil rights legislation of the 1960s, racial exclusion and gender-typing of employment was blatant. The adverse effects of discriminatory practices on the life chances of African Americans, in particular, during that period have been well-documented (Wilson, 1980; Myers and Spriggs, 1997, pp. 32–42; Lieberson, 1980). Cordero-Guzman (1990, p. 1) observes that "up until the early 1960s, and particularly in the south, most blacks were systematically denied equal access to opportunities [and] in many instances, individuals with adequate credentials or skills were

From William A. Darity, Jr., and Patrick L. Mason, "Evidence on Discrimination in Employment: Codes of Color, Codes of Gender," *The Journal of Economic Perspectives*, vol. 12, no. 2 (Spring 1998). Copyright © 1998 by The American Economic Association. Reprinted by permission. References and some notes omitted.

not, legally, allowed to apply to certain positions in firms." Competitive market forces certainly did not eliminate these discriminatory practices in the decades leading up to the 1960s. They remained until the federal adoption of antidiscrimination laws.

Newspaper help-wanted advertisements provide vivid illustrations of the openness and visibility of such practices. We did an informal survey of the employment section of major daily newspapers from three northern cities, the *Chicago Tribune*, the *Los Angeles Times* and the *New York Times*, and from the nation's capital, *The Washington Post*, at five-year intervals from 1945 to 1965. (Examples from southern newspapers are even more dramatic.)...

With respect to gender-typing of occupations, help-wanted advertisements were structured so that whole sections of the classifieds offered job opportunities separately and explicitly for men and women. Men were requested for positions that included restaurant cooks, managers, assistant managers, auto salesmen, sales in general, accountants and junior accountants, design engineers, detailers, diemakers, drivers, and welders. Women were requested for positions that included household and domestic workers, stenographers, secretaries, typists, bookkeepers, occasionally accountants (for "girls good at figures"), and waitresses.[1] The *Washington Post* of January 3, 1960, had the most examples of racial preference, again largely for whites, in help-wanted ads of any newspaper edition we examined. Nancy Lee's employment service even ran an advertisement for a switchboard operator—presumably never actually seen by callers—requesting that all *women* applying be white! Advertisements also frequently in-cluded details about the age range desired from applicants, like men 21–30 or women 18–25. Moreover, employers also showed little compunction about specifying precise physical attributes desired in applicants.[2]

Following the passage of the Civil Rights Act of 1964, none of the newspapers carried help-wanted ads that included any explicit preference for "white" or "colored" applicants in January 1965. However, it became very common to see advertisements for "European" housekeepers (a trend that was already visible as early as 1960). While race no longer entered the help-wanted pages explicitly, national origin or ancestry seemed to function as a substitute. Especially revealing is an advertisement run by the Amity Agency in the *New York Times* on January 3, 1965, informing potential employers that "Amity Has Domestics": "Scottish Gals" at $150 a month as "mothers' helpers and housekeepers," "German Gals" at $175 a month on one-year contracts, and "Haitian Gals" at $130 a month who are "French speaking." Moreover, in the "Situations Wanted" section of the newspaper, prospective female employees still were indicating their own race in January 1965.

The case of the help-wanted pages of the *New York Times* is of special note because New York was one of the states that had a state law against discrimination and a State Commission Against Discrimination in place, long prior to the passage of the federal Civil Rights Act of 1964. However, the toothlessness of New York's State Commission Against Discrimination is well-demonstrated by the fact that employers continued to indicate their racial preferences for new hires in help-wanted ads, as well as by descriptions of personal experience like that of John A. Williams in his semi-autobiographical novel, *The Angry Ones* (1960 [1996], pp. 30–1).

Help-wanted ads were only the tip of the iceberg of the process of racial exclusion in employment. After all, there is no reason to believe that the employers who did not indicate a racial preference were entirely open-minded about their applicant pool. How successful has the passage of federal antidiscrimination legislation in the 1960s been in producing an equal opportunity environment where job applicants are now evaluated on their qualifications? To give away the answer at the outset, our response is that discrimination by race has diminished somewhat, and discrimination by gender has diminished substantially. However, neither employment discrimination by race or by gender is close to ending. The Civil Rights Act of 1964 and subsequent related legislation has purged American society of the most overt forms of discrimination. However, discriminatory practices have continued in more covert and subtle forms. Furthermore, racial discrimination is masked and rationalized by widely-held presumptions of black inferiority.

STATISTICAL RESEARCH ON EMPLOYMENT DISCRIMINATION

Economic research on the presence of discrimination in employment has focused largely on black-white and male-female earnings and occupational disparities. The position typically taken by economists is that some part of the racial or gender gap in earnings or occupations is due to average group differences in productivity-linked characteristics (a human capital gap) and some part is due to average group differences in treatment (a discrimination gap). The more of the gap that can be explained by human capital differences, the easier it becomes to assert that labor markets function in a nondiscriminatory manner; any remaining racial or gender inequality in employment outcomes must be due to differences between blacks and whites or between men and women that arose outside the labor market....

REGRESSION EVIDENCE ON RACIAL DISCRIMINATION

When we consider economic disparities by race, a difference emerges by gender. Using a Blinder-Oaxaca approach in which women are compared by their various racial and ethnic subgroups, Darity, Guilkey and Winfrey (1996) find little systematic evidence of wage discrimination based on U.S. Census data for 1980 and 1990.[3] However, when males are examined using the same Census data a standard result emerges. A significant portion of the wage gap between black and white males in the United States cannot be explained by the variables included to control for productivity differences across members of the two racial groups.

Black women are likely to have the same school quality and omitted family background characteristics as black men (the same is true for white women and men). Hence, it strains credibility to argue that the black-white earnings gap for men is due to an omitted labor quality variable unless one also argues that black women are paid more than white women conditional on the unobservables. The findings of Darity, Guilkey and Winfrey (1996), Rodgers and Spriggs (1996) and Gottschalk (1997) indicate that in 1980 and 1990 black men in the United States were suffering a 12 to 15 percent loss in earnings due to labor market discrimination.

There is a growing body of evidence that uses color or "skin shade" as a natural experiment to detect discrimination. The approach of these studies has been to look at different skin shades within a particular ethnic group at a particular place and time, which should help to control for factors of culture and ethnicity other than pure skin color. Johnson, Bienenstock, and Stoloff (1995) looked at dark-skinned and light-skinned black males from the same neighborhoods in Los Angeles, and found that the combination of a black racial identity and a dark skin tone reduces an individual's odds of working by 52 percent, after controlling for education, age, and criminal record! Since both dark-skinned and light-skinned black males in the sample were from the same neighborhoods, the study *de facto* controlled for school quality. Further evidence that lighter-complexioned blacks tend to have superior incomes and life chances than darker-skinned blacks in the United States comes from studies by Ransford (1970), Keith and Herring (1991) and Johnson and Farrell (1995).

Similar results are found by looking at skin color among Hispanics. Research conducted by Arce, Murguia, and Frisbie (1987) utilizing the University of Michigan's 1979 National Chicano Survey involved partitioning the sample along two phenotypical dimensions: skin color, ranging from Very Light to Very Dark on a five-point scale; and physical features, ranging from Very European to Very Indian on a five-point scale. Chicanos with lighter skin color and more European features had higher socioeconomic status. Using the same data set, Telles and Murguia (1990) found that 79 percent of $1,262

of the earnings differences between the dark phenotypic group and other Mexican Americans was *not* explained by the traditional variables affecting income included in their earnings regression. Further support for this finding comes from Cotton (1993) and Darity, Guilkey, and Winfrey (1996) who find using 1980 and 1990 Census data that black Hispanics suffer close to ten times the proportionate income loss due to differential treatment of given characteristics than white Hispanics. Evidently, skin shade plays a critical role in structuring social class position and life chances in American society, even between comparable individuals within minority groups.

Cross-national evidence from Brazil also is relevant here. Despite conventional beliefs in Brazil that race is irrelevant and class is the primary index for social stratification, Silva (1985) found using the 1976 national household survey that blacks and mulattos (or "browns") shared closely in a relatively depressed economic condition relative to whites, with mulattos earning slightly more than blacks. Silva estimated that the cost of being nonwhite in Brazil in 1976 was about 566 cruzeiros per month (or $104 U.S.). But Silva found slightly greater unexplained income differences for mulattos, rather than blacks vis-à-vis whites, unexplained differences he viewed as evidence of discrimination. A new study by Telles and Lim (1997), based upon a random national survey of 5000 persons conducted by the Data Folha Institute des Pesquisas, compares economic outcomes based upon whether race is self-identified or interviewer-identified. Telles and Lim view interviewer-identification as more useful for establishing social classification and treatment. They find that self-identification underestimates white income and over-estimates brown and black incomes relative to interviewer-classification.

Despite the powerful results on skin shade, some continue to argue that the extent of discrimination is overestimated by regression techniques because of missing variables. After all, it seems likely that the general pattern of unobserved variables—for example, educational quality or labor force attachment—would tend to follow the observed variables in indicating reasons for the lower productivity of black males (Ruhm, 1989, p. 157). As a result, adjusting for these factors would reduce the remaining black-white earnings differential.[4]

As one might imagine, given the framework in which economists tackle the issue of discrimination, considerable effort has been made to find measures of all imaginable dimensions of human capital that could be used to test the presence of labor market discrimination. This effort has uncovered one variable in one data set which, if inserted in an earnings regression, produces the outcome that nearly all of the black-white male wage gap is explained by human capital and none by labor market discrimination. (However, thus far no one has suggested a reasonable missing variable for the skin shade effect.) The particular variable that eliminates evidence of discrimination in earnings against black men as a group is the Armed Forces Qualifying Test (AFQT) score in the National Longitudinal Survey of Youth (NLSY).

A number of researchers have confirmed with somewhat different sample sizes and methodologies that including AFQT scores in an earnings equation virtually will eliminate racial differences in wages. . . .

The conclusion of this body of work is that labor market discrimination against blacks is negligible or nonexistent. Using Neal and Johnson's (1996) language, the key to explaining differences in black and white labor market outcomes must instead rest with "premarket factors." These studies have led Abigail and Stephan Thernstrom (1997) in a prominent *Wall Street Journal* editorial to proclaim that "what may look like persistent employment discrimination is better described as employers rewarding workers with relatively strong cognitive skills."

But matters are not so straightforward. The essential problem is what the AFQT scores are actually measuring, and therefore what precisely is being controlled for. There is no consensus on this point. AFQT scores have been interpreted variously as providing information about school quality or academic achievement (O'Neill, 1990), about previously unmeasured skills (Ferguson, 1995; Maxwell, 1994; Neal and Johnson 1996), and even about intelligence (Herrnstein and Murray, 1994)—although the military did not design AFQT as an intelligence test (Rodgers and Spriggs, 1996).[5] The results obtained by O'Neill (1990), Maxwell (1994), Ferguson (1995), and Neal and Johnson (1996) after using the AFQT as an explanatory variable are, upon closer examination, not robust to alternative specifications and are quite difficult to interpret.

The lack of robustness can be illustrated by looking at how AFQT scores interact with other variables in the earnings equation. Neal and Johnson (1996), for example, adjust for age and AFQT score in an earnings equation, but not for years of schooling, presumably on the assumption that same-age individuals would have the same years of schooling, regardless of race. However, this assumption does not appear to be true. Rodgers, Spriggs and Waaler (1997) find that white youths had accumulated more schooling at a given age than black or Hispanic youths. When AFQT scores are both age and education-adjusted, a black-white wage gap reemerges, as the authors report (p. 3):[6]

> ... estimates from models that use our proposed age and education adjusted AFQT score [show] that sharp differences in racial and ethnic wage gaps exist. Instead of explaining three-quarters of the male black-white wage gap, the age and education adjusted score explains 40 percent of the gap. Instead of explaining the entire male Hispanic-white gap, the new score explains 50 percent of the gap ... [B]lack women no longer earn more than white women do, and ... Hispanic women's wage premium relative to white women is reduced by one-half.

Another specification problem arises when wage equations are estimated using both AFQT scores and the part of the NLSY sample that includes measures of psychological well-being (for "self-esteem" and "locus of control") as explanatory variables. The presence of the psychological variables restores a negative effect on wages of being African-American (Goldsmith, Veum and Darity, 1997).[7]

Yet another specification problem becomes relevant if one interprets AFQT scores as providing information about school quality. But since there is a school survey module of the NLSY which can be used to provide direct evidence on school quality, using variables like the books/pupil ratio, the percent of students classified as disadvantaged, and teacher salaries, it would surely be more

helpful to use this direct data on school quality rather than the AFQT scores. In another method of controlling for school quality, Harrison (1972) compared employment and earnings outcomes for blacks and whites living in the same black ghetto communities, on grounds that school quality would not be very different between them. Harrison found sharp differences in earnings favoring whites.[8]

One severe difficulty in interpreting what differences in the AFQT actually mean is demonstrated by Rodgers and Spriggs (1996) who show that AFQT scores appear to be biased in a specific sense.... [They] create a hypothetical set of "unbiased" black scores by running the mean black characteristics through the equation with the white coefficients. When those scores replace the actual AFQT scores in a wage equation, then the adjusted AFQT scores no longer explain black-white wage differences. A similar result can be obtained if actual white scores are replaced by hypothetical scores produced by running white characteristics through the equation with black coefficients.[9] Apparently, the AFQT scores themselves are a consequence of bias in the underlying processes that generate AFQT scores for blacks and whites. Perhaps AFQT scores are a proxy for skills that do not capture all skills, and thus leave behind a bias of uncertain direction. Or there may be other predictors of the test that are correlated with race but which are left out of the AFQT explanatory equation.

To muddy the waters further, focusing on the math and verbal subcomponents of AFQT leads to inconsistent implications for discriminatory differentials. For example, while a higher performance on the verbal portion of the

AFQT contributes to higher wages for black women versus black men, it apparently has little or no effect on the wages of white women versus white men (Currie and Thomas, 1995). However, white women gain in wages from higher scores on the math portion of the AFQT, but black women do not. Perhaps this says that white women are screened (directly or indirectly) for employment and pay on the basis of their math performance, while black women are screened based upon their verbal skills. Perhaps this is because white employers have a greater "comfort zone" with black women who have a greater verbal similarity to whites. Or perhaps something not fully understood and potentially quirky is going on with the link between these test results and wages.

Finally, since skill differentials have received such widespread discussion in recent years as an underlying cause of growing wage inequality in the U.S. economy—see, for example, the discussion in the Spring 1997 issue of *The Journal of Economic Perspectives*—it should be pointed out that growth in the rewards to skill does not mean that the effects of race have diminished. If the importance of race and skill increase simultaneously, then a rising skill premium will explain more of the changes in *intraracial* wage inequality, which may well leave a larger unexplained portion of interracial wage inequality. For example, when Murnane et al. (1995) ask whether test scores in math, reading, and vocabulary skills for respondents in the National Longitudinal Study of the High School Class of 1972 and High School and Beyond datasets have more explanatory power in wage equations for 1980 graduates than 1972 graduates, their answer is "yes"—the rate of return to cognitive skill (test scores) increased between 1978 and 1986. However, in these same regressions, the absolute value of the negative race coefficient is larger for the 1980 graduates than it is for the 1972 graduates! These results confirm that there are increasing returns to skills measured by standardized tests, but do not indicate that the rise in returns to skills can explain changes in the black-white earnings gap very well.

The upshot is the following. There is no doubt that blacks suffer reduced earnings in part due to inferior productivity-linked characteristics, like skill gaps or school quality gaps, relative to nonblack groups. However, evidence based on the AFQT should be treated with extreme caution. Given that this one variable in one particular data set is the only one that suggests racial discrimination is no longer operative in U.S. employment practices, it should be taken as far from convincing evidence. Blacks, especially black men, continue to suffer significantly reduced earnings due to discrimination and the extent of discrimination.

DIRECT EVIDENCE ON DISCRIMINATION: COURT CASES AND AUDIT STUDIES

One direct body of evidence of the persistence of employment discrimination, despite the presence of antidiscrimination laws, comes from the scope and dispensation of job discrimination lawsuits. A sampling of such cases from recent years... reveals [that] discriminatory practices have occurred at highly visible U.S. corporations often having multinational operations. The suits reveal racial and gender discrimination in employment, training, promotion, tenure, layoff policies, and work environment, as well as occupational segregation.

Perhaps the most notorious recent case is the $176 million settlement reached between Texaco and black employees after disclosure of taped comments of white corporate officials making demeaning remarks about blacks, remarks that revealed an outlook that translated into corresponding antiblack employment practices. Clearly, neither federal antidiscrimination laws nor the pressures of competitive markets have prevented the occurrence of discriminatory practices that have resulted in significant awards or settlements for the plaintiffs.

Another important source of direct evidence are the audit studies of the type conducted in the early 1990s by the Urban Institute (Mincy, 1993). The Urban Institute audit studies sought to examine employment outcomes for young black, Hispanic, and white males, ages 19–25, looking for entry-level jobs. Pairs of black and white males and pairs of Hispanic and non-Hispanic white males were matched as testers and sent out to apply for jobs at businesses advertising openings. Prior to application for the positions, the testers were trained for interviews to minimize dissimilarity in the quality of their self-presentation, and they were given manufactured résumés designed to put their credentials on a par. The black/white tests were conducted in Chicago and in Washington, D.C., while the Hispanic/non Hispanic tests were conducted in Chicago and in San Diego.

A finding of discrimination was confirmed if one member of the pair was offered the position and the other was not. No discrimination was confirmed if both received an offer (sequentially, since both were instructed to turn the position down) or neither received an offer. This is a fairly stringent test for discrimination, since, in the case where no offer was made to either party, there is no way to determine whether employers were open to the prospect of hiring a black or an Hispanic male, what the overall applicant pool looked like, or who was actually hired. However, the Urban Institute audits found that black males were three times as likely to be turned down for a job as white males, and Hispanic males also were three times as likely as non-Hispanic white males to experience discrimination in employment (Fix, Galster and Struyk, 1993, pp. 21–22).

Bendick, Jackson and Reinoso (1994) also report on 149 race-based (black, white) and ethnicity-based (Hispanic, non-Hispanic) job audits conducted by the Fair Employment Council of Greater Washington, Inc. in the D.C. metropolitan area in 1990 and 1991. Testers were paired by gender. The audit findings are striking. White testers were close to 10 percent more likely to receive interviews than blacks. Among those interviewed, half of the white testers received job offers versus a mere 11 percent of the black testers. When both testers received the same job offers, white testers were offered 15 cents per hour more than black testers. Black testers also were disproportionately "steered" toward lower level positions after the job offer was made, and white testers were disproportionately considered for unadvertised positions at higher levels than the originally advertised job.

Overall, the Fair Employment Council study found rates of discrimination in excess of 20 percent against blacks (in the black/white tests) and against Hispanics (in the Hispanic/non-Hispanic tests). In the Hispanic/non-Hispanic tests, Hispanic male job seekers were three times as likely to experience discrimination as Hispanic females. But, surprisingly, in the black/white tests, black females were three times as likely to encounter discrimination as black males. The racial results for women in this particular audit stand in sharp contrast with the results in the statistical studies described above.

The most severe criticisms of the audit technique have come from Heckman and Siegelman (1993). At base, their central worry is that testers cannot be paired in such a way that they will not signal a difference that legitimately can be interpreted by the prospective employer as a difference in potential to perform the job, despite interview training and doctored résumés.[10] For example, what about intangibles like a person's ability to make a first impression or the fact that certain résumés may be unintentionally superior to others?

In an audit study consciously designed to address many of the Heckman and Siegelman (1993) methodological complaints, Neumark, Bank, and Van Nort (1995) examined sex discrimination in restaurant hiring practices. Four testers (all college students, two men and two women) applied for jobs waiting tables at 65 restaurants in Philadelphia. The restaurants were separated into high, medium, and low price, according to average cost of a meal. Waiters at the high price restaurants tend to receive greater wages and tips than their counterparts in low price restaurants; specifically, the authors find that average hourly earnings for waiters were 47 and 68 percent higher in the high price restaurant than the medium and low price restaurant, respectively. One man and one woman applied for a job at each restaurant, so there were 130 attempts to obtain employment. Thirty-nine job offers were received.

One interesting twist to this methodology is that three reasonably comparable résumés were constructed, and over a three-week period each tester used a different résumé for a period of one week. This résumé-switching mitigates any differences that may have occurred because one résumé was better than another. To reduce other sources of unobserved ability—for example, the ability to make a good first impression—the testers were instructed to give their applications to the first employee they encountered when visiting a restaurant. That employee was then asked to forward the résumé to the manager. In effect, personality and appearance were eliminated as relevant variables for the interview decision, if not for the job offer decision.

Neumark et al. (1995) find that in the low-priced restaurants, the man received an offer while the woman did not 29 percent of the time. A woman never received an offer when the man did not. In the high-priced restaurants, the man received an offer while the woman did not in 43 percent of the tests, while the woman received an offer while the man did not in just 4 percent of the tests. Also, at high-priced restaurants, women had roughly a 40 percent lower probability of being interviewed and 50 percent lower probability of obtaining a job offer, and this difference is statistically significant. Hence, this audit study shows that within-occupation employment discrimination may be a contributing source to wage discrimination between men and women....

THE THEORETICAL BACKDROP

Standard neoclassical competitive models are forced by their own assumptions to the conclusion that discrimination only can be temporary. Perhaps the best-known statement of this position emerges from Becker's (1957) famous "taste for discrimination" model. If two groups share similar productivity profiles under competitive conditions where at least some employers prefer profits to prejudice, eventually all workers must be paid the same wage. The eventual result may involve segregated workforces—say, with some businesses hiring only white men and others hiring only black women—but as long as both groups have the same average productivity, they will receive the same pay. Thus, in this view, discrimination only can produce temporary racial or gender earnings gaps. Moreover, alternative forms of discrimination are separable processes; wage discrimination and employment segregation are unrelated in Becker's model.

Despite the theoretical implications of standard neoclassical competitive models, we have considerable evidence that it took the Civil Rights Act of 1964 to alter the discriminatory climate in America. It did not, by any means, eliminate either form of discrimination. Indeed, the impact of the law itself may have been temporary, since there is some evidence that the trend toward racial inequality came to a halt in the mid-1970s (even though interracial differences in human capital were continuing to close) and the momentum toward gender equality may have begun to lose steam in the early 1990s. Moreover, we believe that the forms of discrimination have altered in response to the act. Therefore, it is not useful to argue that either racial or gender discrimination is inconsistent with the operation of competitive markets, especially when it has taken antidiscrimination laws to reduce the impact of dis-

crimination in the market. Instead, it is beneficial to uncover the market mechanisms which permit or encourage discriminatory practices.

Since Becker's work, orthodox microeconomics has been massaged in various ways to produce stories of how discrimination might sustain itself against pressures of the competitive market. The tacit assumption of these approaches has been to find a way in which discrimination can increase business profits, or to identify conditions where choosing not to discriminate might reduce profits.

In the customer discrimination story, for example, businesses discriminate not because they themselves are bigoted but because their clients are bigoted. This story works especially well where the product in question must be delivered via face-to-face contact, but it obviously does not work well when the hands that made the product are not visible to the customer possessing the "taste for discrimination." Moreover, as Madden (1975, p. 150) has pointed out, sex-typing of jobs can work in both directions: "While service occupations are more contact-oriented, sexual preference can work both ways: for example, women are preferred as Playboy bunnies, airline stewardesses, and lingerie salespeople, while men seem to be preferred as tire salespeople, stockbrokers, and truck drivers."

Obviously, group-typing of employment will lead to a different occupational distributions between group A and B, but will it lead to different earnings as well? Madden (1975, p. 150, emphasis in original) suggests not necessarily:

... consumer discrimination causes occupational segregation rather than wage differentials. If the female wage decreases as the amount of consumer contact required by a job increases, women seek employment in jobs where consumer contact is minimal and wages are higher. Only if there are not enough non-consumer contact jobs for working women, forcing them to seek employment in consumer-contact jobs, would consumer discrimination be responsible for wage differentials. Since most jobs do not require consumer contact, consumer discrimination would segregate women into these jobs, but not *cause* wage differentials.

Perhaps the best attempt to explain how discrimination might persist in a neoclassical framework is the statistical discrimination story, which, at base, is a story about imperfect information. The notion is that potential employers cannot observe everything they wish to know about job candidates, and in this environment, they have an incentive to seize group membership as a signal that allows them to improve their predictions of a prospective candidate's ability to perform.

However, this model of prejudicial beliefs does not ultimately wash well as a theory of why discrimination should be long-lasting. If average group differences are perceived but not real, then employers should *learn* that their beliefs are mistaken. If average group differences are real, then in a world with antidiscrimination laws, employers are likely to find methods of predicting the future performance of potential employees with sufficient accuracy that there is no need to use the additional "signal" of race or gender. It seems implausible that with all the resources that corporations put into hiring decisions, the remaining differentials are due to an inability to come up with a suitable set of questions or qualifications for potential employees.

Moreover, models of imperfect competition as explanations of discrimination do not solve the problem completely either. The reason for the immutability of the imperfection is rarely satisfactorily explained—and often not addressed at all—in models of this type (Darity and Williams, 1985). Struggle as it may, orthodox microeconomics keeps returning to the position that sustained observed differences in economic outcomes between groups must be due to an induced or inherent deficiency in the group that experiences the inferior outcomes. In the jargon, this is referred to as a deficiency in human capital. Sometimes this deficiency is associated with poor schooling opportunities, other times with culture (Sowell, 1981).[11] But the thrust of the argument is to absolve market processes, at least in a putative long run, of a role in producing the differential outcome; the induced or inherent deficiency occurs in pre-market or extra-market processes.

Certainly years of schooling, quality of education, years of work experiences and even culture can have a role in explaining racial and gender earnings differences. However, the evidence marshaled above indicates that these factors do not come close to explaining wage differentials and employment patterns observed in the economy. Instead, discrimination has been sustained both in the United States and elsewhere, for generations at a time. Such discrimination does not always even need direct legal support nor has it been eliminated by market pressures. Instead, changes in social and legal institutions have been needed to reduce it.

James Heckman (1997, p. 406) draws a similar conclusion in his examination of a specific sector of employment, the textile industry:

> ... substantial growth in Southern manufacturing had little effect on the labor-market position of blacks in Southern textiles prior to 1965. Through tight and slack labor markets, the proportion of blacks was small and stable. After 1964, and in synchronization with the 1964 Civil Rights Act, black economic progress was rapid. Only South Carolina had a Jim Crow law prohibiting employment of blacks as textile workers, and the law was never used after the 1920s. Yet the pattern of exclusion of blacks was prevalent throughout Southern textiles, and the breakthrough in black employment in the industry came in all states at the same time. Informally enforced codes and private practices, and not formally enforced apartheid, kept segregation in place, and market forces did not break them down.

Nontraditional alternatives to orthodox microeconomic analysis can lead to a logically consistent basis for a persistent gap in wage outcomes. These alternatives typically break down the line between in-market and pre-market discrimination so often drawn in conventional economics. The first of these involves a self-fulfilling prophecy mechanism. Suppose employers believe that members of group A are more productive than members of group B on average. Suppose further that they act upon their beliefs, thereby exhibiting a stronger demand for A workers, hiring them more frequently and paying them more.

Next, suppose that members of group B become less motivated and less emotionally healthy as a consequence of the employment rebuff. Notice that the original decision not to hire may have been completely unjustified on productivity

grounds; nonetheless, the decision made *in* the labor market—a decision not to hire or to hire at low pay—alters the human capital characteristics of the members of group B so that they become inferior candidates for jobs. The employers' initially held mistaken beliefs become realized over time as a consequence of the employers' initial discriminatory decisions. As Elmslie and Sedo (1996, p. 474) observe in their development of this argument, "One initial bout of unemployment that is not productivity based can lay the foundation for continued future unemployment and persistently lower job status even if no future discrimination occurs."

More broadly, depressed expectations of employment opportunities also can have an adverse effect on members of group B's inclination to acquire additional human capital—say, through additional schooling or training. The effects of the past could be passed along by the disadvantaged group from generation to generation, another possibility ignored by orthodox theory. For example, Borjas (1994) writes of the ethnic intergenerational transmission of economic advantage or disadvantage. He makes no mention of discrimination in his work but a potential interpretation is that the effects of past discrimination, both negative and positive, are passed on to subsequent generations. Other evidence along these lines includes Tyree's (1991) findings on the relationship between an ethnic group's status and performance in the past and the present, and Darity's (1989) development of "the lateral mobility" hypothesis based upon ethnic group case histories.

More narrowly, the group-typed beliefs held by employers/selectors also can have a strong effect on the performance of the candidate at the interview stage. In an experiment performed in the early 1970s, psychologists Word, Zanna and Cooper (1974, pp. 109–120) found that when interviewed by "naïve" whites, trained black applicants "received (a) less immediacy, (b) higher rates of speech error, and (c) shorter amounts of interview time" than white applicants. They then trained white interviewers to replicate the behavior received by the black applicants in the first phase of their experiment, and found that "naïve" white candidates performed poorly during interviews when they were "treated like blacks." Such self-fulfilling prophecies are familiar in the psychology literature (Sibicky and Dovidio, 1986).

A second nontraditional theory that can lead to a permanent gap in intergroup outcomes is the noncompeting groups hypothesis advanced by the late W. Arthur Lewis (1979). Related arguments emerge from Krueger's (1963) extension of the trade-based version of the Becker model, Swinton's (1978) "labor force competition" model for racial differences, and Madden's (1975) male monopoly model for gender differences, but Lewis's presentation is the most straightforward. Lewis starts with an intergroup rivalry for the preferred positions in a hierarchical occupational structure. Say that group A is able to control access to the preferred positions by influencing the required credentials, manipulating opportunities to obtain the credentials, and serving a gatekeeping function over entry and promotion along job ladders. Group B is then rendered "noncompeting."

One theoretical difficulty with this argument that its proponents rarely address is that it requires group A to maintain group solidarity even when it may have subgroups with differing interests. In Krueger's (1963) model, for example, white capitalists must value racial group solidarity sufficiently to accept a lower return on their capital as the price they pay for a generally higher level of income for all whites (and higher wages for white workers). In Madden's (1975) model, male capitalists must make a similar decision on behalf of male workers.

This noncompeting group hypothesis blurs the orthodox distinction between in-market and pre-market discrimination, by inserting matters of power and social control directly into the analysis. This approach then links discrimination to racism or sexism, rather than to simple bigotry or prejudice. It leads to the proposition that discrimination—in the sense of differential treatment of those members of each group with similar productivity-linked characteristics—is an endogenous phenomenon. "In-market" discrimination need only occur when all the earlier attempts to control access to jobs, credentials, and qualifications are quavering.

One interesting implication here is that growth in skills for what we have been calling group B, the disadvantaged group, may be accompanied by a surge of in-market discrimination, because that form of discrimination has become more necessary to preserve the position of group A. There are several instances of cross-national evidence to support this notion. Darity, Dietrich and Guilkey (1997) find that while black males were making dramatic strides in acquiring literacy between 1880 and 1910 in the United States, simultaneously they were suffering increasing proportionate losses in occupational status due to disadvantageous treatment of their measured characteristics. Geographer Peggy Lovell

(1993) finds very little evidence of discrimination in earnings against blacks in northern Brazil, where blacks are more numerous, but substantial evidence of discrimination against them in southern Brazil. Northern Brazil is considerably poorer than southern Brazil and the educational levels of northern black Brazilians are more depressed than in the south.[12] It is easy to argue that the exercise of discrimination is not "needed" in the north, since blacks are not generally going to compete with whites for the same sets of jobs. Indeed, there is relatively more evidence of discrimination against mulattos than blacks, the former more likely to compete directly with whites for employment. A third example, in a study using data for males based upon a survey taken in Delhi in 1970, Desi and Singh (1989) find that the most dramatic instance of discriminatory differentials in earnings was evident for Sikh men vis-à-vis Hindu high caste men. On the other hand, most of the earnings gap for Hindu middle caste, lower caste and scheduled caste men was due to inferior observed characteristics. Since these latter groups could be excluded from preferred positions because of an inadequate educational background, it would not be necessary for the upper castes to exercise discrimination against them. Sikh males, on the other hand, possessed the types of credentials that would make them viable contestants for the positions desired by the Hindu higher castes.

A final alternative approach at construction of a consistent economic theory of persistent discrimination evolves from a reconsideration of the neoclassical theory of competition. Darity and Williams (1985) argued that replacement of neoclassical competition with either classical or Marxist approaches to competition—where competition is defined by a tendency toward equalization of rates of profit and where monopoly positions are the consequence of competition rather than the antithesis of competition—eliminates the anomalies associated with the orthodox approach (Botwinick, 1993; Mason, 1995, forthcoming-b). A labor market implication of this approach is that wage diversity, different pay across firms and industries for workers within the same occupation, is the norm for competitive labor markets. In these models, remuneration is a function of the characteristics of the individual and the job. The racial-gender composition of the job affects worker bargaining power and thereby wage differentials. In turn, race and gender exclusion are used to make some workers less competitive for the higher paying positions. This approach emphasizes that the major elements for the persistence of discrimination are racial or gender differences in the access to better paying jobs within and between occupations.

Whatever alternative approach is preferred, the strong evidence of the persistence of discrimination in labor markets calls into question any theoretical apparatus that implies that the discrimination must inevitably diminish or disappear.

NOTES

1. The only significant exception to the help-wanted ads pattern of maintaining a fairly strict sexual division of labor that we could detect was evident in the *Los Angeles Times* employment section of early January 1945, where we found women being sought as aircraft riveters, assemblers, and army photographers. Of course, World War II was ongoing at that stage, and the comparative absence of men produced the "Rosie the Riveter" phenomenon. However, despite wartime conditions, even this temporary breakdown in gender-typing of occupations was not evident in the help-wanted ads for the *Chicago Tribune*, the *New York Times*, or the

Washington Post at the same time. Moreover, racial preferences also remained strongly pronounced in wartime advertisements of each of the four newspapers.

2. The C.W. Agency, advertising in the *Los Angeles Times* on January, 1, 1950, wanted a "Girl Model 38 bust, 25 waist, 36 hips"; "Several Other Types" with physical characteristics unspecified in the advertisement apparently also were acceptable.

3. The 1980 and 1990 Censuses provide only self-reported information on interviewees' race and their ancestry, which makes it possible to partition the American population into 50 different detailed ethnic and racial groups, like Asian Indian ancestry women, Mexican ancestry women, Polish ancestry women, French Canadian ancestry women, and so on. The explanatory variables were years of school, years of college, number of children, married spouse present, years of work experience, years of work experience squared, very good or fluent English, disabled, born in the United States, assimilated (that is either married to a person with a different ethnicity or having claimed two different ethnic groups in the census), location, region, and occupation. Annual earnings was the dependent variable. There was no control for the difference between potential and actual experience; hence, to the extent that the gap between potential and actual experience and the rate of return to actual experience varies by race, the results for the female regressions may be less reliable than the results for the male regression.

4. For a view that unobservable factors might favor black male productivity, thereby meaning that the regression coefficients are underestimating the degree of discrimination, see Mason (forthcoming-a).

5. Indeed, if one uses a measure that, unlike the AFQT, was explicitly designed as a measure of intelligence, it does not explain the black-white gap in wages. Mason (forthcoming-b; 1996) demonstrates this by using in a wage equation an explanatory variable that comes from a sentence completion test given to 1972 respondents to the Panel Study of Income Dynamics (PSID)— a test which was designed to assess "g," so-called general intelligence. Mason finds that the significant, negative sign on the coefficient for

the race variable is unaffected by inclusion of the PSID sentence completion test score as an explanatory variable. Indeed, Mason (1997) finds that although discrimination declined during 1968 to 1973, discrimination grew by 2.0 percent annually during 1973–1991. On the other hand, the rate of return to cognitive skill (IQ) was relatively constant during 1968–1979, but had an annual growth rate of 1.6 percent during 1979–1991.

6. Mason (1997) finds a similar result when age and education-adjusted IQ scores are used.

7. Attention to the psychological measures also provides mild evidence that blacks put forth more effort than whites, a finding consistent with Mason's (forthcoming-a) speculation that there may be unobservables that favor black productivity. Mason argues that effort or motivation is a productivity-linked variable that favors blacks, based upon his finding that blacks acquire more schooling than whites for a comparable set of resources.

8. Card and Krueger (1992) also directly control for school quality. They find that there is still a substantial wage gap left after controlling for school quality.

9. Systematic racial differences in the structural equations for the determination of standardized test scores also are evident in the General Social Survey data. Fitting equations for Wordsum scores separately for blacks and whites also yields statistically distinct structures (White, 1997).

10. Although some of their criticisms along these lines frankly strike us as ridiculous; for example, concerns about facial hair on the Hispanic male testers used by the Urban Institute.

11. To address the effects of culture, following Woodbury (1993), Darity, Guilkey, and Winfrey (1996) held color constant and varied culture by examining outcomes among blacks of differing ancestries. Unlike Sowell's expectation, black males of West Indian and non-West Indian ancestry were being confronted with the same racial penalty in U.S. labor markets by 1990.

12. The portion of the gap that can be explained by discrimination is much lower in the high black region of Brazil, the Northeast, than the rest of Brazil. We know of no evidence which suggests that this is or is not true for the U.S. south.

NO

James J. Heckman

DETECTING DISCRIMINATION

In the current atmosphere of race relations in America, the authors of the three main papers presented in this symposium are like persons crying "fire" in a crowded theater. They apparently vindicate the point of view that American society is riddled with racism and that discrimination by employers may account for much of the well-documented economic disparity between blacks and whites. In my judgement, this conclusion is not sustained by a careful reading of the evidence.

In this article, I make three major points. First, I want to distinguish market discrimination from the discrimination encountered by a randomly selected person or pair of persons at a randomly selected firm as identified from audit studies.

Second, I consider the evidence presented by the authors in the symposium, focusing for brevity and specificity on labor markets. It is far less decisive on the issue of market discrimination than it is claimed to be. Disparity in market outcomes does not prove discrimination in the market. A careful reading of the entire body of available evidence confirms that most of the disparity in earnings between blacks and whites in the labor market of the 1990s is due to the differences in skills they bring to the market, and not to discrimination within the labor market. This interpretation of the evidence has important consequences for social policy. While undoubtedly there are still employers and employees with discriminatory intentions, labor market discrimination is no longer a first-order quantitative problem in American society. At this time, the goal of achieving black economic progress is better served by policies that promote skill formation, like improving family environments, schools and neighborhoods, not by strengthening the content and enforcement of civil rights laws—the solution to the problem of an earlier era.

Third, I want to examine the logic and limitations of the audit pair method. All of the papers in this symposium use evidence from this version of pair matching. However, the evidence acquired from it is less compelling than is often assumed. Inferences from such studies are quite fragile to alternative assumptions about unobservable variables and the way labor markets work. The audit method can find discrimination when in fact none exists; it can also disguise discrimination when it is present. These findings are especially troubling because the Equal Employment Opportunity Commission has recently authorized the use of audit pair methods to detect discrimination in labor markets (Seelye, 1997).

DISCRIMINATION DEFINITION AND MEASUREMENT

The authors of these papers focus on the question of whether society is color blind, not on the specific question of whether there is market discrimination in realized transactions. But discrimination at the individual level is different from discrimination at the group level, although these concepts are often confused in the literature on the economics of discrimination.

At the level of a potential worker or credit applicant dealing with a firm, racial discrimination is said to arise if an otherwise identical person is treated differently by virtue of that person's race or gender, and race and gender by themselves have no direct effect on productivity. Discrimination is a causal effect defined by a hypothetical *ceteris paribus* conceptual experiment—varying race but keeping all else constant. Audit studies attempt to identify racial and gender discrimination so defined for the set of firms sampled by the auditors by approximating the *ceteris paribus* condition.

It was Becker's (1957) insight to observe that finding a discriminatory effect of race or gender at a randomly selected firm does not provide an accurate measure of the discrimination that takes place

in the market as a whole. At the level of the market, the causal effect of race is defined by the marginal firm or set of firms with which the marginal minority member deals. The impact of market discrimination is not determined by the most discriminatory participants in the market, or even by the average level of discrimination among firms, but rather by the level of discrimination at the firms where ethnic minorities or women actually end up buying, working and borrowing. It is at the margin that economic values are set. This point is largely ignored in the papers in this symposium.

This confusion between individual firm and market discrimination arises in particular in the audit studies. A well-designed audit study could uncover many individual firms that discriminate, while at the same time the marginal effect of discrimination on the wages of employed workers could be zero.... Purposive sorting within markets eliminates the worst forms of discrimination. There may be evil lurking in the hearts of firms that is never manifest in consummated market transactions.

Estimating the extent and degree of distribution, whether at the individual or the market level, is a difficult matter. In the labor market, for example, a worker's productivity is rarely observed directly, so the analyst must instead use available data as a proxy in controlling for the relevant productivity characteristics. The major controversies arise over whether relevant omitted characteristics differ between races and between genders, and whether certain included characteristics systematically capture productivity differences or instead are a proxy for race or gender.

HOW SUBSTANTIAL IS LABOR MARKET DISCRIMINATION AGAINST BLACKS?

In their paper in this symposium, [William A.] Darity [Jr.] and [Patrick L.] Mason present a bleak picture of the labor market position of African-Americans in which market discrimination is ubiquitous. They present a quantitative estimate of the magnitude of estimated discrimination: 12 to 15 percent in both 1980 and 1990 using standard regressions fit on Current Population Survey and Census data. Similar regressions show that the black/white wage gap has diminished sharply over the last half century. Comparable estimates for 1940 show a black/white wage gap ranging from 30 percentage points, for men age 25–34 to 42 percentage points, men age 55–64. In 1960, the corresponding numbers would have been 21 percent and 32 percent, for the same two age groups; in 1970, 18 and 25 percent (U.S. Commission on Civil Rights, 1986, Table 6.1, p. 191). The progress was greatest in Southern states where a blatantly discriminatory system was successfully challenged by an external legal intervention (Donohue and Heckman, 1991; Heckman, 1990).

How should the residual wage gap be interpreted? As is typical of much of the literature on measuring racial wage gaps, Darity and Mason never precisely define the concept of discrimination they use. As is also typical of this literature, the phrase "human capital variable" is thrown around without a clear operational definition. The implicit definition of these terms varies across the studies they discuss. In practice, human capital in these studies has come to mean education and various combinations of age and education, based on the available Census and Current Population Survey (CPS) data. However, there is a staggering gap between the list of productivity characteristics available to economic analysts in standard data sources and what is available to personnel departments of firms. Regressions based on the Census and/or CPS data can typically explain 20 to 30 percent of the variation in wages. However, regressions based on personnel data can explain a substantially higher share of the variation in wages; 60–80 percent in professional labor markets (for example, see Abowd and Killingsworth, 1983). It is not idle speculation to claim that the standard data sets used to estimate discrimination omit many relevant characteristics actually used by firms in their hiring and promotion decisions. Nor is it idle speculation to conjecture that disparity in family, neighborhood and schooling environments may account for systematic differences in unmeasured characteristics between race groups.

Consider just one well-documented source of discrepancy between Census variables and the productivity concepts that they proxy: the measurement of high school credentials. The standard Census and CPS data sources equate recipients of a General Equivalence Degree, or GED, with high school graduates. However, black high school certificate holders are much more likely than whites to receive GEDs (Cameron and Heckman, 1993), and a substantial portion of the widely trumpeted "convergence" in measured black educational attainment has come through GED certification. Thus, in 1987 in the NLSY data that Darity and Mason discuss, and Neal and Johnson (1996) analyze, 79 percent of black males age 25 were high school certified, and 14 percent of the credential holders were GED recipients. Among white males, 88 percent were high school certified, and only 8 percent of the white credential holders were GED certified. Given the evidence from Cameron and Heckman that GED recipients earn the same as high school dropouts, it is plausible that standard Census-based studies that use high school credentials to control for "education" will find that the wages of black high school "graduates" are lower than those of whites.

Most of the empirical literature cited by Darity and Mason takes Census variables literally and ignores these issues. The GED factor alone accounts for 1–2 percentage points of the current 12–15 percent black-white hourly wage gap. An enormous body of solid evidence on inferior inner city schools and poor neighborhoods makes the ritual of the measurement of "discrimination" using the unadjusted Census or Current Population Survey data a questionable exercise.

Darity and Mason bolster their case for rampant discrimination by appealing to audit pair evidence. They do not point out that audit pair studies have primarily been conducted for hiring in entry level jobs in certain low skill occupations using overqualified college students during summer vacations. They do not sample subsequent promotion decisions. They fail to point out that the audits under-sample the main avenues through which youth get jobs, since only job openings advertised in newspapers are audited, and not jobs found through networks and friends (Heckman and Siegelman, 1993, pp. 213–215). Auditors are sometimes instructed on the "problem of discrimination in American society" prior to sampling firms, so they may have been coached to find what the audit agencies wanted to find. I have already noted that audit evidence does not translate into actual employment experiences and wages obtained by actors who purposively search markets.

Putting these objections to the side, what do the audits actually show for this unrepresentative snapshot of the American labor market? Table 1 presents evidence from three major audits in Washington, D.C., Chicago and Denver. The most remarkable feature of this evidence is the a + b column which records the percentage of audit attempts where black and white auditors were treated symmetrically (both got a job; neither got a job). In Chicago and Denver this happened about 86 percent of the time. The evidence of disparity in hiring presented in the last two columns of the table suggests only a slight preference for whites over minorities; in several pairs, minorities are favored. Only a zealot can see evidence in these data of pervasive discrimination in the U.S. labor market. And, as I will show in the next section, even this evidence on disparity has to be taken with a grain of salt, because it is based on the implicit assumption that the distribution of unobserved productivity is the same in both race groups.

Darity and Mason go on to dismiss the research of Neal and Johnson (1996) who analyze a sample of males who took an achievement or ability test in their early teens—specifically, the Armed Forces Qualifications Test (AFQT) —and ask how much of the gap in black-white wages measured a decade or so after the test was taken can be explained by the differences in the test scores.[1] It is remarkable and important that this early "premarket" measure of ability plays such a strong role in explaining wages measured a decade after the test is taken.

Table 1

Outcomes from Major Audit Studies for Blacks
(outcome: get job or not)

Number of Audits	Pair	(a) Both Get Job	(b) Neither Gets a Job	Equal Treatment a + b	White Yes, Black No	White No, Black Yes
Chicago*						
35	1	(5) 14.3%	(23) 65.7%	80.0%	(5) 14.3%	(2) 5.7%
40	2	(5) 12.5%	(25) 62.5%	75.0%	(4) 10.0%	(2) 15.0%
44	3	(3) 6.8%	(37) 84.1%	90.9%	(3) 6.8%	(1) 2.3%
36	4	(6) 16.7%	(24) 66.7%	83.4%	(6) 16.7%	(0) 0.0%
42	5	(3) 7.1%	(38) 90.5%	97.6%	(1) 2.4%	(2) 0.0%
197	Total	(22) 11.2%	(147) 74.6%	85.8%	(19) 9.6%	(9) 4.5%
Washington*						
46	1	(5) 10.9%	(26) 56.5%	67.4%	(12) 26.1%	(3) 6.5%
54	2	(11) 20.4%	(31) 57.4%	77.8%	(9) 16.7%	(3) 5.6%
62	3	(11) 17.7%	(36) 58.1%	75.8%	(11) 17.7%	(4) 6.5%
37	4	(6) 16.2%	(22) 59.5%	75.7%	(7) 18.9%	(2) 5.4%
42	5	(7) 16.7%	(26) 61.9%	77.6%	(7) 16.7%	(2) 4.8%
241	Total	(40) 16.6%	(141) 58.5%	75.1%	(46) 19.1%	(14) 5.8%
Denver**						
18	1	(2) 11.1%	(11) 61.1%	72.1%	(5) 27.8%	(0) 0.0%
53	2	(2) 3.8%	(41) 77.4%	81.2%	(0) 0.0%	(10) 18.9%
33	3	(7) 21.2%	(25) 75.8%	97.0%	(1) 3.0%	(0) 0.0%
15	4	(9) 60.0%	(3) 20.0%	80.0%	(2) 6.7%	(2) 13.3%
265	9	(3) 11.5%	(23) 88.5%	100.0%	(0) 0.0%	(0) 0.0%
145	Total	(23) 15.8%	(103) 71.1%	86.9%	(7) 4.8%	(12) 8.3%

Note: Results are percentages; figures in parentheses are the relevant number of audits.
*This study was conducted by the Urban Institute.
**Denver pair numbers are for both black and Hispanic audits. For the sake of brevity, I only consider the black audits. The Denver study was not conducted by the Urban Institute but it was conducted to conform to Urban Institute practice.

Sources: Heckman and Siegelman (1993).

This is as true for studies of white outcomes taken in isolation as it is for black-white comparisons. Their findings are important for interpreting the sources of black-white disparity in labor market outcomes....

The Neal-Johnson story is not about genetic determination. They demonstrate that schooling and environment can affect their measured test score. A huge body of evidence, to which the Neal-Johnson study contributes, documents that human abilities and motivations are formed early and have a decisive effect on lifetime outcomes; the evidence is summarized in Heckman (1995) and in Heckman, Lochner, Taber and Smith (1997). Not only is early ability an important predictor of later success for blacks or whites, it can be manipulated. Early interventions are far more effective than late ones because early skills and motivation beget later skills and motivation. As Heckman, Lochner. Taber and Smith document, however, successful early interventions can be quite costly.

The objections raised by Darity and Mason against the Neal-Johnson study are largely specious. For example, Rodgers and Spriggs (1996) miss the point of the Neal-Johnson article by "adjusting" the test score by a later variable, such as schooling. But ability is known to be an important determinant of schooling (Cawley, Heckman and Vtylacil, 1998), so it should be no surprise that "adjusting" the score for later schooling eliminates an important component of ability and that adjusted scores play a much weaker role in explaining black-white differentials.[2]

Only one point raised by Darity and Mason concerning Neal and Johnson is potentially valid—and this is a point made by Neal and Johnson in their original article. Black achievement scores may be lower than white scores not because of the inferior environments encountered by many poor blacks, but because of expectations of discrimination in the market. If black children and their parents face a world in which they receive lower rewards for obtaining skills, they will invest less if they face the same tuition costs as whites. Poor performance in schools and low achievement test scores may thus be a proxy for discrimination to be experienced in the future.

There is solid empirical evidence that expectations about rewards in the labor market influence human capital investment decisions; for example, the reward to skills held by black workers increased following the passage of the 1964 Civil Rights Act, and a rapid rise in college enrollment of blacks followed (Donohue and Heckman, 1991). But the difficulty with the argument in this context is that it presumes that black parents and children operate under mistaken expectations about the present labor market. Although it was once true

that the returns to college education were lower for blacks than for whites (Becker, 1957; U.S. Civil Rights Commission, 1986), the return to college education for blacks was higher than the return for whites by the mid-1970s, and continues to be higher today. Some parallel evidence presented by Johnson and Neal (1998) shows that the returns to (coefficient on) AFQT scores for black males in an earnings equation are now as high or higher than those for whites, although they used to be lower in the pre-Civil Rights era. Given the greater return for blacks to college education and ability, it seems implausible to argue that a rational fear of lower future returns is currently discouraging black formation of skills.

Ability as it crystallizes at an early age accounts for most of the measured gap in black and white labor market outcomes. Stricter enforcement of civil rights laws is a tenuous way to improve early childhood skills and ability.[3] The weight of the evidence suggests that this ability and early motivation is most easily influenced by enriching family and preschool learning environments and by improving the quality of the early years of schooling.

THE IMPLICIT ASSUMPTIONS BEHIND THE AUDIT METHOD

The method of audit pairs operates by controlling for systematic observed differences across pairs. It does this by attempting to create two candidates for jobs or loans who are "essentially" the same in their paper qualifications and personal characteristics, and then comparing their outcomes in their dealings with the same firm. Averaging over the outcomes at all firms for the same audit pair produces an estimate of the discrimination effect. An average is often taken over audit pairs as well to report an "overall" estimate of discrimination. More sophisticated versions of the method will allow for some heterogeneity in treatment among firms and workers or firms and applicants.

One set of difficulties arise, however, because there are sure to be many unobserved variables. As noted by Heckman and Siegelman (1993), given the current limited state of knowledge of the determinants of productivity within firms, and given the small pools of applicants from which matched pairs are constructed that are characteristic of most audit studies, it is unlikely that all characteristics that might affect productivity will be perfectly matched. Thus, the implicit assumption in the audit pair method is that controlling for some components of productivity and sending people to the same firm will reduce the bias below what it would be if random pairs of, say, whites and blacks were compared using, for example, Census data. The implicit assumption that justifies this method is that the effect of the unobserved characteristics averages out to zero across firms for the same audit pair.

However, the mean of the differences in the unobserved components need not be zero and assuming that it is begs the problem. Nowhere in the published literature on the audit pair method will you find a demonstration that matching one subset of observable variables necessarily implies that the resulting difference in audit-adjusted treatment between blacks and whites is an unbiased measure of discrimination —or indeed, that it is even necessarily a better measure of discrimination than comparing random pairs of whites and blacks applying at the same firm or even applying to different firms....

Consider the following example. Suppose that the market productivity of persons is determined by the sum of two productivity components. These two productivity components are distributed independently in the population so their values are not correlated with each other. Both factors affect employer assessments of employee productivity.[4] Suppose further that average productivity of the sum is the same for both whites and blacks; however, blacks are more productive on average on one component while whites are more productive on average on the other. Now consider an audit pair study that equates only the first component of productivity and equates firm effects by sending the audit pair to the same firm. Under these conditions, the audit estimator is biased toward a finding of discrimination, since in this example, only the characteristic which makes black productivity look relatively high is being used to standardize the audit pair. The condition of zero mean of unobservable productivity differences across race groups is not especially compelling and requires a priori knowledge that is typically not available.

Now consider the case in which the observed and unobserved components of productivity are dependent. In this case, making the included components as alike as possible may accentuate the differences in the unobserved components. As a result, it can increase the bias over the case where the measured components are not aligned.

... [T]hink of pairing up black and white high jumpers to see if they can clear a bar set at a certain height. There is no discrimination, in the sense that they both use the same equipment and have the bar set at the same level. Suppose now that the chance of a jumper (of any race) clearing the bar depends on two additive factors: the person's height and their jumping technique. We can pair up black and white jumpers so that they have identical heights, but we can't directly observe their technique. Let us make the generous assumption, implicit in the entire audit literature, that the mean jumping technique is equal for the two groups. Then, if the variance of technique is also the same for white and black high-jumpers, we would find that the two racial groups are equally likely to clear the bar. On the other hand, if the variance differs, then whether the black or white pair is more likely to clear the bar will depend on how the bar is set, relative to their common height, and which racial group has a higher variance in jumping technique. If the bar is set at a low level so that most people of the given height are likely to clear the bar, then the group with the lower variance will be more likely to clear the bar. If the bar is set at a very high level relative to the given height, then the group with a higher variance in jumping technique will be more likely to clear the bar. A limitation of the audit method is readily apparent from this analogy: there is no discrimination, yet the two groups have different probabilities of clearing the bar.[5] And if there is discrimination —that is, the bar is being set higher for blacks—the differential dispersion in the unobserved component could still cause the minority group to clear the bar more often. The method could fail to detect discrimination when it does exist.

Thus, depending on the distribution of unobserved characteristics for each race group and the audit standardization level, the audit method can show reverse discrimination, or equal treatment, or discrimination, even though blacks and whites in this example are subject to the same cutoff and face no discrimination. The apparent bias depends on whether the level of qualifications set by the audit designer makes it more or less likely that the applicant will receive the job, and the distribution of variables that are unobservable to the audit design. The apparent disparity favoring Washington whites in Table 1 may be a consequence of differences in unobserved characteristics between blacks and whites when there is no discrimination.

Even more disturbing, suppose that there is discrimination against blacks, so the productivity cutoff used by firms is higher for blacks than whites. Depending on the audit designer's choice of what level of qualifications are given to the auditors, the audit study can find no discrimination at all. However, whether the qualifications make it relatively likely or unlikely to get the job is a fact rarely reported in audit studies. . . .

Making audit pairs as alike as possible may seem an obviously useful step, but it can greatly bias the inference about average discrimination or discrimination at the margin. Intuitively, by taking out the common components that are most easily measured, differences in hiring rates as monitored by audits arise from the idiosyncratic factors, and not the main factors, that drive actual labor markets. These examples highlight the fragility of the audit method to untested and unverifiable assumptions about the distributions of unobservables. Similar points arise in more general nonlinear models that characterize other employment decision rules.

THE BECKER MODEL

The papers in this symposium make the erroneous claim that in Becker's (1957) model, market discrimination disappears in the long run. It need not. Entrepreneurs can consume their income in any way they see fit. If a bigoted employer prefers whites, the employer can indulge that taste as long as income is received from entrepreneurial activity just as a person who favors an exotic ice cream can indulge that preference by being willing to pay the price. Only if the supply of entrepreneurship is perfectly elastic in the long run at a zero price, so entrepreneurs have no income to spend to indulge their tastes, or if there are enough nonprejudiced employers to hire all blacks, will discrimination disappear from Becker's model.

However, even if the common misinterpretation of Becker's model is accepted, it is far from clear that the prediction of no or little discrimination in the U.S. labor market in the long run is false. The substantial decline over the past 50 years in wage differentials between blacks and whites may well be a manifestation of the dynamics of the Becker model. It may take decades for the effects of past discrimination in employment and schooling as it affects current endowments of workers to fade out of the labor market. But the evidence from the current U.S. labor market is that discrimination by employers alone does *not* generate large economic disparities between blacks and whites.

APPENDIX

Implicit Identifying Assumptions in the Audit Method

Define the productivity of a person of race $r \in \{1, 0\}$ at firm f, with characteristics $\sim X = (X_1, X_2)$ as $P(\sim X, r, f)$. $r = 1$ corresponds to black; $r = 0$ corresponds

to white. Assume that race does not affect productivity so we may write $P = P(\sim X, f)$. The treatment at the firm f for a person of race r and productivity P is $T(P(\sim X, f), r)$. Racial discrimination exists at firm f if

$$T(P(\sim X, f), r = 1) \neq T(P(\sim X, f), r = 0).$$

As noted in the text, audit methods monitor discrimination at randomly selected firms within the universe designated for sampling, not the firms where blacks are employed.

The most favorable case for auditing assumes that T (or some transformation of it) is linear in f and X. Assume for simplicity that $P = X_1 + X_2 + f$ and $T(P, r) = P + yr$. When $y < 0$ there is discrimination against blacks. y may vary among firms as in Heckman and Siegelman (1993). For simplicity suppose that all firms are alike. Audit methods pair racially dissimilar workers in the following way: they match some components of $\sim X$ and they sample the same firms. Let P_1^* be the standardized productivity for the black member of the pair; P_0^* is the standardized productivity for the white member. If $P_0^* = P_1^*$,

$$T(P_1^*, 1) - T(P_0^*, 0) = y.$$

When averaged over firms, the average treatment estimates the average y.

Suppose that standardization is incomplete. We can align the first coordinate of

Figure 1
Relative Hiring Rate as a Function of the Level of Standardization. Blacks Have More Dispersion. Threshold Hiring Rule: No Discrimination Against Blacks Normally Distributed Unobservables

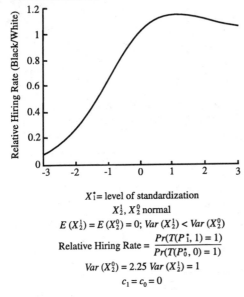

$X_1^* =$ level of standardization
X_2^1, X_2^0 normal
$E(X_2^1) = E(X_2^0) = 0;\ Var(X_2^1) < Var(X_2^0)$
Relative Hiring Rate $= \dfrac{Pr(T(P_1^*, 1) = 1)}{Pr(T(P_0^*, 0) = 1)}$
$Var(X_2^0) = 2.25\ Var(X_2^1) = 1$
$c_1 = c_0 = 0$

Figure 2
Relative Hiring Rate as a Function of the Level of Standardization. Blacks Held to Higher Standard; Blacks Have More Dispersion. Threshold Hiring Rule: No Discrimination Against Blacks Normally Distributed Unobservables

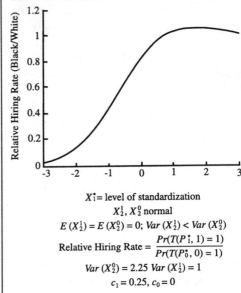

$X_1^* =$ level of standardization
X_2^1, X_2^0 normal
$E(X_2^1) = E(X_2^0) = 0;\ Var(X_2^1) < Var(X_2^0)$
Relative Hiring Rate $= \dfrac{Pr(T(P_1^*, 1) = 1)}{Pr(T(P_0^*, 0) = 1)}$
$Var(X_2^0) = 2.25\ Var(X_2^1) = 1$
$c_1 = 0.25,\ c_0 = 0$

X at $\{X_1 = X_1^*\}$ but not the second coordinate, X_2, which is unobserved by the auditor but acted on by the firm.

$P_1^* = X_1^* + X_2^1$ where X_2^1 is the value of X_2 for the $r = 1$ member and $P_0^* = X_1^* + X_2^1$. In this case

$$T(P_1^*, 1) - T(P_0^*, 0) = X_2^1 - X_2^0 + y.$$

For averages over pairs to estimate y without bias, it must be assumed that $E(X_2^1) = E(X_2^0)$; i.e., that the mean of the unobserved productivity traits is the same. This is the crucial identifying assumption in the conventional audit method. Suppose that this is true so $E(X_2^1) = E(X_2^0) = \mu$. Then the pair matching as in the audit method does not increase bias and in general reduces it over comparisons of two X_1-identical persons at two randomly selected firms. Under these conditions, bias is lower than if two randomly chosen auditors are selected at the same firm if $E(X_1^1) \neq E(X_1^0)$.

However, the decision rule to offer a job or extend credit often depends on whether or not the perceived productivity P exceeds a threshold c:

$T = 1$ if $P \geq T = c$
$T = 0$ otherwise

In this case, the audit pair method will still produce bias even when it does not when T is linear in $\_X$ and f unless the *distributions* of the omitted characteristics are identical in the two race groups. Suppose that $P = X_1 + X_2 . X_2$ is uncontrolled. Then assuming no discrimination ($\gamma = 0$)

$$T(P_1^*, 1) = 1 \text{ if } X_1^* + X_2^1 + f \geq c$$
$$= 0 \text{ otherwise}$$
$$T(P_0^*, 0) = 1 \text{ if } X_1^* + X_2^0 + f \geq c$$
$$= 0 \text{ otherwise.}$$

Even if the distributions of f are identical across pairs, and f is independent of X, unless the *distributions* of X_2^1 and X_2^0 are identical, $\Pr(T(P_1^*, 1) = 1) \neq \Pr(T(P_0^*) = 1)$ for most values of the standardization level X_1^*. The right tail area of the distribution governs the behavior of these probabilities. This implies that even if blacks and whites face the same cutoff value, and in this sense are treated without discrimination in the labor market, even if the means of the distributions of unobservables are the same across race group, if the distributions of the unobservables are different, their probabilities of being hired will differ and will depend on the level of standardization used in the audit study—something that is rarely reported. The pattern of racial disparity in Table 1 may simply be a consequence of the choice of the level of standardization in those audits, and not discrimination.

Worse yet, suppose that the cutoff $c = c_1$ for blacks is larger than the cutoff $c = c_0$ for whites so that blacks are held to a higher standard. Then depending on the right tail area of X_2^1 and X_2^0, the values of

c_1 and c_0, and the level of standardization X_1^*,

$$\Pr(T(P_1^*,) = 1) \gtrless P(T(P_0^*, 0) = 1).$$

In general, only if the *distributions* of X_2^1 and X_2^0 are the same for each race group, will the evidence reported in Table 1 be informative on the level of discrimination in the universe of sampled firms.

Figures 1 and 2 illustrate these two cases for X_2^1 and X_2^0 normally distributed (and independent of each other) where X_1^* is the level of audit standardization and firms are standardized to have $f = 0$. In Figure 1 there is no discrimination in the market. Yet the black hire rate falls short of the white rate if the standardization rate is $X_1^* < 0$, and the lower the value of X_1^*, the greater the shortfall. In Figure 2, which is constructed for a hypothetical economy where there is discrimination against blacks, for high standardization rates, audits would appear to reveal discrimination *in favor* of blacks when in fact blacks are being held to a higher standard. The evidence in Table 1 is intrinsically ambiguous about the extent of discrimination in the market. For further discussion, see Heckman and Siegelman (1993).

NOTES

1. Specifically, Darity and Mason write: "This effort has uncovered one variable in one data set which, if inserted in an earnings regression, produces the outcome that that nearly all of the black male-white male wage gap is explained by human capital and none by labor market discrimination."

2. The Rodgers and Spriggs comment (1997) on Neal-Johnson raises other red herrings. Their confused discussion of endogeneity of AFQT, and their "solution" to the problem end up with an "adjusted" AFQT measure that is poorly correlated

with the measured AFQT, and so is a poor proxy for black ability.

3. However, nothing I have said vindicates abolishing these laws. They have important symbolic value and they addressed and solved an important problem of blatant discrimination in the American South.

4. They need not be perfectly observed by employers but may only be proxied. However, it is easiest to think of both components as fully observed by the employer, but that the observing economist has less information.

5. I owe this analogy to Alan Krueger. This analogy also shows how artificial the audit studies are because one would expect to find athletes choosing their sports based on their chances of success, as in the purposive search in the labor market discussed earlier.

6. For simplicity, assume that y is the same across all firms. Alternatively, assume that it is distributed independently of $_X$ and f.

7. Allowing f to vary but assuming it is normal mean zero and variance σ_f^2 does not change the qualitative character of these calculations assuming that f is distributed independently of the characteristics.

REFERENCES

Abowd, John, and Mark Killingsworth, "Sex, Discrimination, Atrophy, and the Male-Female Wage Differential," *Industrial And Labor Relations Review*, Fall 1983, 22:3, 387–402.

Becker, Gary, *The Economics of Discrimination*. Chicago: University of Chicago Press, 1957.

Cameron. Stephen, and James Heckman, "The Nonequivalence of High School Equivalents," *Journal of Labor Economics*, 1993, 11:1, pt1, 1–47.

Cawley, John, James Heckman, and Edward Vytlacil, "Cognitive Ability and the Rising Return to Education," NBER working paper 6388, January 1998.

Donohue, John, and James Heckman, "Continuous vs. Episodic Change: The Impact of Affirmative Action and Civil Rights Policy on The Economic Status of Blacks," *Journal of Economic Literature*, December 1991. 29:4, 1603–43.

Heckman, James, "The Central Role of the South in Accounting For The Economic Progress of Black Americans," Papers and Proceedings of The American Economic Association, May 1990.

Heckman, James, "Lessons From the Bell Curve," *Journal of Political Economy*, 1995, 103:5, 1091–1120.

Heckman, James, and Peter Siegelman, "The Urban Institute Audit Studies: Their Methods and Findings." In M. Fix and R. Struyk, eds. *Clear and Convincing Evidence: Measurement of Discrimination in America*. Urban Institute, Fall 1993.

Heckman, James, Lance Lochner, Christopher Taber, and Jeffrey Smith, "The Effects of Government Policy on Human Capital Investment and Wage Inequality," *Chicago Policy Review*, Spring 1997, 1:2, 1–40.

Johnson, William R., and Derek Neal, "Basic Skills and the Black-White Earnings Gaps." In Jencks, Christopher and Meredith Phillips, eds. *The Black-White Test Score Gap*. Washington, D.C. Brookings, 1998.

Neal, Derek, and William Johnson, "The Role of Premarket Factors in Black-White Wage Differences," *Journal of Political Economy*, 1996, 104:5, 869–95.

Rodgers III, William, and William Spriggs, "What Does AFQT Really Measure: Race, Wages, Schooling and the AFQT Score," *The Review of Black Political Economy*, Spring 1996, 24:4, 13–46.

Rodgers III, William, William E. Spriggs, and Elizabeth Waaler, "The Role of Premarked Factors in Black-White Differences: Comment," Unpublished Manuscript, College of William and Mary, May 25, 1997.

Seelye, Katherine, "Employment Panel To Send People Undercover to Detect Bias in Hiring," *New York Times*, Sunday, December 7, 1997, p. 22.

U.S. Commission on Civil Rights, *The Economic Progress of Black Men in America*, Clearinghouse Publication 91, 1986.

POSTSCRIPT

Is There Discrimination in U.S. Labor Markets?

Economists assume that markets are anonymous; that is, they assume that rational economic actors would not take race, sex, religious affiliation, or any other personal characteristic into consideration when buying or selling. Consumers are trying to maximize their consumer satisfaction, while producers are in the same marketplace trying to maximize their profits. Just as the often paraphrased axiom of Adam Smith suggests: Each acting for his or her own self-interest advances the well-being of the whole. In the world of neoclassical economics, there is simply no room for discrimination.

Yet the appearance of discrimination, if not the reality of discrimination, is all around us. Why are unemployment rates for African Americans twice those for white Americans? Why, on the average, do African American households earn 60 cents for every dollar earned by white households? Why do U.S. corporations, universities, courthouses, and even military officers' clubs have so many whites? And, more important, why do nearly 40 percent of African American children suffer the life-altering effects of poverty? Is this the product of market discrimination, or is it the consequence of deficient skill levels for African Americans?

In addition to Heckman's many contributions—he is perhaps the most prolific contributor to this debate from the neoclassical position—we suggest that you return to the source of his position, the work of Gary Becker, who in 1957 wrote *The Economics of Discrimination* (University of Chicago Press). Some of Heckman's other recent work is also highly recommended. See, for example, his essay "Lessons from the Bell Curve," *Journal of Political Economy* (vol. 103, 1995), pp. 1091–1120, and the book chapter he wrote with Peter Siegelman, "The Urban Institute Audit Studies: Their Methods," which appeared in Michael Fix and Raymond Struyk, eds., *Clear and Convincing Evidence: Measurement of Discrimination in America* (Urban Institute Press, 1993). Finally, you might read Heckman's paper "The Value of Quantitative Evidence on the Effect of the Past on the Present," *American Economic Review* (May 1997).

Darity and Mason have also contributed extensively to this literature. See, for example, Mason's "Male Interracial Wage Differentials: Competing Explanations," *Cambridge Journal of Economics* (May 1999). You might also look for Darity and Samuel L. Myers, Jr.'s book *Persistent Disparity* (Edward Edgar Publishing, 1999). Lastly, we suggest a coauthored essay by Darity, Jason Dietrich, and David K. Guilkey, "Racial and Ethnic Inequality in the United States: A Secular Perspective," *American Economic Review* (May 1997).

ISSUE 5

Is the Department of Justice Being Too Hard on Microsoft?

YES: Adam D. Thierer, from "The Department of Justice's Unjustifiable Inquisition of Microsoft," *F.Y.I. No. 162* (November 13, 1997)

NO: Richard Wolffe, from "Software Baron," *The New Republic* (November 16, 1998)

ISSUE SUMMARY

YES: Antitrust critic Adam D. Thierer, an Economic Policy Fellow of the Heritage Foundation, charges the U.S. Department of Justice with conducting a vendetta against one of America's most successful companies.

NO: Social critic and author Richard Wolffe argues that Microsoft and Bill Gates have "masterminded a conspiracy" to kill off rivals and establish "control over 90 percent of the world's computers."

Congress's long legislative history of containing the growing economic power of large corporate entities now stretches back more than 100 years. The first legislation in this policy area was the Sherman Act of 1890. This legislation and its companion legislation, the Clayton Antitrust Act of 1914, were intended to impede the progress of the great "merger movement."

Policymakers could not turn a blind eye to the combinations of industrial and commercial firms that were pulled together in what became known as the "trusts." The whisky trust, the sugar trust, the cotton-oil trust, and the Standard Oil trust not only dominated the news in the financial press but also made headlines on the front pages of small-town and big-city daily newspapers. These trusts provided a few shrewd industrialists with the ability to limit industry supply with the explicit intent of sharply increasing industry price. The term *trusts* became synonymous with a small group of individual families: Morgans, Rockefellers, DuPonts, Mellons, and Carnegies. In the process of creating immense wealth for these families, wealth that still benefits many of their heirs five generations later, abuses that conflicted with the prevailing tenets of a free-market economy were inflicted upon society. Thus, immediate and decisive legislative action appeared to be in order.

Such decisive steps were not taken, however. Legislation was passed, but the antitrust policy that flows from that legislation has a long history of vacillation. In the policy's early years under President Theodore Roosevelt, a small staff of antitrust activists was extremely successful in tackling corporate giants. In the process, they established the "rule of reason": Monopolies are not considered illegal unless they establish or exercise their market position in an "unreasonable" manner. After an initial burst of antitrust activity during the early 1900s, public opinion began to sway to the side of big business. It was not until the anti–big business environment of the New Deal era that the antitrust movement picked up momentum again. Under President Franklin D. Roosevelt's administration, antitrust violations were actively prosecuted. This New Deal activism culminated in 1945 with the Aluminum Company of America (Alcoa) case. In this case, the courts went beyond the rule of reason and stated that the mere existence of a monopoly, even if it had been established in a reasonable fashion, was a violation of antitrust law.

In the post–World War II years, the antitrust activism begun by the Roosevelt administration continued. The Celler-Kefauver Antitrust Act was passed in 1950 to strengthen the Clayton Act. In *Brown Shoe Co. v. United States* (1962), the Supreme Court severely limited the extent of vertical mergers. Vertical mergers are mergers of firms at different stages of production within one industry, such as merging a leather tanning firm with a shoe manufacturer, or—as in the *Brown Shoe* case—the manufacturer of shoes with a retail shoe chain. Similarly, *United States v. Bethlehem Steel Co.* (1968) severely limited horizontal mergers (mergers of firms at the same stage of production within one industry, such as merging two steel manufacturers). As a result of the electrical equipment case of 1961, the Supreme Court levied treble damages for price-fixing. Finally, in the Hart-Scott-Rodino Antitrust Improvement Act of 1976, Congress made it mandatory for firms to provide notice to the U.S. Department of Justice concerning their intent to merge.

Despite the strong antitrust mood established in the 1960s and 1970s, public policy was reversed again during the 1980s. These years saw a sharp reduction in the number of antitrust cases brought by the Department of Justice and a return to the view that market decisions were far superior to any decision that antitrust lawyers could devise.

Surprisingly, the reversal of this hands-off policy and the first attempt to investigate Microsoft's market power began in the Federal Trade Commission during the Bush administration. However, when President Bill Clinton took office, his appointee to head the Antitrust Division, Anne Burgaman, co-opted the Federal Trade Commission's case and aggressively pursued its investigation of Microsoft's dominance in providing operating systems for personal computers. The Department of Justice and Microsoft are currently engaged in a titanic struggle. Some predict that this court battle may stretch on for years. Whether or not that comes to pass, this case will surely shape future antitrust litigation.

In the following slections, Adam D. Thierer defends Microsoft, while Richard Wolffe warns that there will be dire consequences if Microsoft is not stopped now.

YES

Adam D. Thierer

THE DEPARTMENT OF JUSTICE'S UNJUSTIFIABLE INQUISITION OF MICROSOFT

INTRODUCTION

On October 20, 1997, officials at the U.S. Department of Justice announced they would seek major penalties against the Microsoft Corporation for supposed violations of a consent decree the latter was forced to sign in 1994. The Department of Justice wants the U.S. District Court in Washington, D.C., to block Microsoft's ability to bundle its own World Wide Web browser software with its popular Windows 95 operating system. Microsoft insists, however, that it has abided by the terms of the consent decree and that its actions are not in violation of antitrust regulations.

According to the Department of Justice's claims, by packaging its Internet software free of charge with its operating system, Microsoft is attempting to squeeze other browser software providers out of the market. To counter this supposed transgression, the Department of Justice wants the District Court to (1) prohibit Microsoft from bundling its Internet Explorer 4.0 software with its operating systems; (2) require Microsoft to inform consumers they do not have to use the Internet Explorer with the Windows 95 operating system; and (3) require the company to provide instructions on how to remove the Internet Explorer icon from a computer's desktop. Until Microsoft complies with this command, the Department of Justice has asked the court to impose an unprecedented fine of $1 million a day on the company.

The Department of Justice's move against Microsoft represents arrogant industrial planning of an industry that exhibits remarkable growth and entrepreneurialism, rapid innovation, and continual price decreases. Microsoft has been one of the most successful companies in its segment of the computer industry, and its products and innovations over the past decade have benefited computer users immensely. In addition, the efforts of the Department of Justice to micromanage the affairs of the Microsoft Corporation represent a shift in the government's rationale behind antitrust enforcement policy.

The new rationale strays far from the original intent of seeking lower prices, higher quality, and increased consumer welfare within an industry. Ironically, in the computer industry, Microsoft's development of products and services positively affected these goals. Consequently, a significant number of industry experts, antitrust scholars, and a surprising diversity of media sources have responded to the ongoing assault on Microsoft with surprise and objections. For example, a recent editorial in *USA Today* noted,

> Who has Microsoft so grievously harmed to earn such condemnation? Not computer makers. Microsoft's packaging of its Web browser costs them nothing. Indeed, Dell, IBM and other computer makers say they'd ask to put in the browser if it weren't part of the package.
> Not other browser firms. Netscape, Microsoft's main rival, has seen its share drop from 80% of the browser market to about 60%. But its profits are up. They beat expectations by 50% last quarter. Meanwhile, new browser companies are building on Microsoft's to provide faster applications.
> And, up to now, not consumers. They are getting more software for the lowest possible price: nothing. And with computer makers providing deals to install Netscape and other browsers as well, they are hardly being denied free choice, either. Indeed, the injuries that the Justice Department complaint indicates have been wrought are hard to find.

Policymakers on Capitol Hill should make every effort to ascertain just how widespread the opposition is— and *why*—before they allow the agency to continue its assault on Microsoft. Congress should take appropriate action to restrain the agency's overzealous inquisition of a company that became a success simply because it strove to respond to the needs of American consumers.

THE HISTORY OF THE DEPARTMENT OF JUSTICE'S FEUD WITH MICROSOFT

The Department of Justice's current move against Microsoft is the latest in a series of antitrust attacks against the Redmond, Washington, company over the past few years. In 1994, the Department of Justice and Microsoft reached a settlement that ended a heated dispute over Microsoft's licensing practices. The consent decree they signed requires Microsoft to change the length of certain licensing and contract agreements as well as to alter its method of collecting royalties from manufacturers of personal computers (PCs) that use Microsoft's products. The Department of Justice argued at the time that Microsoft's power in the software market was so great that it could force its customers and competitors into disadvantageous positions. Specifically, the Department of Justice expressed its concern that Microsoft could tie together the sale of two or more [of] its products, such as Windows and another Microsoft application like Office 95.

Although Microsoft undermined its own business interests by agreeing to settle the dispute in this manner (instead of litigating it in court), concern over the costs of such judicial battles coupled with the costs of the associated delays in product development and deployment may have compelled the company to sign the consent decree. Microsoft now must operate with Department of Justice bureaucrats looking over its shoulders; many of the company's business decisions have been affected by the consent decree. For example, the Department of Justice essentially forced Microsoft to abandon its efforts to acquire financial software manufacturer Intuit, Inc., in mid 1995 just by asking a federal court in San Francisco to prevent the deal from moving forward. The prospect of lengthy delays and constant micromanagement by the Department of Justice was enough for Microsoft to lose interest in the acquisition.

When Microsoft agreed to sign the consent decree, however, it wisely reserved the right to develop "integrated products" to package with its operating systems in order to offer new services to customers or to complement other applications they already possessed. Over time, Microsoft has continued to broaden the range of software applications and services it offers Windows users, much to the benefit of those users. For example, *The Economist* recently noted:

> Microsoft has routinely integrated software into upgrades of Windows that had previously been available only as separate programs. Over the years it has included software for hard-disk defragmenting, disk-compression, calculators, games, graphics and word processing along with software to connect PCs to networks. This may have made life hard for the companies that own those products, but it has been good for consumers. Not only do those products seem to come at no extra cost but they tend to work together seamlessly, thanks to a common standard.

Microsoft has offered Windows users an increasingly wide array of services, seamlessly integrated into one easy-to-use package. Obviously, many competing producers of these software products are not happy with Microsoft's decision and ability to integrate its own version of an application in the Windows sys-

tem. This unhappiness led a handful of lawyers for competing software developers to argue that Microsoft's actions are unfair; bundling their applications directly within Windows might discourage customers from purchasing a competing vendor's products. These rival software developers and the Department of Justice essentially would like to see Microsoft sell only a bare-bones, stripped-down operating system with few Microsoft applications running on top of it. This would be like proclaiming the local ice cream shop can sell only plain vanilla ice cream to customers, not flavored versions or toppings; instead, its customers must take their cones to other stores to buy the toppings or any additional ingredients they desire.

The Department of Justice original case against Microsoft rested on such a premise, even though Microsoft then offered, and still does offer, its competitors the capability to run their own applications on top of its Windows platform. Windows remains an open platform for which all software developers can produce applications. Yet, regardless of this capability, when Microsoft began integrating its Internet Explorer Web browser software into the Windows platform, rival companies and the Department of Justice soon cried foul. They believe that packaging Internet Explorer with the Windows operating system will drive rival Web browser providers —especially Netscape Communications Company with its Netscape Navigator Web browser—from the market, even though Netscape, like any other software provider, is free to offer PC users any Web browser application or software product they desire. The obvious question remains: On what possible grounds does the Department of Justice hope to pursue its case against Microsoft?

PROBLEMS WITH THE ARGUMENTS OF THE DEPARTMENT OF JUSTICE

The Department of Justice's case against Microsoft essentially rests upon two fallacious arguments:

- First, Microsoft is a monopolistic company that threatens the entire future of the Internet and the competitiveness of the computer industry.
- Second, there is something inherently wrong and illegal about efforts by such a company as Microsoft to tie the sale of one product to another.

These faulty arguments can be refuted by examining realities in the marketplace.

Microsoft Is Not a Computer Industry Monopolist

The first faulty argument behind the Department of Justice's suit is that Microsoft is a monopolistic company whose policies threaten the future of the Internet and the computer industry. Microsoft does not possess monopolistic market power within the industry, however; in fact, the computer industry remains remarkably competitive despite Microsoft's success.

The most obvious refutation of the Department of Justice's claim that Microsoft is a computer industry monopolist is the fact that Microsoft controls only a very small portion of the $570 billion computer industry.... Microsoft accounts for less than 2 percent of the entire computer hardware and software industry. It simply is not true that Microsoft is endangering the future of the remaining 98 percent of the industry.

Critics might charge that it is unfair to look at Microsoft's market power over the entire computer sector because Microsoft does not produce much computer hardware. But even if hardware sales are disaggregated from total computer industry sales and only Microsoft's share of the software segment is examined, it will become obvious that Microsoft does not possess overwhelming market power. Far from it,... Microsoft only holds 4 percent of the entire software market.

Even Microsoft's power within the Web browser market—a market the Department of Justice currently accuses it of trying to dominate—is not overwhelming. Netscape, with its popular Netscape Navigator Web browser, remains the dominant software provider with over 60 percent of the market.

Furthermore, Microsoft's overall market power should be examined in the larger context of how well it is doing financially relative to other computer companies. And as Table 1 indicates, according to the most recent *Fortune* 500 survey (in 1996), IBM, Intel, Digital Equipment, and Apple Computer all had higher revenues than Microsoft.

Overall, Microsoft ranked only 172nd on last year's *Fortune* 500 list of the largest corporations in the United States. The survey noted, "Last year IBM generated more revenue from selling software than any other company, some $13 billion. What were total revenues for Microsoft? Just $8.7 billion."

Viewed in this light, it is difficult to understand the claim that Microsoft's market power in the computer industry is destroying competitive opportunities for these larger, more profitable companies, or for any other company in the industry. Moreover, it is difficult to reconcile

Table 1

How Microsoft Ranks in the 1996 *Fortune* 500 Rankings

		Revenues in Billions of Dollars
1st	General Motors	$168,369
2nd	Ford Motor	146,991
3rd	EXXON	119,434
4th	Wal-Mart Stores	106,147
5th	General Electric	79,179
6th	IBM	75,947
7th	AT&T	74,525
8th	Mobil	72,267
9th	Chrysler	61,397
10th	Philip Morris	54,553
43rd	Intel	20,847
51st	Xerox	19,521
72nd	Compaq Computer	18,109
78th	Digital Equipment	14,562
117th	Texas Instruments	11,713
150th	Apple Computer	9,833
172nd	Microsoft	8,671

Source: *Fortune*, April 28, 1997.

the Department of Justice's argument about the industry position of Microsoft with four indisputable facts about the computer industry:

- **First,** prices are low and continuously falling.
- **Second,** quality is high and constantly improving.
- **Third,** innovation and entrepreneurialism are vibrant.
- **Fourth,** competition is cutthroat and ubiquitous.

Many industries in the United States do not exhibit these four trends as strongly and consistently as the computer sector, yet the Department of Justice has been wise in not pursuing antitrust cases against them. For example, relative to the computer software market, far fewer competitors exist within the cola industry, the automobile manufacturing indus-try, the disposable battery market, and the photographic film market. This does not mean these industries are not competitive or that the companies do not serve consumers well in the marketplace. It only shows that hundreds of rivals are not needed for consumers to accrue genuine benefits. Within the computer marketplace, however, hundreds of hardware and software developers already exist and compete with Microsoft, which makes the case against it even more illogical.

Finally, even if the Department of Justice views Microsoft as the proverbial king of the hill in today's operating systems market, there is no guarantee that it will continue to hold such a distinguished position forever. Indeed, the highly publicized case of IBM's fall from power in the 1980s serves as an important reminder of why consumers make better regulators than bureaucrats in Washington, D.C, do.

Remembering IBM's example. The Department of Justice pursued a 13-year antitrust investigation of the IBM Corporation from the late 1960s to 1982. The department had attempted to conjure up enough evidence to take action against the reigning computer giant, but after not being able to do so, it dropped its case in 1982. Michael K. Kellogg, John Thorne, and Peter Huber, authors of *Federal Telecommunications Law*, aptly note that the Department of Justice's case against IBM would "prove to be one of the slowest, most expensive, paper-clogged, and useless antitrust lawsuits ever undertaken."

In hindsight, the futility of the Department of Justice's actions against IBM is even more remarkably evident today. Goliath IBM's own failure to recognize the threat of small entrepreneurs who were creating new PCs for the home right before their eyes proved a greater Achilles' heel. The company lost more than $70 billion, more than two-thirds of its market value, between 1987 and 1992. The Department of Justice's systematic failure to appreciate the dynamic nature of the industry led the agency to waste its time investigating IBM the same way it is pursuing Microsoft.

It is sadly ironic that Microsoft was just getting started when the Department of Justice was dropping its case against computer giant IBM. Microsoft was a small software firm no one had heard of and certainly no one feared back then. As countless computer industry entrepreneurs offer new products every day and many of the major developers collaborate to gain a competitive advantage, it is anybody's guess who will turn out to be tomorrow's king of the computer hill.

Microsoft Is Not Acting Illegally or Unfairly by Tying Products Together

The Department of Justice would like the District Court and the country to believe there is something inherently wrong and illegal about efforts by a company to tie the sale of one product to another. But in reality the practice of tying together products and services for sale within any given market happens every day. There is nothing economically inefficient or anti-competitive about it.

It is important to refute this second argument because it has significant ramifications for the future of antitrust theory and enforcement in general. In theory, illegal tying occurs when a large producer or supplier requires a buyer to purchase one or more additional products or services along with the product it [is] purchasing. Unfortunately for the Department of Justice, however, many antitrust experts and most economists have viewed tying arrangements as an entirely efficient, pro-consumer practice. As noted legal scholar and antitrust expert Judge Robert Bork aptly argues in his 1978 study, *The Antitrust Paradox: A Policy at War With Itself*, economic tying arrangements are used every day by companies to the benefit of consumers. Bork notes:

> Every person who sells anything imposes a tying arrangement. This is true because every product or service could be broken down into smaller components capable of being sold separately, and every seller either refuses at some point to break the product down any further or, what comes to the same thing, charges a proportionally higher price for the smaller unit. The automobile dealer

who refuses to sell only the chassis or the grocer who declines to subdivide a can of pears are engaged in tying. [Antitrust] law ... attempts to avoid this ridiculous conclusion by distinguishing between packages that are inherently one product and those that are inherently more than one. *But the distinction makes no sense. There is no way to state the "inherent" scope of a product.* [emphasis added]

Bork adds, "A review of the cases and the economics of tying leads inescapably to the conclusion that the law in this field is unjustified and is itself inflicting harm upon consumers." Likewise, antitrust expert Dominick T. Armentano, professor of economics at the University of Hartford, argues in his 1982 book, *Antitrust and Monopoly: Anatomy of a Public Policy Failure,* that:

[I]f a group of buyers were unhappy with certain tying contracts, sellers of alternative products would enter the market to offer more favorable terms. Some alternative sellers would offer nontying terms to formerly tied buyers, and over time, a rivalrous process would be expected to purge the relatively undesirable practice from the market. If this did not occur, it must be concluded that buyers prefer such arrangements vis-à-vis other alternatives. It would certainly be incorrect and foolish to believe that buyers are victimized by a system that is voluntarily perpetuated, in the face of open market alternatives, by the very same buyer victims.

The wise words of Bork and Armentano on this issue clearly show how absurd it is to think that requiring a buyer to purchase a bundled good or service is uncompetitive and illegal per se. To the contrary, consider how uncompetitive and inefficient the market would be if tying and bundling arrangements were not allowed in such lines of business as the market for home stereos in which consumers buy stereo components individually or bundled as a single unit, and often at a lower price. Judge Bork notes that the automobile industry is virtually dependent on tying arrangements, because every car purchase presents consumers with a bundled package of styles, colors, and options. Within the computer industry itself, bundling occurs whenever consumers purchase PCs for their homes or offices. Such computer hardware as the central processing unit, the monitor, modems, speakers, and printers are purchased as a single unit from a major retail outlet, although they can be purchased individually. Consumers clearly benefit from such bundling or tying arrangements—and often prefer them.

Similarly, Microsoft hardly can be accused of performing an uncompetitive, inefficient, or illegal act simply by *asking* its customers to accept the Internet Explorer with its Windows operating system. In fact, consumers are benefiting by this tying practice because they are being given a new, competing product free of charge. This factor alone shatters the underpinnings of the Department of Justice's case, because consumer welfare is enhanced by Microsoft products and services. Yet the Department of Justice claims that Microsoft simply is using its current market power to engage in "predatory pricing" of its software applications in order to drive customers from the market and raise prices in the long run. Thus, as this theory goes, Microsoft would continue to price software like Internet Explorer at zero cost, or next to zero, until it drove all competition from the market. Supposedly, then, Microsoft —as the only software provider left in the market—would raise its prices and gouge consumers continually.

Again, this fear is based on another traditional, but discredited, antitrust theory. Predatory pricing is impossible within the dynamic computer industry, just as it is in most other industries. If Microsoft seriously attempted to price all competitors out of the market in order to raise prices and recover profits lost when they gave their products away for free, then it ultimately would lose money as alternative vendors entered the market to offer cheaper substitutes. There simply is no way Microsoft could eliminate all other software entrepreneurs from the software market or force them out of business for good.

Furthermore, it is worth repeating that Microsoft in no way is attempting to restrict access by competitors to its Windows platform. To do so would be economic suicide for the company —Windows customers demand an open operating system platform upon which they can run any type of software they want. Because Windows will remain an open platform for which customers can demand and receive products by other vendors, consumer welfare will not be affected adversely by Microsoft's current business practices.

But therein lies the most disturbing part of the Department of Justice's case against Microsoft: It is not at all clear that consumer welfare is the guiding principle at work in the department's analysis. Rather, the Department of Justice's continuing efforts to micromanage the affairs and operations of the Microsoft Corporation appear to reflect the agency's greater concern for the welfare of its competitors within the software industry. In other words, the Department of Justice's case against Microsoft could be interpreted as

an effort to reinvigorate the old antitrust theory that "big is bad," and to help smaller competing producers who covet the status of industry leader. Microsoft's competitors apparently have been successful in persuading the Department of Justice of the need to stop a normal business practice they do not like because it could cost them customers and profits. The reliance of the Department of Justice on such an outdated and discredited rationale for antitrust enforcement bodes poorly not only for Microsoft, but for any company that gains an advantage within an industry by offering consumers additional choices at a lower price.

CONCLUSION

Clearly, Microsoft possesses a certain degree of market power within the computer operating system sector of the software industry. This is hardly justification, however, for federal antitrust officials to intervene in a fast-paced, rapidly evolving industry and set up industrial policy for software management and development. Microsoft's products and innovations over the past decade have benefited computer users greatly. And although many of their competitors are, understandably, unhappy about this situation, it does not follow that Microsoft should be punished for this success.

Most disturbing, the Department of Justice's actions against Microsoft represent a newfound willingness of federal regulators to interfere in the dynamic and rapidly evolving computer marketplace. The problem with this new approach is explained admirably by American Enterprise Institute scholar J. Gregory Sidak:

> The government's crusade against Microsoft reveals a stunning lack of humil-

ity that in turn indicates a subtle change in the orientation of antitrust policy. The government's multiple cases against Microsoft suggest a tendency to use the consent decree process to establish the Antitrust Division as an ad hoc regulatory agency having jurisdiction over the development of software for personal computers. In effect, this would-be Federal Software Commission could require that Microsoft secure prior approval of every significant strategic endeavor. . . .

The requirement of prior approval in the consent decree process destroys the element of surprise as a tool of competitive rivalry. It makes a competitive industry resemble a regulated industry in which a regulatory commission must issue a certificate of public convenience and necessity before a firm may offer a new service or enter the market. In this respect it is paradoxical that while the telecommunications industry is moving from heavy-handed regulation to competition . . . the Antitrust Division is seeking to impose on Microsoft a regulatory regime that more resembles the one Congress scrapped for telecommunications in 1996.

Many other scholars and media sources of varying orientations agree with this summation and have voiced their opposition to the inquisition of the Microsoft Corporation. Members of Congress should heed these warnings and reject calls by Microsoft's competitors and their backers in the Department of Justice to punish an innovative company simply because it has been so successful.

Punishing Microsoft for its success is a ridiculous use of antitrust law and a dangerous precedent for the future. Congress should communicate its dissatisfaction with the Department of Justice with regard to the Microsoft case. And Congress should consider scaling back the powers of the Antitrust Division at the Department of Justice while simultaneously initiating a comprehensive review of existing antitrust statutes to ensure they cannot be used in such anti-competitive ways in the future.

NO

Richard Wolffe

SOFTWARE BARON

The videotaped interrogation seemed uncannily familiar—a disheveled, pale-faced chief executive parsing his sworn testimony in an attempt to dodge a prosecutor's traps. The federal courthouse in Washington, D.C., had witnessed something similar just two months earlier. But that was a different charge—and a different Bill.

This time it's Bill Gates on the stand. He is accused of abusing the power of his office as chairman of the most successful company of modern times. And, at the start of the biggest antitrust trial in a generation, government lawyers tore into his testimony, even though technically Microsoft—not its founder—is in the dock. The charges might be technologically complex, but the message is clear enough. Gates allegedly masterminded a conspiracy to kill off a rival company, using his monopoly control over 90 percent of the world's computers as the weapon.

The charges facing Gates—in the same building that houses Kenneth Starr's grand jury—are hardly impeachable. After all, Gates will still have his throne when this is all over. But, if proved, they are likely to leave a far more durable mark on the next century, for this is not merely an argument about one company or one very, very rich man. At its heart, the Microsoft monopoly trial will determine who writes the business rules of cyberspace—the government or Microsoft. And, while the current trial concentrates on the conversations of technogeeks in smoke-free rooms, the underlying issue is more basic: Are Gates and company just too powerful for the public good?

The answer lies in the nature of the information highway, which the century-old conceptual world of American antitrust law would treat more like an information railroad. Like the robber barons of the last century, the companies that control the engines and infrastructure of the computer age could wield almost untrammeled power over tomorrow's commercial and social links. And so, the government argues, if Microsoft controls both our desktop computer screens and our means of using the Internet, it is unlikely to stop there. The temptation may be to extend that economic power into other areas, such as payment systems on the Internet, banking services, and Web television. Microsoft would own the metaphorical bridge to the twenty-first century.

In fact, one of the seminal cases in this obscure corner of the law involves two bridges over the Mississippi River. A group of railroads jointly owned the two bridges as well as a ferry for railroad cars and the only terminal in St. Louis. They excluded other railroad companies, thus controlling all traffic through the hub, until the Supreme Court in 1912 ordered the railroads to open up access to their rivals at a reasonable cost. The scenario has become known as the bottleneck monopoly. While Microsoft is unlikely to want to exercise a similar form of control over consumer access to the Internet, the government believes Microsoft could establish a stranglehold over those companies that seek to service the cyber age. But does the government have a point?

* * *

Microsoft's power base lies in two large tracts of computing real estate. One is the computer screen, which users see when they switch on their machines. Microsoft says this is part of its intellectual property, a vital component of the computing experience on which it has built its brand. But, in the Internet age, the humble screen can become a shopping mall, library, newsstand, or telephone kiosk. How that screen is designed and how it operates could affect how consumers use the Internet. Ergo, Microsoft could give an online provider a privileged position on the desktop display in return for other business.

Microsoft's other, and arguably more significant, property is the technical information that software developers require in order to work with Windows, the op-

erating software which drives more than 90 percent of the world's personal computers. By tightly controlling this information and, particularly, the timing of its publication, Microsoft can favor some developers over others. Moreover, it could use that technical edge to merge new products into Windows, as it has already done with the Internet browser. (That argument also provides the basis for the U.S. government's separate lawsuit against Microsoft's principal partner in the personal computer revolution: Intel. Officials at the Federal Trade Commission are suing the world's largest chipmaker for allegedly withholding technical information from rivals in an abuse of its monopoly power.)

The barriers to building a new bridge to rival the one already owned by Microsoft are high. The central role of Windows, managing the operations at the heart of a computer, has been reinforced by hundreds of so-called applications such as Microsoft Word, the word processor that is the most popular software in history. The more widespread Word gets, the more entrenched Windows becomes, as Microsoft reaps the rewards of "network effects." It does so for the same reason that there's no point in developing a new telephone line with just one phone at the end of it. It only works if you can convince millions of customers to buy new phones and be part of the network. According to Joel Klein, head of the antitrust division at the Justice Department, that monopoly control over computer screens is one of the central worries that prompted the lawsuit. "In the new world of the high-tech economy, where so much of what we do will be through interconnectivity and common standards, that will lead to the aggregation of economic power and concerns about bottleneck monopolies," he says.

The government itself estimates that Internet commerce in the United States is likely to exceed $300 billion by 2002. And Microsoft is perfectly placed to take advantage of that: it already enjoys an extraordinary position within the modern economy. Just 23 years old, the company is already one of the largest on the U.S. stock market—neck and neck with General Electric—and is valued at around $260 billion. Its earnings in the first quarter of this year rose by an astonishing 58 percent as the company made $1.52 billion in net profits.

Gates himself is by far the richest man in the United States, worth $58 billion according to the new *Forbes* 400 list—twice the fortune of the second-wealthiest man, his best friend, Warren Buffett. His staggering wealth outstrips even the most notorious antitrust target in U.S. history—John D. Rockefeller, whose Standard Oil Company was broken up into 34 companies at the start of the century. Rockefeller was only worth about $25.6 billion in current prices, according to Ronald Chernow's recent biography of the great tycoon.

The source of Gates's fortune, and Microsoft's vast profits, is Windows— the operating system that has spurred the success of the entire PC industry. Once you have succeeded in establishing the industry standard, everyone must knock on your door, as Gates himself acknowledged at a public conference way back in 1981. "I really shouldn't say this," he announced, "but in some ways it leads, in an individual product category, to a natural monopoly where somebody properly documents, properly trains, properly promotes a particular package."

News of Microsoft's latest profits ironically came on the second day of the trial, as its lawyers were opening the company's defense in court. Responding to the government's charge that Microsoft rakes in monopoly profits, John Warden, its lead attorney, argued that its success in fact sits on a knife-edge. Microsoft was only popular because its products were competitive, but that competition was fierce—and it remains so, despite the company's staggering market share. "Microsoft must constantly innovate to remain viable in each succeeding round of competition, and the pace of that competition is extremely rapid. It is not a comfortable, quiet monopoly backwater," he said. "[Computer makers] have alternatives. They have them today, and there will be plenty of others to come. They install Windows because that is what their customers want, and they . . . are demand driven enterprises in a highly competitive business. Microsoft has not denied consumer choice. It is consumer choice."

Is there really any basis for believing that Microsoft could abuse its effective monopoly power to establish a stranglehold on the Internet? Does the company really have the power to prevent the development of new technologies that could render it as obsolete as, well, the Penn Central Railroad? If the government's evidence about Microsoft's browser wars with Netscape Communications is correct, the answer may really be "yes."

*   *   *

On the one hand, it is true that the company that dominates the industry also fears for its life, strange as that might sound. Microsoft knows that a paradigm shift in technology could bring any giant to its knees. That paranoia was born in its formative experiences with IBM in the '80s, when Microsoft was a mere contractor to the industry leader, supplying the early operating system for IBM's first personal computers. Within ten years, Gates had outstripped his former client in size and power as the PC industry exploded.

Fear of history repeating itself appears to lie behind the battle with Netscape. Microsoft had woken up late to the Internet's appeal and was lagging behind the small, new company. Netscape was storming ahead with its Navigator browser software, which allows computer users to download multimedia information from the World Wide Web. Its threat to Microsoft was not just its rapid success. Its real power lay in its use of Java, a programming language developed by Sun Microsystems, which allows applications to run on all kinds of operating systems, not just Windows. Together, Netscape and Java could make Windows a forgotten piece of plumbing deep inside the computer box.

* * *

Yet, however real Microsoft's fear may have been, it led Microsoft to engage in behavior that, at the very least, skirted the law's limits. By the middle of 1995, Netscape's success had alerted Microsoft to its strategic blunder. While the two companies were already sharing some technical information, Microsoft wanted to develop its own Internet browsing software. In June 1995, with the two companies still engaged in a friendly dialogue, executives from both sides met to discuss technical issues.

What happened at the meeting at Netscape's headquarters is hotly disputed, but the discussions stand at the center of the allegations against Microsoft. For Netscape and the government, Microsoft's abuse of power was clear—it proposed an illegal conspiracy to carve up the market in Internet software. Microsoft would serve Windows customers, while Netscape would mostly sell to business customers using non-Windows systems. In the words of Jim Barksdale, Netscape's chief executive and the government's star witness, Microsoft wanted to draw a line between the two businesses. "Here we are, a little company, and you are a big company with unlimited resources, and you are going to move the line toward our economic interests," he told the court.

Microsoft insists this is a complete fabrication. Netscape concocted the whole idea of a market carve-up because it wanted to protect its 70 percent share of the Internet market. Far from being a big bad monopoly, Microsoft says, it wanted to stop Netscape from strangling the market at birth. All it proposed was a "strategic relationship" where the two would cooperate on technical information and marketing to create new products and expand use of the Internet. In his videotaped deposition, Gates claims the first time he learned of any carve-up claims in the meeting was when he read a *Wall Street Journal* article earlier this year. When asked if he knew of any attempts by his company to carve up the market, Gates said: "I am not aware of any such thing. . . . It is very much against the way we operate."

According to one source close to Microsoft's legal team, the aggressive intent was all Netscape's. "I think what happened is that they wanted a different kind of business," he said. "They had set their goal to take this highly successful browser operation and migrate it into being a platform [like Windows]. They wanted Microsoft's help in destroying Microsoft."

In any event, there was no deal. That prompted Microsoft to unleash its competitive fury—Jeff Raikes, a Microsoft sales executive, said, "Netscape pollution must be eradicated"—and the battle that followed provides a unique insight into how Microsoft wields its formidable market power.

First, Microsoft struck a series of deals with the industry—computer makers, Internet service companies, and Internet content suppliers—to exclude Netscape's browser and promote its own. Manufacturers who challenged the contracts were supposedly threatened with losing their lucrative access to Windows, although Microsoft denies that. Many of these contracts have now lapsed, and Microsoft says it will not renew them.

Just as powerful was Microsoft's use of "reverse bounties," or business favors. In particular, the government accuses the company of being prepared to sacrifice its own online venture—the Microsoft Network—in the greater war against Netscape. Microsoft is accused of offering America Online unique access to the Windows desktop installed on every computer, as long as it committed itself to Microsoft's browser, Internet Explorer. One America Online executive reported a meeting with the Microsoft chairman himself: "Gates offered a characteristically blunt query: 'How much do we need to pay you to screw Netscape? This is your lucky day.' " (Microsoft hasn't challenged this yet, although they may do so in the future.)

Microsoft's crushing blow was to distribute its own Internet browser for free. Netscape made the bulk of its money from licenses for its software. Overnight, Microsoft undercut those revenues and eventually forced its rival to follow suit. As Gates told the *Financial Times* in June 1996: "Our business model works even if all Internet software is free.... We are still selling operating systems. What does Netscape's business model look like [if that happens]? Not very good."

The final weapon came inside the shrink-wrapped package of Windows 98, the latest version of the operating software.... Browsing software no longer exists on its own but is now fully integrated into Windows; those who use Windows 98 can "browse" their own computers using the same tools and graphics as they use to "browse" the Internet. What were once competing products have been crossbred to create a new concept in managing computers. Even Netscape admits it is now impossible to find where one begins and the other ends.

* * *

To be sure, the fact that Microsoft's alleged victim, Netscape, remains alive and relatively healthy would seem to undermine the government's case. Netscape plans to "carpet bomb" consumers with more than 100 million free software copies this year, and the number of its own browser users rose from 40 million to 65 million last year. That hardly connotes competition being crushed. Microsoft also notes, rightly, that its strategy has meant that, in effect, consumers now get for free what Netscape once sold for $39 a copy. If consumers are better off, Microsoft asks, what's the rationale for government intrusion?

In making this argument, Microsoft has the implicit support of such luminaries as Alan Greenspan, the Fed chairman, who has cast doubt on Klein's antitrust agenda by challenging the government's ability to forecast the effects of new technology.

At a Senate Judiciary Committee hearing in June, he praised the entrepreneurs in Silicon Valley for their aggressive, competitive behavior, which, he said, undermines monopoly power as it is traditionally understood. "Forecasting the way markets will evolve and the way technology will evolve is an excruciatingly difficult job," he stated. "History is strewn with people who made predictions that proved to be wrong. I would like to see far more firm roots to our judgments."

Veterans of the pro-market Reagan administration, which was conspicuously reluctant to pursue antitrust cases, are quick to agree. "This is essentially a case of 'big is bad,'" says Rick Rule, a consultant to Microsoft and former head of the Justice Department's antitrust division. "Rather than focusing on the objective of harm to competition and consumers' interests, they are looking after competitors. They are saying this company is too big and the government is going to take it down a couple of notches." Haley Barbour, the former chairman of the Republican National Committee, puts it even more bluntly: "Frankly, what the deal is, despite the Clinton administration's protestations ... is a case of a pro-regulation administration using antitrust enforcement as a guise to try to get its regulatory claws on the technology industry."

Klein, of course, denies any such sentiments. (And, in a strange twist, none other than Robert Bork, intellectual father of conservative anti-regulatory doctrine on antitrust law, has been working on behalf of Netscape.) "We are concerned about the aggregation of market power in a way that could hurt consumers," Klein says. "On the other hand, we are on the side of aggregation of power that is efficient and pro-consumer. There is

not an antipathy to big business. It is a concern about Microsoft's control of the bottleneck monopoly of the desktop."

Klein has a point. It's all well and good that consumers save $39 on their browsers. But, down the road, who will set the prices we pay to shop online? If the marketplace is to shrink to the size of a computer screen, shouldn't we care about who can set up shop on it?

* * *

Unfortunately for Klein, the higher courts may disagree. In a devastating ruling in June, the appeals court in Washington, D.C., ruled that Microsoft was well within its rights to combine its products if it could argue that it provided some plausible consumer benefits. The ruling was based on the earlier consent decree, but the issue of bundling Internet browsers with Windows remains largely the same. "Antitrust scholars have long recognized the undesirability of having courts oversee product design, and any dampening of technological innovation would be at cross-purposes with antitrust law," the court wrote, splitting along political lines —two Republican appointees versus one judge named by Jimmy Carter.

And, even if Klein makes his case successfully, it will merely beg another, equally vexing question: How do you police a company and an industry that have built success on aggressive competition? Is it possible to draft rules that foresee the scope of new technology?

The government's lawsuit ... merely suggested some preliminary actions, like forcing Microsoft to ship Netscape's browser along with its own. Its latest filings talk more ominously of "further remedies" to be decided at further court hearings. Unless the government and Microsoft agree on yet another consent decree about how the company will do business—unlikely, since the past efforts at getting such an agreement have failed —that leaves three options. The first involves breaking the company in two: one of the offspring would produce Windows, and the other would produce applications that run on Windows. It's a neat-enough solution, but it doesn't really address the problem of the all-powerful Windows monopoly.

Another possibility would be to create two or more clones of Microsoft—call them the Baby Bills—each of which would produce its own version of Windows and applications. These companies would engage in equal but vigorous competition on the same turf. A third possibility, which the state attorneys general support, is to leave Microsoft intact but force it to license Windows to several software companies. Microsoft would get royalties and hopefully maintain some incentive to innovate.

The problem with both cloning and licensing is what happens to Windows itself in such a world. The inevitable consequence is that different versions of Windows would evolve, undermining the very strength of the product: its universal acceptance. Perhaps the Internet itself offers a glimpse of such a world in which different computers are able to communicate with one another re-gardless of their operating software—in which case Microsoft was right to identify Netscape as a potential business killer.

* * *

In the end, only one thing seems close to certain. The Microsoft case shows every sign of mirroring the ill-fated IBM case in terms of the tedious length of its legal battles. The IBM case dragged on for 13 years before Reagan's Justice Department dropped it in 1982. Microsoft's first antitrust investigation began in 1990 at the FTC, before the Justice Department picked up the baton. Eight years later, the matter shows few signs of swift resolution. In spite of the expedited preparations, the trial is unlikely to limp its way through the district court much before Christmas.

The smart money backs the government there, in a court that has already sided with it over the consent decree. On the other hand, the appeals court has already ruled in favor of Microsoft on similar issues this year and can reasonably be expected to do the same next year. Both sides expect the case to end in the same place—the Supreme Court. Never mind your computer crashing; the lengthy trials of Microsoft are a far more intractable problem for the year 2000.

POSTSCRIPT

Is the Department of Justice Being Too Hard on Microsoft?

To a considerable degree, whichever side is allowed to define what the "market" is will control this debate. If, as Thierer suggests, the relevant market is the global computer hardware/software market, then the case appears to be open-and-shut and there is little need to worry about Microsoft's integration of a Web browser software system into the Windows platform. However, if the U.S. Supreme Court rules that the relevant market is the world market for personal computer operating systems, then Microsoft's 90 percent share of that market is a real concern.

Even if the Court does side with Microsoft on the question of how to define the market, the antitrust debate will not end. Those fearful of Microsoft will warn the Court of the consequences of "bottleneck monopolies" in an industry with virtually nonexistent marginal costs. Microsoft supporters will likely counter that it is irrational to look to a "perfectly competitive model" in the modern world of fast-paced technological change driven by the lure of immense profits.

Perhaps the best place to begin your search for further information on this issue is to turn on your computer and search the Internet. Note the Web browser you are using. Why are you using it? Once you have resolved that question, you will find more information on the Internet than you will probably care to read. Two good starting points are the home page for the Cato Institute, at http://www.cato.org, and the home page for the Heritage Foundation, at http://www.heritage.org. It is also interesting to note the proliferation of anti-Microsoft Web pages on the Internet.

If you want to explore this debate "in print," you have many alternatives. On the "let's get Gates" side, start with the January/February 1998 issue of *Mother Jones*. This issue contains five articles that are critical of Bill Gates and Microsoft. Also see David Shenk, "Slamming Gates," *The New Republic* (January 26, 1998); Daniel Oliver, "Necessary Gateskeeping," *National Review* (May 4, 1998); and Alan Murray, "Antitrust Isn't Obsolete in an Era of High-Tech," *The Wall Street Journal* (November 10, 1997).

For arguments opposed to the very nature of antitrust, read D. T. Armentano, *Antitrust and Monopoly* (Independent Institute, 1990), as well as his essays "Time to Repeal Antitrust Regulation?" *Antitrust Bulletin 35* (Summer 1990) and "Or Broken Trust?" *National Review* (May 4, 1998). You might also want to read Robert J. Barro, "Why the Antitrust Cops Should Lay Off High Tech," *Business Week* (August 17, 1998) and Gary S. Becker, "Let Microsoft Compete," *Business Week* (December 1, 1997).

ISSUE 6

Is Managed Competition the Cure for Our Ailing Health Care System?

YES: Paul M. Ellwood, Jr., and George D. Lundberg, from "Managed Care: A Work in Progress," *Journal of the American Medical Association* (October 2, 1996)

NO: John H. McArthur and Francis D. Moore, from "The Two Cultures and the Health Care Revolution: Commerce and Professionalism in Medical Care," *Journal of the American Medical Association* (March 26, 1997)

ISSUE SUMMARY

YES: Paul M. Ellwood, Jr., a physician and a long-time advocate of managed health care, and George D. Lundberg, editor of the the *Journal of the American Medical Association*, argue that it is unrealistic to expect a return to unmanaged, autonomous, fee-for-service medicine.

NO: Harvard Business School professor John H. McArthur and Harvard Medical School professor Francis D. Moore warn that, if unchecked, professional commitment to patient care will be subordinated to new rules of practice that ensure the profitability of the corporation.

A quiet revolution has taken place in the U.S. health care industry. Overnight it has gone from a fee-for-service system, where health care users (consumers) had maximum choice and doctors and hospitals (producers) had maximum autonomy, to a system of health maintenance organizations (HMOs) and preferred provider organizations (PPOs), where both consumers and producers of health care are subject to the discipline exercised by those who pay for the large majority of privately provided health care: the insurance industry.

The results have been remarkable. In the 30 years from 1965 to 1995, the consumer price index (CPI) for all items increased almost fivefold. The cost of health care, on the other hand, increased nearly tenfold. Yet if we compare the all-item CPI and the medical care sector of the economy since 1993, the rate of inflation in the latter sector has fallen each year so that by 1996 it was actually less than the overall rate of inflation in the economy.

Those who would like to blame the government for all the problems in the economy are quick to point out that the public sector is no stranger to the health care industry. For more than 30 years the U.S. government has actively shaped both the supply and the demand for services in this industry. Although governmental involvement can be traced back to the passage of the personal income tax in 1913, which explicitly excluded the cost of employer-provided health insurance fringe benefits from taxation—a policy that reduced the relative price of health care—most agree that the real impact of government was not felt until the mid-1960s.

In an attempt to provide access to the U.S. health care system for the aged and often poverty-stricken retired population, Congress amended the Social Security Act in 1965 and created what is known as Medicare. A short time later, it extended these benefits to the non-aged poor by passing Medicaid. These two pillars of President Lyndon B. Johnson's War on Poverty brought about fundamental changes in the health care industry. Few can deny that some of these changes were good. Indeed, large numbers of American citizens were provided with much-needed health care, which they could not otherwise have purchased. But few can also deny that this government intrusion into the marketplace set in motion a tidal wave of price increases in the industry that are easily discernible four decades later.

These increases in price and relatively small (but very significant) increases in consumption of medical services have had major consequences. Consider how much of the U.S. income is devoted to health care. In 1965 it was 5.9 percent. By 1992 it had skyrocketed to 14 percent. Some estimated that without intervention it might have reached 19 percent of the nation's total gross domestic product (GDP) by the year 2000. In the face of these rapidly rising health care costs, President Bill Clinton proposed a new federal initiative: managed health care. This ambitious program, designed to provide universal coverage, was a market-based system that attempted to preserve consumer choice and build upon the employer-based private insurance system that was already in place. When the president's proposals were defeated by Congress, employers took matters into their own hands. They turned to the insurance industry, demanded lower costs, and threatened to take their business elsewhere if their demands were not met.

Seemingly overnight, doctors who were in solo practices or who practiced in small groups found that if they did not join an HMO or a PPO, the large insurance carriers that represented the major employers in their community would not cover their medical charges. Indeed, when they did join these groups out of necessity, they found that they had to agree to a fixed, often low price for their services and abide by a set of medical policies established by the HMO or PPO.

In the following selections, Paul M. Ellwood, Jr., and George D. Lundberg argue in favor of managed competition, while John H. McArthur and Francis D. Moore contend that there are many dangers in allowing such a health care system to prosper.

YES

Paul M. Ellwood, Jr., and George D. Lundberg

MANAGED CARE: A WORK IN PROGRESS

The modern *JAMA* [*Journal of the American Medical Association*] has been working toward comprehensive American health system reform since 1987, emphasizing cost control, access for all, and promotion of quality.[1] One of us (P.M.E.) has been developing market-based health system thinking for more than 25 years.[2] The concept of managed care is hardly new. The Kaiser plans began in the American West in the 1930s.[3] The massive reform that has occurred in the 1990s has been phenomenal and largely unpredicted, although much of it has been called for by many authors.[4-6] Many patients, providers, and purchasers alike consider the system to be in turmoil, some even in chaos. But movement is profound and irreversible, at least in the short run.

As we go forward, we believe that physicians should be more involved and influential in determining where the American health system is going. It is unrealistic to expect to return to unmanaged, autonomous, fee-for-service medicine where those who paid the bill often exerted little influence over medical practice. We should expect a more integrated, selective, epidemiologic data-dependent, and consumer-driven health system. We physicians no longer have a health system that was built by us and sometimes for us.

The new American health system works. It has contained costs, it provides easily accessible comprehensive health care to its insured members, and, on the whole, it has not yet jeopardized quality. But patients, physicians, the uninsured, and the country deserve better. The American health system is a work in progress; it can and, we believe, will get better.

ORIGINS OF THE NEW AMERICAN HEALTH SYSTEM

Only 5 years after the establishment of Medicare, the Nixon administration became alarmed by the program's unanticipated run-up costs. Searching for remedies, the leadership of the Department of Health, Education, and Welfare in 1970 found—and the president accepted—a unique American approach to health reform combining social insurance with market forces.

From Paul M. Ellwood, Jr., and George D. Lundberg, "Managed Care: A Work in Progress," *Journal of the American Medical Association*, vol. 276, no. 13 (October 2, 1996), pp. 1083–1086. Copyright © 1996 by The American Medical Association. Reprinted by permission.

The idea, labeled the "health maintenance strategy,"[7] was to allow Medicare beneficiaries to make a choice between health maintenance organizations (HMOs) and traditional fee-for-service systems that were competing on price and quality. It was anticipated that the government's actions would catalyze similar restructuring in the private, largely employer-financed segment of the health economy that also was having difficulty coping with medical inflation.

The HMOs were designed to take 2 forms: nongroup independent practice associations (IPAs) favored and pioneered by medical societies in the far West, and prepaid group practices (Kaiser Permanente Health Plan was the prototype). Both organizational arrangements were to combine in a variety of ways the health insurance risk-bearing function with the responsibility to deliver health care to voluntary enrollees for 1 year or more. In keeping with the free market philosophy of the Republican administration, rapid expansion of HMOs was encouraged by placing few limitations on the ownership or tax status of the fledgling HMO firms. The suggestion of the architects of the health maintenance strategy, that an independent commission be formed to establish measures to make HMOs publicly accountable for the impact on their enrollees' health, was not incorporated into the Nixon administration proposal.

The health maintenance strategy assumed that IPAs, which resembled more closely the existing arrangement of health care, would initially be more appealing to consumers and most practicing physicians. Later, as competition over prices and the novel approach to quality accountability took hold, the group practices were expected to be better posi-tioned to manage a carefully selected professional workforce and its attendant information systems and capital resources to produce more consistent health value for patients and purchasers. The health delivery function was so much more central, and difficult to manage, than the marketing and insurance activities that physician leadership in managing the health enterprise seemed assured—but it was not guaranteed by law or precedent.

Beyond the structural arrangements and the distribution of power and revenue so important to the supply side of health care, the demand side of the health maintenance strategy represented much more of an experiment. Would consumers be motivated to choose the best value based on a mysterious balance of untested financial incentives and as yet unavailable objective comparisons of health care results? It may seem obvious now, but early advocates of market forces could not prove that demand based on prices of HMO care would be elastic.

THE TRANSITION

After rapid, unheralded passage by the House of Representatives, the more conservative Senate Finance Committee rejected the Nixon administration's proposals for HMO market-based "voucherized" Medicare. Although many years later Medicare risk contracting by HMOs was approved by Congress and the White House, no Health Care Financing Administration (HCFA) administrator has chosen to aggressively sell off to the private sector the opportunity HCFA has to run a huge public conventional health insurance organization. Furthermore, most of the new "health plans" were not quite ready for the high-risk, inevitably sick Medicare population. State-managed Medicaid also lagged despite a contrarian but successful switch to capitation in Arizona in 1982. Far from being the catalyst for public sector and private sector reforms, the government's program preferred the status quo except for complex encounter-based payment tinkering like diagnosis related groups for hospitals and relative value scales for physicians. Unfortunately, these approaches to price controls failed to contain Medicare costs.

The large private-employee-benefits purchasers of health insurance lagged by a decade in taking advantage of the concepts held within the ill-fated employee-oriented 1973 HMO Act. Then, in the mid-1980s, faced with the prospect of intensifying global competition for sale of products and uncontrollable health care costs, employer purchasers began seriously encouraging their employees to join health plans. But the employers, too, defied the health maintenance strategists by offering a very limited number of health plan choices (usually 1 or 2 health plans and an indemnity plan) in each community. The resulting health plans, consisting of rapidly assembled broad provider networks with rich benefit packages and low prices, appealed to employers and employees. Quality was dealt with the old-fashioned way, by word of mouth, and by satisfaction with patient-physician relationships. This approach to purchasing by large corporations more than anything else shaped the new health care marketplace. Large, overlapping provider networks required less financial commitment by health plans and less professional commitment by physicians. Most provider-controlled group practice and hospital-based entities couldn't cover the urgent territorial demands of the typical employer. Their unstandardized, unadjusted, and unaudited claims of qualitative superiority didn't sell to consumers.

The potential unprecedented growth in earnings in the burgeoning, formerly nonprofit, health industry attracted entrepreneurs and venture capital to the hot new health plans. Naturally, for-profit health plans, responding to Wall Street's short-term earnings growth mentality, avoided major capital investments except for acquisitions, and sought to circumvent the uncertainty that objectively competing overtly on quality might bring.

Individual consumers, especially those who had long-standing relationships with physicians, were cautious and slow to switch from the company's traditional indemnity plans. Ultimately they succumbed to the lower out-of-pocket costs, lack of hassle, and aggressive marketing of the new health plans. After all, the physician and hospital panels of the loosely integrated health plans were almost like the familiar Blues. Then, with the advent of point-of-service health plans, the door was open for consumers to go out of their own plan to any provider if it was worth the extra out-of-pocket payments. But they continued to rely on the informal advice of others about the quality of the health plan, supplemented often with information supplied by the health plan about the availability of primary physicians.

In the past 3 years, the Clinton plan of "managed competition" and the Republican "Health Contract for America" foundered on more than politics. Congressional Budget Office (CBO) uncertainty over whether savings would accrue from price competition induced delays and revisions. The arithmetic of the CBO—rather than just political ineptitude and organized backlash—killed major government health reforms.

Following all of this recent political posturing over a market-based approach to medical care was federal government inaction and a demand-side private sector revolution. But the character of the resulting 1996 managed care system (not health maintenance) has been a surprise.

Extraordinarily effective price competition has developed between various health plans. Prices were very elastic and the old system was even more poorly managed and inefficient than anticipated. There remains a moribund indemnity fee-for-service system (mainly Medicare) that may stay alive for a year or 2 on political life support. Consumers, especially healthy families, have been remarkably price sensitive, exhibiting surprisingly little loyalty to physicians or health plans....

THE CURRENT ENVIRONMENT

Thomas Pyle has called health care's revolutionary changes "the unbungling" of health care; others regard it as the rebungling (personal communication, August 10, 1996, Jackson Hole, Wyo). The largest and fastest-growing health plans are national or regional for-profit entities over which providers exert little control. The health plan's power is exercised through legal contracts with purchasers, consumers, and providers. Genuine collaboration between most health plans' management and providers is tenuous, but the understanding of what the health insurance money is buying and its compatibility with sound medical practice have vastly improved. Physicians typically work for several health plans, making it virtually impossible to differentiate between them on the basis of population-based outcome data. The more highly integrated group practice plans (most of them nonprofits and provider controlled) have grown more slowly and locally but think they've found a way to reassert themselves.

Why does the new house of medicine look so different from what the HMO architects designed? The customers weren't ready for a spartan, efficient, high-tech, computerized, Saarinen-like house of scientific medicine. Instead, their tastes were traditional and tended to favor a new home that looked and felt like their old home—cluttered, warm, and secure, close to school, to work, to shopping, and to freeways. The demand side of health care preferred a much more traditional health system than the planners expected —one that was paid for in a new way but felt like the old system.

During the years since Medicare was enacted, American medicine has become, by some calculations, the world's largest business. The pace of restructuring in the American health system has been continuous, responding to innovations in health delivery, advances in medical technology, rising public expectations, and the demands of other sectors of the economy. Now the new health system is faced with a congruence of discontinuities that could produce clinical advances along with economic ones more like the health maintenance strategists envisioned.

There will be no letup in cost-containment pressures. If anything resembling the Republican Medicare plan passes, it will be difficult to rely on the old underfunded Medicare as an income source. Medicare enrollees are already joining risk-based health plans at a record pace, and more plans are becoming risk contractors. Medicare consists of individual purchasers who do not require the broad dispersed networks originally sought by employers. Many have chronic illnesses and are particularly concerned about quality. The rush by states to Medicaid managed care plans opens up yet another individual-choice market that is not attached to any existing insurer except the state.

The public media have chosen to feature some health plans' highly paid executives, gag rules, and physicians' being paid to "undertreat." Anecdotes about skimping on care are hyped enough to make the cover of *Time*. *Barron's, Newsweek,* and *Consumer Reports* all have attempted to rate differences in plan quality based on inadequate information; yet despite anecdotes (some lurid) we have no objective evidence of any overall decline in the quality of care in the new system. Consumers are confused. State legislators—alerted by the headlines encouraged by offbeat and conventional providers—see votes in designing laws to inhibit health plans. More than 100 health care bills have been introduced in the California legislature alone.

Employers continue to demand low price increases in the 1% and 3% range but now want proof of quality. Employers are joining purchasing coalitions on a regional basis (like the Pacific Business Group on Health) and national scale (Washington Business Group on Health) to coordinate contracting and to assess quality. Some (like GTE) are paying higher portions of the premiums for those employees who join what the company believes to be the highest-quality health plans....

The easy ways to cut costs—like shorter hospital stays—are reaching their limits. Now it is time to evaluate the con-

tent of care, but few health plans have information systems or organizational structures to fundamentally challenge traditional approaches to medical care. The IPAs, group practices, and physician management corporations detect an opening. Many believe they can manage quality better than the large, more entrepreneurial health plans. Does quality competition, more choices, and the loyal chronically ill Medicare constituency provide an opportunity for physicians to bypass the managing health plan and contract directly with the purchasers? But even the best of the provider-controlled group practice plans have a long way to go in successfully practicing population-based medicine. At present, their largely uncomputerized clinical record systems and weak epidemiologic perspective leaves them unprepared for population-based medical care. However, advances in medical computing projects, like the Medical Group Management Association's conduct of outcomes management trials, and the accumulation of large open databases, like that of the American College of Surgeons on cancer, give a glimpse of the opportunity.

WHAT'S NEXT

Health plans have become enormous and important actors in the new American health system. They have the capital and character to influence how care is delivered and how resources are used. If pointed in the right direction, even the most entrepreneurial Wall Street–oriented health plan has the opportunity to compete on quality. Such plans can establish extensive premier medical networks (PriMe) within their larger organization, assemble their own selective provider networks, integrate financial management (and rewards) more closely with clinical practice, and build a culture of excellence. Furthermore, they have the capital to buy advanced information technology to support the delivery of more scientifically based and more efficient medical care.

But we have no assurances that the competition of such plans in the current market will reward those who deliver higher-quality care. First, we lack strong national standards that hold these plans accountable for the results they achieve —either in terms of clinical quality, improving the health of their enrolled population, or even satisfying the expectations of their enrollees. Second, we have no evidence that the economic success of these plans is being affected by their clinical performance—purchasers and consumers have not, so far, rewarded or punished plans based on quality. Third, a sound market is always a work in progress. The large for-profit plans that appear to be dominant today may not be as important tomorrow. If purchasers and consumers had tools that allowed them to buy on quality, and if they could actually begin to use that power to shape the market, the thinking that lay behind the original HMO movement may still play out: provider-managed organizations might demonstrate that they are better able to meet patient expectations and get good results and operate more efficiently than their less integrated and disciplined competitors....

Two alternatives exist: strong public policy or effective public interest collaboration. Congress may ultimately be the proper body to articulate standards for health care quality, but it is unlikely to take this on soon or in the short-term. The recently established not-for-profit Foundation for Accountability (FACCT)

is an attempt to meet this need through a voluntary collaboration. Led by purchaser and patient groups, FACCT has just published its first recommended set of patient-oriented outcomes measures. These measures are the product of measurement science that focuses on patients' perceptions of their own function and well-being. Their initial measures cover diabetes, cancer of the breast, major depression, health risk behaviors, and patient satisfaction with care. The foundation will not be in the auditing business but is urging various accrediting and auditing organizations to apply their measures.

At this stage of our health system reconstruction, there is good reason to be hopeful. Compared with 25 years ago, we have achieved a great deal: creation of new organizations that can allocate money and talent in a rational way, reliable and pervasive tools for measuring health outcomes, growing consensus on the importance of preventive services, uniform screening and other "best practices" incorporated into guidelines, initial systems for reporting to the public on the quality of care they are receiving and the impact of the health system on the public's overall health, and information systems that support, monitor, and provide feedback on the effects of health services.

The signs are good for American health care. Consumers are being offered more choices that are more easily understood. Medicare is evolving from a traditional and unorganized array of providers to a more appropriate set of offerings that allow individuals to choose arrangements that best meet their own needs. And we are recognizing that the easiest, crude approaches to cost containment have reached their limits. Purchasers and consumers know that it is possible to compare plans and providers based on quality and are becoming more sophisticated in demanding this information.

Ultimately, this trend may lead to a sound, efficient, and truly effective health system. If we document the benefits achieved by our health care systems, we can respond properly to public concerns about expenditures, entitlements, and reform. At the same time, we will be ensuring that consumers are themselves responsible for their choices and that they are capable of making those choices in an informed manner to the greatest extent possible.

The health care system is coming out of the closet. Professional black boxes and undocumented claims of superior individual credentials and results are no longer enough! Organizational transparency and readily available objective evidence of health improvement is in!

Getting there will require the application of the following principles.

PRINCIPLES OF ACCOUNTABILITY TO THE PUBLIC FOR HEALTH QUALITY

The quality measures must be powerful enough to provide direction to the new American health system. Plans and providers will seek to achieve the results on which they are measured and for which they are accountable. If the measures are sound and the public understands and values them, they will become the central tool of health care reform and redesign.

The measures must anticipate the behavioral changes they induce. If one plan or system proves to be exceptional at treating AIDS or diabetes, it will attract the sickest people in the community—and that's good! We should want the most competent and committed organizations to care

for those most in need. But we should pay them for the additional responsibility and costs they incur. Quality measures and payment systems must be risk adjusted in order to shape the kind of health system we want. Despite its importance, there is no well-funded coordinated effort to devise risk adjustors and to reward health plans that serve the sickest patients well.

Patient opinions should come first. Our patients pay us, receive our services, and have faith in our skill. In the market environment, they increasingly judge us. In the last 20 years, the science of measuring health outcomes and patient satisfaction has made enormous progress.[6,8] Although not without limits, many self-report measures are more reliable and rigorous than traditional clinical measures. The new measures of quality should emphasize consumers' perceptions of their own health function and well-being. At the same time, they should provide the level of feedback to providers that allows them to continuously improve medical practice.

It's time for outcomes accountability. Managed care organizations are structured to facilitate accountability. We finally have the measures and the structures in place to assess whether different practices or systems perform better. And we have an audience in purchasers and patients that is craving that information. As organizations become responsible for outcomes, we will see a growing link between the maturing disciplines of health services research and the clinical practices embraced by health systems.[9] Already many large health plans have created sophisticated research centers to help infuse their practices with evidence-based strategies, and they are building large observational series to continuously refine the care they provide.

The influence of health plans on the measures chosen should be minimized. Health plans are one important device for organizing and financing medical services, but there are others—some not invented yet. The standards for assessing performance must be based on the patient's experience of health and illness, independent of the particular structure or philosophy of the care providers. With billions of competitive dollars at stake, no plan can be objective about how it should be judged. The measures used to assess quality should not be constrained by the self-interest of the provider or financing organizations. We should not ignore the practical experience of health plans that have learned a great deal about measuring and managing quality, and we should remain sensitive to unnecessary burden or cost. But our health system is accountable to the public, and the public must decide what level of reporting or burden is appropriate.

The first phase of the health maintenance strategy was a bold and successful experiment that focused on and produced lower-cost health care. Now we are ready for the next phase that will measure and produce better-quality health care. And, surely, from the enormous savings that have been made through this revolution, we also will be able to find an incremental way to provide access to basic health care for all of our people.[10]

NOTES

1. Lundberg GD, Bodine L. Fifty hours for the poor. *JAMA*. 1987;258:3157.

2. Ellwood PM, Enthoven AC. 'Responsible choices': the Jackson Hole Group plan for health reform. *Health Aff (Millwood)*. 1995;14(2):24–39.

3. Smillie JG. *Can Physicians Manage the Quality and Costs of Health Care? The Story of the Permanente Medical Group.* New York, NY: McGraw-Hill Book Co; 1991.

4. Williams AP. Memorandum to the president-elect: parameters for health system reform. *JAMA*. 1992;268:2699–2700.

5. Lundberg GD. United States health care system reform: an era of shared sacrifice and responsibility begins. *JAMA*. 1994;271:1530–1533.

6. Ellwood PM. The Shattuck Lecture: outcomes management: a technology of patient experience. *N Engl J Med*. 1988;318:1549–1556.

7. Ellwood PM Jr, Anderson NN, Billings JE, Carlson RJ, Hoagberg EJ, McClure W. Health maintenance strategy. *Med Care*. 1971;9:291–298.

8. Ware JE Jr, Bayliss MS, Rogers WH, Kosinski M, Tarlov AR. Differences in 4-year health outcomes for elderly and poor, chronically ill patients treated in HMO and fee-for-service systems: results from the Medical Outcomes Study. *JAMA*. 1996;276:1039–1047.

9. Yelin, EH, Criswell LA, Feigenbaum PG. Health care utilization and outcomes among persons with rheumatoid arthritis in fee-for-service and prepaid group practice settings. *JAMA*. 1996;276:1048–1053.

10. Davis K. Incremental coverage of the uninsured. *JAMA*. 1996;276:831–832.

NO

John H. McArthur and Francis D. Moore

THE TWO CULTURES AND THE HEALTH CARE REVOLUTION

There are two contrasting streams, two distinct cultural traditions, for providing services in the United States: the commercial and the professional. While these two traditions stand in sharp contrast to each other, they have shared a central role in the evolution of our society and its institutions. It is our purpose here to explore threats to the quality and scope of medical care that arise when the tradition of medical professionalism is overtaken by the commercial ethic and by corporations seeking profit for investors from the clinical care of the sick. We also explore the extent to which commercial behavior has invaded the nonprofit sector through the merger of the insurance function with the clinical provider in prepaid health plans. Widespread pressures to reduce the out-of-control costs of health care in this country, as well as the cost to individual patients, families, and employers, have accentuated some of these threats to clinical quality.

Effective communication between the commercial and the professional communities has been wanting with respect to their traditions, technology, and motivation in the medical arena. To the interested public, it appears that people are not listening to each other. It is our hope here to open communication between these two contrasting cultures, an idea expressed by C. P. Snow in his Rede Lecture at Cambridge, in which he contrasted the traditions of science and humanism.[1] . . .

THE TWO CULTURES: PROFESSIONAL AND COMMERCIAL

The fundamental act of professional medical care is the assumption of responsibility for the patient's welfare—an unwritten contract assured by a few words, a handshake, eye contact denoting mutual understanding, or acknowledgment by the physician that "We will take care of you." The essential image of the professional is that of a practitioner who values the patient's welfare above his or her own and provides service even at a fiscal loss and

Excerpted from John H. McArthur and Francis D. Moore, "The Two Cultures and the Health Care Revolution: Commerce and Professionalism in Medical Care," *Journal of the American Medical Association*, vol. 277, no. 12 (March 26, 1997), pp. 985–989. Copyright © 1997 by The American Medical Association. Reprinted by permission.

despite physical discomfort or inconvenience. There is no outside invested capital seeking returns from the physician's work.

The fundamental objective of commerce in providing medical care is achieving an excess of revenue over costs while caring for the sick, ensuring profit for corporate providers, investors, or insurers. A central feature in enhancing net of income over expense in a competitive market is a reduction in volume or quality of services so as to reduce costs, while maintaining prices to the purchaser. While cost reductions often diminish the quality of services, such economies are not always passed along to the public as lowered prices. Many families who seek insurance coverage but are excluded by unaffordable prices are forced to seek public providers outside prepaid plans and the commercial insurance system.

In this setting, the operation of market forces is hampered because patients and families can rarely acquire the information necessary to discriminate as to suitability and quality among alternative clinical services or providers. Without consumer input, market forces often fail completely, or behave perversely, acting strongly on price without regard to quality or breadth.

In purchasing commercial services, the public has learned to beware both of low quality and excessive pricing, as expressed in the Latin phrase *caveat emptor*—"let the buyer beware." The American public is gradually becoming aware that *caveat emptor* may soon become *caveat morbidus*—"let the patient beware."

THE TWO CULTURES IN CONFLICT

When a corporation employing physicians seeks profit by selling their services, the physician-employees cease to act as free agents. Professional commitment to patient care is subordinated to new rules of practice that assure the profitability of the corporation.

Surprisingly, much the same enigma is becoming evident in the voluntary nonprofit private sector, particularly in prepaid health plans and teaching hospitals. Physicians working in such plans, as well as those in fee-for-service plans—both of them in the private, nonprofit sector—are finding themselves increasingly burdened by clinical constraints intended to ensure survival of the hospital, the plan, or the insurance carrier in a fiercely competitive market. While there is no legally defined profit for tax purposes in a nonprofit institution, the same results are threatened by the accumulation of large operating reserves, excessive construction programs, large executive cohorts at high salaries with business support structures, acquisition of other hospitals, or uncontrolled growth of research and teaching programs funded from patient-derived income. A teaching-research hospital that seeks excessive profit from patient care to support its nonprofit activities (teaching, research, community outreach, and education of nurses and paramedical personnel) behaves like a for-profit facility. Both in the commercial and the nonprofit sectors, an appropriate balance must be sought between patient-derived income, reinvestment, scientific and educational obligations.

Prepaid health plans inevitably involve a conflict between the commercial and professional cultures. As Gradison[2] has pointed out, prepaid health plans "merge the insurance function with the delivery function." This mixture is dangerous because when markets are saturated and/or premiums fixed, with costs still rising, financial ruin can be avoided only by reducing quality and breadth of services, endangering the health of individuals, families, or whole communities.

Sensing this inherent conflict, Enthoven and Kronick[3,4] introduced the term "managed competition," which signified protection for the public from exploitation under the pressure of commercial competition, giving further currency to the term "managed care."[3,4]

At the same time, while acting within the framework of professional commitment, some physicians and administrators have taken earnings out of the system that were beyond reasonable and customary rewards for such services.

COMMERCIAL MEDICINE: POTENTIAL HAZARDS

1. Diversion of Funds

Funds for the care of the sick—whether from private sources, employers, or taxation—are intended to support disease prevention, public health, and the care of disease: public health and the health of the public. When a portion of this highly targeted national fund is diverted for corporate objectives (such as dividends, advertising, executive salaries), the resources available for health care are thereby reduced.

The same diversion from health care objectives results from excessive earnings by physicians or administrators in the nonprofit sector and the fee-for-service establishment.

2. Pricing

In the familiar commercial market for everyday goods and services, a less affluent population is assumed to exist that is unable to afford certain products or services and must "get along without." In medical care there is no such population: need is universal. The charity threshold is defined as the income level below which family costs for medical care must be borne by church, charity, or government. Unless regulated, this threshold will inevitably rise as health plans and other insured providers increase prices and/or decrease services to ensure profitability.

3. Risk Avoidance

Exclusion of individuals and families from coverage because of prior disease, genetic constitution, predisposition, or high cost is already noticeable in our health insurance system. Such risk avoidance denies care to those most in need and is not a characteristic of national health insurance plans in other industrialized countries.

4. Increased Load on Public Providers

Exclusion of individuals or families because of high risk or unaffordable prices will shift the burden of their care to other providers, including tax-supported public clinics and hospitals (federal, state, county, or municipal) and charity or church hospitals. Any economic overview of recent trends in the total cost of health care in the nation must quantify the increased burden borne by these public institutions.

5. Downgrading of Personnel

Expertise is expensive. Among physicians, nurses, and paramedical personnel, those who are most highly qualified require the highest compensation. These highly qualified but expensive personnel will be threatened by discharge in favor of others with less experience and fewer credentials but lower income expectations.

6. Loss of Free Speech
Another cause for dismissal is adverse comment or criticism about the quality of care being given. This amounts to a gag rule and is an example of the loss of free speech, not by order of public law but by the dictates of health care corporations that have confused commercial success (and a favorable public image) with professional obligation.

7. Distortions of Clinical Care and Ethical Dilemmas
It is in these areas that most complaints have surfaced, as frequently reported in the media. Problems include delayed admission, premature discharge, sloppy or unskilled services delivered in a shoddy and ill-kempt or unfriendly environment, avoidance of surgery or radiologic scanning, and the overuse of multiple profitable blood tests rather than definitive expert consultation or operation. Limitations in ambulatory care include denying prescriptions written by the physician in favor of similar drugs marketed by favored vendors and strict constraints on the amount of time a physician can spend with each patient. Time limitations on patient-physician contacts are particularly destructive to patient confidence and comfort. Rehabilitation and long-term care including psychiatry and terminal cancer care, care of the frail elderly, and care for those with advanced heart disease or stroke are nonremunerative. In a commercial environment seeking to maximize revenue from each clinical encounter, both volume and quality of such clinical services are inevitably threatened. These economies attract the attention of the media when they occur in a health plan providing extravagant expenditures for executive salaries, public relations, and advertising.

Such compromises and distortions of clinical care place physicians in a severe ethical dilemma: shall they follow the dictates of conscience and known good practice in giving every consideration to the aid and comfort of the patient, or shall they save money for their employers? Such dilemmas are among the most severe ethical challenges in the practice of physicians and surgeons today.

8. Managed Care—Cui Bono?
The term "managed care" came into common currency in the late 1980s to denote clinical practices in prepaid plans. It implied that an element of beneficial professional management, based on concern for patient welfare, would be essential to ensure both equity and quality in the highly competitive environment of corporate medicine. While it was never clearly specified by whom complex management choices would be made, or in whose interest clinical care would be managed, there was a tacit assumption that the provider would supply management in the best interest primarily of the patient, as well as the insurer or parent corporation. Now, only 7 years later, to many the term "managed care" implies the need for concern about the welfare of the patient because they suspect that care is being managed to minimize expense and perhaps even maximize income for the employer, provider, and/or insurer, while masquerading as a benefit for the patient. The term is increasingly interpreted as meaning "managed costs" rather than "managed care."

9. Commercial Insurance in the Nonprofit Sector

As mentioned above, many of the pressures of commercial medicine are already becoming evident even in the nonprofit sector, especially in prepaid health plans, because of their structural combination of the insurance function and the delivery obligation. In addition, indemnity insurance carriers apply continuous pressure on hospitals and physicians to lower costs of diagnosis and treatment, limit hospital stay, and curtail therapy.

10. Physicians as Entrepreneurs in Care and Research

The entry of physicians and biomedical scientists into the world of for-profit commerce is becoming an increasingly prominent feature of this landscape. Many physicians have become owners and managers of commercial hospital chains and treatment centers. Biomedical scientists long accustomed to receiving charitably deductible support from commerce are now becoming the owners, stockholders, and operators of corporations seeking profit from the marketing of their own scientific discoveries.

Sale of securities as well as the sale of products has sometimes led to large earnings for physicians. In some cases, the very scientists whose research was originally supported by public funds are owners of corporations that are often risky and financially unstable but sometimes very profitable. Every taxpayer has made an investment in these biotechnical corporations. It seems inevitable that some sort or repayment to a special government research fund will be mandated for some fraction of the profit accruing to scientific corporations when their product development has been based on research supported by public funds.

11. Neglect of Community Responsibility and Teaching and Research

Many community hospitals were established to include care for the poor, usually at a fiscal loss, accommodated by income from endowment or by shifting funds from other revenue sources within the hospital. As financial insecurity threatens their continuing support, community hospitals are faced with takeover by commercial for-profit corporations. The purchase of such hospitals by for-profit chains (often based in another city or state) generates transition funds that can be used to cover immediate welfare needs. Continuing support is often lacking.

Teaching hospitals have assumed responsibility for a share of the university functions of teaching and research as well as responsibility to the broader community they serve. This support is threatened by commercial takeover.

12. Monopoly: Loss of Free Choice

Free enterprise commerce fosters compensation and encourages consumer choice among alternatives, but these choices cannot operate in rural areas, smaller communities, or inner-city ghettos where the population and financial resources are insufficient to attract more than a single prepaid health plan or HMO. Freedom of choice, long considered an ideal by-product of free competition, is compromised.

STANDARDS

Whether by voluntary self-regulation or by the passage of regional or national legislation, minimum standards will inevitably be required to abate some of the hazards to society and abuses of patient care arising from commercial pressures on professional behavior. These standards address the potential hazards we mentioned in the foregoing.

Acceptable profit levels will require definition, as well as allowable diversion of money to dividends, executive bonuses, promotional expenses, advertising, etc. By the same token, earnings of administrators, business consultants, and physicians in the nonprofit or private sectors will need to be subject to guidelines in the interest of equity and economy. Pricing will necessarily be viewed in light of prevalent income and affordability. Assumption of risk will inevitably be required of all carriers and providers to share the risk for particularly high-cost cohorts such as congenital anomalies, familial disorders, human immunodeficiency virus infection, and chronic vascular disease.

Criteria for effectiveness, quality, and patient satisfaction will need definition. Patient satisfaction, while clearly important, must be viewed with suspicion because approximately 80% of a covered population will, in any one year, be free of any disorder requiring medical care. Their "satisfaction" is easily assured. Only by evaluation of the opinion of those patients and families afflicted with serious illness can patient satisfaction be a meaningful criteria. Morbidity and mortality should never become the principal criteria of effectiveness since they are both subject to manipulation by avoidance of risk.

Staff organization is best served by the unit system common in most teaching hospitals whereby distinct medical and surgical disciplines are under the clinical direction of highly qualified expert physicians rather than administrative executives.

Decoupling the individual physician from the insurance function frees physicians to manage their own clinical care procedures while maintaining the identity of the prepaid plan for business purposes. In decoupling, the physicians, as a group, contract or make other group arrangements with their front office (ie, the insurance function) to deliver patient care or community preventive medicine at a group price to the insurer, thus reestablishing the primacy of professional judgment and supervision of clinical care for individual patients.

Regular input of complaints and suggestions from both patients and physicians must be facilitated. Community responsibility should be accepted by all carriers and prepaid plans to avoid skimming—the enrollment of the low-risk, prosperous segment of a community—leaving newborns, the elderly, and those with prior illness to be cared for at public expense. For teaching hospitals this responsibility to their broader community includes a continuing commitment to share in the support of postgraduate teaching and research. . . .

POTENTIAL BENEFITS OF CORPORATE-COMMERCIAL MEDICINE

Cost control (ie, a decline in the national budget for health care) has been anticipated in the cost-cutting competitive atmosphere of a commercial marketplace. This may become increasingly difficult either to secure or to demonstrate because all patient costs must be embraced in such an accounting, including the increased burden on church, charity, tax-supported institutions, or the patient's own pocketbook. Physician earnings have already shown a decline; total remuneration of executives and administrators appears to have risen over the last decade.

If, as a result of the entry of commerce into American medical care, national standards become a reality—with appropriate agencies for surveillance, reporting, and local assessment of the adequacy of health practices—this will be a major benefit from the commercialization of American medical care.

While access to capital investment will be a benefit from the entry of commerce into medical care, some caution and some years of experience will be necessary before realizing this benefit. Capital investment in medical care that assumes responsibility only for the welfare of stockholders, investors, or executives will arouse public opposition and invite political attack. If private capital disregards community needs, communities will be less well off and the attractiveness of such ventures for investment will decline.

REFERENCES

Snow CP. *The Two Cultures and the Scientific Revolution: The Rede Lectures.* New York, NY: Cambridge University Press; 1959.

Gradison W. Issues in employment and insurance. *Bull N Y Acad Med.* 1995;72:586–594.

Enthoven A, Kronick R. A consumer-choice health plan for the 1990's: universal health insurance in a system designed to promote quality and economy (in two parts). *N Engl J Med.* 1989;320:29–37.

Enthoven A, Kronick R. A consumer-choice health plan for the 1990's: universal health insurance in a system designed to promote quality and economy (in two parts). *N Engl J Med.* 1989;320:94–101.

POSTSCRIPT

Is Managed Competition the Cure for Our Ailing Health Care System?

Ellwood and Alain Enthoven are often considered the two most vocal advocates of managed care. Enthoven served as the principal architect of President Clinton's failed health care reform. Three books by Enthoven that discuss his viewpoint are *Health Plan: The Only Practical Solution to the Soaring Cost of Medical Care* (Addison-Wesley, 1980); *New Directions in Public Health Care: A Prescription for the 1980s* (Institute for Contemporary Studies, 1980); and *Theory and Practice of Managed Competition in Health Care Finance* (Elsevier Science, 1988). Ellwood and Enthoven are coauthors of an essay entitled " 'Responsible Choice': The Jackson Hole Group Plan for Health Reform," *Health Affairs* (Summer 1995).

Finally, there are several books by Henry J. Aaron, director of the Brookings Economic Studies Program, that provide a more middle-of-the-road analysis. In general, he believes that there are still major changes in the future of the health care industry that probably include a regulatory role for government. See *The Problem That Won't Go Away: Reforming U.S. Health Care Financing* (Brookings Institution, 1996) and *Rationing Health Care: The Choice Before Us* (Brookings Institution, 1990).

ISSUE 7

Do Private Prisons Pay?

YES: Adrian T. Moore, from "Private Prisons: Quality Corrections at a Lower Cost," *Reason Public Policy Institute Policy Study No. 240* (April 1998)

NO: Eric Bates, from "Private Prisons," *The Nation* (January 5, 1998)

ISSUE SUMMARY

YES: Social critic and policy analyst Adrian T. Moore maintains that there is extensive evidence to suggest that private sector prisons provide quality correctional services at a lower cost to taxpayers.

NO: Columnist Eric Bates contends that "privatizing prisons is really about privatizing tax dollars [and] about transforming public money into private profits."

Many people feel unsafe walking the streets of urban America or even pitching a tent in a wilderness area. Many believe that the United States is plagued by a terrifying crime rate. We are reminded of this daily by the crime reports we read in local newspapers or see in obscene detail on local and national television news programs. In 1997 the National Crime Victimization Survey reported that 34.8 million crimes were committed against U.S. residents; 74 percent (25.8 million) were property crimes, 25 percent (8.6 million) were crimes of violence, and the remaining 1 percent were personal thefts.

The most stark representation of the crime data generated by the 1997 *FBI Uniform Crime Reports* is the "Crime Clock." In terms of this clock, a criminal offense is committed every 2 seconds in the United States! There is one violent crime every 19 seconds: one murder every 27 minutes, one forcible rape every 6 minutes, one robbery every 54 seconds, and one aggravated assault every 29 seconds. Additionally, there is one property crime every 3 seconds: one burglary every 12 seconds, one larceny-theft every 4 seconds, and one motor vehicle stolen every 23 seconds.

If we took these statistics at face value, we would probably believe that the American criminal justice system is under siege, with no hope in sight. In fact there does appear to be is hope in sight, even though the electronic and print media may be slow to report it. All measures of criminal activity are down, whether we look at violent crimes or crimes against property. This is not something new. Both violent crime and property crime fell by 7 percent from 1994 to 1997, and the mid-year 1998 report suggests that the rate of decline will continue. Perhaps the best measure of criminal activity is the

FBI's "crime index," which, as reported in the *FBI Uniform Crime Reports*, "fell for the 6th straight year in 1997."

The crime index, however, is only half the story. While criminal activity has fallen in the 1990s, America's incarceration rate has continued to increase. This is a trend that began to appear in the mid-1970s. Prior to this, the nation's incarceration rate was relatively stable at about 110 prison inmates per 100,000 U.S. residents. But over time the rate climbed fourfold to its current level of 445 inmates for every 100,000 in the population. Among the adult male population the rate is much higher: 1,100 per 100,000. Thus, while the rate of violent crime in the United States has fallen by 20 percent, the number of prison inmates has risen by 50 percent.

By the end of 1996 the United States had 5.5 million people on probation or in jails and prisons. This represents 2.8 percent of all U.S. residents! Some individual states, such as California, house more prison inmates than many major countries; indeed, California's prison system alone is 40 percent larger than the whole Federal Bureau of Prisons and larger than the combined prison systems of France, Britain, Germany, Japan, Singapore, and the Netherlands.

Thus, in spite of a construction boom in the "corrections industry," prisons are more overcrowded today than they were before the crime rate began to fall. States, sometimes under federal judicial mandates requiring them to reduce overcrowding, have increasingly turned to the private sector for assistance. This has made "privatized corrections" a growth industry. Several dozen corporations have sprung into existence, in an attempt to profit from the shortage of prison beds. Two corporations, Wackenhut Corrections Corporation and Corrections Corporation of America, dominate this new industry. These two companies operate 29 minimum- and medium-security facilities, which imprison 10,000 felons. Others in the industry, like the Pricor Corporation, "rent out" underused county jail capacity—mostly in rural Texas—to any correction facility across the country, as long as it is willing to pay the going rate. Should this privatization trend in the corrections industry be encouraged? Are the economic efficiencies that Adrian T. Moore details in the following selection worth the social and private costs of which Eric Bates warns in the second selection?

YES

Adrian T. Moore

PRIVATE PRISONS: QUALITY CORRECTIONS AT A LOWER COST

BACKGROUND: NOT ENOUGH SPACE OR MONEY

Why are U.S. federal agencies and state and local governments turning to the private sector for correctional services? Because tougher crime policies and budget constraints have combined to create a problem, if not a crisis, in the nation's prisons and jails. Governments are incarcerating more criminals, but they have recently become unwilling to spend sufficient tax dollars for new prisons to house them. The prison system is increasingly characterized by overcrowding, lawsuits, and court orders. Therein lies the problem for federal, state, and local officials—expenditures on corrections have grown rapidly, but the prison population has grown faster.

Corrections is one of the fastest-growing state budget items. In the last 15 years, state spending on corrections grew more than 350 percent—compared to 250 percent growth for spending on public welfare and 140 percent growth for spending on education. More than one-third of the states devote 5 percent or more of their spending to corrections. (See Table 1.)

The Numbers Tell the Story
State spending on corrections has gone up because the number of inmates in the system has skyrocketed. Since 1984 the number of inmates has risen 100 percent in local jails, 213 percent in state prisons, and 290 percent in federal facilities. Incarceration rates are well over double what they were in 1980.

Some states have embarked upon unprecedented prison building programs. Texas and California have led the pack, spending billions of dollars in the last decade building new facilities. According to the Bureau of Justice Statistics, the capacity of state and federal prisons grew 41 percent in the first half of this decade. Local jurisdictions have felt similar pressure: over 800 jurisdictions have identified the need for new construction in the next few years.

But all the building to date has not met the need. Today many state and federal prisons are holding over 20 percent more prisoners than their capacity,

From Adrian T. Moore, "Private Prisons: Quality Corrections at a Lower Cost," *Reason Public Policy Institute Policy Study No. 240* (April 1998). Copyright © 1999 by The Reason Foundation, 3415 S. Sepulveda Blvd., Suite 400, Los Angeles, CA 90034. <www.rppi.org>. Reprinted by permission. Notes omitted.

and a great number of facilities—even entire state and county systems—are under court order to limit or reduce their inmate populations. Nineteen state prison systems are 25 percent or more over capacity, and at least 10 more state systems, and federal prison systems, could be considered very overcrowded. (See Table 2.) In most of these states, the situation is not getting better. Crowding in California's prison system worsened between 1994 and 1996, going from 84 percent over capacity to 96 percent over capacity.

With taxpayers clearly demanding that criminals be put in prison and kept in longer, there seems to be no choice but to increase the capacity of the prison system. But with popular pressure to cut government spending, funding the increase will be difficult. Legislators face a lot of pressure to hold the line on corrections spending, fewer than half of referendums to approve bond financing of new prisons are being approved by voters.

Alternatives

There are alternatives to incarceration. Many states are starting to look at alternative sentencing, including community-based institutions, home confinement, and other programs. But there is a limit to how many criminals such methods can cope with. California's nonpartisan legislative analyst calculates that alternative punishments will be appropriate or possible for only a small share of future convicted criminals. The need for additional prisons and jails will not disappear, and policy makers must look in new directions for corrections policy.

This has led federal, state, and local officials to consider how the private sector can become involved in corrections. The private sector's lower costs and quality services can help cope with the growing number of prisoners without busting the budget. But what do private prisons have to offer? And what evidence is there on how they have performed?

CORRECTIONAL SERVICES OFFERED BY THE PRIVATE SECTOR

There are three basic types of correctional services offered by the private sector:

1. Design and construction of jails and prisons.
2. Services for offenders, such as food service or medical care, and juvenile and community correction centers.
3. Contract management of major detention facilities.

Local, state, and federal governments have contracted with the private sector for each of these types of services. The first two services have been used widely, with little controversy, for decades. The last has grown rapidly, amidst controversy, since the early 1980s.

Design and Construction

Private contractors have long designed and built jails and prisons. In a relatively new development, some governments have accelerated completion of projects by delegating more authority to, and reducing regulatory requirements on, private design-build teams. Even more recent is the appearance of prisons wholly financed and built by the private sector, which offer their bed space on a per-diem contract basis to jurisdictions experiencing an overflow of prisoners.

The per-bed cost of prison space is influenced by many factors, including the security level, location, and jurisdiction

Table 1

States With High Corrections Expenditures as a Percentage of Total Budget (1994)

State	% of Budget to Corrections	Total Annual Corrections Expenditures (in millions)
TX	10	$2,046
CA*	9	$4,042
VA	9	$651
OK	8	$274
RI	8	$130
SC	8	$299
MD	7	$509
NY	7	$2,430
OR	7	$220
TN	7	$372
WY	7	$33
KS	6	$200
NJ	6	$941
CT	5	$392
FL	5	$1,457
ID	5	$60
NM	5	$136
SD	5	$34

*1996 figures

Sources: American Correctional Association; California Department of Corrections.

of the facility. Coming up with useful average costs for government construction is difficult. However, the Criminal Justice Institute has calculated that the average cost of government construction is $80,562 for a maximum-security cell, $50,376 for a medium-security cell, and $31,189 for a minimum-security cell.

Cost Savings

Private companies can build prisons and jails for considerably less than these figures and in less time. Firms in the industry often contend that they can cut between 10 percent and 40 percent off construction costs, with 30 percent being the most common savings estimate. Independent estimates of the cost savings show a similar range of 15 to 25 percent. In addition, private construction can shift a number of risks, including that of cost overruns, to the private sector.

Sources of Cost Savings

Since the final payment does not come until project completion, private firms have an incentive to complete construction more quickly. Construction of a prison or jail takes governments an average of two and one-half years—private firms complete the same type of project in about half the time. One company may have set a record, constructing a new facility in less than 90 days. The firm purchased land, got zoning clearance, lined up financing, and designed, built, and opened a 100-bed maximum-security juvenile facility in just three months.

When a private firm is asked to build a new facility or expand an existing one, only one person has to approve the re-

Table 2

Most Overcrowded Prison Systems (1996)

State	% of Capacity*
CA	196
IA	171
OH	171
DE	163
WA	150
MA	148
MI	146
VA	145
NJ	142
NH	140
IL	138
PA	138
OK	133
WI	133
WY	132
NE	131
NY	131
ND	127
HI	125
FEDERAL	124

*These figures are rough; different states calculate capacity in different ways.

Sources: U.S. Department of Justice; Camille Camp and George Camp, *The Corrections Yearbook, 1997* (South Salem, N.Y.: Criminal Justice Institute, 1997), p. 62.

quest—the CEO. This is in sharp contrast to the often laborious approval process and multiple contract requirements a government construction project must go through. The speediness of private construction gives public officials more flexibility in making corrections policy than does the slower-moving government construction process.

Speed of construction is only one way private firms cut building costs. They also save money because they are free of many costly rules imposed on government projects, such as purchasing restrictions and subcontracting quotas. The most extensive savings are reaped when the private firm is allowed to both design and build a facility. Public-works projects all over the world have used design-build contracts and achieved greater efficiency and cost savings—design-build contracts for corrections projects can do so as well.

Allowing private operating firms to design facilities can lead to considerable long-term operating-cost savings as well. Operating costs are 75 to 85 percent of the overall cost of a prison, and about 60 percent of the operating costs are for personnel. This means that designing a facility to require less staff, while providing the necessary security, can dramatically reduce operating costs. Innovative designs that require fewer personnel are a specialty of private corrections firms, but they have been very slow to catch on with government corrections projects.

Some people object that private prisons are authorized and built so fast that the public has little chance to weigh in on the decision. They say that although public hearings and procurement procedures take time, they are part of the democratic process that many jurisdictions have established. They accuse local officials of avoiding public debate over facility financing by entering into a lease-purchase agreement or by allowing a private firm to build a prison on its own and then contracting on a per-diem basis for each inmate it sends to the facility. Since the capital cost of the facility is embedded in the lease payment or the per-diem rate paid to the private firm, the taxpayers still pay the cost—but the structure of the deal sometimes avoids democratically established review procedures for capital expenditures. This is clearly a problem that local governments have to resolve with their citizens. Some officials that have failed to do so have found themselves facing challenges in court from local citizen groups.

Whichever way the courts come to decide this issue, public officials will continue to find that private construction cuts the cost of new facilities. This will be increasingly important not only to provide space for new prisoners, but also to replace existing aged facilities as needed. Nearly 300 prisons in the United States are over 50 years old, and more than 50 are over 100 years old. These facilities will need replacement or thorough renovation as they decay or become obsolete and inefficient to operate.

Services for Offenders

For-profit and nonprofit private organizations play a major role in providing services to correctional agencies. Most correctional institutions use some form of privatization in such areas as medical services, mental-health services, substance-abuse counseling, educational programs, food services, and management of prison industries.

The use of private services by correctional agencies is most extensive outside institution walls. This reflects the fact that more than 80 percent of convicted offenders in most states are in community supervision, either on parole or on probation.

Private involvement in community corrections (low-security work-release or halfway-house facilities) is a long-standing tradition in most states. In addition, state governments have traditionally let contracts for services such as counseling on abuse of alcohol and other drugs; assessment and treatment of sexual offenders; and job training and placement.

Private involvement in providing services to inmates during detention and after release has brought a new wave of innovation. Florida legislators found the private prisons in their state to be miles ahead of the state prisons in providing effective rehabilitation, education, and other services. Private firms are developing efficient and effective post-release programs aimed at reintegrating inmates into the community and reducing recidivism rates.

Providing these kinds of services does cost money. Inmates will receive these services only if the services are included in the terms of the contract. However, given that a contract with a private firm to house inmates saves money, more funds may be available to pay for specialized services that can reduce recidivism rates.

Management of Detention Facilities

A decade ago, private management of jails and prisons was almost unheard of. The first county, state, and federal prison management contracts were awarded in 1984 and 1985. In 1986, only a fraction of 1 percent of the nation's adult jail and prison population was privately managed.

This has changed. According to the 1997 "Private Adult Correctional Facility Census" (PACFC), at the end of 1996 private firms operated 132 adult facilities in the United States, holding 85,201 inmates. (See Figure 1.) This amounts to around 4 percent of the total U.S. adult prison population and reflects a 25 percent annual growth rate. Experts anticipate that this rate of growth will continue for some time. The PACFC predicts that the capacity of private adult prisons in the United States will exceed 275,000 inmates by the year 2002. Other nations are turning to private

Figure 1

11-Year Growth in Rated Capacity of Private Prisons

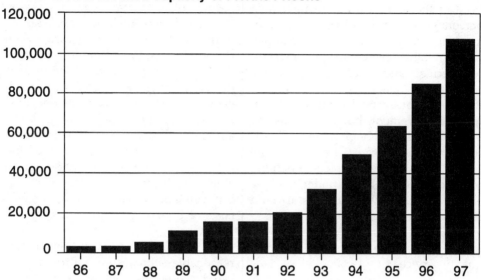

Source: Charles W. Thomas, "Private Adult Correctional Facility Census, 1997," University of Florida, Gainesville 1997, and his unpublished estimated figure for 1977.

prisons as well—the United Kingdom has four in operation and several more under construction, Australia has four in operation, and Canada and South Africa are expected to move forward soon with planned projects.

More states than ever are making use of private corrections—25 states, as well as the District of Columbia and Puerto Rico, have a private facility in operation or under construction. The federal government is also turning to the private sector for corrections services. The Immigration and Naturalization Service and the U.S. Marshals have long contracted with private firms to manage detention centers and other low-security facilities. And in mid-1997, the federal Bureau of Prisons turned a prison over to a private operator for the first time. Just a few weeks after that contract was signed, Congress passed legislation directing the

Bureau of Prisons to take control of most District of Columbia correctional facilities and to place 50 percent of the District's inmates in privately operated facilities by 2003.

There are currently at least 15 firms operating adult correctional facilities in the United States. Two large firms—Corrections Corporation of America and Wackenhut Corrections Corporation—manage the majority of private prisons. Four midsize firms—Correctional Services Corporation, Cornell Correction, Management and Training Corporation, and U.S. Corrections Corporation—each manage a number of facilities and have developed a breadth of experience. Other firms in the industry manage just a few facilities each. Two British firms—Securicor and Group 4 Prison Services—operate prisons in the United Kingdom and Australia and now have subsidiaries in the

United States. A key point: the size of the smaller firms belies their experience. Most of the private firms' management personnel come from careers in government prison systems, so even small private companies can draw upon a wealth of experience and expertise.

Managing major facilities has been the most controversial form of private-sector involvement, but it also has the most potential to help public officials cope with their correctional needs. The rest of this study is devoted to helping public officials and others understand the issues and controversies that surround this use of private-sector corrections—in particular the evidence that private prisons save money, yet still provide quality service.

COST SAVINGS OF PRIVATE PRISONS

There is a growing body of evidence that private prison operating costs are around 10 to 15 percent less than typical government prison operating costs. The number of detailed academic cost comparisons continues to grow, as does the first-hand experience of local officials with tangible cost savings.

Cost Comparison Studies

Any discussion of cost savings must compare private and government facilities. But it is hard to find two facilities that are exactly alike in design, age, personnel, inmate population, and other factors. So adjustments have to be made to data from different facilities to make them comparable.

Government agencies and private firms use different budgeting and accounting methods. Adjustments can help correct for most differences, but the result is a comparison of estimates, not specific expenditure data. Also, there are hidden costs that are hard to account for. A government institution's budget normally does not include various central administrative and support expenses. For example, some state prison budgets do not include the cost of some medical services, legal services, or personnel administration services, many of which are handled on a central accounting basis by other state agencies. On the other hand, a private facility's budget will include administrative and support costs but will not include the government's costs of preparing and monitoring contracts.

By making necessary adjustments, reasonable estimates and approximations can be used to compare government and private costs. The professionals who conduct comparison studies are versed in the difficulties and the adjustments needed to overcome them. They are familiar with the sometimes subjective nature of comparative analysis and point out assumptions and qualifications that readers need to understand. In most cases the authors make it clear that potential savings could be somewhat more or less than identified.

... Of the 14 studies, 12 found private prison costs to be lower than government prison costs—5 percent to 28 percent lower.

Two of the studies ... deserve particular attention. The study by researchers from Louisiana State University (LSU) has been widely acclaimed for overcoming the problem of comparing "apples to oranges." It compared three facilities, two privately operated (by different firms) and one operated by the state of Louisiana. The facilities were built from the same plans and had very similar pop-

Table 3

Staffing and Operating-Cost Comparison: Prairie Correctional Facility (PCF) and Jackson Correctional Institution (JCI) (1995)

	Private (PCF)	Public (JCI)
Inmates	516	663
• Inmates as % of capacity	100%	108%
Staff		
• Correctional officers (C.O.s)	103	163
• Other staff	63	110
• Staff per 100 inmates	32.2	41.2
• C.O.s per 100 inmates	20.0	24.6
Estimated 1995 spending	$7,200,000	$12,000,000
1995 per diem/inmate	$38.23	$49.59
1995 spending/inmate/year	$13,953	$18,100

Local Cost Comparison: An Example. A study of Wisconsin prisons compared the costs of a private prison in Minnesota, Prairie Correctional Facility, to a similar Wisconsin state prison, Jackson Correctional Institution. The two prisons are about the same age, have similar inmate populations, and are geographically close. The study found that the daily cost per inmate in the private facility was 23 percent lower than in the government facility. A summary of the comparison is presented in the table [above]. For more details, see George Mitchell, "Controlling Prison Costs in Wisconsin," Wisconsin Policy Research Institute, December 1996.

ulations—as much "apples and apples" as one could reasonably hope to find. This study found both private prisons to be about 15 percent more cost-effective than their government counterpart.

While not able to directly compare identical facilities, the Arizona study went to considerable lengths to adjust and compensate for differences between the privately run prison and the government-run prisons. Careful steps were taken to account for indirect costs. The state's first private prison, a 444-bed facility, was compared to all 15 government-run prisons in the state. Some government prisons performed better than the private prison, and some performed worse, but the private prison's costs were 17 percent less than the average cost of the state prisons.

In stark contrast to these two studies is a report issued in 1996 by the General Accounting Office (GAO). The GAO examined five studies comparing government and private prison costs and concluded that it "could not draw any conclusions about cost savings or quality of service." ...

The GAO report is important because it is widely cited by privatization opponents, but its methods and conclusions are odd. Of the four studies it examined ..., two found the private facilities to have significantly lower costs. The GAO argued that the results of those two studies should be ignored because they suffered from limitations, specifically: (1) the fact that some comparisons involve actual costs and "hypothetical" costs; and (2) the fact that facilities being compared might be designed differently or operated differently.

The GAO report has been widely criticized for a number of shortcomings, including:

- The GAO, without explaining why, chose to ignore a number of cost comparisons... and focus on only five studies. Among those overlooked were studies from Australia and the United Kingdom, which are not as useful in the United States (although they are certainly relevant). But why ignore the studies by the Texas Criminal Justice Policy Council, the Kentucky Auditor of Public Accounts, and the Florida Office of the Auditor General? The GAO also left out the prominent LSU study. It had not yet been published, but the GAO investigators had been made aware of it by several of the sources they contacted. Ignoring the Louisiana study was particularly egregious because it compared identical facilities —exactly the type of comparison the GAO report said was needed.

- The GAO's insistence that cost comparisons must look at identical facilities, besides being belied by their ignoring the LSU study, misses a crucial point. One of the principal advantages that private firms bring to corrections is that they do things differently. It is precisely the innovative practices of private firms—their breaking away from "the way things have always been done"—that bring about cost savings.

- The GAO report discounts the results of the Texas Comptroller's study because it compared the cost of existing private facilities to the cost of "hypothetical government facilities." Actually, the Texas study compared the cost of the private facilities to the "cost that the TDCJ [Texas Department of Criminal Justice] would incur if it *took over the operation of the four private facilities"* (emphasis added). Moreover, the GAO chose to ignore a subsequent report by the Texas Criminal Justice Policy Council (a state agency) that found the cost advantage of the private facilities to be even greater (21 percent).

- Two of the studies the GAO gave credence are in fact flawed or at least limited. The Washington report was similar to the GAO report in that it reanalyzed earlier data rather than collecting new data—so it is not surprising that it reiterated the results of the Tennessee Legislature's study. The GAO also included a report that compared community corrections facilities in California. This study should not have been included, because it compares halfway-house facilities, not real prisons, and the two "government" facilities were in fact for-profit facilities operated by special agencies of local governments to house state prisoners.

- Finally, the GAO report was not an objective survey of available information, as was requested by the House of Representatives when it asked the GAO to undertake the study. Rather, according to Dr. Charles Logan, it is "so consistently one-sided and negative that it reaches the point of dishonesty."

Other Evidence

To buttress the copious empirical evidence that the private operation of prisons saves money, there are simple commonsense observations. For one thing, why would so many states and federal agencies enter into contracts with private prison firms if not to save money? Tennessee state senator Jim Kyle points out that only the potential cost savings that private prisons offer will entice a politician to take on the battle to contract for correctional services. Indeed, the most frequent reason given for privatization is to save money. Unless we assume that the decision makers in all the governments that contract with private prison firms are willfully stupid, we have to believe that cost savings are being achieved.

This observation is buttressed by the legislation many states have passed to ensure cost savings from prison privatization. For example, Texas and Mississippi both require contracts with private prisons to cost at least 10 percent less than using the state system, Florida requires 7 percent savings, and Tennessee requires payments to private firms to be less than government facility costs. States are refining their methods of assuring savings. Several of the studies... were commissioned by state governments checking to see that cost savings were achieved. The Arizona Department of Corrections, in cooperation with the state Office of Excellence, is developing a new and sophisticated cost comparison model.

How the Private Sector Cuts Costs
Undeniably, the key to the lower costs of the private sector is competition. In order to win contracts—and keep them —a firm must be efficient. Rising costs, or cuts that lead to poor quality, would soon take a firm to where it could win no more contracts.

The private sector saves money by doing a number of things differently from government. Since their success hinges on delivering the same product as the government but at lower cost, or a bet-

ter product at a cost-effective price, they turn to new management approaches, new monitoring techniques, and administrative efficiencies—in a word, innovation. Moving beyond "the way it has always been done" allows them to reduce labor costs, reduce tension between correctional officers and inmates, make full use of a facility's capacity, and make more efficient purchases.

Reducing Labor Costs
About two-thirds of correctional departments' operating budgets are devoted to personnel, so naturally that is where most of the opportunity for savings lies. Private operating firms strive to reduce personnel costs without understaffing a facility. They do this by:

Using more efficient facility design. If a private firm has a role in designing a facility, it is likely to use innovative new design techniques, with sight lines and technology that allow inmates to be monitored with fewer correctional personnel.

Reducing administrative levels. Private operating firms tend to have fewer administrative personnel than the often bureaucratic structures of government correctional departments. One private prison administrator, with 14 years of experience in government corrections, says that private prisons use roughly one-third the administrative personnel government prisons use.

Minimizing the use of overtime. Many correctional departments are understaffed, leading to the use of overtime to ensure sufficient correctional officers for each shift in each facility. Sometimes it is less expensive to use overtime than to hire more employees, but only up to a point. Overtime also increases when employees call in sick. In the public sector, sick time is considered an entitlement, not a privilege, and it is almost rebellious not to use it. With considerable success, private firms use incentives to reduce sick time and the consequent overtime expenditures. While overtime helps raise the take-home pay of existing employees, it can significantly raise operating costs. By using full staffing and more efficient personnel management, private prison firms use less overtime.

Exercising greater freedom to manage personnel. Private operating firms are not bound by civil-service rules in managing their personnel; this significantly reduces personnel management costs. Private operating firms can use both positive and negative incentives to induce employees to perform. Civil-service rules and terms of public-employee union contracts tend to increase costs.

As a rule, private operating firms do not cut costs by cutting personnel quality. Pay for correctional officers at private firms tends to be nearly the same, or only slightly lower, than for government correctional officers. Where compensation is lower, private operating firms make up for it in part by offering opportunity for advancement based on merit rather than civil-service rules. Also, many private operating companies offer employee incentive packages that can be very lucrative. For instance, employee stock ownership plans have reaped tremendous rewards for many employees.

Reducing Incidents
Almost every incident between inmates, or between inmates and correctional officers, costs a prison money. These incidents lead to lawsuits, which also increase personnel costs. Private operating firms respond to these incentives by managing facilities in ways that minimize incidents. This means maintaining tight control of inmates and keeping them well-fed and occupied with work, education, or recreation—in short, establishing in the inmates' eyes the legitimacy of the private correctional officers' authority. Several studies have shown that privately operated facilities tend to have fewer incidents than comparable government facilities. In Florida, "get tough" policies in the state-run prisons have been accompanied by a 62 percent increase in inmate assaults on other inmates and a 250 percent increase in inmate assaults on correctional officers. In the state's private prisons, where the new policies did not apply, there has been no such increase in incidents.

Fully Using Facility Capacity
If a jurisdiction does not use all of the beds in its facility, private operating firms can often lower the per-inmate costs by contracting to hold prisoners from other jurisdictions in the excess space. This allows the local jurisdiction to reduce its share of covering the fixed costs of operating the facility.

Efficient Purchasing and Maintenance
Freedom from bureaucratic purchasing rules and procedures lets private operating firms shop locally for the lowest-cost necessary supplies and services. This saves both time and money. One private prison warden explains that if he needs some item, such as camera film, he doesn't have to order it through a complex state purchasing process or wait for

it to be shipped from a distant supplier—he just goes to a store and buys it.

The story is similar for facility maintenance. Private operators and owners of prisons have incentives to make maintenance decisions that save long-run capital costs as well as current operating costs. Private firms can invest today in ways that generate savings over time, while the public sector often has difficulty getting approval or funds for such investments. For example, in one prison a private company that took over operations switched all lighting over to fluorescent bulbs and refitted the plumbing to stop rampant leaks, generating considerable savings in utility costs.

Competition, Not Private-Sector "Magic," Creates Efficiency and Innovation

When governments contract with the private sector, efficiency and innovation do not come about because private firms have some magic pixie dust, unobtainable by the public sector, to sprinkle about. It is competition that creates efficiency and innovation, because competition punishes inefficiency and inertia. That means two things: first, that the contracting process needs to be competitive in the long run for efficiency to remain, and second, that competition from the private sector makes the public sector more efficient as well. This is the great uncounted benefit of private-sector provision of correctional services. Contracts usually save money not only directly, but also indirectly, by forcing the government corrections departments to tighten up their ships.

There has been little success at quantifying the indirect benefits competition brings to the overall provision of correctional services. Perhaps the best attempt was part of the 1995 cost comparison study in Tennessee. The study compared costs at two government prisons and one private prison at the beginning and at the end of the year of study. When the facilities knew they were being compared, they strove for their best efficiency, and the cost at all three prisons declined over the year—5 and 8 percent at the two government prisons and 15 percent at the private prison.

Anecdotal evidence of competitive pressures and "cross-fertilization" abounds as well. Russ Boraas, Private Prison Administrator for the Virginia Department of Corrections, believes the cross-fertilization benefits of contracting with private firms to run some prisons may be the greatest benefits of contracting. Virginia has two new prisons designed, built, and operated by private firms. Both firms dramatically reduced capital and operating costs of the facilities by replacing expensive external guard towers with high-tech sensors and a roving patrol, and by eliminating a 30-day food storage warehouse and storing just enough food for a week.

For no reason that anyone can remember, Virginia prisons keep 30 days of food on hand in warehouses that are expensive to build, maintain, and operate. Boraas believes it is a practice going back to when prisons were remote and supplied by mule train. No one had ever bothered to question the practice until the private companies came in and did something different. He says that the rest of the state prisons are now adopting the private firms' food storage practices, and that only maximum-security prisons are likely to have external guard towers in the future.

There are plenty of similar stories:

- Responding to a perceived threat from the growth of private prison operation, the Connecticut Department of Corrections (DOC) adopted a philosophy of running its prisons more like businesses and dramatically cut annual spending. At the end of 1996, the department returned $46 million to the state treasury. Savings were realized by cutting staff and increasing revenue generated by inmates. Despite this, Connecticut still spends $65 a day for each inmate, one of the highest per-inmate cost rates in the nation.

- Carl Nink, of the Arizona DOC, explains how the state's prison wardens had never defined the measures that constitute successful performance of a prison until they had to write a contract with the operator of the state's first private prison. The result forced a lot of wardens to go back and reevaluate their own policies and practices to ensure they meet the same standards being asked of the private firm.

- According to Tim Wilson, Head of Contracts for Her Majesty's Prison Service, in the years since the lower costs at new private prisons have become public, costs at government prisons in the United Kingdom have been falling.

The existence of private prisons, and the threat of privatization, changes the incentives for government corrections officials. As long as there is a credible threat of privatization, these incentives to reduce costs and improve quality will remain. It remains to be seen what amount of competition is necessary to maintain these incentives for the public sector.

Conclusion

The evidence from comparative cost studies strongly supports the conclusion that private prisons save an average of 10 to 15 percent on operating costs. The conclusion is also supported by the experience of public officials in many states that use private prisons. Competitive pressure provides the incentive to be efficient that helps drive private-sector costs down, and the firms achieve cost savings through innovative design and management practices.

NO

Eric Bates

PRIVATE PRISONS

A few hours after midnight one August evening last year, Walter Hazelwood and Richard Wilson climbed a fence topped with razor wire at the Houston Processing Center, a warehouse built to hold undocumented immigrants awaiting deportation. Once outside, the two prisoners assaulted a guard, stole his car and headed for Dallas.

When prison officials notified the Houston police that the men had escaped, local authorities were shocked. Sure, immigrants had fled the minimum-security facility near the airport a few times before. But Hazelwood and Wilson were not being detained for lacking the papers to prove their citizenship. One was serving time for sexual abuse; the other was convicted of beating and raping an 88-year-old woman. Both men, it turned out, were among some 240 sex offenders from Oregon who had been shipped to the Texas detention center months earlier—and local authorities didn't even know they were there.

The immigration center is owned and operated by Corrections Corporation of America [C.C.A.], which manages more private prisons than any other company worldwide. While C.C.A. made nearly $14,000 a day on the out-of-state inmates, the company was quick to point out that it had no legal obligation to tell the Houston police or county sheriff about their new neighbors from Oregon. "We designed and built the institution," explained Susan Hart, a company spokeswoman. "It is ours."

Yet like a well-to-do rancher who discovers a couple of valuable head of cattle missing, C.C.A. expected Texas rangers to herd the wayward animals back behind the company's fence. "It's not our function to capture them," Hart told reporters.

Catching the prisoners proved easier, however, than charging them with a crime. When authorities finally apprehended them after eleven days, they discovered they could no more punish the men for escaping than they could lock up a worker for walking off the job. Even in Texas, it seemed, it was not yet a crime to flee a private corporation.

"They have not committed the offense of escape under Texas law," said district attorney John Holmes. "The only reason at all that they're subject to being arrested and were arrested was because during their leaving the facility, they assaulted a guard and took his motor vehicle. *That* we can charge them with, and have."

The state moved quickly to pass legislation making such escapes illegal. But the Texas breakout underscores how the rapid spread of private prisons has created considerable confusion about just what the rules are when a for-profit company like Corrections Corporation seeks to cash in on incarceration. Founded in 1983 with backing from the investors behind Kentucky Fried Chicken, C.C.A. was one of the first companies to push the privatization of public services. The selling point was simple: Private companies could build and run prisons cheaper than the government. Business, after all, would be free of red tape—those inefficient procedures that waste tax dollars on things like open bidding on state contracts and job security for public employees. Unfettered American capitalism would produce a better fetter, saving cash-strapped counties and states millions of dollars each year.

Sooner or later, people realize that "the government can't do anything very well," Thomas Beasley, a co-founder of C.C.A. and a former chairman of the Tennessee Republican Party, said near the start of prison privatization. "At that point, you just sell it like you were selling cars or real estate or hamburgers."

* * *

Not everyone is quite so enthusiastic about the prospect of selling human beings like so many pieces of meat. By privatizing prisons, government essentially auctions off inmates—many of them young black men—to the highest bidder. Opponents ranging from the American Civil Liberties Union to the National Sheriffs Association have argued that justice should not be for sale at any price. "The bottom line is a moral one," says Ira Robbins, who wrote a statement for the American Bar Association opposing private corrections. "Do we want our justice system to be operated by private interests? This is not like privatizing the post office or waste management to provide services to the community. There's something meaningful lost when an inmate looks at a guard's uniform and instead of seeing an emblem that reads 'Federal Bureau of Prisons' or 'State Department of Corrections,' he sees one that says 'Acme Prison Corporation.'"

But such moral concerns have gone largely unheeded in all the excitement over how much money the boys at Acme might save taxpayers. There's only one problem: The evidence suggests that the savings reaped from nearly fifteen years of privatizing prisons are more elusive than an Oregon convict in a Texas warehouse.

* * *

In 1996 the General Accounting Office examined the few available reports comparing costs at private and public prisons. Its conclusion: "These studies do not offer substantial evidence that savings have occurred." The most reliable study cited by the G.A.O. found that a C.C.A.-run prison in Tennessee cost only 1 percent less to operate than two comparable state-run prisons. The track record also suggests that private prisons invite political corruption and do little to improve quality, exacerbating the conditions that lead to abuse and violence.

Although private prisons have failed to save much money for taxpayers, they generate enormous profits for the companies that own and operate them. Corrections Corporation ranks among the top five performing companies on the New York Stock Exchange over the past three years. The value of its shares has soared from $50 million when it went public in 1986 to more than $3.5 billion at its peak last October. By carefully selecting the most lucrative prison contracts, slashing labor costs and sticking taxpayers with the bill for expenses like prisoner escapes, C.C.A. has richly confirmed the title of a recent stock analysis by PaineWebber: "Crime pays."

"It's easier for private firms to innovate," says Russell Boraas, who oversees private prisons for the Virginia Department of Corrections. As he inspects a medium-security facility being built by C.C.A. outside the small town of Lawrenceville, Boraas notes that the prison has no guard towers—an "innovation" that saves the company $2.5 million in construction costs and eliminates twenty-five full-time positions. "Think about it," Boraas says. "A state corrections director who eliminates guard towers will lose his job if a prisoner escapes and molests a little old lady. The president of the company won't lose his job, as long as he's making a profit."

Although corrections officials like Boraas initially viewed the drive to privatize prisons with skepticism, many quickly became converts. The crime rate nationwide remains well below what it was twenty-five years ago, but harsher sentencing has packed prisons and jails to the bursting point. There are now 1.8 million Americans behind bars—more than twice as many as a decade ago—and the "get tough" stance has sapped public resources and sparked court orders to improve conditions.

With their promise of big savings, private prisons seemed to offer a solution. Corporate lockups can now hold an estimated 77,500 prisoners, most of them state inmates. Over the next five years, analysts expect the private share of the prison "market" to more than double.

Corrections Corporation is far and away the biggest company in the corrections business, controlling more than half of all inmates in private prisons nationwide. C.C.A. now operates the sixth-largest prison system in the country—and is moving aggressively to expand into the global market with prisons in England, Australia and Puerto Rico. That's good news for investors. *The Cabot Market Letter* compares the company to a "a hotel that's always at 100% occupancy... and booked to the end of the century." C.C.A. started taking reservations during the Reagan Administration, when Beasley founded the firm in Nashville with a former classmate from West Point. Their model was the Hospital Corporation of America [H.C.A.], then the nation's largest owner of private hospitals. "This is the home of H.C.A.," Beasley thought at the time. "The synergies are the same."

From the start, those synergies included close ties to politicians who could grant the company lucrative contracts. As former chairman of the state G.O.P., Beasley was a good friend of then-Governor Lamar Alexander. In 1985 Alexander backed a plan to hand over the entire state prison system to the fledgling company for $200 million. Among C.C.A.'s stockholders at the time were the Governor's wife, Honey, and Ned McWherter, the influential Speaker of the state House, who succeeded Alexander as governor.

Although the state legislature eventually rejected the plan as too risky, C.C.A. had established itself as a major player. It had also discovered that knowing the right people can be more important than actually saving taxpayers money. The company won its first bid to run a prison by offering to operate the Silverdale Work Farm near Chattanooga for $21 per inmate per day. At $3 less than the county was spending, it seemed like a good deal —until a crackdown on drunk drivers flooded the work farm with new inmates. Because fixed expenses were unaffected by the surge, each new prisoner cost C.C.A. about $5. But the county, stuck with a contract that required it to pay the company $21 a head, found itself $200,000 over budget. "The work farm became a gold mine," noted John Donahue, a public policy professor at Harvard University.

When the contract came up for renewal in 1986, however, county commissioners voted to stick with Corrections Corporation. Several enjoyed business ties with the company. One commissioner had a pest-control contract with the firm, and later went to work for C.C.A. as a lobbyist. Another did landscaping at the prison, and a third ran the moving company that settled the warden into his new home. C.C.A. also put the son of the county employee responsible for monitoring the Silverdale contract on the payroll at its Nashville headquarters. The following year, the U.S. Justice Department published a research report warning about such conflicts of interest in on-site monitoring—the only mechanism for insuring that prison operators abide by the contract. In addition to being a hidden and costly expense of private prisons, the report cautioned, government monitors could "be co-opted by the contractor's staff. Becoming friendly or even beholden to contract personnel could lead to the State receiving misleading reports."

But even when problems have been reported, officials often downplay them. The Justice Department noted "substantial staff turnover problems" at the Chattanooga prison, for instance, but added that "this apparently did not result in major reductions in service quality." The reason? "This special effort to do a good job," the report concluded, "is probably due to the private organizations finding themselves in the national limelight, and their desire to expand the market."

The same year that federal officials were crediting C.C.A. with "a good job" at the undermanned facility, Rosalind Bradford, a 23-year-old woman being held at Silverdale, died from an undiagnosed complication during pregnancy. A shift supervisor who later sued the company testified that Bradford suffered in agony for at least twelve hours before C.C.A. officials allowed her to be taken to a hospital. "Rosalind Bradford died out there, in my opinion, of criminal neglect," the supervisor said in a deposition.

Inspectors from the British Prison Officers Association who visited the prison that year were similarly shocked by what they witnessed. "We saw evidence of inmates being cruelly treated," the inspectors reported. "Indeed, the warden admitted that noisy and truculent prisoners are gagged with sticky tape, but this had caused a problem when an inmate almost choked to death."

The inspectors were even more blunt when they visited the C.C.A.-run immigration center in Houston, where they found inmates confined to warehouselike dormitories for twenty-three hours a day. The private facility, inspectors concluded, demonstrated "possibly the worst conditions we have ever witnessed in terms of inmate care and supervision."

* * *

Reports of inhumane treatment of prisoners, while deeply disturbing, do not by themselves indicate that private prisons are worse than public ones. After all, state and federal lockups have never been known for their considerate attitude toward the people under their watch. Indeed, C.C.A. and other company prisons have drawn many of their wardens and guards from the ranks of public corrections officers. The guards videotaped earlier this year assaulting prisoners with stun guns at a C.C.A. competitor in Texas had been hired despite records of similar abuse when they worked for the state.

Susan Hart, the C.C.A. spokeswoman, insisted that her company would never put such people on the payroll—well, almost never. "It would be inappropriate, for certain positions, [to hire] someone who said, 'Yes, I beat a prisoner to death,'" she told *The Houston Chronicle*. "That would be a red flag for us." She did not specify for which positions the company considers murder an appropriate job qualification.

In fact, C.C.A. employs at least two wardens in Texas who were disciplined for beating prisoners while employed by the state. And David Myers, the president of the company, supervised an assault on inmates who took a guard hostage while Myers was serving as warden of a Texas prison in 1984. Fourteen guards were later found to have used "excessive force," beating subdued and handcuffed prisoners with riot batons.

The real danger of privatization is not some innate inhumanity on the part of its practitioners but rather the added financial incentives that reward inhumanity. The same economic logic that motivates companies to run prisons more efficiently also encourages them to cut corners at the expense of workers, prisoners and the public. Private prisons essentially mirror the cost-cutting practices of health maintenance organizations: Companies receive a guaranteed fee for each prisoner, regardless of the actual costs. Every dime they don't spend on food or medical care or training for guards is a dime they can pocket.

As in most industries, the biggest place to cut prison expenses is personnel. "The bulk of the cost savings enjoyed by C.C.A. is the result of lower labor costs," PaineWebber assures investors. Labor accounts for roughly 70 percent of all prison expenses, and C.C.A. prides itself on getting more from fewer employees. "With only a 36 percent increase in personnel," boasts the latest annual report, "revenues grew 41 percent, operating income grew 98 percent, and net income grew 115 percent."

Like other companies, C.C.A. prefers to design and build its own prisons so it can replace guards right from the start with video cameras and clustered cellblocks that are cheaper to monitor. "The secret to low-cost operations is having the minimum number of officers watching the maximum number of inmates," explains Russell Boraas, the private prison administrator for Virginia. "You can afford to pay damn near anything for construction if it will get you an efficient prison."

At the C.C.A. prison under construction in Lawrenceville, Boraas indicates how the design of the "control room" will enable a guard to simultaneously watch three "pods" of 250 prisoners each. Windows in the elevated room afford an unobstructed view of each cellblock below, and "vision blocks" in the floor are positioned over each entranceway so guards can visually identify anyone being admitted. The high-tech panel at the center of the room can open any door at the flick of a switch. When the prison opens next year, C.C.A. will employ five guards to supervise 750 prisoners during the day, and two guards at night.

Another way to save money on personnel is to leave positions unfilled when they come open. Speaking before a legislative panel in Tennessee in October, Boraas noted that some private prisons in Texas have made up for the low reimbursement rates they receive from the state "by leaving positions vacant a little longer than they should." Some C.C.A. employees admit privately that the company leaves positions open to boost profits. "We're always short," says one guard who asked not to be identified. "They do staff fewer positions—that's one way they save money." The company is growing so quickly, another guard explains, that "we have more slots than we have people to fill them. When they transfer officers to new facilities, we're left with skeletons."

* * *

At first glance, visitors to the South Central Correctional Center could be forgiven for mistaking the medium-security prison for a college campus. The main driveway rolls through wooded hills on the outskirts of Clifton, Tennessee, past picnic benches, a fitness track and a horse barn. But just inside the front door, a prominent bulletin board makes clear that the prison means business. At the top

are the words "C.C.A. Excellence in Corrections." At the bottom is "Yesterday's Stock Closing," followed by a price.

* * *

In addition to employing fewer guards, C.C.A. saves money on labor by replacing the guaranteed pensions earned by workers at state-run prisons with a cheaper—and riskier—stock-ownership plan. Employees get a chance to invest in the company, and the company gets employees devoted to the bottom line. "Being a stockholder yourself, you monitor things closer," says Mark Staggs, standing in the segregation unit, where he oversees prisoners confined for breaking the rules. "You make sure you don't waste money on things like cleaning products. Because it's your money you're spending."

Warden Kevin Myers (not related to C.C.A. president David Myers) also looks for little places to cut costs. "I can save money on purchasing because there's no bureaucracy," he says. "If I see a truckload of white potatoes at a bargain, I can buy them. I'm always negotiating for a lower price."

But what is thriftiness to the warden is just plain miserly to those forced to eat what he dishes out. "Ooowhee! It's pitiful in that kitchen," says Antonio McCraw, who was released from South Central last March after serving three years for armed robbery. "I just thank God I'm out of there. You might get a good meal once a month. The rest was instant potatoes, vegetables out of a can and processed pizzas. C.C.A. don't care whether you eat or not. Sure they may cut corners and do it for less money, but is it healthy?"

The State of Tennessee hoped to answer that question when it turned South Central over to C.C.A. in 1992. The prison was built at roughly the same time as two state-run facilities with similar designs and inmate populations, giving officials a rare opportunity to compare daily operating costs—and quality—under privatization.

The latest state report on violence at the three prisons indicates that South Central is a much more dangerous place than its public counterparts. During the past fiscal year, the C.C.A. prison experienced violent incidents at a rate more than 50 percent higher than state facilities. The company also posted significantly worse rates for contraband, drugs and assaults on staff and prisoners.

"If that doesn't raise some eyebrows and give you some kind of indication of what the future holds, I guess those of us who are concerned just need to be quiet," says John Mark Windle, a state representative who opposes privatization.

Corrections officials note that under-staffing can certainly fuel violence, which winds up costing taxpayers more money. The state legislature has heard testimony that employee turnover at South Central is more than twice the level at state prisons, and prisoners report seeing classes of new recruits every month, many of them young and inexperienced. "The turnover rate is important because it shows whether you have experienced guards who stick around and know the prisoners," says inmate Alex Friedmann, seated at a bare table in a visitation room. "If you have a high turnover rate you have less stability. New employees come in; they really don't know what's going on. That leads to conflicts with inmates."

Internal company documents tell a similar story. According to the minutes of an August 1995 meeting of shift supervisors at South Central, chief of security Danny Scott "said we all know that we have lots of new staff and are constantly in the training mode." He "added that so many employees were totally lost and had never worked in corrections."

A few months later, a company survey of staff members at the prison asked, "What is the reason for the number of people quitting C.C.A.?" Nearly 20 percent of employees cited "treatment by supervisors," and 17 percent listed "money."

Out of earshot of their supervisors, some guards also say the company contributes to violence by skimping on activities for inmates. "We don't give them anything to do," says one officer. "We give them the bare minimum we have to."

Ron Lyons agrees. "There's no meaningful programs here," says Lyons, who served time at state-run prisons before coming to South Central. "I can't get over how many people are just laying around in the pod every day. I would have thought C.C.A. would have known that inmate idleness is one of the biggest problems in prisons—too much time sitting around doing nothing. You definitely realize it's commercialized. It's a business. Their business is to feed you and count you, and that's it."

Given all the penny-pinching, it would seem that C.C.A. should easily be able to demonstrate significant savings at South Central. Instead, a study of costs conducted by the state in 1995 found that the company provided almost no savings compared with its two public rivals. The study—cited by the General Accounting Office as "the most sound and detailed comparison of operational costs"— actually showed that the C.C.A. prison cost *more* to run on a daily basis. Even after the state factored in its long-term expenses, C.C.A. still spent $35.38 a day per prisoner—only 38 cents less than the state average.

The study contradicted what is supposed to be the most compelling rationale for prison privatization: the promise of big savings. But the industry champion dismissed its defeat by insisting, much to the amazement of its challengers, that it hadn't tried very hard to save tax dollars. "When you're in a race and you can win by a few steps, that's what you do," said Doctor R. Crants, who co-founded C.C.A. and now serves as chairman and chief executive officer. "We weren't trying to win by a great deal."

* * *

The comment by Crants, as remarkable as it seems, exposes the true nature of privatization. When it comes to savings, the prison industry will beat state spending by as narrow a margin as the state will permit. To a prison company like C.C.A., "savings" are nothing but the share of profits it is required to hand over to the government—another expense that cuts into the bottom line and must therefore be kept to a minimum, like wages or the price of potatoes. At its heart, privatizing prisons is really about privatizing tax dollars, about transforming public money into private profits.

That means companies are actually looking for ways to keep public spending as high as possible, including charging taxpayers for questionable expenses. The New Mexico Corrections Department, for example, has accused C.C.A. of overcharging the state nearly $2 million over the past eight years for operating the women's prison in Grants. The company fee of $95 a day for each inmate, it turns

out, includes $22 for debt service on the prison.

* * *

Last summer, a legislative committee in Tennessee calculated that state prisons contribute nearly $17.8 million each year to state agencies that provide central services like printing, payroll administration and insurance. Since company prisons usually go elsewhere for such services, states that privatize unwittingly lose money they once counted on to help pay fixed expenses.

The "chargebacks," as they are known, came to light last spring when C.C.A. once again proposed taking over the entire Tennessee prison system. This time the company offered to save $100 million a year—a staggering sum, considering that the annual budget for the system is only $270 million.

Like many claims of savings, the C.C.A. offer turned out to be based on false assumptions. Crants, the company chairman and C.E.O., said he derived the estimate from comparing the $32 daily rate the company charges for medium-security prisoners at South Central with the systemwide average of $54. But the state system includes maximum-security prisons that cost much more to operate than South Central. "It's almost like going into a rug store," says State Senator James Kyle, who chaired legislative hearings on privatization. "They're always 20 percent off. But 20 percent off what?"

Yet the sales pitch, however absurd, had the intended effect of getting Kyle and other lawmakers into the store to look around. Once there, the prison companies kept offering them bigger and better deals. Given an opportunity to submit cost estimates anonymously, firms offered fantastic savings ranging from

30 percent to 50 percent. Threatened by the competition, even the state Department of Corrections went bargain basement, offering to slash its own already low cost by $70 million a year. Despite opposition from state employees, legislators indicated after the hearings that they support a move to turn most prisoners over to private companies—a decision that delighted C.C.A. "I was pretty pleased," Crants said afterward. The governor and legislators are wrangling over the details, but both sides have agreed informally to privatize roughly two-thirds of the Tennessee system. A few prisons will be left in the hands of the state, just in case something goes wrong.

Lawmakers didn't have to look far to see how wrong things can go. South Carolina decided last February not to renew a one-year contract with C.C.A. for a juvenile detention center in the state capital. Child advocates reported hearing about horrific abuses at the facility, where some boys say they were hogtied and shackled together. "The bottom line is the staff there were inexperienced," said Robyn Zimmerman of the South Carolina Department of Juvenile Justice. "They were not trained properly."

Once again, though, such stark realities proved less influential than the political connections enjoyed by C.C.A. The chief lobbyist for the company in the Tennessee legislature is married to the Speaker of the state House. Top C.C.A. executives, board members and their spouses have contributed at least $110,000 to state candidates since 1993, including $1,350 to Senator Kyle. And five state officials—including the governor, the House Speaker and the sponsor of the privatization bill—are partners with C.C.A. co-founder Thomas Beasley in several Red

Hot & Blue barbecue restaurants in Tennessee.

The political clout extends to the national level as well. On the Republican side, Corrections Corporation employs the services of J. Michael Quinlan, director of the federal Bureau of Prisons under George Bush. On the Democratic side, C.C.A. reserves a seat on its seven-member board for Joseph Johnson, former executive director of the Rainbow Coalition. The Nashville *Tennessean* points to Johnson as evidence that the company "looks like America.... Johnson is African-American," the paper observes, "as are 60% of C.C.A.'s prisoners."

Johnson played a pivotal behind-the-scenes role earlier..., using his political connections to help C.C.A. swing a deal to buy a prison from the District of Columbia for $52 million. It was the first time a government sold a prison to a private company, and C.C.A. hopes it won't be the last.... [W]ith backing from financial heavyweights like Lehman Brothers and PaineWebber, the company formed C.C.A. Prison Realty Trust to focus solely on buying prisons. The initial stock offering raised $388.5 million from investors to enable C.C.A. to speculate on prisons as real estate.

* * *

Why would cities or states sell their prisons to the C.C.A. trust? PaineWebber cites the lure of what it calls "free money." Unlike many public bond initiatives earmarked for specific projects like schools or sewage systems, the broker explains, "the sale of an existing prison would generate proceeds that a politician could then use for initiatives that fit his or her agenda, possibly improving the chances of re-election." Companies building their own prisons certainly receive friendly treatment from officials. Russell Boraas invited companies bidding on a private prison to a meeting and asked what he could do to help. "I said, 'Guys, I know quite a bit about running construction projects, but I don't know much about private prisons. What are you looking for? What can I do to make this user-friendly for you?' They said it would be nice if they could use tax-exempt bond issues for construction, just like the state." So Boraas allowed companies to finance construction with help from taxpayers, and a local Industrial Development Authority eventually aided C.C.A. in getting $58 million in financing to build the prison.

Such deals raise concerns that private prisons may wind up costing taxpayers more in the long run. Although governments remain legally responsible for inmates guarded by public companies, firms have little trouble finding ways to skirt public oversight while pocketing public money. Instead of streamlining the system, hiring corporations to run prisons actually *adds* a layer of bureaucracy that can increase costs and reduce accountability. Prison companies have been known to jack up prices when their contracts come up for renewal, and some defer maintenance on prisons since they aren't responsible for them once their contract expires.

Even more disturbing, private prisons have the financial incentive—and financial influence—to lobby lawmakers for harsher prison sentences and other "get tough" measures. In the prison industry, after all, locking people up is good for business. "If you really want to save money you can lock prisoners in a box and feed them a slice of bread each day," says Alex Friedmann, the prisoner at South Central. "The real question is, Can you run programs in such a way that people don't commit more crime? That should be the mark of whether privatization is successful in prisons—not whether you keep them locked up but whether you keep them out."

C.C.A. officials dismiss such concerns, confident the current boom will continue of its own accord. "I don't think we have to worry about running out of product," says Kevin Myers, the warden at South Central. "It's unfortunate but true. We don't have to drum up business."

Perhaps—but Corrections Corporation and other company prisons already have enormous power to keep their current prisoners behind bars for longer stretches. Inmates generally lose accumulated credit for "good time" when they are disciplined by guards, giving the C.C.A. stockholders who serve as officers an incentive to crack the whip. A 1992 study by the New Mexico Corrections Department showed that inmates at the women's prison run by C.C.A. lost good time at a rate nearly eight times higher than their male counterparts at a state-run lockup. And every day a prisoner loses is a day of extra income for the company—and an extra expense for taxpayers.

Some C.C.A. guards in Tennessee also say privately that they are encouraged to write up prisoners for minor infractions and place them in segregation. Inmates in "seg" not only lose their good time, they also have thirty days added to their sentence—a bonus of nearly $1,000 for the company at some prisons. "We will put 'em in seg in a hurry," says a guard who works at the Davidson County Juvenile Detention Facility in Nashville.

The prison holds 100 youths—"children, really," says the guard—most of them teenage boys. "They may be young, but they understand what's going on," he adds. One day, as a 14-year-old boy was being released after serving his sentence, the guard offered him some friendly advice.

"Stay out of trouble," he said. "I don't want to see you back here."

"Why not?" the kid responded. "That's how you make your money."

POSTSCRIPT

Do Private Prisons Pay?

There are many concerns about private prisons that are not addressed in the selections by Moore and Bates. One issue that is repeatedly noted by those who write in this area concerns legality; that is, can the "state" incarcerate its inmates in a private facility? Consider the difficulties with the "rent-a-cell" business. Has a prisoner broken the law by escaping from a private prison? Can a corrections officer use "deadly force" to control prison riots? Is it "cruel and unusual punishment" to force a prisoner to serve her or his time 1,500 miles away from friends and family? Are correctional officers adequately trained in private facilities? Who is responsible for regulating private prisons? Will private prison corporations make their records open to the public?

The answers to these and other questions are found in the growing body of literature on the development of the private prison system. One source of information is the Prison Privatization Research Site at http://www.ucc.uconn.edu/~Logan/. This Internet site addresses many of these questions by looking at the more than 100,000 prison beds in the nearly 200 private corrections facilities currently under contract or under construction in the United States, the United Kingdom, and Australia as of the end of 1997. For views that agree with Moore's enthusiastic support of private prisons, see the Texas Public Policy Foundation's *Bexar County Opportunity Analysis,* which can be found online at http://www.tppf.org/bexar/bexartoc.htm. On the other side, see Phil Smith's critique of private prisons entitled "Private Prisons: Profits of Crime," *Covert Action Quarterly* (Fall 1993). You can find this on the Internet at http://www.mediafilter.org/MFF/prison.html.

There are many other good sources of information. For example, in "The Prison-Industrial Complex," *The Atlantic Monthly* (December 1998), Eric Schlosser likens the developments in the corrections industry to the development of President Dwight Eisenhower's military-industrial complex. Schlosser suggests that the "confluence of special interests" has given America a "prison-industrial complex." Or you might wish to go directly to the U.S. Department of Justice and look for their Bureau of Justice Statistics, which can be found at http://www.ojp.usdoj.gov/bjs/. Finally, for a good annotated bibliography, see the Web site Cashing in on Criminality, at http://speech.csun.edu/ben/news/karyl.html.

On the Internet . . .

Financial Reports and the Financial Condition of the Federal Government
Available at this site is a daily Treasury statement, information on the federal budget from the Office of Management and Budget, a collection of statistics on social and economic conditions in the United States, and much more. *http://www.fms.treas.gov/conditn.html*

Joint Economic Committee
Start here to explore the work and opinions of the members of the Joint Economic Committee on many topics— tax reform and government spending, the economic situation in Japan, and who is benefiting from economic growth, to name just a few.
http://www.senate.gov/~jec/jechmpgt.html

The Public Debt Online
Here you will find links to the public debt of the United States "to the penny," historical debt, interest expense and the public debt, and frequently asked questions about the public debt.
http://www.publicdebt.treas.gov/opd/opd.htm

U.S. Macroeconomic and Regional Data
Hosted by the State University of New York, Oswego, Department of Economics, this site contains the full text of recent economic reports to the president and links to various global and regional economic indicators.
http://www.oswego.edu/~economic/mac-data.htm

U.S. Treasury Department
In addition to information about the U.S. Treasury Department itself, this site features the latest news and speeches from the Treasury Department, a calendar of important events in the department's history, and a public engagement schedule to find out where and when Treasury Department officials will speak.
http://www.ustreas.gov

PART 2

Macroeconomic Issues

Government policy and economics are tightly intertwined. Fiscal policy and monetary policy have dramatic input on the economy as a whole, and the state of the economy can often determine policy actions. Decisions regarding tax cuts, the minimum wage, and welfare reform must be made in the context of broad macroeconomic goals, and the debates on these issues are more than theoretical discussions. Each has a significant impact on our lives.

■ Is Deflation Coming?

■ Is the Current U.S. Social Security Program Securely Anchored?

■ Does the Consumer Price Index Suffer from Quality and New Product Bias?

■ Should Federal Government Budget Surpluses Be Used to Reduce Taxes?

■ Is It Time to Abolish the Minimum Wage?

■ Has Wisconsin Ended Welfare As We Know It?

ISSUE 8

Is Deflation Coming?

YES: Charles W. McMillion, from "Meltdown in the Making," *The New Republic* (November 2, 1998)

NO: Martin Feldstein and Kathleen Feldstein, from "Don't Panic," *The New Republic* (November 2, 1998)

ISSUE SUMMARY

YES: Charles W. McMillion, president of MBG Information Services, asserts that a sharp decline in consumer spending is very possible and that this will intensify the deflationary pressures that already exist in the U.S. economy.

NO: Professor of economics Martin Feldstein and Kathleen Feldstein, president of Economic Studies, Inc., argue that deflation is unlikely because the forces that have put downward pressure on prices have abated, and any future declines in aggregate demand will be quickly countered by expansionary monetary and fiscal policy.

Aggregate price stability is an economic goal for almost every nation. Aggregate price stability is defined as the situation where the average level of prices, usually measured by a price index—such as the Consumer Price Index (CPI)—remains constant. It is important to note that aggregate price stability does not mean that all prices are constant. This kind of price stability is simply inconsistent with the notion of a healthy and dynamic market economy. In such an economy there should be increases in the prices of goods for which demand is increasing and decreases in the prices of goods for which demand is decreasing. When the price increases of certain goods and services are averaged against price decreases for other goods and services, then the aggregate price level should be constant.

There are two kinds of price instability. *Inflation* represents the case where the average level of prices is increasing, while *deflation* is the term used for the situation where the average level of prices is decreasing. Generally speaking, inflation has been the more frequent type of aggregate price instability encountered by economies. In every year since 1955, for example, the United States has experienced some inflation. In some years inflation was quite modest; for example, in 1955 the rate of inflation (the percentage increase in the CPI) was less than 1 percent. In other years inflation was much stronger, reaching double-digit levels in 1974 and 1979.

With inflation identified as the much more frequent version of price instability, it is not surprising that there is a great deal of literature that examines the causes of inflation, the consequences of inflation, and the actions that might be taken to prevent or eliminate inflation. Economists have designed a number of models to explain why the average level of prices might be increasing. Economists have also advocated various types of policies to combat inflation.

After more than 40 years of concern about inflation, a series of events, both in the United States and abroad, raised the possibility that the U.S. economy might be exposed to the other type of price instability—deflation. One of these events was a pattern of disinflation in the United States. *Disinflation* is defined as a pattern of decline in the rate of inflation. The data indicate that the United States has entered a period of disinflation: the average rate of price increase, again measured as the percentage change in the CPI, fell from 3.3 percent in 1996, to 1.7 percent in 1997, and to 1.6 percent in 1998. A simple extrapolation of this pattern suggests that the United States might be heading for a period of decreasing average prices; that is, disinflation may evolve into deflation.

A second event was not really a single event but rather a combination of international considerations. For example, the Japanese economy was in a period of recession; the advanced economies of Western Europe were experiencing periods of high unemployment; a number of economies in the Far East, including Thailand, Indonesia, and Korea, suffered significant financial and economic problems; the Russian economy edged closer to economic collapse; and there were concerns about future prospects for the Brazilian economy. In the context of today's global economy, events in one part of the world affect other parts of the world. As a consequence, there was little doubt that these international considerations would impact the U.S. economy. Most observers agree that these international events are likely to have deflationary consequences for the U.S. economy.

To most economists a period of deflation is a problem in and of itself because it generates redistributions of income and wealth, which interfere with the efficient and equitable operation of the economy. But beyond this, the interference with the efficient and equitable operation of the economy is likely to be associated with a decline in production and an increase in unemployment. This is best illustrated by an examination of the data for the last year in which the United States experienced deflation. That year was 1954, with the CPI falling by a bit less than 1 percent. During this mild and brief episode of deflation, the production of goods and services (real Gross Domestic Product) fell by approximately 1 percent, while the number of unemployed persons increased from 1.8 million to just over 3.5 million.

So, is deflation likely for the U.S. economy? In the following selections, Charles W. McMillion contends that a set of circumstances are in place that will push the economy over the brink into a period of declining prices, falling output, and rising unemployment. Martin Feldstein and Kathleen Feldstein maintain that although the United States faces some economic problems, conditions are such that deflation is unlikely.

YES

Charles W. McMillion

MELTDOWN IN THE MAKING

Effects have begun to spread quickly from what is already the worst global debt crisis in more than 50 years. Many of the once most bullish stock markets in the world are down 60 to 80 percent. Nearly 40 percent of the world's economy is in a recession or depression, and one-third of the world's labor force is either unemployed or severely underemployed. A worldwide recession suddenly seems possible. How hard could it hit the United States?

As Federal Reserve Chairman Alan Greenspan noted on October 7, [1998], this crisis poses a set of risks to the U.S. economy unlike anything that we have seen since the 1930s. Deflation, a decline in the general level of prices, is one of those unfamiliar perils now facing Japan, China, and others in Asia. It has not occurred in the United States since 1933, but it could happen again soon.

If inflation is the result of too many dollars chasing too few goods, deflation can be seen as the result of too few buyers chasing too many goods and services. Recent years have seen great price cuts in the United States, from $1,000 computers to 90-cents-a-gallon gas. The losers in this competition were generally ignored in a growing economy with a booming stock market.

All this could change quickly if deflationary pressures spread. Just as a virtuous cycle of growth and prosperity feeds on itself, a deflationary cycle can intensify a decline and be difficult to stop. The best way to assure that it does not occur in the United States, or, if it does, that it is short and mild, is to recognize the risks and act forcefully now.

However, many still dismiss the risks. Only [recently], Greenspan himself was repeating his habitual warning that accelerating inflation was still the greatest danger. The orthodox argument has been that unemployment is well below the levels at which inflation previously accelerated and that job growth remains strong. Real wages have been inching ahead faster than the anemic growth of productivity. Surely, increased costs would soon be passed along to consumers, and, despite all the previous false warnings, inflation is just around the corner.

This view was widely held until the effects of Asia's collapse on lenders' soaring risk premiums forced Russia to default and Wall Street to rescue the too-big-to-fail hedge fund Long-Term Capital Management. U.S. credit standards, which had been criticized as too lax, suddenly gave way to a credit crunch.

The Fed changed course and responded at the end of September, but with a grossly inadequate interest rate cut of only 0.25 percent. With the federal funds rate still at 5.25 percent and a federal budget surplus, it is certainly possible to stimulate the economy through further interest rate cuts, tax cuts, and new spending initiatives. The finance and trade ministers who gathered in Washington last week for the annual IMF [International Monetary Fund] and World Bank meetings also seemed ready to respond to bold U.S. leadership.

But none was evident. While concern is spreading rapidly over the effects of the world crisis, years of constant triumphalism about our "Goldilocks" economy have created dangerous complacency about the extent of U.S. vulnerabilities and our capacity to serve as a market for the world's excess production.

One reason this complacency is so unfounded is that U.S. consumer spending—which currently accounts for more than 60 percent of the U.S. economy—is already running at very high levels. Since 1984, the world economy has grown faster than the U.S. economy every year —circumstances under which you might expect the United States to be running a trade surplus. Yet this year's current account deficit is expected to widen to $230 billion.

Ironically, foreign borrowing to finance these massive annual deficits has converted the United States from the world's banker to the world's largest annual borrower, with net foreign obligations of $1.3 trillion. These trade deficits and finance charges are a large and constant drag on the U.S. economy, raising interest rates and limiting policy options. If U.S. consumers buy even more foreign goods and services, will there also be enough domestic spending to drive U.S. job and income growth?

A sharp slowdown in domestic consumer spending risks spreading deflation. Even strong spending has not led to significant inflation up until now. For instance, though strong consumer spending (which grew at a real annual rate of 6.1 percent), the GDP deflator used to measure inflation of personal consumption expenditures was zero percent in the first three months of the year and rose at an annual rate of only 0.9 percent in the second quarter. The consumer price index was also virtually flat early in the year (although it bounced back to an annualized rate of about 1.6 percent during the spring and summer).

Similarly, wholesale prices have been falling for two years, and, even excluding oil, import prices are plunging. Imports of manufactured goods costing $800 billion will equal more than half the value of U.S. manufacturing.... The price to consumers of most physical goods, from cars to clothes, has been falling at an accelerating rate for at least a year with all of our inflation coming from services such as cable television, health care, and financial services.

Meanwhile, it seems quite probable that U.S. consumer spending will soon substantially slow down. U.S. households are up to their eyeballs in record levels of debt. They are saving virtually nothing. Mortgage (including home equity), credit card, auto, and other household debt has soared far beyond any previous share of disposable income. Lower mortgage rates in recent years have helped moderate the rising cost of debt service for many, but credit card rates remain exorbitant, currently averaging 15.8 percent.

At the same time, notoriously low levels of personal savings have fallen from eight to ten percent of disposable income 20 years ago, to a range of five to six percent ten years ago, to 2.1 percent last year and less than 0.3 percent in recent months. As skyrocketing bankruptcy figures already show, such highly indebted consumers are unusually vulnerable to job or income loss.

Households have also shifted an unprecedented share of their savings out of their homes and insured savings accounts into the stock market, where irrational exuberance may have created strong but false expectations. This is particularly the case now, as overall corporate profits have fallen in 1998 after enjoying strong growth for most of the decade.

The positive effects of growth and a booming stock market encouraged consumers to spend down their savings over the past five years. It is now likely that, without prompt and strong policy steps, rising uncertainties could lead to a sharp decline in spending with very unhappy consequences, thereby spreading perilous deflationary pressures more broadly through the economy.

NO

Martin Feldstein and Kathleen Feldstein

DON'T PANIC

For more than a year now, we've been hearing dire warnings about deflation, coupled with calls for the Federal Reserve to cut interest rates sharply to prevent such a fall in prices. The stock market's decline has no doubt contributed to the public's fear of deflation. Ironically, the Federal Reserve's recent small interest-rate cut may also have added to these worries. And Japanese Finance Minister Kiichi Miyazawa recently declared that the deflationary spiral is worldwide.

We see things differently. There is at present no deflation either in the United States or in the world economy as a whole. And, looking to the future, the likelihood of deflation remains remote, even if there is a recession in the next year. There have been seven U.S. recessions in the past 40 years, and prices have continued to rise in every one of them. If we had to bet, we'd say that the U.S. rate of inflation a few years from now will be higher, not lower, than it is today.

Deflation is the opposite of inflation and shouldn't be confused with "disinflation." An economy experiences deflation when the *overall* price level falls. That's different from "disinflation," which means a decline in the *rate* of inflation. The United States has benefited from disinflation since the early '80s with inflation declining from more than ten percent then to about four percent in the early '90s and about two percent in recent years. But this nevertheless remained a time of inflation, not deflation.

Changes in the level of the stock market are also distinct from changes in the prices of things we buy and use. So the recent fall in share prices doesn't signify or predict deflation any more than the tenfold rise in share prices since the early '80s constituted inflation.

Now to the data. The consumer price index increased by 1.6 percent in the twelve months leading up to August [1998] and by 2.2 percent in the three months [since]. That's a low rate of inflation, but it is not deflation. Even with an adjustment for the statistical problems that cause the price index to overstate the true rise in the cost of living, the rate of inflation remains positive.

As for the rest of the world, Japan is alone among the industrial countries in experiencing actual deflation, with consumer prices there falling 0.3 percent over the past year and at a rate of 2.2 percent in the past three months. In Europe, inflation is low but positive. Among the emerging markets, China is the outlier with consumer prices down 1.4 percent over the past year. But China's price decline reflects the restructuring of state industries, and China remains very different from the market economies in the rest of the world. Although the "crisis" economies of Southeast Asia are in recession, they are still experiencing substantial rates of inflation, ranging from 5.6 percent in Malaysia to 81 percent in Indonesia. Latin American inflation rates vary widely from Argentina's 1.1 percent to more than 30 percent in Venezuela. This is not global deflation!

So what accounts for the perception of deflation? The most obvious reason is that *some* prices *are* falling. Energy costs are the most obvious, with the prices of gasoline and other fuels down about ten percent in the past year in response to the decline in the world price of oil. Americans are also paying about one percent less for apparel than they did a few years ago. Many manufacturers are very vocal about the fact that the prices that they receive at the wholesale level are actually down significantly. But even these wholesale price declines do not translate into lower consumer prices because of the rising costs of transportation and marketing.

The price of services in general—including such things as restaurant meals, transportation, and personal ser-vices like haircuts—rise faster than the prices of manufactured goods. That persistent difference reflects the fact that most service prices do not benefit from the kind of technical change that helps to lower the prices of manufactured goods. A haircut still takes as many barber minutes as it did a decade or two ago, while the employee time needed to make a car declines every year.

Looking ahead, several indicators lead us to think that inflation over the next few years is more likely to rise than to decline or to turn into deflation. Normally, the acceleration in wage and salary increases that has occurred over the past few years would have translated into higher consumer prices already. But the fall in world oil prices and the rising value of the dollar relative to other currencies have depressed import prices and put downward pressure on domestic prices. The restructuring of health care has reduced health insurance costs, an important part of total employee compensation. Finally, unusually rapid productivity gains have kept unit labor costs from rising in line with wage inflation.

These anti-inflationary forces are coming to an end. The dollar's rise has been reversed with sharp falls relative to the yen and the European currencies. There are signs world oil prices will rise over the next year. Health care costs appear to be rising more rapidly again. And the higher productivity growth rate that has kept unit labor costs down is probably reverting to its earlier low level.

The expected slowdown in economic activity in 1999 will help restrain the rate of price increases, but the most likely market pressures will still be for inflation to be higher a year from now than the 1.6 percent inflation rate of the past year. Even if a credit crunch or some external surprise to the economy does lead to a recession, we would continue to see positive inflation. Only in the extreme case of the economy falling into a deep depression like that of the 1930s with an unemployment rate above ten percent would the level of prices actually begin a sustained decline. But there is no reason to believe that such a depression is coming. And, at the first sign of a major credit crunch or outside shock, the Federal Reserve would take the further steps necessary to raise total demand.

Deflation, like inflation, does not just happen. The behavior of prices reflects the monetary policies of the Federal Reserve. Inflation rose from about two percent in the 1960s to more than ten percent in the early '80s because the Federal Reserve was then unwilling to raise interest rates enough to halt the inflationary spiral. Only when inflation got bad enough in the early '80s did the Fed bite the bullet and accept the costs, in terms of high unemployment, of reversing several decades of inappropriate policies.

By comparison, fighting deflation would be much easier. Cutting interest rates stimulates economic growth, raises employment, and, by lowering the relative value of the dollar, makes American products more competitive internationally. If deflation ever becomes a serious threat, we have little doubt that the Fed would act decisively. And, if Fed policy alone were not enough, the administration and Congress would willingly join in the tax cuts needed to stimulate demand.

Japanese efforts to reverse deflation have failed because the government there has been unwilling to deal directly with the banking crisis and to cut taxes to stimulate consumer demand. Experience shows that America wouldn't make those mistakes.

There are many economic problems to worry about today and for the future. But deflation is not one of them.

POSTSCRIPT

Is Deflation Coming?

McMillion begins his argument with some international considerations. He mentions a global debt crisis, declines in foreign stock markets, recession in 40 percent of the world's economy, and unemployment and underemployment of one-third of the world's labor force. He thinks that a worldwide recession is possible, with deflationary consequences for the United States. Many in the United States are ignoring the possibility of deflation—they seem complacent about the risks of deflation. But there are some reasons why this complacency may be unfounded: consumer spending is already very high, even though the world economy has grown faster than the U.S. economy in every year since 1984, and the United States continues to run a huge trade deficit. McMillion notes that the prices consumers pay for the bulk of their "physical goods" have been falling and that the rate at which they are falling has accelerated. The CPI continues to show inflation instead of deflation because these prices have been more than offset by increases in the prices of the services consumers purchase. McMillion believes that consumer spending is likely to fall. He concludes that among the factors that might contribute to this decline, and ensure deflation, is a probable decline in the stock market.

The Feldsteins admit that some countries, including Japan and China, are currently experiencing deflation. But they point to several countries, including some in Southeast Asia and Latin America, that continue to experience inflation. On the basis of these data, the Feldsteins conclude that there is presently no global deflation. They then ask why, given these data, there is a perception of deflation. Their answer is that some prices are indeed falling and that much is made of these decreases. Looking to the future, they see inflation to be more likely than deflation. One reason for this outlook is that a number of deflationary forces are coming to an end—the fall in world oil prices, unusually large productivity gains, restructuring of health care, and increases in the international value of the dollar. The Feldsteins think that deflation could result only if events lead to a replay of the Great Depression. But they consider this a remote possibility because the Federal Reserve System stands ready to take corrective action in the form of expansionary monetary policy, and Congress and the president stand ready to cut taxes and engage in expansionary fiscal policy.

Additional readings related to this issue include "The Price Is Right," by George Selgin, *National Review* (March 23, 1998); "The Forces Making for an Economic Collapse," by Thomas I. Palley, *The Atlantic Monthly* (July

1996); "The Zero Inflation Economy," by Michael J. Mandel, *Business Week* (July 19, 1998); "Deflation, the Real Enemy," by Robert B. Reich, *The Financial Times* (January 15, 1998); "Is Deflation the Worry?" by George L. Perry, *Brookings Institution Policy Brief No. 41* (December 1998); and "The Deflation Debate," by Dimitri B. Papadimitriou and L. Randall Wray, *Economic Policy* (January/February 1999).

ISSUE 9

Is the Current U.S. Social Security Program Securely Anchored?

YES: Robert M. Ball, from "Social Security: Keeping the Promise," An Original Essay Written for This Volume (1997)

NO: Sylvester J. Schieber, from "Social Security: Avoiding the Downstream Catastrophe," An Original Essay Written for This Volume (1997)

ISSUE SUMMARY

YES: Robert M. Ball, former commissioner of Social Security, asserts that Social Security is in good shape financially and that the projected imbalances can be addressed through a series of minor adjustments.

NO: Sylvester J. Schieber, a business executive, sees a serious Social Security funding problem and calls for fundamental change: movement from a completely defined benefits program to a partially defined benefits program.

It is not surprising, in retrospect, that an event as catastrophic as the Great Depression of the 1930s would produce fundamental changes in the American economy. The reality of the human suffering generated by the collapse of one-third of the nation's banks, an unemployment rate of 25 percent, and 30 percent declines in the production of goods, services, and household net worth led to a rush of legislation, which, in general terms, was intended to achieve two objectives: to restore confidence in the economy and to provide greater economic security. The institutions and programs created by this legislative avalanche are today familiar to almost all Americans: the Federal Deposit Insurance Corporation (FDIC), the Securities and Exchange Commission (SEC), and Social Security.

Social Security, more formally Old Age, Survivors, and Disability Insurance (OASDI), was signed into law on August 14, 1935, by President Franklin D. Roosevelt. As originally designed, OASDI provided three types of benefits: retirement benefits for the elderly who were no longer working, survivor benefits for the spouses and children of persons who have died, and disability benefits for people who experience non-work-related illness or injury. The Medicare portion of Social Security, which provides benefits for hospital, doctor, and medical expenses, was not created until 1965.

There are many terms used to describe OASDI. It is an entitlement program; that is, everyone who satisfies the eligibility requirements receives benefits. Eligibility is established by employment and contributions to the system (in the form of payroll taxes) for a minimum period of time. It is also a defined benefits program; that is, the level of benefits is determined by legislation. The opposite of a defined benefits program is a defined contributions program where benefits are determined by contributions and whatever investment income is generated by those contributions. OASDI is also described as a pay-as-you-go system; this means that payments received by recipients are financed primarily by the contributions of current workers. Still another description of OASDI is that it is an income security program. This refers to a whole set of government programs designed to provide minimum levels of income to various people. Other income security programs include workmen's compensation, unemployment compensation, supplemental security income (SSI), and general assistance. Finally, OASDI is described as a social insurance program to distinguish it from private insurance programs. The insurance feature rests on the fact that OASDI protects against certain unforeseen events like disability or early death. The social feature arises from the fact that contributions and the level of benefits are determined by legislation as well as the fact that the contributions are mandatory (payroll taxes that must be paid).

With respect to the administration of OASDI, there are several components to consider. One component is the Social Security and Medicare Trustees. This six-member panel annually prepares estimates of the inflows and outflows of funds and examines the long-term actuarial soundness of the system. A second component is the Social Security Advisory Council, which is constituted every four years and reviews the projections of the trustees. In the process the council may offer suggestions for changes in the program. The third component involves both Congress and the president because any changes to the system, in terms of contributions and benefits, require the passage of legislation.

All this serves as background for understanding the current issue. For the last several years the trustee projections have indicated that OASDI trust funds would fall below the "safe level" by the year 2030. These predictions were widely reported by the media as the "Social Security crisis." The Advisory Council that was formed in 1994 met periodically during 1994 and 1995 to explore alternative solutions to the crisis and in early 1996 issued its own report. But the 13-member council could not agree on a single overall strategy to resolve the crisis; instead, it offered three different strategies.

In this issue two members of the Advisory Council present their views on the magnitude of the Social Security underfunding and then detail and defend their strategies for dealing with it. Robert M. Ball supports what has been called the "Maintenance of Benefits" option, which retains the basic structure of OASDI as a completely defined benefits program. Sylvester J. Schieber supports a fundamental restructuring of OASDI involving partial privatization with the creation of personal security accounts.

YES

Robert M. Ball

SOCIAL SECURITY: KEEPING THE PROMISE

For 60 years, the United States has had a deliberate policy of promoting income security in retirement through a four-tier system: (1) a nearly universal, wage-related, contributory, defined-benefit Social Security plan; (2) supplementary employer-sponsored private pensions (now covering about one-half of the workforce); (3) individual savings; and (4) underlying the whole, a means-tested safety-net program, now called Supplemental Security Income (SSI). Social Security and SSI are federally-operated and financed, and private pensions and savings are explicitly promoted by federal tax policy.

Over 30 years ago, the Medicare program was added to this four-tier system because it was recognized that while a cash income could meet regular and recurring expenses, only a health insurance system could meet the unpredictable and sometimes very heavy cost of health care in retirement and during disability. So we now have a five-tier federally-promoted system for retirement security, each tier with a distinct mission and complementing the others.

Unlike Medicare, Social Security is in quite good shape financially, and can rather easily be brought into long-range balance. It is important that this be done promptly because what is now easy will become difficult if unattended to. The recently released 1997 report of the Trustees is the third in a row to report that *without any changes of any kind in the program*, the system will be able to pay full benefits on time until about 2030, and that after that date the continuing income from the payments of employers and employees (augmented by income from the taxes on benefits) would meet three-fourths of the cost. Even with the cost of benefits rising, after 75 years these sources of income alone would still meet about two-thirds of the cost.

Social Security is not "going broke." The long-range financing challenge is how to cope with a shortfall. In designing a financing plan we aren't starting from scratch after 2030 but rather with 75 percent of benefit costs already being financed by the tax rates in current law.

Another point about Social Security financing that is greatly misunderstood concerns the ratio of workers (those paying in) to the number of beneficiaries (those taking out). This ratio is dropping, and the change accounts for the increasing cost of Social Security in future years as the baby-boom generation retires. However, this ratio has always been recognized as the most important factor in the program's long-range costs and has been addressed in all the long-range estimates and provisions for financing. There are no surprises here. Yet commentators routinely treat the changing ratio as though we had suddenly discovered a situation that will make it overwhelmingly difficult to meet rising costs as the baby-boomers retire.

This is not the case. The current anticipated deficit has to do entirely with other factors. Half the new deficit is the result of a change in actuarial methods and in new sources of data, and half in changes in assumptions about the future growth of real wages, disability incidence, and other cost-controlling factors. (And it is entirely possible, of course, that similar adjustments resulting in either higher or lower cost estimates will need to be incorporated in future forecasts made over a 75-year period.)

STRATEGIES TO STRENGTHEN SOCIAL SECURITY

A deficit of 2.23 percent of payroll could be eliminated by simply raising contribution rates 1.12 percentage points for workers and employers alike. It is doubtful, however, that such a big increase in taxes would be generally accepted as the best way of meeting the shortfall, and it is not necessary. There are other ways. Yet it is to be noted that the two groups of Advisory Council members advocating partial privatization of Social Security call for very large tax increases—deductions of an additional 1.6 percent from earnings

in one case and an increase of 1.52 percent in the combined payroll tax in the other case. As a matter of fact, if tax increases of this size were adopted, there would be no need for benefit cuts and certainly no financial reason for basic changes in Social Security, such as partial privatization. These tax increases alone would bring Social Security very close to the long-range balance; the remaining gap would be 0.6 percent of payroll in one plan and only slightly more in the other. If coupled with a correction of about −0.2 percent in the Consumer Price Index, which governs Social Security's cost-of-living adjustments—a correction very likely to be made as the result of the current reevaluation of the CPI by the Bureau of Labor Statistics—these tax increases would bring Social Security well within the definition of close actuarial balance as traditionally defined, i.e., with estimated benefit expenditures falling within 5 percent of estimated income. No other changes in benefits or taxes would be needed.

But instead of relying on big tax increases, there are several more attractive alternatives. The most important change would be to shift from pay-as-you-go financing to partial reserve financing so that part of the increasing costs in the future can be met from earnings on a fund build-up. The recent Advisory Council was unanimous on the desirability of this shift. And once partial reserve financing is adopted, the rate of return in the funds' investments becomes important.

In Social Security, the government is the administrator and fund manager of an enormous pension and group insurance plan. It collects dedicated taxes which are the equivalent of the premiums in a private insurance plan and the payments into the defined benefits plan of a private corporation or state retirement system. And it administers benefits which, like the dedicated tax contributions, are spelled out in detail in the law. There are, of course, important differences between Social Security's defined-benefit plan and the defined-benefit plans managed by the private sector and the states, but the broad characteristics are similar.

The administration of Social Security is very efficiently handled, costing less than one percent of income. But the government is not doing as well as it might in its role as fund manager. This is not because of any failure on the part of those managing the system but because Social Security by law is allowed to invest only in the most conservative of all investments: long-term, low-yield government bonds. Trustees of private pension systems and managers of state pension systems who have the authority to invest much more broadly would surely be replaced if they were to pursue such an ultraconservative investment policy.

To deny Social Security managers the same investment opportunities available to private fund managers means that Social Security will pay smaller benefits than private pensions can pay for each dollar of contribution (except to the extent that Social Security's low administrative costs offset the smaller investment gain). This differential, caused by prohibiting investments in private securities, accounts for much of the pressure to switch to a system of private savings plans as a partial substitute for Social Security. It leads to the cry, "Give me the money—I can do better on my own."

Yet increasing the investment return on Social Security contributions cannot be the whole answer to balancing Social Security nor is it a necessary part of the answer. The attached table shows a series of changes which together with an increase in the investment return would bring the program into long-range balance. The items in the chart alone eliminate about two-thirds of the long-range deficit and postpone the date of Trust Fund exhaustion from 2030 to 2050. Investing 40 percent of the fund build-up in stocks would do the rest.

If for whatever reason it were decided to keep all Trust Fund investments in government bonds, balance over the 75-year estimating period could still be maintained by implementing additional moderate tax increases or benefit cuts now or providing for gradual benefit cuts in the future by scheduling increases in the normal retirement age beyond the age 67 provided in present law.

Proposals to substitute a compulsory savings plan for part of Social Security seem undesirable for a variety of reasons and certainly unnecessary. But before looking more closely at the issues raised by privatization, it is important to put the debate in context by examining the nature of the Social Security system—both in law and by tradition.

SOCIAL SECURITY AS AN ENTITLEMENT

Social Security is an "entitlement" program. In spite of the fact that entitlements on the whole have recently been given a bad name, the concept is of great importance to the future economic security of those covered by Social Security. The term deserves to be rehabilitated. In the case of Social Security, "entitlement" means that all people without distinction of sex, race, income, or behavior receive benefits in an amount specified by law once they have met the objective criteria of having worked in employment cov-

STRENGTHENING SOCIAL SECURITY:
RECOMMENDED STEPS FOR CONSIDERATION[1]

- **Starting point:** Over the long run (75 years), Social Security revenues are expected to fall short of outlays by . . . 2.23% of payroll.[2]
- **Goals:** Preserve long-term balance without making major changes in the program, and improve the benefit-contribution ration for younger workers.
- **Initial Steps:**

Proposed Change	Rationale for Change	Impact on Deficit
1. Increase taxation of benefits	Benefits should be taxed to the extent they exceed what the worker paid in, as is done with other contributory defined-benefit pension plans.	− 0.31
2. Change Cost of Living Adjustment (COLA) to reflect corrections to Consumer Price Index (CPI)	COLA is determined by CPI, which is widely believed to overstate inflation; anticipated corrections should result in downward adjustment of at least 0.2%.	− 0.20
3. Extend Social Security coverage to all newly hired state and local employees	Most state and local employees are already covered; the 3.7 million who are not are the last major group in labor force not covered.	− 0.22
4. Change wage-averaging period for benefits-computation purposes from 35 to 38 years.	Reduces benefits for future retirees an average of 3%.	− 0.28
5. Increase contribution rate 0.50% (0.25% for workers and employers alike)	Future workers as well as current and future beneficiaries should share modestly in correction of imbalance.	− 0.50

(Box continued on next page)

ered by the program for a specified period of time and have met other objective qualifications—by reaching age 62 for reduced retirement benefits, or by reaching age 65 for full benefits, or by having a total disability estimated to last for a long and indefinite period, or by having a relationship with a covered worker that gives them entitlement to benefits as a widow or widower, or by being the child of an insured worker.

In the case of Social Security and Medicare, as distinct from certain other entitlement programs such as food stamps, there is not only a *legal* entitlement, but since the benefits grow out of past earnings and contributions, they are looked on as an *earned* entitlement. Thus, although benefits and conditions for payment can be changed by law if the changes affect a broad category of participants in ways that are reasonable and

- **Long-term deficit remaining** after implementation of above changes... 0.75% of payroll.[3]
- **Conventional options** to eliminate this remaining deficit include: additional moderate tax increases or benefit cuts now or providing for gradual benefit cuts in the future by scheduling increases in the normal retirement age beyond the age 67 provided in present law. But all of these changes have the disadvantage of making Social Security less attractive to younger workers (by lowering the ratio of benefits to contributions),which strengthens the case for—
- **Investing some of Social Security's accumulating funds in equities:** Under present law, funds may be invested only in low-yield government bonds. Passively investing 40% of these funds in stocks indexed to the broad market would yield higher returns, closing the deficit and improving the benefit/contribution ratio for younger workers.[4]

[1]By Robert M. Ball, commissioner of Social Security 1962–73 and member of the Social Security Advisory Council 1994–96. [2]1997 estimate by the Social Security trustees, expressed as a percent of total covered payrolls: in other words, if Social Security payroll-tax rates had been increased by 2.23 percentage points in 1997, the long-term deficit would be eliminated. [3]Adjusted for interaction of proposed changes. [4]To help maintain the program in balance even beyond the traditional 75-year estimating period, a contribution-rate increase of 1.6% should be scheduled to go into effect in 2045, with the understanding that at that time, depending on actual experience, the increase may not be needed.

nondiscriminatory, there is a considerable reluctance on the part of Congress or the President to reduce protection or make radical changes. There is good reason for this. Social Security commitments are very long-term. People are contributing now to pay for benefits that may not be due for more than 40 years in the future, and a high degree of stability in both contribution rates and benefit levels is a valued part of the Social Security tradition—so much so that discussions of possible benefit reductions or other major changes make participants very uneasy.

The opposite of an entitlement is a discretionary payment, which if applied to Social Security could mean—as it does in some programs—that benefit levels would be determined not by long-term considerations but by short-term budget cycles, in which various programs compete against each other for funding. It could even mean—as once was the case in welfare programs and may soon be again in some states (now that basic welfare policy has been turned back to the states) —that payments could vary according to the policies of individual administrators seeking to encourage or discourage certain behavior. Social insurance is designed to get away from all that, and the fundamental principle that determines the character of the program is that it is an *earned entitlement*. There would be little security in a Social Security system if benefits were to be altered every few years to adjust to short-term budget considerations. To make Social Security work, it has to be backed by long-term commitments —an entitlement, but an entitlement in return for work and contribution, not an entitlement granted simply by legislative fiat.

It is important also to the concept of Social Security that it have its own financing through earmarked contributions by participants. Thus, over the years, the test of adequate financing for Social Security has not been short-run, as with other programs, but rather whether the best estimates, projected across a very long period—75 years—show an approximate balance between earmarked income and benefits as specified in law.

WHAT PARTIAL PRIVATIZATION MEANS

Proponents of partial privatization on the 1994–1996 Advisory Council on Social Security would significantly reduce the guarantee of an entitlement by, in one case, limiting benefits to what could be supported by present tax rates and, in the other proposal, by substituting a low, flat benefit. The first approach would require, over time, an average cut of 30 percent in the guaranteed benefit, and the second would cut the guaranteed benefit even more on average. Both plans call for substituting, for a part of the entitlement, a compulsory savings plan that would guarantee only that the worker be given an amount taken from his or her wages to invest, as with a 401(k) plan, for future income in retirement. So there would be two major changes: the Social Security en-

titlement would be cut back and, instead of being entitled to a full defined *benefit*, contributors would make defined *contributions* to various investment vehicles, with future income dependent in part on the success or failure of individual investment strategies. Under one plan, individual investments would be limited to a number of government-operated plans; under the other, investors could channel their deductions from wages to virtually any generally available investment account or broker.

The argument over privatization divides into two parts. First, why not invest part of the Social Security fund directly in private stocks? This increases the return on contributions and thus substantially improves the benefit/contribution ratio for younger workers as well as helping with the long-range balance. The main fear expressed by some is that if Social Security invests in stocks, Congress would force Social Security to make politically motivated investments. The fear is that instead of following a neutral policy of passive investment in indexed funds, Congress would steer investments toward or away from particular stocks according to some political agenda and would interfere in other ways with the best interest of the participants and with the operations of individual companies or industries.

Based on experience to date, this fear is entirely unwarranted. Managers of the Thrift Savings Plan (TSP), a major retirement plan for federal employees, and of the defined benefit plans of the Federal Reserve System and the Tennessee Valley Authority, all of which have been investing in private securities for many years, have remained entirely independent in their fund management. However, to provide additional safeguards, it would be possible to create an organization, modeled on the Board of Governors of the Federal Reserve System, to have broad responsibility for Social Security Trust Fund investments. The board would consist of experts confirmed by Congress and appointed for lengthy, staggered terms. By law the board would be required to pursue a policy of investment neutrality, a policy buttressed by being required to invest in broadly indexed funds and to select private portfolio managers experienced in handling large indexed accounts. While under our political system there can obviously be no absolutely iron-clad guarantees against attempts at political manipulation, the record of the Board of Governors of the Federal Reserve makes clear that this approach can insulate decision-makers and protect the principle of independence in policy-making.

Second, what, if anything, is wrong with shifting part of Social Security protection over to personal savings-and-investment accounts? There are several problems.

Individual Accounts

First let us consider the plan of one group within the Advisory Council called "Individual Accounts" (IA). This plan, it should be noted, would modify the present program less than just about any of the other proposals for privatization that have been discussed both within and outside of the Advisory Council, but it still seems entirely unsatisfactory.

In discussing the IA plan, it is important to bear in mind that, as previously noted, the plan requires an additional deduction from workers' earnings of 1.6 percent. I am inclined to think that this alone might well be enough to make the proposal unacceptable to the public,

since no corresponding increase in Social Security protection is proposed. The whole objective of the IA plan is to reduce the benefits covered by the government guarantee to a level where over the long run they can be financed by present Social Security contribution rates, while hoping that the new Individual Accounts will, on average, make up for the cuts in the guaranteed Social Security plan. Since the objective is only to make up for the cuts *on average*, it may be assumed that for many people, in spite of the increase in deductions from their earnings, the combined benefits of the residual government plan and the savings benefits will actually be substantially lower than those of the government plan under present law. This does not seem to be a very attractive proposition: higher deductions from workers' earnings than under present law, but a considerable risk that one might be in the group that will get less in benefits than the present government guarantee.

To be fair, in making comparisons with today's guarantees it needs to be recognized that the present level of benefits is not adequately funded for the long run. So people will need to choose—to decide whether a menu of modest proposals to bring the present program into balance is as onerous as having earnings reduced an additional 1.6 percent coupled with lower benefits for those who get a less-than-average return from their individual account and in all cases lose guaranteed defined benefit protection.

Under the IA plan, individual savers would have a limited choice of investment vehicles, perhaps five to ten indexed funds, managed and invested by the federal government as in the case of the Thrift Savings Plan. At retirement age, the retiree would be required to take out a lifetime annuity underwritten by the government with a guaranteed period of payment and with protection against inflation by price indexing. The annuitant also would be required to take out a joint and survivors annuity to protect the annuitant's spouse—unless, as is the case under the Employee Retirement Income Security Act (ERISA) requirement for private pension plans, the spouse agrees in writing to waive this right. It should be noted that with the government directly handling the investment of the funds in the savings accounts, this plan does not do much for the financial industry. The Advisory Council assumed that the cost of financial management would be low—only 10 basis points.

Perhaps the worst thing about this plan is that it increases the risk that retirement income will be inadequate. The IA plan shifts Social Security away from a defined-*benefit* plan toward a defined-*contribution* plan. This is a bad idea. By definition, defined-contribution plans contain no guarantees regarding the amount of the benefit. With more and more private-sector employers offering only defined-contribution 401(k) pension plans, it is all the more important that the nation's *basic* plan be maintained as a defined-benefit plan with amounts available in retirement determined by law rather than by the risks and uncertainties of individual investment.

The increased risk arises, of course, not solely from the general risk of picking investments that perform badly but also from the fact that individuals are inevitably exposed to the risk of being forced to begin or end an investment period at a bad time. Workers are required to start making the investments when they go to work and end them when they re-

tire and convert the accumulation to an annuity. But they have no control over conditions in the stock market at these times.

Moreover, although the intent of the IA plan is to create a nationwide system of individual retirement accounts, with both the principal and the income available only in retirement, it is very doubtful that this objective could be preserved in practice. As with today's IRAs and 401(k) plans, people will want to use individual savings accounts for medical, educational, housing, or other needs. With funds going into *individually-named* accounts, as provided for under the IA plan, account holders will assuredly find it unreasonable to be denied access to their "personal" funds in an emergency situation—or indeed for any purpose that seems worthwhile—and Congress and the Executive Branch can be expected to go along, as is already happening with IRAs and 401(k)s. As a result, the amounts that would actually be available at retirement under the IA plan would almost certainly be much lower than predicted by the plan's proponents.

Looking at the two parts of the plan together—the part guaranteed by the government plus the individual savings part—the IA plan would achieve a better return on total investment than the current Social Security system, assuming pay-as-you-go increases in the contribution rates to make up for the shortfall under present law. However, the residual Social Security part of the IA plan, looked at separately, would not do at all well on this test—a fact that could lead to the unraveling of the whole plan.

As the plan developed over time, with beneficiaries doing less and less well under the reduced Social Security plan compared to individual accounts (at least in the case of the more successful investors), there would be every reason for many above-average earners to press for further reductions in contributions to Social Security in order to be able to shift more of their Social Security contributions to their individual accounts. Thus the IA plan is inherently unstable, and would probably lead to further cutbacks in government-guaranteed benefit levels.

This approach to retirement security raises another troubling issue. How far should we go in compelling people to save for retirement? It is not doing average and below-average earners any favors to make them save more for the sole purpose of trying to increase their income in retirement. Millions of workers are living from paycheck to paycheck, spending whatever they have on food, clothing, shelter, schooling and other immediate needs—and still falling short of an adequate standard of living. And for many workers, protecting against the unforeseeable cost of health care may be a higher priority than setting aside more income for retirement. Yet the IA plan's sponsors take no note of these needs.

Partial-privatization proponents simply accept, as a given, that more should be deducted from workers' wages now to improve their cash income in retirement. But many workers, if asked, might prefer to earmark any deductions from earnings beyond those needed to support the present level of Social Security either for current health insurance or for Medicare in their retirement. After all, Medicare is just as important as cash benefits to the financial security of retirees and the disabled, and the Medicare Hospital Insurance (HI) fund faces problems in the near term. To ignore Medicare's immediate needs in order to finance a long-term re-

design of Social Security strikes me as a serious inversion of priorities.

If Congress is willing to support a payroll tax increase of 1.6 percent (which is doubtful), directing it to Medicare would be sufficient to postpone the HI's fund exhaustion by about 15 years, thus providing a substantial planning period in which to design and implement needed structural changes. When combined with these changes, a tax rate increase of a small fraction of 1.6 percent is enough to support the present level of Social Security benefits. The IA plan puts the whole burden of maintaining the present benefit level on deductions from worker wages.

Personal Security Accounts
The other plan proposed by some members of the Advisory Council to privatize a part of Social Security—the "Personal Security Accounts" (PSA) plan—would, over time, completely abolish the present Social Security system and substitute a flat benefit payment varying only by the length of time under the system—with full coverage, one would have a guaranteed benefit of $410 a month, increased over time to keep up with rising wages—augmented by 5 percent of earnings invested by the individual in any generally available investment vehicle.

The combined payroll tax on employers and employees would be increased 1.52 percent, with the increase maintained over the next 70 years or so to meet the cost of paying benefits to current retirees and others with a stake in the present system while at the same time funding a new compulsory savings plan for those under age 55. This 1.52 percent of payroll is the so-called "transition" cost of switching from a pay-as-you-go system (Social Security today) to a funded savings plan. It is a very long and very costly "transition." For many years —across the span of two generations— workers must pay twice: once for their own protection and once for the protection of those already retired and older workers with an investment under the old system.

In addition, to make the financing of the plan work, it is necessary to borrow very large amounts from the federal government—as much as $2 trillion in 1997 dollars at the peak, $15 trillion in nominal dollars. Borrowing on this scale is required because, although the payroll tax increase of 1.52 percent meets the *average* transition cost over some 70 years, the cost is above average at first—for about 30 years, in fact. Then, with the cost gradually declining after 30 years, it becomes possible to gradually repay the loan out of the tax increase.

This larger privatization scheme has all the disadvantages of the IA plan —plus many more. In the first place, it is doubtful whether such a plan could be administered. The government would need to see that 5 percent of workers' earnings were deducted each payday and sent to any of thousands of financial institutions or brokers and kept invested until retirement, while at the same time allowing workers to shift from one investment arrangement to another and adding new funds each payday to the same or a different account. It is difficult to see how this would work with smaller employers and an unlimited number of investment opportunities. And administration also entails trying to make clear to people what their individual benefits would be: how benefits are computed under the old plan, how the transitional benefits work, and how this new hybrid system's

benefits all fit together. Each part of the plan is complicated within itself and when combined with the others creates a situation that defies explanation. The total job of administration would be chaotic, expensive, and quite likely unmanageable at any price. (It should be noted, however, that no allowance has been made for administration in the estimated cost of this plan except for an allowance of 100 basis points for the cost of investing.)

There are other problems. The PSA plan does not provide for inflation protection or annuitization. (Individuals desiring annuities would have to buy them in the private market, which necessarily has to charge an extra premium to protect against the fact that those who buy annuities ordinarily have longer than average life expectancies.) Moreover, the plan does not require protection for a spouse. And, although survivors and disability protection are continued as part of the government guaranteed plan, over time the disability benefits would be cut about 30 percent below present law.

Finally, a government system supported by a wage tax but with a benefit unrelated to wages will clearly be a bad deal for above-average earners, who are therefore likely to give the government part of the PSA plan little support. Thus this whole plan could easily end up as simply a compulsory individual savings plan—without the present program's ability to redistribute income from the higher-paid to the lower-paid— supplemented by a government safety-net program testing individual need (as in the case of SSI). This would represent a major loss of security for many workers, particularly those with lower-than-average lifetime earnings. For society as a whole, that loss of security would mean greater reliance on welfare programs, with all their flaws, difficulty of administration, and lack of political support.

BUILDING ON WHAT WORKS

Whatever their attractions, partial-privatization schemes have seemingly insurmountable disadvantages. They are a high-cost, high-risk approach to retirement security. In essence, they require workers to contribute more of their wages than at present in order to fund two distinct systems: one offering reduced benefits and the other promising uncertain returns. One can imagine workers and beneficiaries choosing this approach only if they believe the present system is going broke and needs to be replaced, and only if they are unaware of the philosophy that has made Social Security so successful for so long.

Social Security is a blend of reward for individual effort and, at the same time, a strong affirmation of community solidarity. Social Security is based on the premise that we're all in this together, with everyone sharing responsibility not only for contributing to their own and their family's security but also to the security of everyone else, present and future.

There is nothing sentimental about this approach; it is neither liberal nor conservative. It simply makes sense. Lacking a crystal ball—unable to know in advance who will succeed and who will struggle unsuccessfully, who will suffer early death or disability and who will live long into retirement, in good health or ill—we pool our resources and are thus able to guard against the average risk at manageable cost to each of us. Social Security's redistributive benefit formula, feasible only in a system in which nearly everyone participates, not only helps to protect us all against impoverishment but, because it is part of a universal system, does so at much lower administrative cost than private insurance and without the stigma of a welfare program.

The unique strengths of this approach argue for retaining our traditional multi-tier retirement system with Social Security as the foundation. Basic protection that one can count on is particularly important in a dynamic, risk-taking economy such as ours, in which long-established businesses, sometimes whole industries, may fade even as new ones are springing up. More than most, our economy rewards rapid adaptation to changing conditions; that is one reason why it functions well at the aggregate level. But the more dynamic the economy, the greater the need for individuals to be protected against economic circumstances beyond their control. In short, we need the basic security that Social Security uniquely supplies regardless of downsizing, mergers, bankruptcies, the volatility of the job market, and the uncertainty of individual investments.

Social Security as presently constituted clearly meets the test of what Lincoln described as the legitimate objective of government: "to do for a community of people whatever they need to have done but cannot do at all or cannot do so well for themselves in their separate and individual capacities." Compulsory individual savings plans do not meet this test—and we would be well advised to keep Lincoln's wise words in mind as we consider various proposals to "individualize" our Social Security system.

NO

Sylvester J. Schieber

SOCIAL SECURITY: AVOIDING THE DOWNSTREAM CATASTROPHE

INTRODUCTION

For more than 20 years now, the movie *To Fly* has been shown several times each day at the Air and Space Museum of the Smithsonian Institution in Washington, DC. The beginning of the movie is set in 1876 and in an early scene a balloonist is seen floating over a very peaceful river as he notices a trapper paddling below in a canoe. After a bit, from his high perch the balloonist sees some dangerous white water and waterfalls down river. The balloonist, seeing that the trapper has no clue of the pending danger, screams down to the trapper that there is white water down river and he must get to shore for his own safety. In the movie, the trapper paddles safely toward shore. This scene is a good analogy for the nature and scope of the financing problem now facing Social Security.

THE NATURE AND SCOPE OF THE SOCIAL SECURITY FINANCING PROBLEM

This year Social Security will collect approximately $60 billion more in revenues than it will incur in expenses through the Old Age and Survivors Insurance and the Disability Insurance (OASDI) programs. Trust fund balances in the combined programs currently exceed $500 billion. Social Security's current funding flows and trust fund balances might encourage us to be tranquil about the downstream prospects of its operations. But its actuaries and trustees have been telling us for some time that the program is significantly underfunded for future generations of retirees. The most recent Trustees Report suggests that the payroll tax would have to be about 2.23 percentage points higher than it is today to provide promised benefits over the next 75 years.[1]

Some students of the program trivialize its underfunding by saying that 2.23 percent of covered payroll over the next 75 years is no big deal; that current law tax rates would meet two-thirds of promised benefits even after the trust funds are depleted; and that there are some very simple marginal adjustments that can rebalance the system. These arguments are misleading.

If the current actuarial imbalance is to be made up through a tax increase, it would represent an 18 percent increase in the program's cost over the next 75 years. Such an increase in the tax that has become the largest federal tax for many workers is no trivial matter. If it were imposed this year, it would amount to $72 billion and it would grow at the compound rate of average wage growth in the future. In addition, the 2.23 percent figure assumes that we could have raised the payroll tax rate 2.23 percentage points early in 1997 and "banked" the added accumulation, or cut benefits by a comparable amount. This assumption is problematic for several reasons: it does not consider the deteriorating funding status of the program at the end of the 75-year projection period; there are questions about the government's ability to convert added payroll tax collections into national savings; and by the time action is finally taken, the funding gap will be much larger than it is currently.

Social Security today is no more in "crisis" than the man in the canoe described earlier. But the man in the canoe, with the benefit of the downstream perspective of the balloonist, realized that he would be in danger if he did not change his course. Our situation with Social Security is similar to that of the man in the canoe. The program's actuaries have warned us several times that there is a significant problem downstream. Not only have they warned us repeatedly of Social Security's actuarial imbalance, their estimates of the magnitude of the imbalance have consistently worsened over the last 15 years as reflected in Table 1.

The table shows that since 1983 the projected accumulation in the trust funds has diminished significantly in virtually every subsequent valuation of the ongoing operations of the program. The actuarial underfunding of the program, stated as a percentage of covered payroll over the 75-year projection period, has also worsened in almost every projection year since 1983. The year that we expect the trust fund to be depleted has also worsened significantly over the the projection period. Finally, the projected underfunding of the program has grown by more than $3 trillion since 1983. We have been told repeatedly that this program is significantly underfunded downstream, and each subsequent valuation tells us that the underfunding is worse than that revealed in the last valuation. One Canadian actuary characterizes the unfolding picture as a "predictable surprise." The essence of his characterization is that the problems we face are highly predictable, but it is likely that we will still be surprised when we finally experience them because we have refused to deal with them.

BALANCING SOCIAL SECURITY WITHIN THE CONTEXT OF GOVERNMENT'S TOTAL OPERATIONS

In 1997, total expenditures under the OASDI programs will be an estimated 4.66 percent of our gross domestic product (GDP). By 2030, the OASDI claim on the economy is expected to rise to 6.57 percent of GDP and by 2035 to 6.64 percent. In other words, over the next 30 to 35 years, we expect Social Security's claim on the economy

Table 1

Projected Maximum OASDI Trust Fund Accumulations in Current Dollars, Projected 75-Year Actuarial Balance as a Percentage of Covered Payroll, and Estimated Year Trust Funds Will Be Depleted by Year of Actuarial Estimate and Present Values of 75-Year Surpluses of OASDI Funds Relative to Obligations

Year of Estimate	Projected Maximum Trust Fund Balance ($ billions)	Actuarial Balance as Percent of Payroll	Year Trust Fund Projected to Be Depleted	Present Value of Tax Income **plus** Current Fund **minus** Obligations ($ billions)
1983	$20,750	0.02	2063	$148.3
1984	18,393	−0.06	2059	37.4
1985	11,955	−0.41	2049	−268.8
1986	12,739	−0.44	2051	−342.6
1987	12,411	−0.62	2051	−377.6
1988	11,838	−0.58	2048	−664.0
1989	11,930	−0.70	2046	−849.5
1990	9,233	−0.91	2045	−1,242.7
1991	8,020	−1.08	2041	−1,185.1
1992	5,535	−1.46	2036	−1,772.6
1993	4,923	−1.46	2036	−1,863.7
1994	2,976	−2.13	2029	−2,841.9
1995	3,275	−2.17	2030	−2,832.7
1996	2,829	−2.19	2029	−3,094.2
1997	2,834	−2.23	2029	

Sources: 1983 to 1997 Annual Reports of the Board of Trustees of the Federal Old-Age and Survivors Insurance and Disability Insurance Trust Funds (Washington, DC: Social Security Administration) and the Office of the Actuary, Social Security Administration.

to grow by about 2 percentage points. Some analysts would have us believe that such a shift in national resources to this vital retirement program can be achieved without significant difficulty. One of the problems that we face in rebalancing Social Security is that it is only one of several governmental programs that will be affected by the aging of our society. The combination of these programs, including Social Security, Medicare, Medicaid, and other federal retirement programs, will place a tremendous strain on the government's fiscal operations.

Figure 1 shows three-year averages of the total receipts of the federal government as a percentage of gross domestic product (GDP) starting with Fiscal Year 1951 through Fiscal Year 1996. Three-year averages are used here rather than the actual annual data to smooth the effects of economic cycles on tax revenues. Over the 45-year period from the end of the Korean War, total federal tax receipts have varied from a low of 17.1 percent of GDP to a high of 19.3 percent, only about a 2 percentage point variation in the claim that the federal government has made on

Figure 1

Three-Year Averages of Total Federal Receipts as a Percentage of GDP

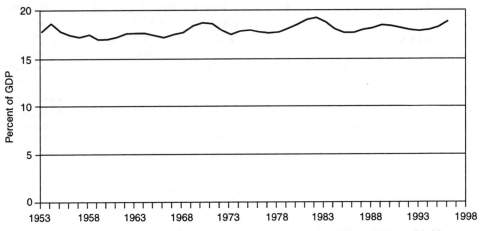

Source: *Historical Tables: Budget of the United States Government, Fiscal Year 1998*, pp. 21–22.

taxpayers. Even looking at actual year-to-year numbers, the maximum claim in any year was 19.7 percent of GDP.

While there is no natural limit to government's claim on the economy, there are clearly political forces that have narrowly limited the amount U.S. taxpayers have rendered to it over virtually all of the last half century. If total government revenue claims on the economy are narrowly limited and Social Security is scheduled to make a bigger claim than currently, then some other government expenditures must shrink. It is here that projected expansions in Social Security's economic claims would seem to be particularly constrained.

Figure 2 shows the projected increases in the claims on the economy by various federal entitlement programs between 1996 and 2030. The graphic shows the projected increasing claim of Social Security as discussed earlier. The projected relative growth in Medicare claims is expected to far outstrip that of OASDI. Some analysts conclude from this picture that we should really focus our energies for managing entitlement growth on federal medical programs in general and Medicare in particular. They claim that if we can restrain the rapid growth in the health care programs, we can sustain projected growth in the cash retirement programs.[2]

While constraining federal health programs for the elderly may be desirable, it will be more difficult to do so than constraining the cash programs for retirees for four reasons. First, old people simply use more health care services than younger ones. Second, the percentage of our population over age 65 is expected to grow by as much between 2010 and 2030 as it had in the prior 80 years. The third factor that will make it difficult to reduce Medicare expenditures is the excessive price inflation that persists in the health sector of our economy. The fourth factor that will drive up future health costs is the continued technological development in the health sector and increasingly intensive treatment of patients.[3]

These four factors are all compounding factors that will drive up the cost of Medicare claims even in the face of program reforms. Current projections suggest that under present law Medicare's claim on the economy will grow from 2.5 percent of GDP today to 7.5 percent by 2030. The underlying assumptions in that projection, however, assume that the added price inflationary pressures and the increased costs of treatment due to cost expanding technologies will largely be eliminated by the end of the first decade of the next century, just as the first of the baby boomers begin to turn age 65. In other words, current Medicare projections assume we will have an amelioration in inflationary pressures on this program just as the baby boomers begin to bring on tremendous levels of new demand.

The point of this discussion is that the potential rededication of 2 percent of GDP to rebalance OASDI might be tenable if that were the only imbalance that the government were facing. But it is not. As we look for policy options to deal with Social Security, we have to consider rebalancing it in the larger context of the total federal government's claim on the economy and within the context of other entitlements that must be financed out of total government revenues.

SOCIAL SECURITY REFORM OPTIONS

Social Security is financed largely by the earmarked payroll tax, and promised benefits are defined in current law. The problem of insufficient revenues to meet the promised benefit stream can be addressed in a number of ways. One would be to simply raise the payroll tax by the necessary amount to meet benefit

Figure 2

Current and Projected Levels of Entitlement Program Operations as a Percent of GDP

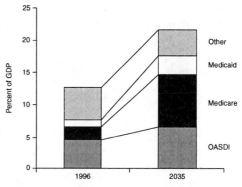

Source: Congressional Budget Office, *Long-Term Budgetary Pressures and Policy Options* (Washington, DC: The Congress of the United States, March 1997), Executive Summary, Table 2.

promises. There is very little support for this option even among the staunchest supporters of the current system.[4] An alternative way would be to reduce benefits by a sufficient amount to live within the current payroll tax rates. The Advisory Council actually considered a proposal along these lines, but no one on the Council was willing to support the proposal because of the resulting low levels of benefits that would be provided by the program and because of the relatively low rates of return that future generations of workers would receive under this approach to reform.[5]

Given the reluctance to address the shortfalls explicitly through straightforward tax increases or benefit reductions, a number of Advisory Council members opted to impose a set of implicit charges on workers and beneficiaries to cover the actuarial shortfalls under the auspices of the "Maintenance of Benefits" (MB) option. They advocated: (1) increasing the number of years of earnings used in determining benefits from 35 to 38; (2) diverting income tax revenues on Social Security benefits now going to the Medicare HI trust fund to the OASDI funds; (3) taxing all benefits above workers' own lifetime nominal payroll tax contributions—i.e., their own basis in benefits; (4) investing 40 percent of the trust funds in the private equity markets to get a higher rate of return than that provided by current investments; and (5) raising the payroll tax rate by 1.6 percentage points in 2045. While only the last of these could be characterized as an explicit tax increase, each of the others would implicitly increase taxes or reduce benefits for program participants.

The majority of the Advisory Council members opposed the MB option largely because of its last two elements. The proposal to invest Social Security trust funds in the private equity markets would make the federal government by far the largest owner of private capital in our economy. Such a policy might result in politically motivated investment of such capital for reasons other than the economic interests of the program's participants. Even as the Advisory Council's debate was unfolding, Secretary of Labor Robert Reich was advocating that some of the assets in employer-based pensions should be used for "economically-targeted investment" purposes. At the height of the debate within the Advisory Council over this proposal, the Clinton Administration actually tapped federal workers' pension funds to avoid debt ceiling limits that were being exceeded during the budget battle with Congressional Republicans early in 1996. Concerns about the political use of retirement funds held by the federal government is not a pipe dream; it has already been a reality. An OASDI trust fund holding more than a trillion dollars worth of equities in today's dollars would be much more tempting for such uses than the relatively small existing federal retirement funds that hold only a few billion dollars today. There are many cases, from California to Kansas to New York where the investment of assets in public retirement plans at the state and local levels has been influenced or dictated by political rather than economic considerations. Around the world, there are also cases from Singapore to Sweden where the assets in partially funded national retirement systems have been used for social investing purposes. While the advocates of Social Security becoming our economy's largest private investor dream up ways to insulate the investing from political directives, there is no way that a current Congressional limitation in this regard could preclude future Congresses from undoing it.

In addition to the problems of politicizing investment decisions, the MB proposal would also raise conflict of interest questions as the government reconciled its role as a fiduciary responsible for protecting the economic value of its portfolio while at the same time fulfilling its responsibility as a regulator of businesses in the interest of public welfare. Finally, it would raise issues of corporate governance. The advocates of this proposal suggest that the government would not vote its shareholder interests in proxy voting matters. Such a policy would change the relative balance of other stockholders on proxy votes and would be contrary to the government's own position on employer-based retirement program fiduciaries voting their ownership position for shares in their pension programs. Some members of the Advisory Council found it ironic that

U.S. policymakers would be considering a massive governmental buy-up of our economy's private capital as we enter the 21st century while many other governments around the world are moving in exactly the opposite direction because of lessons learned from the U.S. experience during the 20th century. The majority of the Advisory Council members opposed the proposed tax increase in 2045 because they felt it was patently unfair to propose tax rates on our grandchildren that we were not willing to pay ourselves.

Those Advisory Council members opposed to the MB proposal, 7 out of the total 13 members on the Council, proposed substantial reform of the current structure of Social Security as the means to salvage the system. They recommended that part of the solution include some funding of benefits through individual accounts. Two members developed an "Individual Account" (IA) proposal where the individual accounts would be financed by an added employee contribution of 1.6 percent of covered payroll with the accounts being held and managed by the Social Security Administration. Although workers would be given some discretion in directing where the individual account funds would be invested under this proposal, the other five members of the Council felt that it was inappropriate to have Social Security managing the funds for the same set of reasons that they opposed the MB proposal.

These latter five members of the Council, including me, felt that the accounts should be financed by the workers' share of the payroll tax contributions now going to finance retirement benefits through Social Security—namely 5 percent of covered payroll. Under our proposal, workers would have considerable discretion in investing their retirement assets held

in the form of "Personal Security Accounts" (PSAs) just as they do in the investment of individual retirement accounts and 401(k) assets.[6] The PSA proposal raises a transitional financing issue because current benefits are largely financed by current payroll tax revenues. If workers are allowed to keep their portion of the payroll tax that finances retirement benefits, added revenues would be required to meet current benefit commitments.

Figure 3 indicates the magnitude of the transition costs under the PSA proposal if it were to be financed on a pay-as-you-go basis through a supplemental payroll tax. The top line in the figure is the combined employer and employee tax rates that would be required in each year of the transition. The lower line shows the current law rate of 12.4 percent of covered payroll. If the transition is financed on a pay-as-you-go basis, the payroll tax to support the non-Medicare portion of the total benefit package would have to increase to roughly 15.9 percent of payroll shortly after the transition begins. Under this transition approach, virtually all of the transitional costs would be paid off within the span of a regular working lifetime. Workers near the end of their careers when the plan was implemented would incur a relatively high cost for a few years at the end of their careers. Workers who were young when the proposal was adopted would bear the full burden of the transition costs throughout their lives. Those entering the work force near the end of the transition would bear little of the cost. While all generations might benefit from this proposal under the right circumstances, it seemed unfair to distribute the costs

Figure 3

Pay-As-You-Go Payroll Tax to Fund Transition to Personal Security Accounts

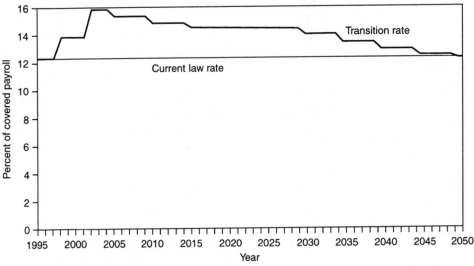

Source: Office of the Actuary, Social Security Administration.

of transition so heavily onto a single generation of workers.

To address the concerns about intergenerational fairness, we proposed that the transition not be financed purely on a pay-as-you-go basis. We proposed levying a flat 1.52 percent payroll tax over roughly 70 years with transitional borrowing when the transitional payroll tax supplement is insufficient to meet pay-as-you-go costs. Under this transition proposal, the burden on any single worker would not increase more than 12.3 percent (i.e., 1.52 percent payroll tax supplement divided by the base rate of 12.4 percent) in any given year. This compares with the pay-as-you-go transition where some workers would incur payroll tax increases of as much as 28.2 percent (i.e., 3.5 percent supplement divided by 12.4 percent). Spreading the transition costs over a larger number of cohorts of participants would make the transition less

onerous for those caught at the early part of the transition. Of course, it increases the cost for those at the end of the transition, but the workers adversely affected have the most to gain from the proposal under consideration.

Under the PSA proposal, the transitional federal borrowing would reach about 2 percent of GDP in 2007 and then gradually decline to zero around 2030 or so. The transitional borrowing would add to formal government debt. The added debt would peak at around 20 percent of GDP by 2020 and decline after that. At its peak, the present value of the added government debt would be equal to about $1.1 trillion. In the context of today's dollars, the borrowing would peak at $2.4 trillion. The added debt would be completely paid off by 2070 under the transition program.

Critics of the PSA proposal argue that the transitional costs are simply too great to be borne by workers and by the government. Their arguments seek to obfuscate the actual obligations that are implied by the current operations of Social Security and to confuse people about the financial transactions that would be involved in the various reform approaches. They argue that lower- and average-wage workers cannot afford to pay the extra cost of transitioning out of the current system. They argue that a government striving to balance its budget cannot afford to take on the transitional debt that would be involved in the PSA proposal. Both arguments are misleading.

If anyone disputes the Social Security's actuaries' estimates of the program's underfunding, they argue that the estimates are overly optimistic. They point to the continuous deterioration in the projections reported in Table 1 to support their case. Taking the actuaries' estimates as reasonable, however, even the MB proponents agree that the current system is underfunded over the next 75 years by about 20 percent. Their proposal would basically protect almost all of the benefits promised under current law. They would have us believe that they can accomplish this without increasing the payroll tax rate. From an economic perspective though, the 2.23 percent of payroll actuarial deficit can only be closed by imposing a real economic cost on the economy. Someone has to pay it regardless of whether it is borne through an explicit tax on workers, an explicit reduction in payments to beneficiaries, or some other hidden claim. The MB proposal would rely heavily on the latter route. Many analysts believe that the MB proposal would lead to higher interest rates on government borrowing because it would have the government buy up $1 trillion worth

of equities without creating significant new savings in the economy.[7] Such an increase in interest rates would undoubtedly carry over into increased interest rates on home mortgages, consumer debt, and other borrowing, directly affecting the well being of lower- and middle-wage workers. In short, there is no magic way to close this deficit without imposing costs on someone. The question is on whom we want to impose costs and how to impose them.

The confusion over the creation of "federal debt" under the PSA transition proposal arises because the government does its accounting purely on a cash basis. Under cash accounting the only governmental debt that is recognized in a given year is the difference in cash receipts and expenditures for the year. As such debt arises, the holders of the debt are issued government bonds. These bonds represent a claim on future revenue streams of the government and, as such, they represent obligations that will have to be met by future taxpayers. The cash accounting that recognizes the government's formal debt, however, only recognizes part of the true operations under federal financing and expenditure programs. It does not recognize the unfunded obligations that arise under various federal programs such as Social Security. For example, looking back to Table 1, the unfunded obligations in the OASDI programs have risen from zero at the end of 1984 to more than $3 trillion at the end of 1996. Just as in the case of formal federal debt, these obligations also represent a claim on future revenue streams of the government and, as such, they also represent obligations that will have to be met by future taxpayers. The only difference between them and the formal debt is that one is accounted for and the other is not when we calculate the annual budget flows and balances. Some analysts claim that there is a difference in the two forms of obligations because Congress can restructure Social Security, thus wiping out the statutory obligations under the program. While that is technically true, the thought of completely reneging on accrued benefits under the program has never been proposed by anyone. That means that much, if not most, of these statutory unfunded obligations will be every bit as burdensome to future taxpayers as the servicing of the formal debt obligations will be. Indeed, the MB proposal would have us cover virtually all of Social Security's current unfunded obligations.

When the total economic costs of the various proposals developed by the Social Security Advisory Council are considered, the proposed borrowing in the PSA plan can be seen in an appropriate perspective. Table 2 shows the estimated present value of the 75-year total federal obligations under the three proposals put forward by Council members. The PSA plan, including the full cost of transition financing cuts the obligations to future taxpayers by significantly more than either of the other proposals. The formal debt that would be created under the PSA would arise because of a restructuring of total federal obligations in a way that would ultimately reduce those obligations.

Table 2 is quite clear that either the PSA or IA proposals would significantly reduce the "entitlement" obligations of the federal government through reformation of Social Security. While some people believe that would be inadvisable policy, they have failed to address the issues raised by the projected growth in federal entitlement claims on the economy that

were discussed earlier. The only way we can keep Social Security, Medicare, and other federally sponsored retirement programs from making a larger claim on the economy than historical levels of total government funding is by constraining them. In that regard, the MB proposal and others like it are a total failure. It is likely that we can only accomplish the kinds of reductions in costs necessary to maintain Social Security's future viability by significantly restructuring it to meet the needs of workers and retirees in the 21st century.

SHIFTING FROM A DEFINED BENEFIT TO A PARTIAL DEFINED CONTRIBUTION REGIME

The individual account approaches included in the IA and PSA plans would change the defined benefit nature of Social Security. Once again, some people see this as an undesirable change to the existing system. They raise the specter of individual financial risk and argue that exposing workers to such risk would be bad public policy. What they fail to address in their arguments is that the current system is fraught with risks that are not accounted for in their analysis. The implications of these risks are clear when the last two major policy adjustments to the Social Security Act are considered.

During the early 1970s the Social Security system faced a severe short-term financing crisis because of rapid growth in new retirees' benefit levels. The 1977 Amendments addressed this problem by reducing by about 25 percent the benefits of workers who would become eligible to retire five years after the implementation date of the Amendments. Despite the severe benefit reductions they imposed, the 1977 Amendments failed to completely

Table 2

Present Value of OASDI's 75-Year Obligations Under Alternative Policy Options

	Obligations	Change from current law	Percent change
	(dollar amount in billions)		
Present law	$ 21,345	—	—
PSA flat benefit plus transition tax	16,487	4,858	22.8
OASDI benefit under IA proposal	18,867	2,478	11.6
MB proposal	21,177	228	1.1

Source: Derived from tables prepared by the Social Security Administration, Office of the Actuary for 1994–1996 Social Security Council.

address the short-term financing problem and by the early 1980s the program faced trust fund insolvency. In addition, by the early 1980s there was growing awareness of the long-term financing problems facing the program. The 1983 Amendments were meant to address both of these by further curtailing benefits. While the 1983 Amendments supposedly "fixed" Social Security's financing problems for at least the next 80 years, here we are again less than 15 years later worrying about the system's underfunding. In a little over a decade, Social Security will begin to run a cash flow deficit, and it is projected to be facing insolvency before the youngest members of the baby boom generation are eligible to receive full benefits.

The risks that we face under the current system are that benefits are going to be cut significantly or that the taxes on workers are going to be increased significantly. Implicitly, if not explicitly, one or the other has to happen because the system is 20 percent out of actuarial balance today and is projected to be much further out of balance in the future.

If current law benefits were secure, we would not be carrying on a national debate about how to fix Social Security. The fact is that current law benefits are significantly under-financed for the majority of people that are contributing to the system today. While policymakers have not been willing to address this issue yet, those that have been willing to put proposals on the table have tended toward benefit reductions in their recommendations to rebalance the system. And these proposals are not all coming from the libertarian end of the political spectrum whose devotees would like to see the current program significantly curtailed on philosophical grounds alone.

Contemporary proposals to reduce Social Security benefits are coming from policymakers anchored in the political mainstream. Before he retired in 1994, Representative Jake Pickle, a Democrat from Texas and Chairman of the Social Security Subcommittee of the House Ways and Means Committee, proposed to rebalance the system virtually completely through benefit reductions. Senator Bob Kerrey, a Democrat from Nebraska, has reached across party lines to cosponsor a proposal to reduce benefits in the traditional Social Security program in order to finance the creation of individual accounts that would be held by workers. And as mentioned earlier, within the

Advisory Council there was virtually no support for a straightforward payroll tax increase to deliver future Social Security benefits defined by current law. Maybe some proposals advocating tax increases to deliver currently promised benefits will ultimately be tabled by policymakers but general reluctance to increase tax rates in this society suggests that such proposals will face major opposition in the legislative process.

Virtually all of the members of the Advisory Council sought to improve the rates of return in the Social Security system for younger cohorts of workers. In addition, the majority of the members of the Council were also concerned about the implications of reform proposals on national savings rates. As Bosworth and Burtless point out, both of these goals can conceivably be achieved either within the current defined benefit system or outside it through the creation of individual accounts.[8] As they note, from an economic perspective the important factor in achieving the goals of improved returns and higher national savings is the prefunding of benefits, not how those funds are held. But they also note that many people involved in the debate about Social Security reform are skeptical that the two different approaches are equivalent from a political perspective. The ultimate question that we face is whether the government can be the accumulator of a vast pool of private economic wealth and can be expected to invest it in a fashion that is neutral to the performance of financial markets and the independent operations of business. The supporters of the PSA plan within the Advisory Council thought that the government could not accumulate the pools of wealth in question nor remain neutral in the operations of a free economy

if it held the large pools of private assets implied by the MB or IA proposals. While economic considerations were extremely important to this group, it was ultimately political considerations that drove them to suggest the individual account option that they did. They simply did not believe the economic goals that they thought were important could be achieved within our political framework through any mechanism other than individual accounts managed outside government.

The creation of individual accounts, of course, would expose workers to greater financial market risks in the accumulation of their base pensions than the financial market risks they currently face. But it is not clear that their overall risks would be any greater than they are in the current environment. If policymakers are reluctant to increase payroll taxes at all to simply sustain the current structure of benefits, the political probability of the Maintain Tax Rate Benefit (MTR), the benefit that could be provided to a worker if benefits were scaled back to live within the tax rate levels in current law, approaches one. In this regard, the Advisory Council's unwillingness to advocate a straightforward increase in payroll tax rates to deliver currently promised benefits is important.

The advocates of the MB plan sought to secure current benefit promises and the current benefit structure by crafting a proposal that would minimize the explicit costs of doing so to workers. But as we pointed out earlier, there is no way to cover the real deficit that exists in the current system without incurring real costs. If the only way policymakers can get society to bear these costs is to hide them, the proposal itself acknowledges that there is tremendous political risk that the public will be unwilling to deliver on current promises. The advocates of the individual account options developed by the Advisory Council believed that policymakers might be willing to explicitly increase the cost of providing benefits under the proviso that the added levies go into individual accounts. If they are correct, the political probability of a benefit greater than MTR increases significantly, but it would only do so at the expense of the worker taking on some investment risk.

A simulation approach has been used to determine benefit levels for selected birth cohorts of average age workers.[9] The simulation results suggest that there are tradeoffs between political risks and market investment risks that might make the choice between the two difficult for the older birth cohorts, especially the baby-boom birth cohorts. For those birth cohorts born after the baby boom, however, the advantages of prefunding a portion of the benefits through individual accounts are much clearer. And this does not take into account the added improvements in economic welfare that should result from the added savings that would be stimulated by the IA or PSA plans.

Critics of the PSA proposal argue that it would be costly if not impossible to administer. In this regard, the experience of the employer-based 401(k) system is instructive. Although this system is completely voluntary, it has experienced explosive growth over the period since it was first made available to workers in the early 1980s. The system went from virtually nothing to accounting for more than half the total contributions going into private employer-sponsored retirement programs in 1993. Under current law, these programs allow young and old workers alike to contribute from a few dollars a week or up to nearly $200 per week into them. In the aggregate, workers pour more than $1 billion per week into private 401(k) plans. Most workers are free to direct the investment of their own retirement savings in these plans, and they do so on a fully accounted basis that costs much less than 1 percent per year.

Critics also argue that the PSA plan is flawed because it does not require the annuitization of the benefit at retirement. While the PSA proposal did not call for forced annuitization, it did not preclude it either. Indeed, its authors suggested that it might make sense to require retirees to show that they had a lifetime annuity income that would equal 1.5 times the poverty line, or some other similar multiple of the poverty level income before they could liquidate their PSA accumulation at retirement. At some level of income that protects taxpayers from having injudicious consumers demanding welfare support, however, it is not the government's business how private consumers choose to distribute their lifetime savings.

Finally, critics of Social Security reform proposals that include an individual account element argue that Congress would be unlikely to force workers to keep the money in the accounts until they reach retirement. They suggest that our political leaders could not withstand the pressure to allow workers to tap retirement savings in cases of personal and financial hardship. The fact is that a wide range of countries around the world have adopted Social Security reforms of the sort recommended under the PSA proposal. Such reforms have swept across Latin America. A much larger, fully funded individual account program is being phased in currently in Australia. A similar approach is used in Singapore and is being considered by a number of other Asian countries including China. Sweden, the mother of all social welfare states, is moving toward a system very similar to the one recommended by the authors of the IA proposal. The UK has allowed workers to "contract out" of the second tier of their national retirement program for some years, essentially allowing voluntary PSAs in their national retirement system. The UK is beginning to discuss moving further down this path in the direction that Australia has gone. A wide range of other countries around the world are carrying on similar deliberations.[10] If our political system or our national policymakers are so politically incontinent that they cannot do what a wide range of countries around the world have been able to achieve, we may have a much larger problem to resolve than figuring out how to secure the retirement benefits of today's workers at a cost that future workers will be able to bear.

Possibly the most amazing aspect of what is going on all around the world is the range of other countries that have recognized the downstream perils of payroll tax financed pay-as-you-go retirement security systems. These countries are paying attention to the predictable demographics they face and changing the course of their national retirement programs—often much older than ours —generally by adopting some form of individual account program. They are amending existing systems to avoid the perils that taxpaying workers and dependent retirees face from retirement security systems that are not sustainable for aging populations. What is going on elsewhere in the world is not incompatible with the early direction of our own Social Security program.

The father of the U.S. Social Security system, Franklin D. Roosevelt, felt strongly that a significant portion of the system's promises should be funded. When he discovered that the original proposal submitted to Congress by his Committee on Economic Security did not provide for such funding, he made the Committee revise the legislative package to include it. While his proposed funding was included in the original Social Security Act, the levels of funding that FDR had insisted upon for his beloved Social Security program were never achieved, largely for two reasons. The first was Congressional worries that the accumulated funds would be used to buy up significant shares of private capital, a move many in Congress thought was incompatible with the nature of our government and the private ownership of capital. The second was that it was always easier for Congress to delay tax increases that would have led to the trust fund build-up that FDR envisaged than to bear the pain of imposing the necessary taxes; or it was more politically expedient to use excess tax revenues as they arose to raise benefits than to allow the trust fund to accumulate.

FDR was right; a healthy fund backing our national retirement system would be good for the economy and its participants' economic security. What more than 60 years of experience has told us, however, is that we can only achieve FDR's vision by significantly reforming the current system. We were among the last of the countries in the Western Hemisphere to adopt a Social Security program. We should not be the last to reform it.

NOTES

1. *The 1997 Annual Report of the Board of Trustees of the Federal Old-Age and Survivors Insurance and Disability Insurance Trust Funds* (Washington, DC: US Government Printing Office, April 1997), p. 24.

2. Henry Aaron, "Is a Crisis Really Coming? (Social Security and...)," *Newsweek* (December 9, 1996).

3. For a full discussion of those issues, see Roland D. McDevitt and Sylvester J. Schieber, *From Baby Boom to Elder Boom: Providing Health Care for an Aging Population* (Washington, DC: Watson Wyatt Worldwide, 1996).

4. For example, the members of the 1994–1996 Social Security Advisory Council who advocated maintaining the current system and benefit structure to the maximum extent possible argued that any increase in the payroll tax should be largely devoted to supporting the Medicare program. See Robert M. Ball, et al., "Social Security for the 21st Century: A Strategy to Maintain Benefits and Strengthen America's Family Protection Plan," *Report of the 1994–1996 Advisory Council on Social Security*, vol. 1, Findings and Recommendations, p. 64.

5. Transcript of the Public Meeting of the Social Security Advisory Council, December 14, 1995 (Social Security Administration).

6. For a complete description of this proposal and its financing and benefits implications, see Sylvester J. Schieber and John B. Shoven, "Social Security Reform Options and Their Implications for Future Retirees, Federal Fiscal Operations, and National Savings," a paper prepared for a public policy forum, "Tax Policy for the 21st Century," sponsored by the American Council for Capital Formation, Washington, DC, December 1996. Copies available from the author on request.

7. For example, see Alan Greenspan, speech at the American Enterprise Institute's Public Policy Conference, January 1997, Joan T. Bok et al., "Restoring Security to Our Social Security Program," and Edward M. Gramlich and Marc M. Twinney, "The Individual Accounts Plan," in *The Report of the 1994–1996 Advisory Council on Social Security*, vol. 1, pp. 128, 155.

8. Gary Burtless and Barry Bosworth, "Privatizing Social Security: The Troubling Tradeoffs," *Brookings Policy Brief* (March 1997), No. 14.

9. For a full discussion of the simulation approach and the results of simulations for lower- and higher-wage workers, see Gordon P. Goodfellow and Sylvester J. Schieber, "Social Security Reform: Implications of Individual Accounts on the Distribution of Benefits," Pension Research Council Working Paper, Philadelphia: The Wharton School, University of Pennsylvania, May 1997.

10. For a more in-depth discussion of what is going on in the international arena, see Sylvester J. Schieber and John B. Shoven, "Social Security Reform: Around the World in 80 Ways," *The American Economic Review* (May 1996), vol. 86, no. 2, pp. 373–377.

POSTSCRIPT

Is the Current U.S. Social Security Program Securely Anchored?

Ball believes that Social Security is basically in good shape and that financing can easily be brought into long-range balance. He identifies the sources of the projected deficits: 50 percent from changes in actuarial methods and new sources of data and 50 percent from changes in assumptions. The problem is to eliminate the projected deficit of 2.23 percent of covered payroll. Ball's solution, which would maintain the basic structure of OASDI as a completely defined benefits program, involves six elements: increase taxation of benefits, change the cost of living adjustment, extend Social Security coverage, increase the wage-averaging period, increase the overall tax rate, and allow the investment of trust fund balances in equities. Ball rejects the two partial privatization proposals— individual accounts and private savings accounts —for a number of reasons: they require too drastic a reduction in basic benefits, they require too high an increase in current taxes, they increase risk, they are too complex, they are too costly, and they are politically unstable. In conclusion, Ball argues that his position on Social Security reform is consistent with community solidarity and the proper role of government in a market economy.

Schieber, unlike Ball, believes that the projected underfunding is a very serious problem that requires a fundamental restructuring of OASDI. He rejects the solution favored by Ball; in particular, Schieber rejects the investment of trust funds in equities by government officials on the grounds that such an arrangement will politicize investment decisions, create conflicts of interest, and lead to problems of corporate governance. Moreover, Ball's "Maintenance of Benefits" option, because it requires a 1.6 percent increase in the payroll tax in 2045, shifts the tax burden to future generations. As an alternative, Schieber proposes transforming Social Security from a completely defined benefits program to a partially defined benefits program through the partial privatization of OASDI. In defending his alternative, the "Personal Savings Account" option, Schieber argues that it will actually reduce risk and that it is consistent with reforms that are occurring in a number of countries across the globe. But, most important, he believes that his proposal of partial privatization is the only way in which important economic goals can be achieved within a democratic political framework.

Additional readings on this issue include "How Not to Fix Social Security," by Mark Weisbrot, *Dollars and Sense* (March/April 1997); "The Great Social Security Scare," by Jerry L. Mashaw and Theodore R. Marmor, *The American Prospect* (November/December 1996); "A Secure System," by Robert M. Ball,

The American Prospect (November/December 1996); "Different Approaches to Dealing With Social Security," by Edward M. Gramlich, *Journal of Economic Perspectives* (Summer 1996); and "Proposals to Restructure Social Security," by Peter A. Diamond, *Journal of Economic Perspectives* (Summer 1996). Also see three articles in *Economic Commentary, Federal Reserve Bank of Cleveland*: "Should Social Security Be Privatized?" by Jagadeesh Gokhale (September 1995); "Social Security: Are We Getting Our Money's Worth?" by Jagadeesh Gokhale and Kevin J. Lansing (January 1, 1996); and "A Simple Proposal for Privatizing Social Security," by David Altig and Jagadeesh Gokhale (May 1, 1996).

ISSUE 10

Does the Consumer Price Index Suffer from Quality and New Product Bias?

YES: Michael J. Boskin et al., from "Consumer Prices, the Consumer Price Index, and the Cost of Living," *Journal of Economic Perspectives* (Winter 1998)

NO: Katharine G. Abraham, John S. Greenlees, and Brent R. Moulton, from "Working to Improve the Consumer Price Index," *Journal of Economic Perspectives* (Winter 1998)

ISSUE SUMMARY

YES: Economist Michael J. Boskin and his colleagues argue that the Consumer Price Index (CPI) suffers from quality and new product bias, which means that the CPI overstates inflation and increases in the cost of living.

NO: Economists Katharine G. Abraham, John S. Greenlees, and Brent R. Moulton argue that the conclusions drawn about the upward bias of the CPI are either based on weak evidence, based on improper inference from the evidence, or based on the identification of problems that have no practical solution.

Each month the Bureau of Labor Statistics (BLS) releases a new estimate of the Consumer Price Index (CPI). This release usually merits front-page attention in U.S. newspapers because changes in the CPI are interpreted as changes in the cost of living of Americans. If nominal income does not increase to keep pace with increases in the cost of living, as determined by increases in the CPI, then real income falls.

Because of this connection between changes in the CPI and changes in the cost of living, a number of monetary arrangements in the economy are altered when the CPI changes; that is, they are indexed. For example, some private sector collective bargaining agreements tie wages to changes in the CPI. If the CPI increases, then wages automatically rise by the same percentage. But indexing is not limited to the private sector of the economy; the federal government has resorted to indexing in a variety of areas. In counting the number of poor persons, the poverty thresholds (the income levels that separate poor from nonpoor) are adjusted upward each year by the percentage increase in the CPI. With the individual income tax, the dollar value of the personal exemption is adjusted to reflect changes in the cost of living as determined by changes in the CPI. Social Security benefits are also adjusted each year to reflect changes in the cost of living and the CPI. So from the government's perspective, if changes in the CPI overstate changes in the cost of living, then its tax receipts will be lower than they should be and its Social Security payments will be higher than they should be.

It is clearly important, then, to measure changes in the CPI and in the cost of living accurately. This issue addresses the question of the extent to which this accuracy is achieved. As a first step in understanding this debate, it is important to know how the CPI is calculated. The CPI, in technical terms, is a Laspeyres fixed-weight index. Accordingly, the first step in the calculation of the CPI is to determine the fixed weights—the goods and services that consumers purchase at a particular point in time known as the base period. This is known as the market basket and is accomplished by surveys of consumer purchasing behavior. The market basket can be considered the expenditure pattern of the typical consumer. The market basket currently used in the CPI was determined by surveys conducted in the early 1980s; that is, the base period for the CPI is the 1982–1984 period. The second step is to gather information regarding the prices of the goods and services in the market basket, and this is done every month. The price information is necessary to determine the cost of the market basket. The cost of the market basket changes as prices change, but the market basket itself does not (it is fixed). If the cost of the market basket increases, then it costs the typical consumer more to buy an unchanged bundle of goods and services; that is, the cost of living has increased. The ratio of the cost of the market basket in the current period to the cost of the market basket in the base period (multiplied by 100) provides the current numerical value of the CPI. The percentage change in the CPI between any two periods represents the rate of inflation in consumer prices between those two periods and, by extension, the percentage change in the cost of living between those two periods. But to be an accurate measure of price and cost of living changes, the market basket must either remain unchanged or it must be properly adjusted to account for new products or changes in the quality of old products.

The BLS recognizes this problem and attempts to make adjustments to rectify it. The issue is whether or not the adjustments are appropriate and sufficient. In the following selections, Michael J. Boskin et al. assert that the adjustments are insufficient and that the CPI therefore suffers from quality and new product bias and, as a consequence, overstates price and cost of living changes. Katharine G. Abraham, John S. Greenlees, and Brent R. Moulton have a different opinion. In exploring the debate between the two groups, the affiliations of the opposite sides should be noted. Boskin et al. were members of the Advisory Commission to Study the Consumer Price Index (the Boskin commission), constituted by the Senate Finance Committee. The selection by Boskin et al. is based on the commission's final report, *Toward a More Accurate Measure of the Cost of Living,* which was submitted early in 1996. On the other side, Abraham and Greenlees work for the BLS, and Moulton is a former employee of the BLS.

YES
Michael J. Boskin et al.

CONSUMER PRICES, THE CONSUMER PRICE INDEX, AND THE COST OF LIVING

Accurately measuring prices and their rate of change, inflation, is central to almost every economic issue. There is virtually no other issue that is so endemic to every field of economics. Some examples include aggregate growth and productivity; industry prices and productivity; government taxes and spending programs that are indexed to inflation; budget deficits and debt; monetary policy; real financial returns; real wages, real median incomes and poverty rates; and the comparative performance of economies.

In mid-1995, the Senate Finance Committee, pursuant to a Senate Resolution, appointed an Advisory Committee to study the Consumer Price Index (CPI) with the five authors of this article as its members. The CPI Commission concluded that the change in the Consumer Price Index overstates the change in the cost of living by about 1.1 percentage points per year, with a range of plausible values of 0.8 to 1.6 percentage points (Boskin et al., 1996). That is, if inflation as measured by the percentage change in the CPI is running 3 percent, the true change in the cost of living is about 2 percent. This bias might seem small, but when compounded over time, the implications are enormous. Over a dozen years, the cumulative additional national debt from overindexing the budget would amount to more than $1 trillion. The implications of overstating inflation for understanding economic progress are equally dramatic. Over the last quarter-century, average real earnings have risen, not fallen, and real median income has grown, not stagnated. The poverty rate would be lower. Because the CPI component price indexes are inputs into the national income accounts, an overstated CPI implies that real GDP (gross domestic product] growth has been understated (Boskin and Jorgenson, 1997)....

Since the publication of our report, in a series of professional meetings, Congressional hearings, and other events, there has been much support for, and criticism of, the findings and recommendations of the CPI Commission. The purpose of this paper is to provide a readily accessible and self-contained discussion of the issues involved.

At this point in the debate, we see no reason to change our original estimate of a 1.1 percentage point per annum upward bias in the change in the Consumer Price Index. We strongly endorse the proposed improvements the Bureau of Labor Statistics (BLS) is currently planning to make, research, or explore (Abraham et al., 1998), but believe it can and should, if given the appropriate resources, do far more to improve the CPI than it currently contemplates....

The Debate Over Quality Change and New Product Bias

Most of the criticism has focused on our extensive analysis of quality change and new product bias. On the question as to whether estimates of quality change bias are inevitably too "subjective" and "judgmental" to be taken seriously, it is, of course, at least as subjective to assume that every CPI category not subject to careful research has a zero bias as to extrapolate research-based estimates from one category to another. The notion that assuming zero bias is scientific, whereas attempting to generalize cautiously from related goods or practical reasoning is not precise enough, strikes us as unreasonable. Even though we will never precisely measure the value of the invention of, say, the jet airplane, as economists we *know* the consumer surplus triangles are positive, not zero. Likewise, we have known for years that PC's with Pentium processors are objectively higher quality (faster) than the 386 and 486 machines they replaced.

Hence, the Commission examined 27 subcomponents of the CPI, and most of our estimates of quality change are based on the collection of price data from independent sources and the care-ful quality adjustment of those independent data. Independent sources of price data are employed in our bias estimates for shelter, appliances, radio-TV, personal computers, apparel, public transportation, prescription drugs, and medical care. Estimates derived from these categories are extrapolated, sometimes partially rather than fully, to other house furnishings, nonprescription drugs, entertainment, commodities, and personal care. This leaves only a few remaining categories where we added a bias estimate to the CPI category in which there are already quality adjustments, rather than computing the bias estimate indirectly by subtracting an independent estimate from the CPI estimate for the same category. These categories are food and beverages, other utilities, new and used cars, and motor fuel, and personal expenses. The BLS does not object to our "down in the trenches" approach to the problem. Indeed, Moulton and Moses (1997) state, "This is the first time that a systematic analysis of quality bias has been done category by category, which we consider to be a noteworthy accomplishment of the Commission.... [the] overall approach seems to us to be a sensible and useful way to approach the problem of coming up with an overall assessment of bias, and we expect this type of structure will prove to be useful in the future."

Some outside critics of the Commission have argued that the BLS already does a great deal of quality adjustment, and that the Commission report is flawed for ignoring the extent of the BLS adjustments. However, for most categories, the extent of current BLS quality adjustments is irrelevant to an assessment of the Commission report's treatment of quality change. We were comparing our own evidence to the corresponding CPI indexes—however they are quality-adjusted, in a major or minor way—and thus our estimates of quality change bias are a residual that remains after the BLS has completed its efforts.

However, it is still instructive to discuss what the BLS calls quality adjustment, since it illustrates the substantive and communication difficulties in this field. There is presently very little explicit adjustment for quality change (Nordhaus, 1998). Most of the reported "quality adjustment" by the BLS comes from "linking" procedures, where a missing item is replaced by another.[1] No judgment at all is made about the quality differential between the new and old item. The price change during the link period is imputed, by using either the inflation rate in the overall CPI or of other commodities in the particular class. Roughly one out of three items in the same general class, such as a larger versus a smaller package of yogurt, a blue raincoat versus black, a 12-cubic-foot refrigerator with its freezer at the bottom rather than at the top. But this churning is not what we had in mind by "quality change," which rather involves the appearance of new and improved goods, greater speed, durability, variety, convenience, safety, energy efficiency, and so on. Some examples include the increased variety and freshness of vegetables and fish due to improving transport facilities and the globalization of trade, the substitution of laparoscopic procedures for gallstone operations, and many more.

Yes, the BLS does lots of "price adjustments." It is forced to by its sampling framework and the product turmoil in the markets. However, the BLS is not looking for the "quality change"

that we were worried about. And it does not adjust explicitly for quality *change,* as we were defining it, except in the case of automobiles, apparel, and possibly rental apartment units and the occasional truly new goods caught by their substitution procedures.[2] While some of the Commission's estimates can be questioned—in both directions—there is very little overlap between them and the recent numbers produced by the BLS.

The helpful Moulton and Moses (1997) discussion of several categories would probably lead us to reduce our overall quality change bias estimate by perhaps 0.1 of the total 0.6 percentage points, if that were the only new information since the report, but other new research information and criticism goes in the opposite direction. Eventually, even though it may turn out that some of our estimates of quality change may be too high, others are likely to be too low.[3] Remember that except for a few cases, with low overall weight in the index, we did not explicitly estimate the additional welfare gain of the numerous new commodities in the economy. In the Commission's report, we indicate this is, in our view, a major source of the improvement in living standards. We also indicate that major problems occurred with the very late introduction of VCRs, microwave ovens, personal computers, and the soon to be introduced cellular telephone service. We indicated that the appropriate way to deal with new products is to value the consumer surplus from their introduction, as first demonstrated by Hicks (1940), and recently nicely elaborated and applied by Hausman (1996). However, we were *cautious* in this regard because, while we conjecture that the rate of introduction of new products is likely to be no different in the foreseeable future than it has been in the past (and some would even argue that the pace of introduction of new products is accelerating), it is difficult to predict which new products will become important that will not be picked up with the current BLS procedures. Perhaps many Internet-related activities are candidates. In any event, we chose to deal with this by being deliberately cautious, but indicating that there was an asymmetrical bias with more potential bias on the upside than the downside because of the likely future new product introductions which were unlikely to be captured in the CPI program.

Nor did we try to quantify all of the intangible aspects of quality change, such as the improved safety of home power tools or the improved quality of stereo sound and TV pictures. But we did try to do so in some cases; for example, the increased freshness and timeliness of fruits and vegetables.

Our report considered that new goods may drive out older goods which are still valued by a subgroup of the population, or the loss of economies of scale may drive up their price. Existing goods and services may deteriorate in quality, although only a few examples can be found, as on balance, the improvement in quality is overwhelming. For example, despite the recent complaints about how health maintenance organizations have tightened up the rules of access to medical care, few would argue that unrestricted access to the technologies of yesteryear is preferable to more restricted access to the recent improvements in bypass operations, ulcer treatments, or cataract surgeries. . . .

CONCLUSION

While the CPI is the best measure currently available, it is not a cost-of-living index and it suffers from a variety of conceptual and practical problems. Despite important BLS updates and improvements over time, the change in the CPI has substantially overstated the actual rate of inflation, and is likely to continue to overstate the change in the cost of living for the foreseeable future. This overstatement will have important unintended consequences, including overindexing government outlays and tax brackets and increasing the federal deficit and debt. Moreover, such revisions as have occurred have not been carried out in a way that can provide an internally consistent series on the cost of living over an extended span of time.

The CPI Commission's report and findings have, in our opinion, held up to criticism and scrutiny quite well. Our overall estimate of about 1.1 percentage point of upward bias per year in the growth of the CPI still seems right to us, especially because we were so cautious in the treatment of the bias from new products. The purposes of our Commission's report included: disseminating information about the complexity of constructing a cost-of-living index; generating additional intellectual capital from academe and the private sector; and suggesting potential improvements. But these improvements must be considered, as we said in the report, with more appreciation of the efforts of our colleagues in the BLS and other government statistical agencies and an understanding of the constraints under which they are working. The BLS and other government statistical agencies have a remarkably complex task in a dynamic flexible market economy.

The analytical and econometric research done over recent decades has dramatically improved economists' understanding of the issues surrounding a cost-of-living index. We believe that improvements in geometric means, superlative indexes, more rapid introduction of new goods and new outlets, speedier updating of consumption weights, making use of hedonics and of related statistical tools, the use of scanner data, and other recommendations made here can substantially reduce the bias in the CPI going forward. Now, the time has come for governments in the United States and elsewhere to recognize these problems and to commit the resources to dealing with them. Virtually every major private firm in the world is spending heavily on information technology, and we should not expect better statistics from our government agencies without a corresponding investment.

We had hoped to provide an opportunity for the BLS (and the related statistical community) to implement an agenda for the most fundamental improvements in the nation's price statistics in many decades and to obtain financing (as necessary) for it. While we strongly support the modest improvements BLS is hoping to make (BLS, 1997; Abraham et al., 1998), we would hope that over time the size and scope of the reform agenda will expand.[4]

Ultimately, the president and Congress must decide whether they wish to continue the widespread overindexing of government programs. If the purpose of the indexing is to compensate recipients of the indexed programs or taxpayers from changes in the cost of living, no more and no less, they should move to wholly or partly adjust the indexing formulas, taking due account of the partial improvements BLS will make along the way. Such changes will have profound ramifications for our fiscal futures, but these changes should be made even if the budget was in surplus and there was no long-run entitlement cost problem. They should be made first and foremost in the interest of accuracy not only for the budget and the programs, but for the economic information upon which citizens depend.

NOTES

1. In Moulton and Moses (1997), 1.65 out of the 1.76 percentage points in BLS quality adjustments come from linking procedures. If one excludes outliers, defined as commodity pairs where the implicit price-quality differential exceeds 100 percent, the quality adjustment number shrinks to 0.3 percentage points.

2. In Moulton and Moses (1997), such explicit quality adjustments account for only about 6 percent of the total "treatment of substitutions" effect, and amount to only 0.08 percent per year in the "outlier-cleaned" recomputations.

3. Recent evidence that we may have underestimated the biases in some of the areas we did examine comes from an alternative measure of consumer prices, the PCE (personal consumption expenditures) deflator, which has been rising by about one-third percent less per year (since 1992) than the CPI. An unpublished examination of this difference by the BLS indicates that most of it arises from the use by the BEA of alternative price indexes for hospital expenditures and airfares. These indexes do not adjust for any of the quality changes mentioned by us.

4. We have been told by leaders in government statistics agencies around the world that they were surprised that the BLS initially reacted defensively to the Commission Report, and failed to capitalize fully on the opportunity it presented.

REFERENCES

Abraham, Katherine G., John S. Greenlees, and Brent R. Moulton, "Working to Improve the Consumer Price Index," *Journal of Economic Perspectives*, Winter 1998, 12:1.

Boskin, Michael J., and Dale W. Jorgenson, "Implications of Overstating Inflation for Indexing Government Programs and Understanding Economic Progress," 1997 Papers and Proceedings, *American Economic Review,* May 1997, *87*: 2, 89–93.

Boskin, Michael J., E. Dulberger, R. Gordon, Z. Griliches, and D. Jorgenson, "Toward a More Accurate Measure of the Cost of Living," Final Report to the Senate Finance Committee, December 4, 1996.

Hausman, Jerry, "Valuation of New Goods Under Perfect and Imperfect Competition." In Bresnahan, T. and Robert J. Gordon, eds. *The Economics of New Goods.* Chicago: University of Chicago Press, 1996.

Hicks, John R., "The Valuation of the Social Income," *Economica,* May 1940, 7:26, 105–24.

Moulton, Brent R., and Karin E. Moses, "Addressing the Quality Change Issue in the Consumer Price Index," forthcoming in *Brookings Papers on Economic Activity,* 1997.

Nordhaus, William D., "Quality Changes in Price Indexes," *Journal of Economic Perspectives,* Winter 1998, *12:*1.

U.S. Bureau of Labor Statistics, "Measurement Issues in the Consumer Price Index." Response to the U.S. Congress, Joint Economic Committee, June 1997.

NO
Katharine G. Abraham, John S. Greenlees, and Brent R. Moulton

WORKING TO IMPROVE THE CONSUMER PRICE INDEX

The Advisory Commission believes that the failure to make adequate adjustment for changes in the quality of the goods and services people buy and to account properly for value to consumers of newly available goods, together with deficiencies in the way the CPI [Consumer Price Index] treats differences in the prices charged at different retail outlets, creates an upward bias in the CPI of 0.7 percentage points per year.

The BLS [Bureau of Labor Statistics] does have procedures in place that are designed to purge the effects of changes in item quality that occur when a new item must be substituted for an item that is no longer available for pricing in the CPI. In the case of certain item categories (most notably automobiles and apparel), these procedures involve direct adjustment for the observed price differential associated with the differences in the old and new items' characteristics. For example, since 1992, direct adjustments made in the CPI for the changing quality of autos include adjustments for improved corrosion protection, improved warranties, sealing improvements, stainless steel exhaust, longer-life spark plugs, improved steering gears, rust-resistant fuel injection, clearcoat paint, and more. In other item categories, the procedures most commonly applied, which are referred to as "linking" procedures, remove any difference in price between the new item and the disappearing item at the changeover point from measured price change. In essence, these procedures assume that the difference in price between the items at the time the substitution occurs reflects the difference in their value to consumers.[1]

It is clear that the linking procedures do not work perfectly. In the case of personal computers and other "high tech" consumer goods affected by rapid innovation, they fail to capture the full value of quality improvements (Berndt, Griliches and Rappaport, 1995). Still, absent evidence for a particular index component to the contrary, there is no a priori basis for concluding that linking necessarily leads to overstatement of the rate of growth of prices. Indeed, there may be some presumption in the opposite direction. As already noted, the linking approach to quality adjustment treats the difference in price between the original and the replacement item as wholly attributable to a difference in quality. Price increases for many goods occur intermittently and often are timed to coincide with model replacements or other quality improvements. By attributing the full price difference between the old and new items to a difference in quality, the linking approach may lead to overadjustment for quality change and a resulting understatement of the rate of price growth (Triplett, 1971). Indeed, direct quality adjustments were introduced for apparel items as evidence emerged that linking procedures had led to a significant understatement of price change in that item category (Armknecht and Weyback, 1989; Liegey, 1993, 1994; Reinsdorf, Liegey and Stewart, 1996). Methods have been introduced to try to minimize the possibility of overadjusting for quality differences in the linking process more generally, but we cannot say it has been eliminated.[2]

In addition to the procedures put in place to account for changes in items' quality, the BLS also has established procedures for bringing new items and new outlets into the index. The expenditure share information used to aggregate the CPI subindexes historically has been updated only once every ten years or so, but the specific stores in which prices are collected and the specific items priced are reselected on a five-year cycle. It may be possible by using scanner data or other approaches to identify new product introductions sooner and rotate them into the index more quickly (Bradley, Cook, Leaver and Moulton, 1997). Although more frequent sample rotations undoubtedly would be desirable, it is already true that a considerable share of the resources available for producing the CPI

are devoted to ensuring that the sample of items priced is representative of what consumers actually are purchasing.

The Advisory Commission does not argue, of course, that the BLS does not attempt to address quality/new goods biases, but rather that, in spite of the BLS efforts, residual bias remains. The report's approach to assessing this residual bias is to divide the index into 27 categories, and then to make a judgment about the magnitude of the bias in each case. Unfortunately, the evidence applicable to many of these categories is rather sparse. In a number of cases the Commission draws conclusions from the existing evidence with which we do not agree.

In the food and beverages categories, for example, the Commission's estimates of upward biases rest exclusively on unsubstantiated judgments regarding the value to consumers of increased variety on grocery and liquor store shelves, together with the value of greater choice in restaurants. Moulton and Moses (1997) have examined evidence pertaining specifically to the value of the increased seasonal availability of fruits and vegetables; based on the magnitude of observed changes in consumption, they conclude that the Commission's estimates of that value are implausibly large. For new and used cars, the Commission estimates that the growth in prices has been overstated by 0.6 percentage point per year in the recent past, based on data showing that the average age of cars on the road has risen, together with an assumption that current CPI procedures do not capture any of the increases in automobile durability that may have occurred. This latter assumption, however, is incorrect;... a large number of direct quality adjustments related to auto durability has been made in the CPI over the past few years. For apparel, the Commission estimates that the CPI has overstated the rate of growth of prices by 1.0 percentage point per year since 1985, but this estimate rests on a comparison of the official CPI data with price indexes constructed using Sears catalogue prices for items remaining unchanged from one year to the next. We have serious reservations about drawing any general conclusions based upon the prices charged by a single catalogue merchant, and are very skeptical of any index based only on the prices of unchanging items, particularly in a market segment where changing fashion is as important as it is in apparel.

To move beyond the particular examples, our reading of the Advisory Commission report is that the efforts made to identify possible positive biases in the CPI were considerably more systematic than those made to identify possible negative biases. Other analysts have pointed to reduced convenience and comfort of air travel, deteriorating quality of higher education, increases in travel time and driver irritation resulting from growing traffic congestion, and widespread declines in the quality of customer service as examples of quality decreases that are not accounted for in the CPI.

All of this, however, leaves us a long way from solving the quality/new goods problems the Commission believes exist with the CPI. There is much of what the Commission discusses that we do not know how to measure—or, to put it another way, for which economists simply have not developed operational procedures to correct the problems cited —and the Commission offers little in the way of practical assistance. Let us try to illustrate what we mean.

Surely, the variety of goods and services available to consumers has grown, and, surely, this variety is of value to consumers. Unfortunately, the techniques available for measuring the gains in consumer welfare from those new products (and the losses from product disappearances) are in their infancy, and may never be adaptable for implementation in a large, ongoing price measurement program like the CPI. To take another example, we would readily acknowledge that there have been major improvements in the medical treatment available for many serious health problems—improvements that have been of indubitable value to those suffering from the afflictions in question. Unfortunately, as a general matter, the BLS has no good way to measure the value of these improvements (say, increased mobility from improved knee surgery techniques).

Close to half of the quality/new goods bias the Commission believes exists in the overall CPI is judged to occur in just two areas of the index: medical care and high-tech consumer goods. These clearly are components of the index in which the BLS faces particularly difficult measurement problems. The Commission does not view ongoing BLS efforts in these areas as sufficient, but offers few concrete suggestions toward solutions to the difficult problems identified.

The report also discusses the question of new outlet bias, namely, how changes in the mix of retail outlets at which consumers shop ought to be treated. Current CPI procedures treat purchases of a particular item at different retail outlets as distinct transactions; the prices at the different stores are never directly compared. This could impart an upward bias to the CPI if, for example, stores offering lower prices but comparable service gained in market share. It also could impart a downward bias to the CPI if, for example, entry by low-priced outlets offering reduced services caused incumbent establishments to reduce their services in turn. As a practical matter, however, measurement of any such bias is complicated by the fact that different types of outlets commonly offer quite different shopping environments. Research on the factors affecting consumers' choices about where to shop ultimately may be helpful in devising appropriate procedures for dealing with changes in outlet mix.

For the BLS, the primary task is not to evaluate the bias estimates set forward by the Advisory Commission or other groups, but rather to employ the most accurate methods available for dealing with quality change and with new goods and outlets. Those methods must be rigorous, objective and reproducible, minimizing the role of analyst judgment. We recognize that there may be changes in consumer well-being associated with particular product or service innovations that are difficult or even impossible to capture using methods that meet these standards. We also believe, however, that adhering to the use of such methods is critical to maintaining the credibility of our official statistics.

NOTES

1. It is not correct to say that, in the application of these procedures, "No judgment at all is made about the quality differential between the new and old item," as do Boskin and his co-authors in their... paper in [*Journal of Economic Perspectives*, Winter 1998]. Rather, there is an implicit judgment that quality differences can be inferred from market price differences.

2. Recent research by Moulton and Moses (1997) provides some interesting evidence on the combined impact of the various steps taken to adjust for quality change on the overall rate of growth of the CPI. As they document, the rate of growth of the CPI would be significantly larger were these procedures not applied. As they also make clear, however, these findings carry no direct implications concerning any quality-adjustment bias in the CPI.

REFERENCES

Armknecht, Paul A., and Donald Weyback, "Adjustments for Quality Change in the U.S. Consumer Price Index," *Journal of Official Statistics*, 1989, 5:2, 107–23.

Berndt, Ernst R., Zvi Griliches, and Neal J. Rappaport, "Econometric Estimates of Price Indexes for Personal Computers in the 1990s," *Journal of Econometrics*, July 1995, 68:1, 243–68.

Bradley, Ralph, Bill Cook, Sylvia G. Leaver, and Brent R. Moulton, "An Overview of Research on Potential Uses of Scanner Data in the U.S. CPI," paper presented at the Third Meeting of the International Working Group on Price Indices, Voorburg, Netherlands, April 16–18, 1997 (Washington, D.C., Bureau of Labor Statistics).

Liegey, Paul R., Jr., "Adjusting Apparel Indexes in the Consumer Price Index for Quality Differences." In Foss, M. F., M. E. Manser, and A. H. Young, eds. *Price Measurements and Their Uses.* Chicago: University of Chicago Press, 1993, 209–26.

Liegey, Paul R., Jr., "Apparel Price Indexes: Effects of Hedonic Adjustment," *Monthly Labor Review*, May 1994, 117:5, 38–45.

Moulton, Brent R., and Karin E. Moses, "Addressing the Quality Change Issue in the Consumer Price Index," *Brookings Papers on Economic Activity*, 1997, 1, 305–49.

Reinsdorf, Marshall, Paul Liegey, and Kenneth Stewart, "New Ways of Handling Quality Change in the U.S. Consumer Price Index." Working Paper No. 276, Bureau of Labor Statistics, 1996.

Triplett, Jack E., "Quality Bias in Price Indexes and New Methods of Quality Adjustment." In Zvi Griliches, ed. *Price Indexes and Quality Change: Studies in New Methods of Measurement.* Boston: Harvard University Press, 1971.

POSTSCRIPT

Does the Consumer Price Index Suffer from Quality and New Product Bias?

Boskin et al. begin by stressing the importance of accuracy in measuring price change. They provide several examples of economic measurement that rely on such accuracy, especially those bearing on economic progress. They then reaffirm their original estimates of the extent of upward bias in the CPI: current measurement procedures employed by the BLS overstate the overall upward movement of prices by 1.1 percent per year, with quality change and new product bias accounting for more than half of the overall upward bias. Boskin et al. defend their estimate of the magnitude of quality change and new product bias with two fundamental arguments. First, they dismiss as unreasonable the criticism that estimates of such bias are too subjective. Second, they contend that the procedures used by the BLS are irrelevant because the Boskin et al. estimates are "a residual that remains after the BLS has completed its efforts." Boskin et al. note that most of the quality adjustments made by the BLS involve linking procedures when a new item replaces an old item. They contend that in these linking procedures there is no effort to judge the quality difference between the new and old items. This procedure thereby misses real quality differences associated with the "greater speed, durability, variety, convenience, safety, [and] energy efficiency" accompanying the introduction of new and improved goods. In addition, they assert that their original estimate of the extent of quality change and new product bias did not include all the factors needed to estimate the improvement in consumer well-being associated with the introduction of new products. Thus, they conclude, their estimate of the overall bias and its most important component —quality change and new product bias—"still seems right to us, especially because we were so cautious in the treatment of the bias from new products."

Abraham et al. begin by describing the procedures that the BLS uses when a new item must be substituted for an item in the CPI that is no longer available for pricing. In some cases—most notably in the categories of automobiles and apparel—the BLS employs a direct procedure. For example, there has been a direct adjustment for such changes in automobiles as "improved corrosion protection, improved warranties, sealing improvements, stainless steel exhaust, longer-life spark plugs, improved steering gears, rust-resistant fuel injection, clear-coat paint, and more." In other categories a linking procedure is used. Contrary to Boskin et al., these do involve a judgment about quality— the difference in price measures the difference in consumer value. Abraham et al. cite arguments by Boskin et al. that they believe are inconsistent with or negated by other evidence. For example, the upward bias associated with an increased variety in grocery and liquor stores and restaurants is implausible; the upward bias associated with apparel involves a general comparison based on the prices charged by a single retailer; and the upward bias associated with automobiles incorrectly assumes no adjustment for increased durability. Abraham et al. also argue that Boskin et al. seem to have ignored possible negative bias in the CPI and concentrated exclusively on positive or upward bias; examples are the decreased quality of air travel and higher education. Finally, Abraham et al. argue that many of the problems associated with the proper measurement of price and cost-of-living adjustments cannot be accomplished by the BLS because "economists simply have not developed operational procedures to correct the problems cited."

Additional readings on this issue include "The Overstated CPI—Can It Really Be True?" by Dean Baker, *Challenge* (September/October 1996); "Presto Change-O! On the Consumer Price Index," by Audrey Freedman, *Challenge* (March/April 1996); "The Downside of Bad Data," by Everett Ehrlich, *Challenge* (March/April 1997); "How Right is the Boskin Commission? Interview With Janet Norwood," *Challenge* (March/April 1997); "Quality Changes in the CPI: Some Missing Links," by Charles Hulten, *Challenge* (March/April 1997); "The Boskin Commission's Trillion-Dollar Fantasy," by Wynne Godley and George McCarthy, *Challenge* (May/June 1997); and "Bias in the Consumer Price Index: What Is the Evidence?" by Brent R. Moulton, *Journal of Economic Perspectives* (Fall 1996). For additional perspectives from the members of the Boskin commission, see "Quality Change and New Products," by Robert J. Gordon and Zvi Griliches, *American Economic Review* (May 1997) and "Implications for Overstating Inflation for Indexing Government Programs and Understanding Economic Progress," by Michael J. Boskin and Dale W. Jorgenson, *American Economic Review* (May 1997). Additional readings include "Getting Price Right: What Should Be Done?" by Angus Deaton; "The Consumer Price Index: A Research Agenda and Three Proposals," by Robert Pollak; and "Quality Changes in Price Indexes," by William D. Nordhaus, all of which appeared in *The Journal of Economic Perspectives* (Winter 1998).

ISSUE 11

Should Federal Government Budget Surpluses Be Used to Reduce Taxes?

YES: Daniel J. Mitchell, from "Return the Revenue Surplus to the Taxpayers," *The Heritage Foundation Backgrounder* (February 11, 1998)

NO: Office of Management and Budget, from *A Citizen's Guide to the Federal Budget: Budget of the United States Government Fiscal Year 2000* (1999)

ISSUE SUMMARY

YES: Political economist Daniel J. Mitchell argues that current and projected federal government budget surpluses should be used for tax cuts because this will promote economic growth and lead to rising living standards.

NO: In constructing the U.S. fiscal year 2000 budget, the Office of Management and Budget argues that current and projected surpluses should be used to invest in America's future; most important, 62 percent of the surpluses over the next 15 years should be used to strengthen Social Security.

The Full Employment and Balanced Growth Act of 1978 lists a number of economic goals for the U.S. federal government. Besides the macroeconomic objectives of full employment, price stability, and increased real income, the act specifically mentions the goal of a balanced budget. This means that the government must collect in taxes an amount equal to its expenditures. Despite this legislative call to action, the U.S. federal government's budget was in deficit in every fiscal year from 1978 through 1997. In fiscal year 1978 the deficit stood at $59 billion and reached a record level of $290 billion in 1992. Since fiscal year 1992, however, the government's budget position has gradually improved: by fiscal year 1997, the deficit was down to $22 billion.

When the U.S. federal government runs a deficit, it sells securities—treasury bills, notes, and bonds—just like a business firm that sells securities to raise funds. When the government runs a deficit, the public debt increases by the amount of the deficit. The public, or national, debt represents the total value of outstanding government securities. Accordingly, the public debt at any point in time is a summary of all prior deficits (offset by the retirement of securities if the government chooses to repurchase its securities when it has a budget surplus). By September 1998 the gross U.S. federal debt was approximately $5.5 trillion, and the net interest on this debt amounted to approximately $243 billion. The debt is owned by (the government securities have been purchased by) different groups, including individuals, commercial banks, pension funds, life insurance companies, federal government agencies, state and local governments, and corporations. Some of the government's debt has also been purchased by foreign individuals, businesses, and governments.

Fiscal year 1998 marked what some have called a historical turning point in the U.S. federal government's budget position. Instead of another deficit and additional debt, the government's budget ran a surplus for the first time since fiscal year 1969. This surplus represented the excess of revenues of $1.722 trillion over spending of $1.653 trillion, a difference of $69 billion. Current projections indicate that without changes in the basic structure of various taxes and spending programs, the U.S. federal government's surplus position will extend far into the future. The estimated surplus is $80 billion for fiscal year 1999 and $117 billion for fiscal year 2000. Over the next 15 years the Clinton administration projects a cumulative surplus of more than $4.8 trillion.

U.S. federal government budget surpluses mean that taxpayers are paying more to the government than the government is spending. This is not a comforting position for taxpayers. This discomfort arises from the belief that taxpayers' disposable income and consumption are being reduced for no apparent reason; that is, taxpayers are paying more in taxes than is necessary to finance current government programs. Thus, it comes as no surprise that many taxpayers want something done with these surpluses. The options are either reduce taxes to bring revenues down to the level of outlays or raise spending to match the level of revenues. The latter option includes using the surpluses to reduce or buy back part of the federal debt. But within either of these fundamental choices there are many options. If the tax reduction option is chosen, which taxes should be reduced, and by what amounts? If the surpluses are to be used for spending increases, then which programs should be expanded, and by what amounts?

So instead of opposing views on how to eliminate government budget deficits and balance the budget, there is now a debate on how the surpluses should be used—whether the best course of action is to cut taxes or to maintain taxes and use the surpluses for other purposes. In the following selections, Daniel J. Mitchell argues that the surpluses should be used for tax reduction. He believes that this will work to the benefit of the larger economy, stimulating economic growth and raising living standards. The Clinton administration's Office of Management and Budget argues that the surpluses would be better used for "investments in America"; targeting a significant portion of the surplus to fix Social Security is one of these investments.

YES

Daniel J. Mitchell

RETURN THE REVENUE
SURPLUS TO THE TAXPAYERS

Although the federal government has run budget deficits every year for nearly three decades, recent government estimates indicate that revenues will exceed spending by 2001. Indeed, both President Bill Clinton and congressional leaders have stated their intention to balance the budget as early as 1999. Even if lawmakers do nothing more than control future spending to the limited degree called for in [the 1997] budget deal—admittedly, a bold assumption—the projected budget surplus will climb to more than $100 billion by 2006. This emerging surplus has created a three-way battle in Washington, D.C. Some policymakers would like to spend the surplus money on new government programs. Others recommend using it to reduce the national debt. A third group, meanwhile, prefers returning the money to U.S. taxpayers.

If policymakers wish to increase economic growth and improve living standards, they should dedicate the surplus revenues to the option that will generate the highest returns. In simpler terms, they should ask themselves how the surplus money could get the "most bang for the buck." Economic research continues to show that tax cuts, particularly reducing marginal tax rates on work, savings, and investment, would generate large returns. Debt reduction also would have positive returns, but the benefit would be modest because the government's inflation-adjusted borrowing costs are relatively low. Increasing spending, by contrast, would be the least desirable way to dispose of surplus revenues. Indeed, most government programs have negative returns, meaning that the economy's overall performance falls as government spending increases....

Why the Size of Government Is the Real Issue
Two decades of budget battles in Washington, D.C., have created a bipartisan myth that balancing the budget is the most important goal of fiscal policy. This is a deeply flawed assumption. Budget deficits are neither good nor bad. They simply measure the extent to which government is financed through borrowing instead of taxes. To be sure, there are some good reasons to avoid large and persistent deficits, such as a moral concern about imposing costs on

From Daniel J. Mitchell, "Return the Revenue Surplus to the Taxpayers," *The Heritage Foundation Backgrounder*, no. 1155 (February 11, 1998). Copyright © 1998 by The Heritage Foundation. Reprinted by permission.

future generations and a political concern about whether taxpayers recognize the true cost of government. Nonetheless, a myopic obsession with balancing the budget distracts policymakers from more important issues—such as the size of government and the burden of the tax system.

In reality, the battle over the surplus is a battle over the size of government. Advocates of bigger government want the tax burden to remain high so that excess tax revenues can be used to create new programs and expand existing ones. The Clinton Administration, for example, has proposed expanding the Medicare program and creating new federal childcare programs. In fact, the Administration's budget proposals include $100 billion in additional taxes over five years in order to finance additional increases in the size of government. Some policymakers, by contrast, want the tax burden to remain high in order to keep government on its current growth path while balancing the budget faster and/or paying off some of the national debt.

Why Cutting Taxes Is the Better Option
Advocates of tax reduction believe that surplus tax revenues should be returned to those who earned the money in the first place—the taxpayers. This view also holds that a tax cut should be equal, at the very least, to any projected surplus, thus precluding politicians from spending the money. In this scenario, tax cuts would keep government from growing any larger. Many tax cut proponents today hope to go beyond such a point, however, and urge tax reductions that exceed the estimated surplus. The benefit of this approach is that lawmakers would be under pressure to reduce federal

spending in order to limit or preclude increases in government borrowing.

In addition to constraining the growth of government, tax cuts are desirable because lower tax rates increase incentives to work, save, and invest. The degree to which the economy benefits, however, will depend on how the tax cut is structured. In order to maximize the increase in family income and improvement in standards of living, tax reductions should be designed to move the tax code toward a single rate consumption-based tax, such as the flat tax. Alternatively, tax cuts could help facilitate the transition to a private Social Security system that would boost retirement income, increase national savings, and reduce the unfunded liabilities of the current system. Furthermore, cutting taxes has a more beneficial impact on the economy, dollar for dollar, than reducing the debt. Although scholars have failed to find any significant relationship between government borrowing and growth, the academic literature is rife with studies that illustrate the ways in which high tax rates reduce incentives to engage in productive economic behavior.[1]

Finally, the tax burden should be reduced because Americans are overtaxed. Despite the tiny tax cut approved [in 1997], federal taxes are expected to consume 19.9 percent of economic output in 1998, a peacetime record.[2] To put this issue in perspective, taxes totaled 19.7 percent of gross domestic product (GDP) in 1981, the year Ronald Reagan took office in part because of a nationwide tax revolt.

Not only are taxes at record highs today, the trend is in the wrong direction. Since Bill Clinton took office in 1993, the tax burden as a percent of GDP has climbed by 2.1 percentage points. This may not sound like a large amount, but

2.1 percent of an $8.461 trillion economy is $177.7 billion. Just reducing taxes to their level when Clinton took office would mean that the average family of four would receive more than $2,500 in annual tax relief.

HOW TO CUT TAXES

The burden of government in the United States is smaller than in many other countries. U.S. labor markets are much more flexible, and the country has comparatively small amounts of economic regulation. Inflation is at very low levels, and Americans enjoy the benefits of expanded international trade. These factors help to explain why the United States is prosperous, with reasonable growth and low unemployment. Nevertheless, several reforms could accelerate the economy's performance. Two of these reforms involve taxes, and in both cases the reforms almost certainly would require a reduction in the country's tax burden.

First, the income tax system suffers from serious moral and economic shortcomings. With respect to the moral question, the current income tax code fails a simple test of justice and fairness because it does not treat everyone equally. In terms of the economic shortcomings, the present system undermines the economy's performance by levying punitive tax rates, imposing double taxation on savings and investment, and burdening taxpayers with more than $150 billion of compliance costs. The best solution to the tax code's myriad problems is the flat tax. In order to minimize political opposition to a flat tax, however, the tax rate under a flat tax should be set at a sufficiently low level so that a substantial majority of taxpayers would receive a tax cut. The upcoming budget surplus makes such a tax cut more feasible.

Second, the Social Security system is a financial disaster. Not only is it actuarially bankrupt, with trillions of dollars of unfunded liabilities, it also is a bad deal for workers, offering them meager retirement benefits in exchange for the huge amount of taxes they pay into the system.[3] The only way to solve both problems is to reduce payroll taxes substantially and then require workers to place that money in private retirement accounts. Workers who chose this option would have no problem foregoing their promised Social Security benefits, because their private retirement investments would generate a nest egg that would give them much more income in retirement than would be possible in the government's system. Surplus tax revenues could help facilitate the transition to a private system while ensuring the benefits payments to current retirees would continue.

Regardless of whether fundamental reform of either Social Security or the internal revenue code is politically practical in the near future, incremental changes could move the United States closer to a tax code that treats all citizens equally or to a Social Security system that provides workers with more retirement security.

In the case of Social Security, lawmakers could begin the process of reform by allowing workers to divert a portion of the existing payroll tax into private pension accounts. This option would reduce the government's long-term debt problem because workers who choose this option would agree to forego a portion of the future benefits they currently are promised. Workers would be better off under this option because private pension accounts earn better returns, thus accruing more income for retirement. Future taxpayers would be better off as well, because even partial privatization would reduce the huge unfunded liability of the system.

Using surplus tax revenues to begin moving to a flat tax is somewhat more complicated, but only because there are many problems with the current tax code. Its high tax rates, pervasive double taxation of savings and investment, and mind-numbing complexity cry out for attention. Policymakers need to be sure, however, that their incremental changes to the tax code are consistent with their efforts to move to a fair and simple flat tax. In other words, any revisions should move the country closer to a system that taxes all income, but only taxes it one time and at one low rate.

Among the reforms that would satisfy these objectives are:

- The repeal of the marriage penalty. The current tax system penalizes marriage. A married two-earner couple will pay more in taxes than an otherwise identical couple of two income earners who choose to live together. For the 21 million couples affected, this marriage penalty averages about $1,400 annually. Because there is no marriage penalty under the flat tax, repeal of the marriage penalty would be an important step toward fundamental reform.
- The repeal of the death tax. A core principle of tax reform is that the Internal Revenue Service (IRS) should get only one bite of the apple. Once taxpayers pay tax on their earned income, the government should not be allowed to impose an additional layer of tax on parents who choose to save that after-tax money to leave a nest egg for their children. Repealing the

death tax would be a major step toward establishing a tax code that treats all income and all taxpayers the same.
- An end to double taxation of savings. The current tax code does not wait until a taxpayer's death before imposing double taxation on his or her income. With some exceptions, such as individual retirement accounts (IRAs), the current system imposes a second layer of tax on income that is saved by taxing the interest earned. Because there is no second layer of tax on income that is consumed, this creates a bias against saving. The ideal way to end that bias would be to extend IRA treatment to all savings.[4] To the extent that comprehensive IRA expansion is not feasible, lawmakers could move in this direction by eliminating the double taxation on certain kinds of savings, such as money set aside for purposes of higher education.

CONCLUSION

The government is collecting near-record amounts of tax revenue. This windfall, combined with rather modest levels of fiscal restraint, could generate a budget surplus. The potential existence of a surplus, however, is not nearly as important as the questions of whether government already is too big or the U.S. tax code is too destructive. Thorough analysis of these questions strongly suggests that the tax burden should be reduced, preferably by reforming the tax code and/or privatizing the Social Security system.

NOTES

1. Roger H. Gordon and Dale Jorgenson, "The Investment Tax Credit and Countercyclical Policy," Harvard Institute of Economic Research Discus-

sion Paper No. 373, Cambridge, Mass., June 1974; James M. Poterba and Lawrence Summers, "Dividend Taxes, Corporate Investment, and 'Q'," National Bureau of Economic Research Working Paper No. 829, December 1981; Martin Feldstein, "Inflation, Tax Rules, and the Accumulation of Residential and Non-Residential Capital," Institute for International Economic Studies *Seminar Paper* No. 186, University of Stockholm, Sweden, November 1981; Dale Jorgenson, "Taxation and Technical Change" in Ralph Landau and N. Bruce Hannay, eds., "Taxation, Technology, and the U.S. Economy" (New York: Pergamon Press, 1981); Robert E. Hall and Dale Jorgenson, "Tax Policy and Investment Behavior," *American Economic Review*, Vol. 58, No. 3, pp. 391–414; Charles W. Bischoff, "The Effect of Alternative Lag Distributions," in Gary Fromm, ed., *Tax Incentives and Capital Spending* (Washington, D.C.: The Brookings Institution, 1971); Keith Marsden, "Links Between Taxes and Economic Growth: Some Empirical Evidence," World Bank Staff Working Paper No. 605, Washington, D.C., 1983.

2. U.S. Government Printing Office, Historical Tables, *Budget of the United States Government*, FY1999, February 1998.

3. William W. Beach and Gareth G. Davis, "Social Security's Rate of Return," *A Report of the Heritage Center for Data Analysis*, No. CDA98–01, The Heritage Foundation, January 15, 1998.

4. This can be achieved through traditional IRAs, which allow a deduction when the income is first earned, but then impose the one layer of tax on withdrawals, or back-ended (or Roth) IRAs, which impose the one layer of tax when income is first earned, but then do not impose a second layer of tax on subsequent withdrawals.

Office of Management and Budget

THE PRESIDENT'S 2000 BUDGET

The President's 2000 budget promises the third balanced budget of this Administration. With it, the Nation's fiscal house is in order and we are prepared to meet the challenges of the next century. It continues on the path the President has followed for the past six years of maintaining fiscal discipline and investing wisely in our Nation's priorities.

It invests in education and training so Americans can make the most of this economy's opportunities. It invests in health and the environment to improve our quality of life. It invests in our security at home and abroad, strengthens law enforcement and provides our Armed Forces with the resources they need to safeguard our national interests in the next century.

The President's budget makes these investments while maintaining the fiscal discipline that allowed the Federal Government to record its first surplus in a generation last year. The budget forecasts that the Government will produce a surplus again this year, and will continue to do so for decades to come. Our success in eliminating the budget deficit proves that we are capable of fulfilling great responsibilities, and there is now every reason for us to rise to the next challenge. The President believes it is now time to work together to save Social Security.

INVESTING IN THE FUTURE

In his State of the Union address, the President proposed a framework for a comprehensive, bipartisan solution to the long-term financing problems of Social Security. The President's plan proposes using 62 percent of the unified budget surplus of the next 15 years to strengthen Social Security. It would tap the power of financial markets by investing roughly one-fifth of the surplus dedicated to Social Security in private financial instruments, including corporate equities. This proposal would substantially improve the program's fiscal position, strengthening it until the middle of the next century. Then, in a bipartisan effort envisioned by the [recent] national dialogue, the President is urging Congress to join him to make the difficult but achievable choices to save Social Security until 2075.

From Office of Management and Budget, *A Citizen's Guide to the Federal Budget: Budget of the United States Government Fiscal Year 2000* (1999). Washington, DC: U.S. Government Printing Office, 1999.

Once Social Security is on sound financial footing, the President proposes saving and improving Medicare, the Federal program that finances health care for millions of seniors and disabled Americans. The President's framework will reserve 15 percent of the projected budget surplus of the next 15 years for Medicare, ensuring that its trust fund is secure for 20 years.

The President is also committed to helping all Americans save and invest so that they will have additional sources of income in retirement. Dedicating just over 10 percent of the surplus of the next 15 years to Universal Savings Accounts will help Americans save for the future by allowing them to invest as they choose and receive matching contributions.

And looking ahead to the Nation's other vital needs that will arise in the future, the President's framework will reserve 11 percent of the projected surplus for military readiness, education, and other critical domestic priorities.

The President's budget builds on efforts to invest in the skills of the American people. It continues his policy of helping working families with their basic needs —raising their children, sending them to college, and expanding access to health care. It also invests in education and training, the environment, science and technology, law enforcement, and other priorities to help raise the standard of living and quality of life of Americans.

In this budget, the President is proposing major initiatives that will continue his investments in high-priority areas— from helping working families with their child care expenses to allowing Americans from 55 to 65 to buy into Medicare; from helping States and school districts recruit and prepare thousands more teachers and build thousands more classrooms to making every effort to fight tobacco and its use among young people.

For six years, the President has sought to help working families balance the demands of work and family. In this budget he proposes a major effort to make child care more affordable, accessible and safe, by expanding tax credits for middle-income families and for businesses to expand their child care resources, assisting parents who want to attend college meet their child care needs, and increasing funds with which the Child Care and Development Block Grant can help more poor and near poor children. The budget proposes an Early Learning Fund, which would provide grants to communities for activities that improve early childhood education and the quality of child care for those under age five.

The President has worked hard to expand health care coverage and improve the Nation's health. The budget gives new insurance options to hundreds of thousands of Americans aged 55 to 65 and it advocates bipartisan national legislation that would reduce tobacco use among the young. The President's budget proposes initiatives to help patients, families, and care givers cope with the burdens of long-term care; and it helps reduce barriers to employment for individuals with disabilities. The budget also enables more Medicare beneficiaries to receive promising cancer treatments by participating more easily in clinical trials. And it improves the fiscal soundness of Medicare and Medicaid through new management proposals, including programs to combat waste, fraud, and abuse.

The President's efforts have also enhanced access to, and the quality of, education and training. The budget takes the next steps by continuing to help States and school districts reduce class size by recruiting and preparing thousands more teachers and building thousands more new classrooms. The President's budget proposes improving school accountability by funding monetary awards to the highest performing schools that serve low-income students, providing resources to States to help them identify and change the least successful schools, and ending social promotion by funding additional education hours through programs like the 21st Century Community Learning Centers. The budget also proposes further increases in the maximum Pell Grant to help low-income undergraduates complete their college education and more funding for universal reemployment services to help train or find jobs for all dislocated workers who need help.

The budget proposes a historic interagency Lands Legacy initiative to both preserve the Nation's Great Places, and advance preservation of open spaces in every community. This initiative will give State and local governments the tools for orderly growth while protecting and enhancing green spaces, clean water, wildlife habitat and outdoor recreation. The Administration also proposes a Livability Initiative with a new financing mechanism, Better America Bonds, to create more open spaces in urban and suburban areas, improve water quality, and clean up abandoned industrial sites. In addition, the budget would restore and rehabilitate national parks, forests, and public lands and facilities; expand efforts to restore and protect the water quality of rivers and lakes; and better protect endangered species.

The President has worked to bring peace to troubled parts of the world, and

has played a leadership role in Northern Ireland, Bosnia, and most recently in the Wye River Memorandum on the Middle East. The budget reinforces America's commitment to peace in the Middle East by providing for an economic and military assistance package arising from the Wye River Memorandum. The work of diplomacy, advancing peace and United States interests, has inherent dangers, as the death toll from the terrorist attacks on two U.S. Embassies in Africa [recently] reminds us. The budget proposes increased funding to ensure the continued protection of American embassies, consulates and other facilities, and the valuable employees who work there. It supports significant increases in funding for State Department programs to address the threats posed by weapons of mass destruction. The budget also increases programs that support U.S. manufacturing exports and continues our long standing policy of opening foreign markets.

The mission of our Armed Forces has changed in this post-Cold War era, and in many ways it is more complex. Today, the U.S. military must guard against major threats to the Nation's security, including regional dangers like cross-border aggression, the proliferation of the technology of weapons of mass destruction, transnational dangers like the spread of drugs and terrorism, and direct attacks on the U.S. homeland from intercontinental ballistic missiles or other weapons of mass destruction. The U.S. Armed Forces are well prepared to meet this mission. Military readiness —the ability to engage where and when necessary—is razor sharp, and this budget provides resources to make sure that it stays that way for years to come. The budget provides a long term, sustained increase in defense spending to enhance the military's ability to respond to crises, build for the future through programs for weapons modernization, and take care of military personnel and their families by enhancing the quality of life, thereby increasing retention and recruitment.

IMPROVING PERFORMANCE THROUGH BETTER MANAGEMENT

A key element in the Administration's ability to making these investments, while balancing the budget, is the reinvention of Government—doing more with less. Efforts led by Vice President Gore's National Partnership for Reinvention have streamlined Government, reduced its work force, and focused on performance to improve operations and delivery of service. And these efforts, by reducing the cost of Government operations, have improved the bottom line and contributed to our strong economy.

Since 1993, the Administration, working with the Congress, has eliminated and reduced hundreds of unnecessary programs and projects. The size of Government, that is, the actual total of Government spending, has equaled a smaller share of GDP [gross domestic product] than in any year of the previous two Administrations, and in 2000 will drop to 19.4 percent of GDP, its lowest level since the early 1970s. Finally, the Administration has cut the size of the Federal civilian work force by 365,000, creating the smallest work force in 36 years and, as a share of total civilian employment, the smallest since 1933. . . .

The Administration, however, is working to create not just a smaller Government, but a better one, a Government that best provides services and benefits to its ultimate customers—the American people. It has not just cut the Federal work force, it has streamlined layers of bureaucracy. It has not just reorganized headquarters and field offices, it has ensured that those closest to the customers can best serve them.

For 2000, the Administration once again is turning its efforts to the next stage of "reinventing" the Federal Government. It plans to dramatically overhaul 32 Federal agencies to improve performance in key services, such as expediting student loan processing and speeding aid to disaster victims. It also plans to continue tackling critical challenges, such as ensuring that Government computers can process the year 2000 date change and making more Government services available electronically.

Under the 1993 Government Performance and Results Act, Cabinet departments and agencies have prepared individual performance plans that they will send to Congress with the performance goals they plan to meet in 2000. These plans provided the basis for the second Government-wide Performance Plan which is contained in this budget. In 2000, for the first time, agencies will submit to the President and the Congress annual reports for 1999 that compare actual and target performance levels and explain any difference between them.

POSTSCRIPT

Should Federal Government Budget Surpluses Be Used to Reduce Taxes?

Mitchell states that government budget surpluses can be used in three different ways: spend the surpluses on new government programs, use the surpluses to reduce the national debt, or eliminate the surpluses by cutting taxes. He then rates the three alternatives: the first alternative is the least desirable because government programs have negative returns and will hurt the overall performance of the economy. The second alternative will only produce modest benefits because "the government's inflation-adjusted borrowing costs are relatively low." The third alternative is the best because it will generate large returns in the form of more saving and investment as well as a greater return to work. Mitchell contends that the debate of what to do with the budget surpluses is really a debate over the size of government, and cutting taxes will be a step in reducing the role of government in the economy.

The Clinton administration's Office of Management and Budget outlines the general goals of the president's budget for fiscal year 2000: to improve education and training, health and the environment, and security both at home and abroad. The administration proposes that budget surpluses over the next 15 years be used as follows: 62 percent should be used to strengthen Social Security; 15 percent should be used to strengthen and improve the Medicare program; 10 percent should be dedicated to Universal Savings Accounts; and 11 percent should be allocated to "military readiness, education, and other critical domestic priorities." The Clinton administration believes that the use of the budget surpluses for these investments in America's future will better prepare the nation for the challenges it will face as it enters the new millennium.

For more detailed information on the U.S. federal government's budget, see *The Economic and Budget Outlook: Fiscal Years 2000–2009* (January 1999). Additional readings include "New Surplus Projections Will Allow Deep Tax Cuts and Social Security Reform" by Ronald D. Utt, *The Heritage Foundation Backgrounder* (July 27, 1998); "How Congress Can Use the Surpluses to Cut Taxes and Begin Fundamental Tax Reform," by William W. Beach, *The Heritage Foundation Backgrounder* (April 13, 1999); "Does the Budget Surplus Justify a Large Scale Tax Cut?" by William G. Gade and Alan J. Auerbach, *Brookings Institution Tax Notes* (March 22, 1999); "Budget Surpluses? What to Do With the Surplus," by Max B. Sawicky, *Challenge* (January/February 1998); and "The Great Surplus Debate," by Alice Munnell, Dean Baker, and Robert Eisner, *The American Prospect* (May–June 1998).

ISSUE 12

Is It Time to Abolish the Minimum Wage?

YES: Thomas Rustici, from "A Public Choice View of the Minimum Wage," *Cato Journal* (Spring/Summer 1985)

NO: Charles Craypo, from "In Defense of Minimum Wages," An Original Essay Written for This Volume (1997)

ISSUE SUMMARY

YES: Orthodox neoclassical economist Thomas Rustici asserts that the effects of the minimum wage are clear: it creates unemployment among the least-skilled workers.

NO: Labor economist Charles Craypo argues that a high minimum wage is good for workers, employers, and consumers alike and that it is therefore good for the economy as a whole.

In the midst of the Great Depression, Congress passed the Fair Labor Standards Act (FLSA) of 1938. In one bold stroke, it established a minimum wage rate of $.25 an hour, placed controls on the use of child labor, designated 44 hours as the normal workweek, and mandated that time and a half be paid to anyone working longer than the normal workweek. Fifty years later the debates concerning child labor, length of the workweek, and overtime pay have long subsided, but the debate over the minimum wage rages on.

The immediate and continued concern over the minimum wage component of the FLSA should surprise few people. Although $.25 an hour is a paltry sum compared to today's wage rates, in 1938 it was a princely reward for work. It must be remembered that jobs were hard to come by and unemployment rates at times reached as high as 25 percent of the workforce. When work was found, any wage seemed acceptable to those who roamed the streets with no "safety net" to protect their families. Indeed, consider the fact that $.25 an hour was 40.3 percent of the average manufacturing wage rate for 1938.

Little wonder, then, that the business community in the 1930s was up in arms. Business leaders argued that if wages went up, prices would rise. This would choke off the little demand for goods and services that existed in the marketplace, and the demand for workers would be sure to fall. The end result would be a return to the depths of the depression, where there was little or no hope of employment for the very people who were supposed to benefit from the Fair Labor Standards Act.

This dire forecast was demonstrated by simple supply and demand analysis. First, as modern-day introductory textbooks in economics invariably show, unemployment occurs when a minimum wage greater than the equilibrium wage is mandated by law. This simplistic analysis, which assumes competitive conditions in both the product and factor markets, is predicated upon the assumptions that as wages are pushed above the equilibrium level, the quantity of labor demanded will fall and this quantity of labor supplied will increase. The result is that this wage rigidity prevents the market from clearing. The end result is an excess in the quantity of labor supplied relative to the quantity of labor demanded.

The question that should be addressed in this debate is whether or not a simple supply and demand analysis is capable of adequately predicting what happens in real-world labor markets when a minimum wage is introduced or an existing minimum wage is raised. The significance of this is not based on idle curiosity. The minimum wage has been increased numerous times since its introduction in 1938. Most recently, effective September 1, 1997, legislation establishing the current minimum wage of $5.15 was signed into law by President Bill Clinton.

Did this minimum wage increase, and other increases before it, do irreparable harm to those who are least able to defend themselves in the labor market, the marginal worker? That is, if a minimum wage of $5.15 is imposed, what happens to all those marginal workers whose value to the firm is something less than $5.15? Are these workers fired? Do firms simply absorb this cost increase in the form of reduced corporate profits? What happens to productivity?

This is the crux of the following debate between Thomas Rustici and Charles Craypo. Rustici argues that the answer is obvious: there will be an excess in the quantity of labor supplied relative to the quantity demanded. In lay terms, there will be unemployment. Craypo rejects this neoclassical view. He recommends judging the minimum wage on the intent of the original legislation: increased aggregate demand and elimination of predatory labor market practices.

YES

Thomas Rustici

A PUBLIC CHOICE VIEW OF
THE MINIMUM WAGE

Why, when the economist gives advice to his society, is he so often cooly ignored? He never ceases to preach free trade ... and protectionism is growing in the United States. He deplores the perverse effects of minimum wage laws, and the legal minimum is regularly raised each 3 to 5 years. He brands usury laws as a medieval superstition, but no state hurries to repeal its laws.

—George Stigler

INTRODUCTION

Much of public policy is allegedly based on the implications of economic theory. However, economic analysis of government policy is often disregarded for political reasons. The minimum wage law is one such example. Every politician openly deplores the spectacle of double-digit teenage unemployment pervading modern society. But, when economists claim that scientific proof, a priori and empirical, dictates that minimum wage laws cause such a regretful outcome, their statements generally fall on deaf congressional ears. Economists too often assume that policymakers are interested in obtaining all the existing economic knowledge before deciding on a specific policy course. This view of the policy-formation process, however, is naive. In framing economic policy politicians will pay some attention to economists' advice, but such advice always will be rejected when it conflicts with the political reality of winning votes....

ECONOMIC EFFECTS OF THE MINIMUM WAGE

Economic analysis has demonstrated few things as clearly as the effects of the minimum wage law. It is well known that the minimum wage creates unemployment among the least skilled workers by raising wage rates above free market levels. Eight major effects of the minimum wage can be discussed: unemployment effects, employment effects in uncovered sectors of the economy,

From Thomas Rustici, "A Public Choice View of the Minimum Wage," *Cato Journal*, vol. 5, no. 1 (Spring/Summer 1985). Copyright © 1985 by The Cato Institute. Reprinted by permission.

reduction in nonwage benefits, labor substitution effects, capital substitution effects, racial discrimination in hiring practices, human capital development, and distortion of the market process with respect to comparative advantage. Although the minimum wage has other effects, such as a reduction in hours of employment, these eight effects are the most significant ones for this paper.

Unemployment Effects

The first federal minimum wage laws were established under the provisions of the National Recovery Administration (NRA). The National Industrial Recovery Act, which became law on 16 June 1933, established industrial minimum wages for 515 classes of labor. Over 90 percent of the minimum wages were set at between 30 and 40 cents per hour.[1] Early empirical evidence attests to the unemployment effects of the minimum wage. Using the estimates of C. F. Roos, who was the director of research at the NRA, Benjamin Anderson states: "Roos estimates that, by reason of the minimum wage provisions of the codes, about 500,000 Negro workers were on relief in 1934. Roos adds that a minimum wage definitely causes the displacement of the young, inexperienced worker and the old worker."[2]

On 27 May 1935 the Supreme Court declared the NRA unconstitutional, burying the minimum wage codes with it. The minimum wage law reappeared at a later date, however, with the support of the Supreme Court. In what became the precedent for the constitutionality of future minimum wage legislation, the Court upheld the Washington State minimum wage law on 29 March 1937 in *West Coast Hotel v. Parrish*.[3] This declaration gave the Roosevelt administration and Labor Secretary Frances Perkins the green light to reestablish the federal minimum wage, which was achieved on 25 June 1938 when President Roosevelt signed into law the Fair Labor Standards Act (FLSA).

The FSLA included legislation affecting work-age requirements, the length of the workweek, pay rates for overtime work, as well as the national minimum wage provision. The law established minimum wage rates of 25 cents per hour the first year, 30 cents per hour for the next six years, and 40 cents per hour after seven years. The penalty for noncompliance was severe: violators faced a $10,000 fine, six months imprisonment, or both. In addition, an aggrieved employee could sue his employer for twice the difference between the statutory wage rate and his actual pay.[4]

With the passage of the FLSA, it became inevitable that major dislocations would result in labor markets, primarily those for low-skilled and low-wage workers. Although the act affected occupations covering only one-fifth of the labor force,[5] leaving a large uncovered sector to minimize the disemployment effects, the minimum wage was still extremely counterproductive. The Labor Department admitted that the new minimum wage had a disemployment effect, and one historian sympathetic to the minimum wage was forced to concede that "[t]he Department of Labor estimated that the 25-cents-an-hour minimum wage caused about 30,000 to 50,000 to lose their job. About 90% of these were in southern industries such as bagging, pecan shelling, and tobacco stemming."[6]

These estimates seriously understate the actual magnitude of the damage. Since only 300,000 workers received an increase as a result of the minimum wage,[7] estimates of 30,000–50,000 lost jobs reveal that 10–13 percent of those covered by the law lost their jobs. But it is highly dubious that only 30,000–50,000 low-wage earners lost their jobs in the entire country; that many unemployed could have been found in the state of Texas alone, where labor authorities saw devastation wrought via the minimum wage on the pecan trade. The *New York Times* reported the following on 24 October 1938:

> Information received today by State labor authorities indicated that more than 40,000 employees of the pecan nut shelling plants in Texas would be thrown out of work tomorrow by the closing down of that industry, due to the new Wages and Hours Law. In San Antonio, sixty plants, employing ten thousand men and women, mostly Mexicans, will close.... Plant owners assert that they cannot remain in business and pay the minimum wage of 25 cents an hour with a maximum working week of forty-four hours. Many garment factories in Texas will also close.[8]

It can reasonably be deduced that even if the Texas estimates had been wildly inaccurate, the national unemployment effect would still have exceeded the Department of Labor's estimates.

The greatest damage, however, did not come in Texas or in any other southern state, but in Puerto Rico. Since a minimum wage law has its greatest unemployment effect on low-wage earners, and since larger proportions of workers in poor regions such as Puerto Rico tend to be at the lower end of the wage scale, Puerto Rico was disproportionately hard-hit. Subject to the same national 25-cents-per-hour rate as workers on the mainland, Puerto Rican workers suffered much more hardship from the minimum wage law. According to Anderson:

> It was thought by many that, in the first year, the provision would not affect many industries outside the South, though the framers of the law apparently forgot about Puerto Rico, and very grave disturbances came in that island.... Immense unemployment resulted there through sheer inability of important industries to pay the 25 cents an hour.[9]

Simon Rottenberg likewise points out the tragic position in which Puerto Rico was placed by the enactment of the minimum wage:

> When the Congress established a minimum wage of 25 cents per hour in 1938, the average hourly wage in the U.S. was 62.7 cents.... It resulted in a mandatory increase for only some 300,000 workers out of a labor force of more than 54 million. In Puerto Rico, in contrast... the new Federal minimum far exceeded the prevailing average hourly wage of the major portion of Puerto Rican workers. If a continuing serious attempt at enforcement... had been made, it would have meant literal economic chaos for the island's economy.[10]...

After two years of economic disruption in Puerto Rico, Congress amended the minimum wage provisions.[11] The minimum wage was reduced to 12.5 cents per hour, but it was too late for many industries and for thousands of low-wage earners employed by them, who suddenly found unemployment the price they had to pay for the minimum wage.

In sum, the tragedy of the minimum wage laws during the NRA and the FLSA was not just textbook-theorizing by academic economists, but real-world disaster for the thousands who became the victims of the law. But these destructive effects have not caused the law to be repealed; to the contrary, it has been expanded in coverage and increased in amount.

... Evidence for the unemployment effects of the minimum wage continues to mount. Many empirical studies since the early 1950s—from early research by Marshall Colberg and Yale Brozen to more recent work by Jacob Mincer and James Ragan—have validated the predictions of economic theory regarding the unemployment effects of the minimum wage law. In virtually every case it was found that the net employment effects and labor-force participation rates were negatively related to changes in the minimum wage. In the face of 50 years of evidence, the question is no longer *if* the minimum wage law creates unemployment, but *how much* current or future increases in the minimum wage will adversely affect the labor market.

Employment in Uncovered Sectors

The labor market can be divided into two sectors: that covered by the minimum wage law, and that not covered. In a partially covered market, the effects of the minimum wage are somewhat disguised. Increasing it disemploys workers in the covered sector, prompting them to search for work in the uncovered sector if they are trainable and mobile. This then drives down the wage rate in the uncovered sector, making it lower than it otherwise would have been. Since perfect knowledge and flexibility is not observed in real-world labor markets, substantial unemployment can occur during the transition period.

Employees in the covered sector who do not lose their jobs get a wage-rate increase through the higher minimum wage. But this comes only at the expense

of (1) the disemployed workers who lose their jobs and suffer unemployment during the transition to employment in the uncovered sector, and (2) everyone in the uncovered sector, as their wage rate falls due to the influx of unemployed workers from the covered sector. While increasing the incomes of some low-wage earners, increasing the minimum wage tends to make the lowest wage earners in the uncovered sector even poorer than they otherwise would have been.

Yale Brozen has found that the uncovered household sector served to absorb the minimum wage-induced disemployed in the past.[12] But the "safety valve" of the uncovered portion of the economy is rapidly vanishing with the continual elimination of various exemptions.[13] Because of this trend we can expect to see the level of structural unemployment increase with escalation of the minimum wage.[14]

Nonwage Benefits

Wage rates are not the only costs associated with the employment of workers by firms. The effective labor cost a firm incurs is usually a package of pecuniary and nonpecuniary benefits. As such, contends Richard McKenzie,

> employers can be expected to respond to a minimum wage law by cutting back or eliminating altogether those fringe benefits and conditions of work, like the company parties, that increase the supply of labor but which do not affect the productivity of labor. By reducing such non-money benefits of employment, the employer reduces his labor costs from what they otherwise would have been and loses nothing in the way of reduced labor productivity."[15]

If one takes the view that employees desire both pecuniary and nonpecu-

Table 1

Value of the Minimum Wage, 1955–1995

Year	Value of the Minimum Wage, Nominal Dollars	Value of the Minimum Wage, 1995 Dollars†	Minimum Wage as a Percent of the Average Private Nonsupervisory Wage
1955	$0.75	$3.94	43.9%
1956	1.00	5.16	55.6
1957	1.00	5.01	52.9
1958	1.00	4.87	51.3
1959	1.00	4.84	49.5
1960	1.00	4.75	47.8
1961	1.15	5.41	53.7
1962	1.15	5.36	51.8
1963	1.25	5.74	54.8
1964	1.25	5.67	53.0
1965	1.25	5.59	50.8
1966	1.25	5.43	48.8
1967	1.40	5.90	52.2
1968	1.60	6.49	56.1
1969	1.60	6.21	52.6
1970	1.60	5.92	49.5
1971	1.60	5.67	46.4
1972	1.60	5.51	43.2
1973	1.60	5.18	40.6
1974	2.00	5.89	47.2
1975	2.10	5.71	46.4
1976	2.30	5.92	47.3
1977	2.30	5.56	43.8
1978	2.65	6.00	46.6
1979	2.90	5.99	47.1
1980	3.10	5.76	46.5
1981	3.35	5.68	46.2
1982	3.35	5.36	43.6
1983	3.35	5.14	41.8
1984	3.35	4.93	40.3
1985	3.35	4.76	39.1
1986	3.35	4.67	38.2
1987	3.35	4.51	37.3
1988	3.35	4.33	36.1
1989	3.35	4.13	34.7
1990	3.80	4.44	37.9
1991	4.25	4.77	41.1
1992	4.25	4.63	40.2
1993	4.25	4.50	39.2
1994	4.25	4.38	n/a
1995	4.25	4.25	n/a

† Adjusted for inflation using the CPI-U-X1.

Source: Center on Budget and Policy Priorities.

niary income, then anything forcing them to accept another mix of benefits would clearly make them worse off. For example, suppose worker A desires his income in the form of $3.00 per hour in wages, an air-conditioned workplace, carpeted floors, safety precautions, and stereo music. If he is *forced* by the minimum wage law to accept $3.25 per hour and fewer nonpecuniary benefits, he is worse off than at the preminimum wage and the *higher* level of nonpecuniary income. A priori, the enactment of minimum wage laws must place the worker and employer in a less-than-optimal state. Thus it may not be the case that only unemployed workers suffer from the minimum wage; even workers who receive a higher wage and retain employment may be net losers if their nonpecuniary benefits are reduced.

Labor Substitution Effects

The economic world is characterized by a plethora of substitutes. In the labor market low-skill, low-wage earners are substitutes for high-skill, high-wage earners. As Walter Williams points out:

Suppose a fence can be produced by using either one high skilled worker or by using three low skilled workers. If the wage of high skilled workers is $38 per day, and that of a low skilled worker is $13 per day, the firm employs the high skilled worker because costs would be less and profits higher ($38 versus $39). The high skilled worker would soon recognize that one of the ways to increase his wealth would be to advocate a minimum wage of, say, $20 per day in the fencing industry.... After enactment of the minimum wage laws, the high skilled worker can now demand any wage up to $60 per day... and retain employment. Prior to the enactment of the minimum wage of $20 per day, a

demand of $60 per day would have cost the high skilled worker his job. Thus the effect of the minimum wage is to price the high skilled worker's competition out of the market.[16]

Labor competes against labor, not against management. Since low-skill labor competes with high-skill labor, the minimum wage works against the lower-skill, lower-paid worker in favor of higher-paid workers. Hence, the consequences of the law are exactly opposite its alleged purpose.

Capital Substitution Effects

To produce a given quantity of goods, some bundle of inputs is required. The ratio of inputs used to produce the desired output is not fixed by natural law but by the relative prices of inputs, which change continuously with new demand and supply conditions. Based on relative input prices, producers attempt to minimize costs for a given output. Since many inputs are substitutes for one another in the production process, a given output can be achieved by increasing the use of one and diminishing the use of another. The optimal mix will depend on the relative supply and demand for competing substitute inputs.

As a production input, low-skill labor is often in direct competition with highly technical machinery. A Whirlpool dishwasher can be substituted for low-skill manual dishwashers in the dishwashing process, and an automatic elevator can take the place of a nonautomatic elevator and a manual operator. This [is] not to imply that automation "destroys jobs," a common Luddite myth. As Frederic Bastiat explained over a century ago, jobs are obstacles to be overcome.[17] Automation shifts the *kinds* of jobs to be done in society but does not reduce their total number. Low-skill jobs are done away with, but higher-skill jobs are created simultaneously. When the minimum wage raises the cost of employing low-skill workers, it makes the substitute of automated machinery an attractive option.

Racial Discrimination in Hiring Practices

At first glance the connection between the level of racial discrimination in hiring practices and the minimum wage may not seem evident. On closer examination, however, it is apparent that the minimum wage law gives employers strong incentives to exercise their existing racial preferences.[18] The minimum wage burdens minority groups in general and minority teenagers most specifically. Although outright racism has often been blamed as the sole cause of heavy minority teenage unemployment, it is clearly not the only factor. William Keyes informs us that

> In the late 1940's and early 1950's, young blacks had a lower unemployment rate than did whites of the same age group. But after the minimum wage increased significantly, especially in 1961, the black youth unemployment rate has increased to the extent that it is now a multiple of the white youth unemployment rate.[19]

To make the case that racism itself is the cause of the employment and unemployment disparity among blacks and whites, one would have to claim that America was more racially harmonious in the past than it is now. In fact, during the racially hostile times of the early 1900s 71 percent of blacks over nine years of age were employed, as compared with 51 percent for whites.[20] The minimum wage means that employers are not free to decide among low-wage workers on the basis of price differentials; hence, they face fewer disincentives to deciding according to some other (possibly racial) criteria.

To see the racial implications of minimum wage legislation, it is helpful to look at proponents of the law in a country where racial hostility is very strong, South Africa. Since minimum wage laws share characteristics in common with equal pay laws, white racist unions in South Africa continually support both minimum wage and equal-pay-for-equal-work laws for blacks. According to Williams:

> Right-wing white unions in the building trades have complained to the South African government that laws reserving skilled jobs for whites have been broken and should be abandoned in favor of equal pay for equal work laws.... The conservative building trades made it clear that they are not motivated by concern for black workers but had come to feel that legal job reservation had been so eroded by government exemptions that it no longer protected the white worker.[21]

The reason white trade unions are restless in South Africa is a $1.52-per-hour wage differential between black and white construction workers.[22] Although the owners of the construction firms are white, they cannot afford to restrict employment to whites when blacks are willing to work for $1.52 per hour less. As minimum wages eliminate the wage differential, the cost to employers of hiring workers with the skin color they prefer is reduced. As the cost of discrimination falls, and with all else remaining the same, the law of demand would dictate that more discrimination in employment practices will occur.

Markets frequently respond where they can, even to the obstacles the minimum wage presents minority groups. In fact, during the NRA blacks would frequently be advanced to the higher rank of "executives" in order to receive exemptions from the minimum wage.[23] The free market demands that firms remain color-blind in the conduct of business: profit, not racial preference, is the primary concern of the profit-maximizing firm. Those firms who fail the profit test get driven out of business by those who put prejudice aside to maximize profits. When markets are restricted by such laws as the minimum wage, the prospects for eliminating racial discrimination in hiring practices and the shocking 40–50 percent rate of black teenage unemployment in our cities are bleak.

Human Capital Development

Minimum wage laws restrict the employment of low-skill workers when the wage rate exceeds the workers' marginal productivity. By doing so, the law prevents workers with the least skills from acquiring the marketable skills necessary for increasing their future productivity, that is, it keeps them from receiving on-the-job training.

It is an observable fact, true across ethnic groups, that income rises with age.[24] As human capital accumulates over time, it makes teenagers more valuable to employers than workers with no labor-market experience. But when teenagers are priced out of the labor market by the minimum wage, they lose their first and most crucial opportunity to accumulate the human capital that would make them more valuable to future employers. This stunting reduces their lifetime potential earn-

ings. As Martin Feldstein has commented:

> [F]or the disadvantaged young worker, with few skills and below average education, producing enough to earn the minimum wage is incompatible with the opportunity for adequate on-the-job learning. For this group, the minimum wage implies high short-run unemployment and the chronic poverty of a life of low wage jobs.[25]

Feldstein also finds a significant irony in the minimum wage: "It is unfortunate and ironic that we encourage and subsidize expenditure on formal education while blocking the opportunity for individuals to 'buy' on-the-job training."[26] This is especially hard on teenagers from the poorest minority groups, such as blacks and hispanics—a truly sad state of affairs, since the law is instituted in the name of the poor.

Distortion of the Market Process

Relative prices provide the transmission mechanism by which information is delivered to participants in the market about the underlying relative scarcities of competing factor inputs. They serve as signals for people to substitute relatively less scarce resources for relatively more scarce resources, in many cases without their even being aware of it.[27]

Whenever relative price differentials exist for input substitutes in the production process, entrepreneurs will switch from higher-priced inputs to lower-priced inputs. In a dynamically changing economy, this switching occurs continually. But when prices are not allowed to transmit market information accurately, as in the case of prices artificially controlled by government, then distorted in-

Table 2
Dates and Amounts of Minimum Wage Changes

Date	Amount	As a Percent of the Average Wage in Manufacturing (Old Minimum/New Minimum)
February 1967	$1.40	44.8% / 50.2%
February 1968	$1.60	47.6% / 54.4%
May 1974	$2.00	37.8% / 47.3%
January 1975	$2.10	42.7% / 44.9%
January 1976	$2.30	41.7% / 45.6%
January 1978	$2.65	38.5% / 44.4%
January 1979	$2.90	40.8% / 44.6%
January 1980	$3.20	41.7% / 44.5%
January 1981	$3.35	40.1% / 43.3%
April 1990	$3.80	31.4% / 35.6%
April 1991	$4.25	33.6% / 37.6%

formation skews the market and guides it to something clearly less than optimal.[28]

Minimum wages, being such a distortion of the price system, lead to the wrong factor input mix between labor and all other inputs. As a result, industry migrates to locations of greater labor supply more slowly, and labor-intensive industries tend to remain fixed in non-optimal areas, areas with greater labor scarcity. Large labor pools of labor-abundant geographical areas are not tapped because the controlled price of labor conveys the wrong information to all the parties involved. Thus, the existence of price differentials, as knowledge to be transmitted through relative prices, is hidden.[29] The slowdown of industrial migration keeps labor-abundant regions poorer than they otherwise would be because economic growth there is stifled. As Simon Rottenberg explains for the case of Puerto Rico:

The aggregate effect of all these distortions was that Puerto Rico could be expected to produce fewer goods and services than would have otherwise been produced and that the rate at which insu-

lar per capita income rose toward mainland United States income standards could be expected to be dampened. In sum, the minimum wage law could be expected to reduce the rate of improvement in the standard of life of the Puerto Rican people and to intensify poverty in the island.[30]

In summary, the evidence is in on the minimum wage. All eight major effects of the minimum wage examined here make the poor, disadvantaged, or young in society worse off—the alleged beneficiaries turn out to be the law's major victims....

CONCLUSION

George Stigler may have startled some economists in 1946 when he claimed that minimum wage laws create unemployment and make people who had been receiving less than the minimum poorer.[31] Fifty years of experience with the law has proven Stigler correct, leaving very few defenders in the economics profession.[32]

But economists have had little success in criticizing this very destructive law. Simon Rottenberg demonstrated the government's disregard for what most economists have to say about this issue in his investigation of the Minimum Wage Study Commission created by Congress in 1977. He noted the numerous studies presented to the commission that without exception found that the law had a negative impact on employment and intensified the poverty of low-income earners. The commission spent over $17 million to conduct the investigation and on the basis of the evidence should have eliminated the law. What was the outcome? The commission voted to *increase the minimum wage by indexing and expanding coverage.* As dissenting commissioner S. Warne Robinson commented about the investigation:

The evidence is now in, and the findings of dozens of major economic studies show that the damage done by the minimum wage has been far more severe than even the critics of forty years ago predicted. Indeed, the evidence against the minimum wage is so overwhelming that the only way the Commission's majority was able to recommend it be retained was to ask us not to base any decisions on the facts.[33]

It cannot be that our elected representatives in Congress are just misinformed with respect to the minimum wage law. To the contrary, the *Congressional Record* demonstrates that they fully understand the law's effects and how the utilization of those effects can ensure reelection. Economists would do well to realize that governments have little interest in the truth when its implementation would contradict self-serving government policies. Rather than attempting to bring gov-

ernment the "facts," economists should educate the public. This is the only solution to the malaise created when people uncritically accept such governmental edicts as the minimum wage.

NOTES

1. Leverett Lyon et al. *The National Recovery Administration: An Analysis and Appraisal* (New York: Da Capo Press, 1972), pp. 318–19.
2. Benjamin M. Anderson, *Economics and the Public Welfare: A Financial and Economic History of the United States, 1914–1946* (Indianapolis: Liberty Press, 1979), p. 336.
3. Jonathan Grossman, "Fair Labor Standards Act of 1938: Maximum Struggle for a Minimum Wage," *Monthly Labor Review* 101 (June 1978): 23.
4. "Wage and Hours Law," *New York Times*, 24 October 1938, p. 2.
5. Grossman, "Fair Labor Standards Act," p. 29.
6. Ibid., p. 28.
7. Ibid., p. 29.
8. "Report 40,000 Jobs Lost," *New York Times*, 24 October 1938, p. 2.
9. Anderson, *Economics and the Public Welfare*, p. 458.
10. Simon Rottenberg, "Minimum Wages in Puerto Rico," in *Economics of Legal Minimum Wages*, edited by Simon Rottenberg (Washington, D.C.: American Enterprise Institute, 1981), p. 330.
11. Rottenberg, "Minimum Wages in Puerto Rico," p. 333.
12. Yale Brozen, "Minimum Wage Rates and Household Workers," *Journal of Law and Economics* 5 (October 1962): 103–10.
13. Finis Welch, "Minimum Wage Legislation in the United States," *Economic Inquiry* 12 (September 1974): 286.
14. Brozen, "Minimum Wage Rates and Household Workers," pp. 107–08.
15. Richard McKenzie, "The Labor Market Effects of Minimum Wage Laws: A New Perspective," *Journal of Labor Research* 1 (Fall 1980): 258–59.
16. Walter Williams, *The State Against Blacks* (New York: McGraw-Hill, 1982), pp. 44–45.
17. Frederic Bastiat, *Economic Sophisms* (Irvington-on-Hudson, N.Y.: Foundation for Economic Education, 1946), pp. 16–19.
18. Walter Williams, "Government Sanctioned Restraints That Reduce the Economic Opportunities for Minorities," *Policy Review* 22 (Fall 1977): 15.
19. William Keyes,"The Minimum Wage and the Davis Bacon Act: Employment Effects on Minorities and Youth," *Journal of Labor Research* 3 (Fall 1982): 402.
20. Williams, *State Against Blacks*, p. 41.

21. Ibid., p. 43.

22. Ibid., pp. 43–44.

23. Lyon, *National Recovery Administration*, p. 339.

24. U.S. Department of Commerce, Bureau of the Census, *Statistical Abstract of the United States 1982–83*, p. 431.

25. Martin Feldstein, "The Economics of the New Unemployment," *The Public Interest*, no. 33 (Fall 1973): 14–15.

26. Ibid., p. 15.

27. Thomas Sowell, *Knowledge and Decisions* (New York: Basic Books, 1980), p. 79.

28. Ibid.

29. Ibid., pp. 167–68.

30. Rottenberg, "Minimum Wages in Puerto Rico," p. 329.

31. George Stigler, "The Economies of Minimum Wage Legislation," *American Economic Review* 36 (June 1946): 358–65.

32. Although there are a few supporters left such as John K. Galbraith, many "liberal" economists such as Paul Samuelson and James Tobin have recently come out against the minimum wage. See Emerson Schmidt, *Union Power and the Public Interest* (Los Angeles: Nash, 1973).

33. Simon Rottenberg, "National Commissions: Preaching in the Garb of Analysis," *Policy Review* no. 23 (Winter 1983): 139.

NO

Charles Craypo

IN DEFENSE OF MINIMUM WAGES

This article refutes the dominant view held by orthodox neoclassical economists such as Thomas Rustici. These economists assert that minimum wage laws should be abolished because they misallocate resources and cause production inefficiencies. I reject Rustici's conclusion and instead take the position that in most instances high minimum wages are good for workers, employers and consumers alike and hence are good for the economy as a whole.

Three things are wrong with Rustici's neoclassical view of things. It depends on an idealized world that by assumption favors more rather than less market competition as the solution to economic problems. Second, it ignores the reasons why governments enact minimum wage laws in the first place and instead interprets and judges them on inappropriate grounds. Third, the neoclassical argument against minimum wages is supported by contradictory empirical evidence that casts doubt on its theoretical validity and practical significance.

Critics of the orthodox neoclassical interpretation of minimum wages include both neoclassical and institutional applied labor economists. In fact, most of the contradictory empirical studies in recent years have [been] produced by neoclassical economists whose findings prompt them to question the dominant view. In addition to the research of mainstream economists, research critical of the orthodox position has come from the various institutional schools of thought which emphasize evolutionary change and systemic rather than deductive reasoning from an idealized model.

Most of the debate surrounds the federal minimum wage law contained in the Fair Labor Standards Act (FLSA) of 1938, which represented an essential part of President Roosevelt's agenda to get the nation out of the Great Depression. Labor law reformers had long advocated federal wage and hour laws in response to an historic pattern of low earnings among working families and intense wage competition among employers. The courts, however, struck down early attempts to establish federal standards on grounds the separate states had constitutional primacy in such matters. Individual states were reluctant to pass regulatory laws, however, because they feared industry would avoid locating there. The enormities of the depression nevertheless drove working people to strike employers and protest politically. Soon the Supreme Court changed directions and ruled that the constitution does in fact allow Congress to regulate interstate commerce; Congress responded with numerous regulatory laws including the FLSA.

The inherent bias in neoclassical analysis. When polled, a large majority of American economists support Rustici in his opposition to minimum wage increases. This reflects their prior training in the neoclassical wage model, which generally rejects labor standards legislation on grounds that market outcomes are superior to anything government can achieve through regulation. Employers and others lobbying to abolish or weaken minimum wage laws therefore can count on the support of orthodox economists, despite widespread public approval of these laws. Indeed, in 1993, three-fourths of economists polled said that an increase in the minimum wage would increase unemployment, while a similar poll in 1996 found that 84% of the public favored an increase.

This vastly different view of the world underscores the first problem with Rustici's neoclassical analysis. The competitive market model it uses simply does not depict real labor markets accurately. It imagines all sorts of things that do not exist and ignores a great many other things that do. When this analysis is applied to particular labor market problems, such as declining real wages, it is likely to misdiagnose the ailment and to prescribe inappropriate public policy.

The problem is that in explaining how the interaction between worker skill and output determines wages the neoclassical model uses circular reasoning. It presumes that if we know the wage we also know the worth of the worker because market competition ensures that each worker is paid the value of his or her worth, as measured by the value of what each produces. It further presumes that the worker's productive value is determined by his or her level of skill and education, that is, by their accumulated "human capital." Therefore, if one worker is paid more than another worker, then the first worker must be worth more (that is, must have more skill and education) than the second; because the wage is, by definition, equal to output value, which in turn is determined by skill and education. Consequently, every worker must be worth what he or she is being paid, no more and no less. Workers who think they are not being paid enough must be wrong, because if they possessed more human capital they would be worth more therefore paid more.

This is tautological reasoning. It explains everything and nothing because it uses the thing it is trying to explain as the evidence with which to explain it. It does, however, allow neoclassical economists to reject any attempt to regulate wages on the grounds that the worker currently is being paid what he or she is worth. In the world of the neoclassical economist, forcing employers to pay a higher wage will simply place the individual employer at a competitive disadvantage and at the same time discriminate against workers who did not benefit from the regulated wage increase. As a result, neoclassical investigations of minimum wage effects usually ask a single question. How many workers will become unemployable following an increase in the minimum wage. The question derives from the competitive wage model, not from observed experiences or policy objectives.

With this mind-set, it is understandable that Rustici and other orthodox neoclassical economists see the solution to labor market problems, such as low earnings and unemployment, as more rather than less market determination and the elimination of existing regulations. If labor markets deliver less than ideal results it is because they are not free enough. Public policy must be to remove the imperfections. Unions and minimum wages are logical targets in this regard.

The problem with such deductive reasoning is that employers and employees seldom meet as equals in the labor market, although the model assumes that they do. In blue-collar settings, for example, the employment relationship favors employers, who typically offer jobs on a take-it-or-leave-it basis. Individual workers find there are far more workers than there are good jobs and they take what they can get on the terms that are offered. Employers simply have more options in the hiring process than do workers—except perhaps when unemployment is low and workers scarce in the lowest paying, least desirable occupations and industries, at which point employers turn to immigrant labor to fill job vacancies at the going wage levels. Additionally, employers know far more than hourly workers do about supply and demand conditions in local labor markets and are more mobile in terms of where and when to hire. They also can hold out much longer financially than can workers in the event of differences over wages and working conditions. Finally, and importantly, because they own the plant and equipment upon which the worker's livelihood depends, they can threaten to relocate the workplace or to replace the workers with machines or other workers.

In the absence of institutional protections such as union contracts and minimum wages, workers are in constant danger of having to compete with one another to see which of them will work for less pay and under the worst conditions. If one or a few employers are able to reduce labor standards by taking advantage of labor's inherent bargaining weakness, and in the process they expand markets and increase their profits, then the race is on among all employers to take down labor standards. The labor market degenerates into what institutional labor economists call destructive competition. As two institutional labor economists observed decades ago, "When an employer can hire workers for practically his own price, he can be slack and inefficient in his methods, and yet, by reducing wages, reduce his cost of production to the level of his more able competitor" (Commons and Andrews, 1936:48).

The irrelevancy of the neoclassical analysis. This demonstrates the second thing wrong with Rustici's neoclassical interpretation. It examines and evaluates minimum wage laws only on the basis of what would result in a competitive market model. In doing so, it ignores the reasons why such laws are enacted in the first place and whether or not they solve the problems they were intended to solve. The problem with this approach is that it focuses on only one of the three forms of economic efficiency that are essential for a nation to sustain high-levels of production and consumption: a nation's need to provide high standards of living for its citizens.

Robert Kuttner (1997) argues that neoclassical preoccupation with allocative efficiency prevents an examination of macroefficiency and technical efficiency. Macroefficiency concerns a nation's ability to sustain or enhance total production, employment, and family living standards; whereas technical efficiency refers to the ability to generate new products and production methods through industrial invention and innovation. Allocative efficiency, on the other hand, is limited to looking after the immediate interests of the consumer by minimizing production costs and product prices. If only allocative efficiency is taken into account, the long-term interests of both producers and consumers is ignored as the nation neglects its overall economic growth, job and earnings performance, and progress in research/development.

It must be remembered that neither macro- nor technical efficiency necessarily results in optimal allocation efficiency in the short run, that is, in the lowest possible costs of production and consumer prices. Nor does optimal allocative efficiency necessarily help to maximize either macro- or technical efficiency. The postwar success of certain West European and Asian economies, led by Germany and Japan, testifies to the need to distinguish between alternative forms of economic efficiency and between short- and long-run goals and performance. Japanese industrial strategists made these distinctions for example when they targeted the global auto market in the late 1950s. They gave up short-run cost efficiency in return for long-term product and workforce quality on their way to world supremacy in autos by the 1980s (Halberstam 1986).

Because neoclassical economists largely ignore macro- and technical efficiency in their analysis of competitive labor markets, their competitive model cannot estimate the macroeffects of incremental changes in prices and quantities in particular markets. The 1930s, for example, were characterized by the kind of intense wage and price competition that neoclassical economists associate with allocative efficiency. Consequently, the economy should have been performing at its best. But we still refer to what happened instead as the Great Depression.

Remember that the question deriving from the neoclassical market model is "How many workers are made unemployable because the new wage prices them out of competitive labor markets?" That is not, however, the question that advocates of the FLSA were concerned with in 1938, nor what people are concerned with today in view of the long-term decline in median real wages and the increase in unstable jobs. The problem then and now is not the ability to produce enough goods and services, but rather it is creating jobs at wages high enough to buy back what is produced and in the process sustain high living standards for everyone.

This was the task of the 1938 federal minimum wage. It was designed to do two things: (i) increase employment and purchasing power in order to stimulate the slumping economy; and (ii) drive out of the market employers who competed on the basis of cheap labor instead of through better products and state-of-the-art production methods. The country had been in economic crisis for the better part of a decade. It had become increasingly clear that much of the problem was due to low pay, long workweeks, and growing use of child rather than adult labor.

Advocates of minimum wages were not the least dissuaded by neoclassical forecasts that some jobs would be lost and some employers driven out of business. That is precisely what they wanted to do, on grounds that a job that does not pay enough to support a family should not exist and an employer who cannot pay a living wage, even though other employers in that industry can and do pay the mandated living wage, should be driven from the marketplace.

In brief, if a job pays less than enough to sustain workers and their dependents at the customary standard of living, then that job is not paying its way in a productive economy because it is being subsidized by some household, charitable organization, or government transfer payment. The beneficiary of this subsidy is either the employer paying the low wage and making a profit by doing so, or the customer paying a low price for the good or service. Fast-food restaurant fare, for example, is cheap in part because fast-food workers earn poverty level wages. Home owners in wealthy suburbs can get their houses cleaned cheaply because the women who clean them live in low-income areas, need the money, and have few job options. A subsidy is a subsidy, whether the worker is part of a poor household or an affluent household and whether the employer is a large or a small business.

If you work for a fast-food restaurant why should your family subsidize the owners of that restaurant? In a like manner, why should taxpayers subsidize manufacturers that employ fathers and mothers who cannot support their families without receiving food stamps or a tax rebate from the government? Why should the large employer have to compete with a smaller rival that is being sub-sidized by low-income households and taxpayers?

This subsidization does not have to occur. In Australia, for example, restaurant workers, "bag boys" in grocery stores, bartenders in taverns, and other workers who are generally low paid in the United States are paid in excess of $12 an hour. Nevertheless, McDonalds hamburgers and Pizza Hut pizzas still abound in Australia. In the United States unionized waitresses in Las Vegas also earn $12 an hour, before tips, and Las Vegas is one of the fastest growing economic regions in America. Waitresses in other parts of the country commonly receive about half the level of the minimum wage, before tips, which forces them to show a certain amount of servitude in order to earn enough tips to make the job worthwhile (a subsidy to the employer from the customer) and leaves the worker unsure of her or his earnings from day-to-day and week-to-week. Such market outcomes reflect the low-status, devalued nature of these workers and occupations more than it does their value to both customers and employers.

Contradictory evidence for the neoclassical view. Rustici's neoclassical approach necessarily ignores the economic and social problems associated with low-wage jobs because it concentrates on workers rather than jobs. Such focus also shifts responsibility for low-wage incomes from jobs to workers by focusing on worker behavior rather than industrial strategies and government policies. Recall that the theory assumes the individual worker's wage is determined by his or her worth on the job; it further presumes that this worth is determined in large part by the amount of human capital the worker possesses in terms of formal education (college degrees) and occupational training (vocational and on-the-job training). Thus the job and its requirements are excluded from the analysis and low-wages are linked to the worker's efforts to acquire skill and education. When neoclassical researchers like Thomas Rustici want to verify their theory they study the earnings and employment experiences of groups of workers having low educational and vocational skills on grounds such workers are most likely to lose jobs as a result of minimum wage raises. Most neoclassical studies do indeed find greater unemployment among such groups following minimum wage increases.

But the findings of empirical studies themselves pose the third problem with Rustici's analysis. The results of far too many empirical studies—those conducted by neoclassical as well as institutional labor economists—have contradicted the neoclassical model for it to remain very convincing. During the Progressive Era prior to World War I, for example, government economists surveyed jobs before and after passage of state minimum wage laws covering women workers (Obenauer and von der Nienburg 1915). This and a later study conducted by Commons and Andrews (1936), found that mandated wages alleviated the degenerative effects of low wages and actually enhanced productivity by increasing worker desire and ability to produce. Only "parasitic" employers were threatened by minimum wages and relatively small numbers of jobs were eliminated.

Some years later, Princeton labor economist Richard Lester surveyed southern manufacturing employers after World War II and found they had not laid-off marginal workers in response to minimum wage increases, but instead had maintained their workforces and tried to offset the higher labor cost by increasing output and sales. This allowed them to take advantage of the economies of scale (lower per-unit costs of production) that accompany higher levels of plant and equipment utilization. Lester went on to note that workers doing the same jobs in different plants received different wages over long periods of time—another finding at odds with neoclassical reasoning—therefore, it was not possible to predict the employment effects of a minimum wage raise. His and other studies thus refuted the neoclassical notion of a single competitive wage. Workers with comparable skills often make quite different wages over long periods of time and those with different skills often earn the same wages. "Such matters are elementary and commonplace to a student of labor, but they seem to be largely overlooked by theorists of the [neoclassical] marginalist faith," he concluded (1947:148).

In the 1990s, another group of neoclassical revisionists using much the same investigative methods as Lester, but with more sophisticated equipment and techniques at their disposal, produced similar findings and came to much the same conclusion. Princeton economists David Card and Alan Krueger demonstrated that modest increases in minimum wage rates have little if any negative impact on the most exposed workers—teenagers. Instead of analyzing what happens to workers following minimum wage increases, they, like Lester before them, asked what happened to the jobs themselves. And like Lester, they discovered that employers did not respond as anticipated. Jobs in fast-food restaurants and other low-wage establishments did not decline, and in fact they even increased slightly in New Jersey when that state increased its minimum wage above the federal level. More surprising perhaps, in adjacent Pennsylvania, where no increase in the state minimum wage had occurred, fast-food employment actually fell slightly! Card and Krueger substantiated these findings in similar studies involving fast-food restaurant jobs in Texas and teenage workers in all industries in California (Card and Krueger 1995: Chapters 2 and 3).

These results, clearly at odds with the neoclassical literature, prompted one somewhat shaken but faithful neoclassical reviewer of Card and Krueger's work to conclude in 1995, just as the debate was getting underway on a proposal to raise the federal minimum wage to $5.15, that "we just don't know how many jobs would be lost if the minimum wage were increased to $5.15" (Kennan 1995:1964). Orthodox certainty was beginning to be eroded by the contradictory findings, but the basic model was not questioned. Many neoclassical economists hold doggedly to the view that jobs *must be* lost if minimum wages are increased. Consider, for example, a standard neoclassical labor economics text now in its sixth edition. The authors dismiss the Card-Krueger findings and insist instead that: "While the impact of the minimum wage on employment, especially that of young workers will undoubtedly continue to receive a great deal of research and public policy discussion, the best evidence remains that the overall impact of the law is to lower employment of unskilled workers while increasing the earnings of those who are able to get jobs" (Filer, Hamermesh, and Rees 1996:175).

In sum, neoclassical economists like Rustici find fault with the minimum wage because they contrast it with a theoretical system that is said to provide optimal results; but it is a system that ultimately is nonfalsifiable because of its tautological nature. They purport to refute the minimum wage on grounds it destroys low-wage jobs despite the fact that this is precisely what it is supposed to do. Finally, by limiting the inquiry to the dictates of a model that is inherently hostile to government regulation, they preclude serious debate on regulation as a policy tool.

Alternative analyses of minimum wage laws. The shortcomings of traditional neoclassical analysis become apparent when considered in terms of macro- and technical efficiency. Wage-based competition during the 1930s reduced already depressed earnings and worker purchasing power, which in turn decreased product demand and caused additional workers to be unemployed. The effect was to cut output, incomes, and profits. With no recovery in sight, large firms could not be expected to make more cars, radios, and appliances than they could sell, nor could they be expected to design and manufacture new products when consumers could afford neither old nor new models.

Economic recovery did not occur until total war production during 1940–45, when all the neoclassical rules of allocative efficiency were repealed: industry was cartelized, wages and prices were controlled, and productive decision making was centralized. Yet, despite the total violation of market rules, the defense plants were running day and night, workers were acquiring formal and informal education and training, incomes and profits were high. Then, from the late 1940s until the mid-1970s, industrial oligopolies and labor unions replaced government in administering the productive system, again in violation of allocative efficiency. But we look back fondly on those decades as the golden age of increased living standards and job security.

Since then, however, the economy has been deregulated in keeping with neoclassical doctrine and both product and labor markets made more competitive by domestic and global changes in industrial structure and behavior. Labor productivity has been increasing, albeit modestly, and labor resources probably have been allocated more efficiently than in the postwar decades, but real earnings are falling, job security declining, and living standards stagnating (Mishel, et al. 1996).

As a society we have three broad policy responses. One, we can remove a certain portion of the population from the productive system by offering social insurance and welfare benefits to able-bodied individuals including laid-off or displaced males and single mothers. This should raise wages by reducing the supply of workers. Two, we can force some idle workers into productive roles by abolishing their financial support and subsidy systems, giving them no practical choice but to work under the terms offered. This should lower wages by putting the new low-wage workers in competition with existing ones. Finally, we can legislate high minimum wages and other protective labor measures to ensure the lowest paid workers a conventional standard of living. This would raise wages directly.

The first alternative has been the favorite of conservative economists and moral reformers since the early 1880s when industrial poverty appeared in Britain (Persky 1997). Free market advocates urged the abolition of welfare support and wage supplements on grounds that its elimination would increase the number of laborers and their productivity while also lowering taxes and birth rates. As a secondary benefit, they went on to claim, this would also enhance family stability and values by making parents responsible for their children and both children and mothers/wives dependent on and therefore respectful of and obedient to wage-earning fathers/husbands. Conservatives still argue generally along these lines.

The second alternative is preferred by liberal economists and policy makers. It seeks to assure low-wage workers a living income by supplementing their inadequate earnings through the Earned Income Tax Credit, a tax rebate of up to several thousand dollars a year to the employee based on his or her payments into the Social Security fund. Advocates favor this approach because it effectively increases the employee's real wage rate and at the same time it offsets undesirable market outcomes of low wages without distorting wage and employment structures and obstructing allocative efficiency. They also believe that the long-run solution is worker training and education to enhance human capital. Conservative and liberal economists and policy makers tend to agree on that. They differ, however, on whether it should be publicly financed and broadly available.

In view of the bipartisan support for more education, a word of caution is in order. More education is always laudable, but by itself cannot solve the problem of low wages. This is because employers use formal educational credentials, especially college degrees, to screen applicants for good jobs. Therefore, as the overall educational level of the workforce rises, the amount of education needed to get a given job also increases. This jeopardizes the effectiveness of education as the justification for high pay. For if a college degree were to be conferred magically upon the entire working population tomorrow, who would bus and wait tables the day after? Employers would find and apply other screening criteria, perhaps a graduate or professional degree, in order to determine which college grads would manage restaurants and which would bus and wait tables.

Moreover, the supply of educated workers does not automatically create the demand for them. American engineering students, for instance, may wonder exactly what it is they are going to engineer when they read about U.S. companies hiring pools of low wage but college trained information technologists in developing countries to work on computer software projects using high-speed satellite information links, or when they hear about domestic aerospace companies transferring technology overseas in exchange for sales contracts, or of NASA purchasing rocketry equipment from other industrialized countries in order to get the lowest possible price (Barlett and Steele 1996: 49–52, 93–9).

The third alternative favors policies that increase earnings and incomes directly, that is, before taxes and transfer payments. High minimum wages are a logical policy choice in this analysis because they contribute directly to sustained economic growth (macroefficiency) and industrial capitalization and innovation (technical efficiency). It is based on the premise that with rare exceptions people want the dignity and independence that comes with gainful employment, and therefore they should work because it is good for them as individuals and good for the society in which they are stakeholder producers and con-

sumers. But this is true only if the jobs available to them pay wages that afford a decent living.

In addition, the high wage economy is most consistent over time with the three economic efficiencies. It is true that minimum wages are inconsistent with the neoclassical definition of allocative efficiency in the short run; but it is the long term that should concern us as a nation. High-paid workers stay with their employers, which encourages the latter to invest in worker skill and education, which in turn encourages employers to adopt state-of-the-art production methods and sophisticated product design and performance. High-paid workers also have the purchasing power to buy the goods and services that they and other high-paid workers produce.

A high wage policy is the best hope for a bright future for the American economy. It ensures a proficient labor force in a stable macroeconomy and encourages steady technological advancement. The larger society is only as prosperous as its individual parts. Thus when labor standards are high the larger society prospers.

REFERENCES

Barlett, Donald L., and James B. Steele. 1996. *America: Who Stole the Dream?* Kansas City: Andrews & McMeel.

Card, David Edward, and Alan B. Krueger. 1995. *Myth and Measurement: The New Economics of the Minimum Wage.* Princeton, NJ: Princeton University Press.

Commons, John R., and John B. Andrews. 1936. *Principles of Labor Legislation* (fourth edition). New York: Augustus M. Kelley (1967 Reprint).

Filer, Randall K., Daniel S. Hamermesh, and Albert Rees. 1996. *The Economics of Work and Pay*, sixth edition. New York: Harper Collins.

Halberstam, David. 1986. *The Reckoning.* New York: Morrow.

Kuttner, Robert. 1997. *Everything For Sale: The Virtues and Limits of Markets.* New York: Alfred A. Knopf.

Lester, Richard A. 1947. "Marginalism, Minimum Wages, and Labor Markets." *American Economic Review* 37 (March) pp. 135–48.

Mishel, Lawrence, Jared Bernstein, and John Schmitt. 1977. *The State of Working America, 1996–97.* Armonk, NY: M. E. Sharpe.

Obenauer, Marie L., and Bertha von der Nienburg. 1915. *Effect of Minimum Wage Determinations in Oregon.* Bureau of Labor Statistics, Bulletin No. 176. Washington: GPO.

Persky, Joseph. 1997. "Classical Family Values: Ending the Poor Laws as They Knew Them." *Journal of Economic Perspectives* 11 (Winter) pp. 179–89.

POSTSCRIPT

Is It Time to Abolish the Minimum Wage?

The impact of the minimum wage can be expressed in many ways. Two particularly rewarding ways of looking at such legislative initiatives are to examine minimum wages over time in real dollars and as a percentage of manufacturing wages.

A clear pattern should emerge from an examination of this data. The 1965–1970 period saw the highest level of the minimum wage in real terms. In constant 1982–84 dollars, the minimum wage for these years was approximately four dollars an hour and reached nearly 50 percent of the prevailing manufacturing wage. For the next 20 years, however, the value of the minimum wage in real terms and as a percentage of the manufacturing wage fell. It is only in recent years that it has begun to recover.

The renewed interest in the minimum wage can be traced in part to the research findings of David Card and Alan Krueger. These economists, as Craypo points out, have shaken the economics profession with their empirical research findings that moderate increases in the minimum wage have few negative consequences on employment patterns and in some cases are associated with the increases in employment. Their work has been published widely in professional journals: *Industrial and Labor Relations Review* (October 1992 and April 1994) and the *American Economic Review* (1994 and 1995). They have also detailed their findings in a book entitled *Myth and Measurement: The New Economics of the Minimum Wage* (Princeton University Press, 1995).

Two vocal critics of Card and Krueger's research are David Newmark and William Wascher. Their empirical studies are supportive of the traditional neoclassical findings that the minimum wage causes unemployment, particularly among teenagers and young adults. See their work published in *Industrial and Labor Relations Review* (September 1992 and April 1994); *NBER Working Paper No. 4617* (1994); *Journal of Business and Economic Statistics* (1995); and *American Economic Review Papers and Proceedings* (May 1995). Still often considered the best anti–minimum wage statement, however, is George J. Stigler's 1946 essay "The Economics of Minimum Wage Legislation," *American Economic Review*.

ISSUE 13

Has Wisconsin Ended Welfare As We Know It?

YES: Robert Rector, from "Wisconsin's Welfare Miracle," *Policy Review* (March/April 1997)

NO: Michael Wiseman, from "Welfare Reform in the United States: A Background Paper," *Housing Policy Debate* (vol. 7, no. 4, 1996)

ISSUE SUMMARY

YES: Heritage Foundation senior policy analyst Robert Rector contends that Wisconsin has already won more than half the battle against dependence on Aid to Families with Dependent Children (AFDC) and is proceeding with the other half with breathtaking speed.

NO: Economist Michael Wiseman concludes that not even the governor of Wisconsin has found the key to welfare savings by means other than cutting benefits and active broad-based efforts at job placement and training.

Given American society's traditional commitment to a market system and its fundamental belief in self-determination, Americans are generally uncomfortable enacting social welfare legislation that appears to give someone "something for nothing," even if that individual is clearly in need. Thus, when we trace the roots of the existing U.S. social welfare system back to its origins in the New Deal legislation of President Franklin D. Roosevelt during the Great Depression of the 1930s, we see that many of the earliest programs linked jobs to public assistance. One exception was Aid to Families with Dependent Children (AFDC), which was established as part of the 1935 Social Security Act. This program provided money to families in which there were children but no breadwinner. In 1935, and for many years thereafter, this program was not particularly controversial. There are two reasons for this: the number of beneficiaries was relatively small, and the popular image of an AFDC family was that of a white woman with several young children whose husband had died as the result of an illness or an industrial accident.

In the early 1960s, as the U.S. economy prospered, poverty—and what to do about it—captured the attention of the nation. The Kennedy and Johnson administrations declared a War on Poverty: major legislative initiatives focused social welfare programs on the plight of the poor, who represented about one-fifth of the population and were white by a ratio of two to one. This pattern is often overlooked because the incidence of poverty among African Americans exceeded 50 percent of that community.

The policies of the Kennedy and Johnson administrations were designed to address the needs of those trapped in "pockets of poverty," a description popularized in the early 1960s by Michael Harrington (1929–1989), a political theorist and prominent socialist. Between 1964 and 1969 the number of AFDC recipients increased by more than 60 percent, and the costs of the program more than doubled. The number of AFDC families grew throughout the 1970s and 1980s, and the program became increasingly controversial.

The controversy grew for several reasons: the increase in the number of recipients, the increase in costs, and a change in perceptions. During the Reagan years, a welfare mother was characterized as a woman in a big-city public housing project whose children had been deserted by their father, or as an unmarried woman who bore more children only to get more financial assistance through welfare. By the late 1980s and early 1990s, AFDC had become one of the most controversial social welfare programs.

Social critics used this negative image of the welfare mother to attack AFDC. Charles Murray, for example, charged AFDC with encouraging welfare dependency, teenage pregnancies, the dissolution of the traditional family, and an erosion of the basic American work ethic. Such criticism set the stage for the first major reforms in AFDC in 25 years. In 1988 the Family Support Act was passed. The intent of this legislation was to develop state-run programs that would help individuals who receive welfare assistance to break away from their dependency through work, training, and education.

Within a few short years, most states had nearly 20 percent of their welfare caseload either working or in a work training program. The use of waivers became widespread. These waivers, which allowed states to experiment with federal rules governing AFDC eligibility, work incentives, and work mandates, were either approved or pending in all but four states by mid-1996.

In the face of this sea change in public attitudes and state public policy, President Bill Clinton pledged to "end welfare as we know it." Within eight months of the start of his second term, Congress obliged. In a bold legislative move it passed the Personal Responsibility and Work Opportunity Act. This act abolished the AFDC entitlement that had guaranteed poor families a standardized set of welfare benefits for 60 years and replaced AFDC with a new block grant program entitled Temporary Assistance for Needy Families (TANF), which allowed individual states far more discretion in determining which families would be supported and how much each of these families would get.

No single state pursued these options more aggressively and with more apparent success than the state of Wisconsin. In the selections that follow, Robert Rector and Michael Wiseman debate what works and what does not in the Wisconsin waivers and, more important, what the future holds for states that follow Wisconsin's lead.

YES

Robert Rector

WISCONSIN'S WELFARE MIRACLE

Everyone wants—or professes to want—to "end welfare as we know it." Despite such lofty proclamations, welfare is still thriving. [In 1996], federal and state governments spent $411 billion on means-tested welfare programs that provide cash, food, housing, medical care, and social services to poor and low-income Americans. This greatly exceeded the $324 billion spent in 1993, the first year of the Clinton presidency.

At the core of America's vast, dysfunctional welfare system is Aid to Families with Dependent Children (AFDC). At present, nearly one out of seven children in the United States receives AFDC, residing with a mother married to a welfare check rather than a working husband. The typical family now on AFDC will spend nearly 13 years in the program.

"Ending welfare" must begin with reform of AFDC. Congress enacted major new legislation last summer that will start this process. The new law promises three major changes. First, it eliminates the entitlement system of AFDC funding, under which states that increased their AFDC caseloads received automatic increases in federal funding, while states that reduced dependence faced a fiscal penalty.

Second, the new law establishes performance standards that will require each state to reduce its AFDC caseload, or at least, if the caseload does not decline, require some recipients to work in return for their benefits.

Third, the law sets a new goal of reducing illegitimacy and will reward states that reduce out-of-wedlock births without increasing the number of abortions.

Although the new federal legislation sets the proper framework for reform among the states, the liberal welfare establishment and its allies in the media incessantly warn that reform will prove to be difficult, if not impossible. But one state has already proven the naysayers wrong: Wisconsin. Wisconsin's experience with welfare reform provides an unparalleled model for implementing reform that other states would be wise to follow.

In the last 10 years, while AFDC caseloads in the rest of the nation were rising steeply, the caseload in Wisconsin has dropped by half. In inner-city Milwaukee, the caseload has fallen by 25 percent, but in the rest of the state,

From Robert Rector, "Wisconsin's Welfare Miracle," *Policy Review* (March/April 1997). Copyright © 1997 by *Policy Review*, published by The Heritage Foundation. Reprinted by permission.

caseloads have fallen by nearly 70 percent. In 28 of Wisconsin's 77 counties, the welfare rolls have already dropped by 80 percent or more.

And if all this weren't remarkable enough, the pace of Wisconsin's reduction in welfare dependency is accelerating. In Milwaukee, the AFDC caseload is now shrinking 2 percent per month; in the rest of the state, 5 percent. Wisconsin's achievements are utterly unprecedented in the history of AFDC. Liberal welfare experts used to insist that a successful work program might reduce welfare caseloads by 5 percent over five years; in much of Wisconsin, the number of people on welfare is steadily falling by that amount every 30 days.

Wisconsin has thus won more than half the battle against AFDC dependence and is proceeding with the other half with breathtaking speed. This victory is crucial, since welfare dependency severely hampers the healthy development of children. In the long term, the greatest beneficiaries of Wisconsin's dramatic achievements in reforming welfare will be the children themselves.

THE ROAD LESS TRAVELED

This remarkable story begins in 1987, when a major congressional debate on welfare culminated in the Family Support Act (FSA). Touted as yet another "end of welfare," the FSA was a complete bust. The Act did, however generate the expectation among voters that welfare recipients would be required to work. In the same year a second unheralded event occurred with far greater significance for the future of welfare: Tommy Thompson took office as governor of Wisconsin.

Following a gubernatorial campaign largely about welfare, Thompson entered office with a firm commitment to reform. Figure 1 tells the rest of the story. Despite the rhetorical promises of the Family Support Act, the nationwide AFDC caseload remained constant in the late 1980s and then grew by more than a third between 1990 and 1994. The nationwide caseload has eased downward over the last two years, but the majority of states still suffer higher levels of welfare dependency than before the Family Support Act became law.

Wisconsin has been the only clear exception to this pattern. Upon taking office, Thompson initiated a series of reforms that cut welfare dependency during the late 1980s and blocked any resurgence during the 1990–93 recession. Starting in 1994, a second round of more sophisticated work-related reforms has caused the caseload to nosedive further. But the raw figures understate Thompson's achievements. As noted, welfare rolls across the country ballooned by some 35 percent during the early 1990s. There is every reason to believe that, without Thompson's reforms, Wisconsin would have followed this national trend. If it had, its AFDC caseload would have surged from around 100,000 recipients in 1987 to a peak of 135,000 in 1993. It is reasonable to conclude that Thompson has not merely cut his state's caseload in half (from 98,295 recipients to 48,451) but has reduced it by some two-thirds relative to the potential peak in dependence that Wisconsin would have experienced in the early 1990s in the absence of reform.

Many states brag about their recent declines in welfare dependency. In the past 24 months, for example, Indiana has cut its caseload by 32 percent, Oregon by 30 percent, Maryland by 29 percent, Massachusetts by 25 percent, Oklahoma by 24 percent, and Michigan

Figure 1

AFDC Families: Wisconsin vs. the Nation

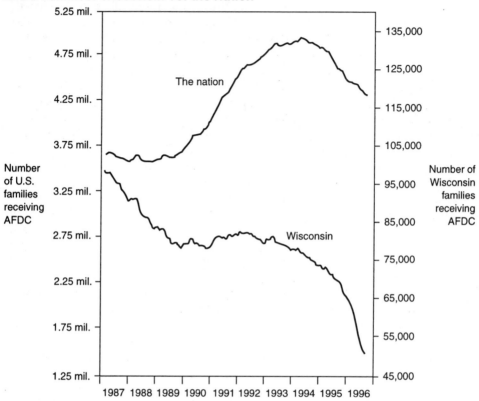

Source: U.S. Department of Health and Human Services.

by 22 percent. But, in almost every case, these successes merely represent a pruning back of the explosive surge in welfare dependency of the early 1990s. In reality, other reforming states lag a half-decade behind Wisconsin; they are only now engaging in the initial stages of dependency reduction that Wisconsin accomplished in the late 1980s. We might say that the reforms in most states have merely blown the foam off the top of the beer mug, while Wisconsin has already drained the mug halfway to the bottom.

Having cut its caseload in half, Wisconsin's reformers are now grappling with a more difficult, less employable group of welfare recipients. Skeptics argued that after Wisconsin weaned the most employable recipients off the rolls in the early stages, the decline in the caseload would slow and then stop. Yet the opposite has occurred. As new reforms have been implemented over the last three years, the decline has accelerated sharply. Wisconsin continues to reduce dependency at a rate surpassing all other states.

REFORM INITIATIVES

The general thrust of welfare reform in the Thompson administration has been to require reasonable behavior by recipients as a condition of receiving aid. An early example was *Learnfare*. Enacted in 1987, the *Learnfare* program required welfare recipients to ensure that their school-age children attended school regularly, and reduced welfare payments to families with truant children. Although *Learnfare* did not reduce the AFDC rolls directly, it did have a symbolic importance, sending a clear message to both the bureaucracy and the welfare clientele that, for the first time, the government seriously intended to demand constructive behavior of welfare recipients and to sanction those who were derelict.

The centerpiece of reform, however was the requirement that a growing share of those on the AFDC rolls engage in employment-related activities such as training and tightly supervised job search. By the 1990s, many Wisconsin counties were operating sophisticated systems aimed at pushing welfare recipients quickly into the labor market. For example, a particularly effective program in Sheboygan County required most AFDC recipients to undertake closely supervised job search immediately after applying for benefits. Individuals who failed to find employment within a few weeks were required to perform community-service work until they could find a private-sector job.

Beginning in 1994, Thompson's staff initiated a more sophisticated and successful round of reforms. His administration instructed county welfare directors to de-emphasize education and job training in the classroom and to concentrate on activities leading to immediate work. The state created new incentives to guide the welfare bureaucracies: Counties would no longer be simply allocated work, training, and day-care funds but would be required to earn those funds by increasing the number of recipients placed in jobs or community-service work.

The governor's staff also understood that many applicants entering the welfare system had other options. The easiest way to break this group of the debilitating habit of dependency was to prevent it from forming in the first place, by reducing the number of new AFDC enrollments. The state began a pilot program based on this principle in 18 counties in 1994 (gradually expanded to cover 60 by early 1996). The program, *Work First,* provided new applicants with counseling on the negative effects of dependence, offered short-term aid (such as car repairs) that might eliminate the need to enroll in AFDC, and required most new applicants to begin working in private-sector jobs or community-service jobs almost immediately after enrolling in welfare. (Once a recipient starts a full-time job in the private sector AFDC benefits are eliminated; however AFDC benefits generally continue at a reduced level while the recipient works part time. By contrast, a recipient performing community-service work continues to receive full AFDC payments but must work for the benefits obtained.)

Another pilot program called *Work Not Welfare* (WNW) began in January 1995 in two counties, Fond du Lac and Pierce. WNW placed an absolute time limit of 24 months on receiving AFDC. Although this program obviously had no direct impact on dependency in most of the state, it did send a strong symbolic message to welfare recipients: Long-term dependence would no longer be tolerated. (Still, caseloads in those two counties have fallen only slightly more rapidly than in most other counties.)

In December 1995, the governor's staff instituted a radical new system for rewarding good performance in county welfare offices. The new system employed competitive bidding for the management of each county's welfare system. Governmental or private organizations currently running AFDC in each county were thus threatened with competition and could be replaced by outside organizations. The current welfare organizations, however could escape the competitive bidding process if they fulfilled new performance criteria specified by the state. Chief among these criteria was a requirement that each county reduce its AFDC caseload by roughly 15 to 25 percent (requirements varied by county) over the subsequent 12 months.

DECISIVE NEW POLICIES

In April 1996, Wisconsin unveiled two more decisive reforms. *Work First* (renamed Self-Sufficiency First) went into effect in all counties including Milwaukee, and a new *Pay for Performance* (PFP) system was implemented statewide. For decades politicians have talked about making welfare recipients work while creating regulations that made this impossible. With *Pay for Performance*, Wisconsin closed the loopholes, creating for the first time a real work requirement for AFDC recipients. Prior to PFP, a recipient who failed to obtain a private-sector job might be required to perform community service. If the recipient failed to actually perform this service work, however, the state could only cut AFDC benefits slightly. Under PFP, a recipient would see his welfare check reduced in direct pro-

portion to the number of hours of community work he fails to perform. An individual who performs no work would receive no AFDC or food stamps. Critically, the PFP principle was also applied to other constructive activities such as class attendance or supervised job search.

PFP effectively eliminated the freedom of most Wisconsin AFDC recipients to receive welfare without working. Caseloads, already in rapid decline, began to plummet. In the first seven months after the implementation of *Pay for Performance* and *Self-Sufficiency First,* the AFDC caseload dropped 14 percent in Milwaukee and 33 percent in the rest of the state. If the trends continue, the welfare rolls statewide will drop by an additional one-third over the next 12 months.

REFORM SKEPTICS

Apologists for big welfare have naturally sought some pretext for ignoring or trivializing Wisconsin's achievement. The most common ploy is to attribute the decline in AFDC caseload to a "good economy." Although Wisconsin has enjoyed low unemployment and healthy growth in jobs, it is ridiculous to claim that this has brought about a dramatic reduction in caseload. After all, over the past 40 years states have often experienced robust economic growth without any significant drop in the welfare rolls, let alone a drop of 50 percent.

The limited role of economics in Thompson's victory over dependence can be seen by comparing Wisconsin with the 13 states that have experienced lower levels of unemployment than Wisconsin over the past decade. In these states, the welfare rolls, on average, actually increased by some 20 percent. None

Table 1

Wisconsin Leads the Nation

Rank	State	Jan. 1987	Sep. 1996	Change in Caseload
1.	Wisconsin	98,295	49,930	−49.2%
2.	Michigan	214,273	167,210	−22.0%
3.	Iowa	39,697	31,010	−21.9%
4.	Louisiana	85,047	66,540	−21.8%
5.	Mississippi	57,082	44,840	−21.4%
6.	Alabama	47,817	40,640	−15.0%
7.	South Dakota	6,620	5,670	−14.4%
8.	Nebraska	16,246	13,950	−14.1%
9.	Maryland	66,248	57,130	−13.8%
10.	Ohio	227,035	201,950	−11.0%
11.	Illinois	240,764	217,130	−9.8%
12.	New Jersey	117,694	106,500	−9.5%
13.	North Dakota	5,069	4,660	−8.1%
14.	Kansas	25,256	23,390	−7.4%
15.	Indiana	53,156	49,500	−6.9%
16.	Massachusetts	87,195	81,260	−6.8%
17.	South Carolina	45,640	42,640	−6.6%
18.	Wyoming	4,640	4,340	−6.5%
19.	Oregon	30,368	28,530	−6.1%
20.	Pennsylvania	187,946	179,880	−4.3%
21.	Arkansas	22,797	22,060	−3.2%
22.	Montana	9,410	9,490	0.9%
23.	Maine	19,329	19,700	1.9%
24.	Utah	13,720	14,030	2.3%
25.	West Virginia	36,485	37,470	2.7%
26.	Minnesota	54,699	57,150	4.5%
27.	Virginia	56,751	60,340	6.3%
28.	Oklahoma	32,653	35,230	7.9%
29.	Colorado	31,079	33,550	8.0%
30.	Vermont	7,678	8,660	12.8%
31.	New York	358,083	412,720	15.3%
32.	Missouri	67,690	78,980	16.7%
33.	Kentucky	59,579	69,840	17.2%
34.	Dist. of Col.	19,988	25,140	25.8%
35.	Washington	75,697	96,800	27.9%
36.	Rhode Island	15,843	20,420	28.9%
37.	Delaware	7,810	10,450	33.8%
38.	Idaho	6,215	8,500	36.8%
39.	Georgia	87,329	120,520	38.0%
40.	Tennessee	65,296	90,520	38.6%
41.	Connecticut	38,919	57,040	46.6%
42.	California	585,321	870,230	48.7%
43.	Hawaii	14,498	21,890	51.0%
44.	Texas	153,934	238,340	54.8%
45.	North Carolina	67,360	107,480	59.6%
46.	Alaska	7,163	12,320	72.0%
47.	New Mexico	18.207	32,970	81.1%
48.	Florida	102,013	200,290	96.3%
49.	New Hampshire	4,329	8,920	106.1%
50.	Arizona	29,114	61,790	112.2%
51.	Nevada	5,575	13,120	135.3%
	U.S. Total	**3,735,386**	**4,267,926**	**14.3%**

Change in number of families receiving Aid to Families with Dependent Children, January 1987 through September 1996, by state.

Source: U.S. Department of Health and Human Services.

produced a substantial decline in welfare caseloads. Although a robust economy has undoubtedly helped Wisconsin to reduce welfare dependency, it is far from the principal cause.

Another common dodge of the skeptics is to claim that reform has raised welfare costs. This charge is no surprise; defenders of the status quo have always claimed that taxpayers must "invest" more funds in order to "end welfare." But Wisconsin's reforms did not result in increased spending in either the short or long term. Although the state has increased its outlays on welfare administration, job training, and day care, these expenditures have been more than offset by the rapidly shrinking caseload. Wisconsin spends more per family on welfare now than in 1987, but it has half the number of families on welfare. The greatest expenditure increase has been for welfare administration; although day-care costs have also increased modestly, they still constitute only 6 percent of the total. Today Wisconsin's aggregate spending on AFDC benefits, administration, training, and day care, in current dollars, is some 5 to 10 percent lower than in 1986, the last year before Thompson became governor. But in the rest of the nation, similar expenditures have nearly doubled in the same period: Clearly, Wisconsin's reforms have produced huge de facto savings, not higher costs. In inflation-adjusted terms, Wisconsin's spending is actually down by a third since 1986.

LESSONS LEARNED

The Wisconsin experience provides a cornucopia of lessons for the rest of the nation. In reforming welfare, Wisconsin has rediscovered a philanthropic philosophy once ubiquitous in American charities, but largely abandoned over the past 40 years. This philosophy regards dependence and idleness as harmful to the welfare recipient and insists that he perform useful labor in exchange for benefits he receives.

Thus a serious work requirement provides not only a sound moral foundation, but also performs a crucial gatekeeping function. A key problem for rational charity is separating those who truly need aid from those who do not but are willing to take a free handout if one is offered. Work requirements serve that purpose. For example, in the 19th century, religious organizations throughout the United States provided food and shelter to persons who would today be called "homeless." Before providing a free meal and a bed, however, the shelter would require the man seeking aid to perform some useful chore such as chopping firewood. Charity workers had discovered that such a requirement greatly reduced the numbers seeking aid. This "work test" winnowed out those who did not need aid and allowed the philanthropists to focus limited resources on the truly needy.

With one out of seven children enrolled in AFDC, the current system is so large that serious reform will be impossible. The initial task in transforming welfare is to shrink the AFDC caseload to manageable proportions. Culling those who do not truly need aid from the welfare rolls will allow the system to focus its efforts on those who have the most difficulty becoming self-sufficient, and will free up resources and energy needed to deal with the underlying problems, such as educational failure and illegitimacy, that promote future dependence.

Wisconsin's example provides nine clear rules on how to sharply reduce dependency:

1. Set the right goal. If the ultimate aim of reform is to reduce dependence, the official goal must be to reduce the welfare caseload. A large drop in caseload entails dramatic administrative change and threatens the financial self-interest of the welfare industry. Ingenious welfare bureaucrats will thus propose other performance criteria that allow them to claim success in reducing dependence while caseloads continue to rise. Such ersatz benchmarks generally include: the length of time spent on welfare; the number of recipients in training, part-time employment, or make-work jobs; or the number who leave welfare. Decisionmakers should not be fooled: It is the size of the caseload that matters.

2. Focus on the size of the caseload, not welfare exits. Measuring the number of recipients who leave welfare—or "exits" —is misleading. Large numbers of "exits" from welfare will occur even when welfare caseloads are rising. States with liberal welfare systems may have larger numbers of exits because they encourage highly employable persons to enroll in welfare. By contrast, a serious work requirement may actually reduce welfare exits since it will discourage the most employable persons from enrolling in welfare in the first place.

3. Avoid education and training. Government training and remedial education programs in general do not increase recipients' wage rates and do little to reduce dependence. A recent Labor Department study of the government's largest training program, the Job Training Partnership Act (JTPA), found that the program had little or no effect on the wages of trainees: The average hourly wage rate of trainees rose 3.4 percent, while the hourly wages of males did not increase at all.

4. Use work requirements to reduce welfare applications. The most important effect of a work requirement is to reduce dramatically the number of persons who apply for welfare. This is called the "dissuasion" effect of work requirements. By operating programs such as Self-Sufficiency First and by requiring most new applicants to find private-sector employment or perform community-service work shortly after enrolling in welfare, Wisconsin has cut the number of new AFDC entrants almost in half over the last two years.

5. Require continuous activity. In the private sector, employees are expected to work continuously, not intermittently. This principle must be duplicated in welfare. Once a recipient begins supervised job search, training, or work, some activity should be required without interruption or lessened intensity until the recipient leaves AFDC. In order to reduce welfare recidivism, the work obligation should resume as soon as a former welfare recipient returns to the AFDC rolls.

6. Establish a pay-after-performance benefits system. Welfare should be based on "pay-after-performance": Recipients will not receive the welfare check until after they have performed work or other required activity. If they fail to perform the required number of hours of activity, the welfare check must be reduced on a pro-rata basis.

7. Use community-service "workfare" as an enforcement mechanism. Upon applying for welfare, employable recipients should be required to begin a supervised search for employment. If they have not found a private-sector job within six weeks, they should be required to perform community-service work. Of course, the real goal of reform is to see that recipients obtain private-sector employment, not to push them into make-work jobs. But in a conventional welfare system, large numbers of recipients will claim they cannot find private-sector jobs. If such "unsuccessful job seekers" are permitted to remain idly on the rolls, reform will fail. Instead, all individuals who fail to obtain private-sector jobs should be placed immediately in community service slots on a pay-for-performance basis.

This effectively eliminates any recipient's chance of receiving a welfare income without working, and pushes recipients into private-sector jobs while dissuading other individuals from entering welfare. Mandatory community service is thus the crucial backstop to a serious work requirement. Of course, this does not mean that large numbers of recipients will end up in make-work community service. In Wisconsin few do, but the threat of community work is the key to propelling recipients into the private sector.

8. Impose work requirements on the most employable recipients first. The initial goal of welfare reform should be to restrict welfare to those who truly need it and to eliminate from the rolls those who do not. In order to accomplish this goal and to shrink welfare caseloads, work requirements should be focused on the most employable welfare recipients first. These would include two-parent families (10 percent of the caseload in a typical state) and mothers who do not have preschool children (typically 50 percent).

This strategy may seem counterintuitive, but it is essential to reducing dependence. The number of crucial community-service work slots (where the recipient is required to work for benefits) in the first phases of reform will be quite small in relation to the overall caseload. If the least employable recipients occupy these slots, they will remain there for long periods, clogging up the system. When highly employable recipients, by contrast, are faced with the prospect of performing community-service work, most will respond by quickly leaving AFDC, freeing the work slots for others, who will in turn leave the rolls. Through this revolving process, the caseload will begin to shrink quickly. (A variant of this principle is to focus work requirements on recent applicants who are, in general, more employable than the rest of the caseload.)

9. Establish bureaucratic incentives and competition. Throughout the United States, most of the welfare industry is liberal, regards welfare recipients as victims of social injustice, and is threatened by reforms that will sharply reduce its welfare clientele. In order to ensure the faithful and efficient implementation of conservative reforms, decisionmakers must establish precise performance criteria linked to rewards and sanctions for the welfare bureaucracies. In Wisconsin, welfare offices were forced to compete with one another to earn funding, and ultimately each county office faced the threat of elimination if it failed to meet high performance standards set by the governor.

LOOKING TOWARD THE FUTURE

The lessons from Wisconsin greatly influenced the national welfare reform enacted in Washington [in 1996]. The new federal law encourages states to pursue work policies similar to Wisconsin's. Among the specific features of the new federal law drawn from Wisconsin are the federal performance standards based on caseload reduction, the use of workfare to "dissuade" new applicants, and a requirement that states set up pay-for-performance systems.

Tommy Thompson has shown that state governments can overcome AFDC dependency. The greatest benefit will accrue to children. In the past, liberals have been mesmerized by the belief that "poverty" somehow harms children and that welfare, by "combating poverty," is therefore good for kids. Hence they are timid, if not outright adversarial, in their attitude toward serious efforts to reduce welfare dependency. But studies that compare children on welfare with poor children not on welfare show that it is actually welfare dependency, not poverty, that harms children. A childhood of welfare dependency lowers children's IQs, increases their likelihood of academic failure, and diminishes their future earnings as an adult. Welfare is a system of child abuse; by radically reducing dependence, Wisconsin's reforms will improve the future well-being of children.

There is, however, one very important shortcoming to Wisconsin's welfare achievement: The current reforms have not cut the state's illegitimate birth rate. Illegitimacy does much more harm to children's development than does welfare dependency. The ultimate goal of reform must be not only to reduce dependency but to rebuild marriage. One can only hope that over the next decade, Wisconsin's reformers will tackle the problem of out-of-wedlock births with the ingenuity and diligence they have already applied to the question of dependence.

Throughout his tenure as governor, Tommy Thompson has routinely accomplished what the welfare industry declared impossible. He has demolished many of the fables buttressing the welfare status quo. Among the venerable myths debunked by Wisconsin are the following: Recipients really want to work but jobs are not available; the lack of day care makes employment impossible; education and training are the key to reducing dependence; and it costs more to reform than to continue the status quo. Thompson has not only rewritten the rule book on fighting dependence; he has invented a new language in which future rules will be written.

Perhaps the most surprising aspect of Wisconsin's story is the extraordinary outcomes produced by mundane policies. There is nothing radical about initiatives like *Self-Sufficiency First* or *Pay for Performance*. Indeed, these policies are pretty much what most voters have in mind when they hear talk of making welfare recipients work. It is true that in the fall of 1997, Thompson will inaugurate a new set for reforms termed Wisconsin Works, or W2. This will abolish AFDC entirely and replace it with a pure employment-based system of assistance. Although great things are expected of W2, its arrival should not overshadow the fact that the current reforms will have already eliminated a vast portion of the Wisconsin AFDC caseload before W2 even begins.

Other states that are in early stages of reform need not leap as far as W2. Any state that will enact *Pay for Performance* and *Self-Sufficiency First*, and follow the nine principles outlined above, will dramatically reduce the welfare dependency of its citizens. Wisconsin has shown the way; it is now up to rest of the nation to apply the lessons learned.

NO

Michael Wiseman

WELFARE REFORM IN THE UNITED STATES: A BACKGROUND PAPER

INTRODUCTION

... This article surveys the major issues surrounding welfare reform, outlines the competing proposals for reform, reviews PRWORA [Personal Responsibility and Work Opportunity Reconciliation Act], and comments on the outlook for further reform. I argue that the likely outcome of the coming struggle over welfare reform is, at least over the next few years, increased hardship for the poor. Contrary to popular wisdom, however, I also argue that the new legislation is likely to produce a larger federal role in welfare and more difficulty for governors than would have been the case given continuation of the programs ended by welfare reform. Because so many poor families using public assistance are located in central cities, many of the consequences, both positive and negative, of the reform effort will be concentrated there. Welfare reform is in essence an urban policy issue....

By convention, the term welfare is applied to programs of public assistance that give aid to individuals or families on the basis of need and means. There are many such programs in the United States, including locally funded and state-funded general relief; various housing assistance programs; the Low-Income Home Energy Assistance Program; school lunch and breakfast programs; and the Special Supplemental Food Program for Women, Infants, and Children (WIC). The four means-tested programs most important to the national welfare reform debate are Aid to Families with Dependent Children (AFDC), food stamps, supplemental security income (SSI), and Medicaid. AFDC gives cash to needy families with children; food stamps are special coupons that indigent families and individuals can use to purchase food; SSI provides income to needy aged, blind, and disabled persons; and Medicaid provides health care for the poor. PRWORA replaced AFDC with block grants to states for Temporary Assistance for Needy Families (TANF) and altered eligibility standards for food stamps and SSI. The TANF block grant allows states to sustain the AFDC program for at least the coming fiscal year, and as a result the changes have yet to affect either programs or caseloads sig-

From Michael Wiseman, "Welfare Reform in the United States: A Background Paper," *Housing Policy Debate*, vol. 7, no. 4 (1996). Copyright © 1996 by The Fannie Mae Foundation. Reprinted by permission. Notes and references omitted.

nificantly. Thus I begin with discussion of welfare before PRWORA. I then turn to predictions of how states will change the welfare system under block grants. . . .

I choose 1993, the year between the election of President Clinton and the landmark congressional election of 1994, as point of reference.

Caseload trends. Political concern about welfare has been driven in part by exceptionally rapid recent caseload growth. Between 1980 and 1989, the AFDC caseload grew by about 5.5 percent (figure 1). Between 1989 and 1993, the caseload grew by 33 percent. Part of this acceleration is attributable to the recession of 1990 to 1992. However, the economic downturn at the beginning of this decade was by most measures no more severe than that of 1980 to 1982, when the caseload response was much less.

These trends produced a substantial increase in the proportion of American children living in families at least partly dependent on welfare. In a typical month in 1980, about 1 child in 10 lived in a family receiving AFDC; by 1993 the odds had increased to 1 child in 8. Almost 14 percent of American families with children received AFDC during an average month in 1993; a higher proportion received such benefits at some time during the year.

Welfare costs. Between 1980 and 1993, the welfare caseload grew by 39 percent. Over the same interval, real outlays for the "big four" transfer programs grew by 116 percent, and the composition of welfare outlays changed in ways that affect both the state and federal share of outlays and the effect of the system on poverty. These changes have

had important consequences for welfare politics in the 1990s.

A number of observations can be made by examining constant-dollar expenditures on AFDC, food stamps, SSI, and Medicaid for 1980 through 1995:

1. *Effort has increased.* It is difficult to argue that the national antipoverty effort has diminished since President Carter's last year of office. In addition to outstripping the rate of growth in the AFDC caseload over this interval, the 116 percent growth in overall real outlays for public assistance substantially exceeded growth in population (13 percent), in real gross domestic product (36 percent), and in the number of poor children (29 percent). The rate of growth accelerated after 1985.

2. *Medicaid is the villain.* While national effort at public assistance may not have decreased, it has been redirected. Most (80 percent) of the increase in assistance outlays is attributable to rising costs of Medicaid. In 1980, Medicaid accounted for 45 percent of outlays in the four categories identified here; by 1993 this share had grown to 63 percent and was continuing to rise. While approximately 36 percent of Medicaid recipients are in AFDC households, this group accounts for only about 30 percent of Medicaid outlays. Costs for members of other served groups (the elderly, the disabled) are typically much greater. From 1980 to 1988, the share of payments on behalf of AFDC recipients in Medicaid costs fell. Between 1988 and 1993, the share grew by 25 percent. Thus, while AFDC-related Medicaid costs are slightly less than a third of Medicaid outlays, the growth of this segment during the period leading up

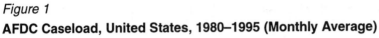

Figure 1

AFDC Caseload, United States, 1980–1995 (Monthly Average)

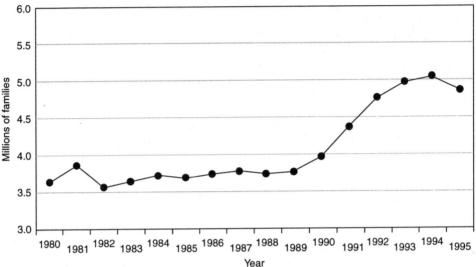

Note: Data for 1995 are preliminary.

Source: U.S. House Committee on Ways and Means (1994).

to the Contract with America was exceptionally rapid.

3. *AFDC is the loser.* Outlays for AFDC benefits grew more slowly than the number of AFDC recipients from 1980 to 1993 (a 14 percent increase compared with a 33 percent increase). Thus, real cash benefits received by individual families declined. States set the level of AFDC benefits. Between January 1985 and January 1994, the maximum AFDC grant for a family of three in the median state (based on benefits) fell from $461 to $367 (a 20 percent decrease) in constant (January 1994) dollars....

The bottom line is that "spendable" welfare (i.e., food stamps and AFDC) has become increasingly federalized over the past 13 years as states have lowered AFDC benefits while food stamp benefits have been sustained.

4. *SSI lost, too.* The basic SSI benefit is wholly federally funded. The law permits (and, in some instances, requires) states to supplement the federal payment. Currently, all but eight states provide some type of supplement to the federal benefit. However, over time state SSI supplements have not kept up with inflation, while the federal benefit has. The result is that the direct federal share in overall SSI costs has increased and food stamp benefits paid to SSI recipients have also gone up. This too has increased the federal share of the costs of aiding the SSI target population.

5. *The state share remains unchanged.* The federalization of spendable welfare cited above would be expected to increase the federal share in overall assistance payments. In fact, the federal share of the cost of AFDC, food

stamps, SSI, and Medicaid combined did not change at all over the 1980–95 interval. The... culprit has already been identified. Medicaid outlays grew much faster than food stamp and SSI benefits combined. The federal government still pays only slightly more than half the costs of Medicaid. The rapid growth in total Medicaid outlays kept the overall federal share at slightly less than two-thirds. . . .

In sum, despite cutbacks, states have not found substantial fiscal relief in public assistance policy. Although the states were clearly attempting to reduce their fiscal contribution to social welfare costs, the rapid increase in Medicaid offset the attempt so that as late as 1995 the states' apparent share was virtually the same as it had been 13 years earlier. Given the failure of national health insurance reform, it was likely that states would seek fiscal relief in other ways. The fact that states do respond strategically to the incentives created by federal assistance policy is important, because PRWORA changes state incentives substantially.

Welfare and poverty.   At the same time that outlays for public assistance were increasing, so too were poverty rates. In 1980, 18 percent of all children lived in families with reported incomes below the federal poverty standard (approximately $12,000 in current dollars for a family of three); by 1993, the proportion was 23 percent. The 1995 poverty rate among all persons, children and adults, was 13.8 percent; in 1980, it was 13 percent, and it has not fallen below that level since. . . .

THE PROBLEM OF REFORM

The litany of indictments suggests that the U.S. welfare system is a ripe target for government reinventing. The lesson of recent American history is that welfare reform is hard to accomplish, and as bad as some problems are, the system can be made worse by ill-considered fixes. There are several reasons for this.

Poverty Is Complex
The welfare system in part mirrors the complexity of poverty in general. Simple solutions for many, if not most, poverty issues are elusive, and the enthusiasm of even the most zealous reformer often dims as special case after special case is identified. In general, the less experienced the author is with poverty and welfare operation and the farther the author is from the nearest welfare office, the simpler the solution proffered. . . .

WELFARE REFORM IN THE STATES

The Bush initiative.   ... In 1991, the Bush administration made a strategic decision to encourage state welfare demonstrations [or experiments] as a means of establishing an initiative in this area at minimal federal cost.

In his 1992 State of the Union Address, President Bush encouraged states to continue efforts to "replace the assumptions of the welfare state and help reform the welfare system" and promised to make the waiver process "easier and quicker." The response was swift and substantial. Between the State of the Union message and the end of the Bush administration the following January, 22 state applications for waiver-based welfare reform demonstrations were received. Of these,

14 were approved and the remaining 8 proposals were carried over to the Clinton administration. None were denied.

Following precedents established by the Reagan administration's Interagency Low-Income Opportunity Advisory Board, the Bush administration applied two standards in dealing with these initiatives. To be approved, waiver-based demonstrations had to be cost neutral and rigorously evaluated. A demonstration was cost neutral if it would not add to federal welfare outlays. Rigorous evaluation meant, for the most part, evaluation by random assignment. The two criteria were linked: A demonstration's effects on costs were assessed by comparing costs between control and experimental groups. States were obligated to cover the difference between federal per-case costs for the controls and federal per-case costs for recipients in the experimental group. Content did not play a major role in waiver strategy.

Clinton policy. Since the ambitious waiver program was largely a Republican initiative, one might have expected the new Democratic administration to curtail waiver-based welfare demonstration activity. Instead, two weeks after his inauguration, President Clinton promised the National Governors' Association that his own administration would continue to support state demonstrations, as long as the results were "honestly evaluated." The result was rapid growth in the number of waiver applications and waiver-based demonstrations approved. In the interval between Clinton's inauguration and the 1994 congressional elections, the administration approved 21 more waiver demonstrations in 20 states. By mid-1996, on the eve of PRWORA's passage, it had approved waivers for 43 states and the District of Columbia.

These state initiatives featured an extraordinary collection and combination of interventions, ranging from benefit reductions to cash incentive schemes for encouraging inoculation of children against disease. Objective evaluation of this avalanche of novelties is difficult. A defensible summary is that few will ever produce any results usable in the process of policy development. In general, the interventions were too poorly planned, the number of program changes too large, and the evaluation schemes too limited in scope to encompass the range of possible program effects. In some ways this outcome was politically desirable. In state welfare reform initiatives, the political payoff from demonstration activism may be more important than the modest gain in knowledge that might be attained. Moreover, in most cases the political payoff seems to come early, while assessment is postponed virtually indefinitely.

The waiver leader: Wisconsin. A prime example of the difference in timing between political attention and demonstration outcomes is provided by Wisconsin's Work Not Welfare initiative. Proposed in early 1993 following President Clinton's address to the National Governors' Association, Work Not Welfare is an experiment designed to test the impact of a time limit for welfare receipt. The program was approved by HHS [U.S. Department of Health and Human Services] in November; it began in two small Wisconsin counties in January 1995 with a target number of experimental cases under 1,000. The final report is scheduled for the year 2006.

Work Not Welfare is one of nine Wisconsin welfare reform demonstrations initiated since Governor Tommy Thompson took office in January 1987. Overall, Thompson's record on welfare has been extraordinary: Between his inauguration and January 1994, the AFDC caseload in Wisconsin fell by 21 percent. The Thompson administration is understandably willing to attribute this decline to the welfare reform initiatives. However, most of the reduction was accumulated before the state's waiver-based initiatives were under way, and like Work Not Welfare, some of the more celebrated of the Thompson initiatives have involved only a small proportion of the caseload. Contrary to the image of the Thompson administration beyond the state's borders, a significant proportion of the Wisconsin waiver-based demonstrations have actually increased the generosity of the welfare system by improving services and extending eligibility to two-parent families without application of the 100-hour rule. It is the Thompson administration's benefit strategy and income tests that have been restrictive.

While definitive assessments are complicated, it appears that at least through 1994 the overall Wisconsin achievement is attributable to the combination of a robust economy (the September 1994 unemployment rate in Wisconsin was 4.5 percent, compared with 5.9 percent for the nation), a gradual tightening through inflation of the welfare eligibility standard in the state, a freeze on welfare benefits, and aggressive use of the funds for recipient job assistance provided by FSA [Family Support Act of 1988]. In 1994, *Rising Tide*, the Republican National Committee's news magazine, reported that Thompson considered the JOBS program his "favorite" in the welfare arena. *Rising Tide* failed to note that JOBS [Job Oppor-

tunities and Basic Skills] is a product of FSA, not the waiver process.

Since 1994, both Wisconsin's unemployment rate and its welfare caseload have continued to decline. The state has launched two additional initiatives—Self Sufficiency First and Pay for Performance—intended to increase efforts by local operating agencies to move persons applying for assistance into employment and to facilitate penalizing recipients who fail to participate in JOBS programs. Between December 1994 and mid-1996, the AFDC caseload fell an additional 29 percent. The state is conducting an evaluation of these initiatives based on comparison of outcomes for cases subject to the Self Sufficiency First–Pay for Performance initiative with outcomes for a set of cases selected at random to be exempt, but results are not yet available. The evaluation may be terminated as the state moves to its latest initiative, Wisconsin Works, to be discussed later.

Conclusion: Image and reality.   Perhaps the most important conclusion to be drawn from the plethora of state initiatives is that no one, not even Thompson, has really found the key to welfare savings by means other than cutting benefits and active and broad-based efforts at job placement and training. As politically significant as the state initiatives may be, both the content and the scale of implementation of most have been modest, and states like Wisconsin that have undertaken more ambitious efforts have done so in an exceptionally favorable economic context. Governors know that political hyperbole is one thing, budget consequences another. An index of real state commitment to welfare-to-work efforts is provided by the JOBS program. While most states appeared eager to pursue welfare demonstrations, as of March 1996 only 12 states (including Wisconsin) had claimed all federal funds available for the JOBS operation, even though such funds required very little in state matching expenditure.

The record of the Thompson administration and the panoply of state initiatives spawned by Bush and Clinton waiver policy were important elements of the politics of welfare in the aftermath of the 1994 election. Wisconsin's achievement was generally cited as representative of what states could do when not hampered by federal regulation. In 1995, Thompson became chairman of the National Governors' Association, and he used this position to promote award of even greater latitude to states to structure their welfare programs. This gubernatorial effort might have been cast as the leading alternative to the strategy set forth in the Clinton administration's WRA [Work and Responsibility Act], were it not for the emergence on the stage of welfare reform of a third set of players, the House Republicans, led by Speaker Newt Gingrich. Since the congressional Republican initiative was originally aimed at the Clinton reform, it is the Clinton plan that is discussed first.

THE CLINTON PLAN

Welfare politics caused the Clinton administration's WRA to be pitched as "ending welfare as we know it." This characterization was disingenuous, since much of the proposal was a continuation of the reform trajectory established by FSA. What was new, of course, was the time limit. But the significance of even this centerpiece, as proposed by Clinton, should not be exaggerated. Its billing had more to do with the political strategy of the 1992 presidential campaign than with the substance of the program.

The Time Limit

Prior to assuming national office, President Clinton was actively involved in welfare reform, both in Arkansas and as part of a task force of the National Governors' Association. During the presidential campaign, Bruce Reed (then a volunteer speech-writer) brought the work of Harvard scholar David Ellwood to Clinton's attention. With the support of the Ford Foundation, Ellwood had recently published a book, *Poor Support* (Ellwood 1988), that offered a plan for welfare reform.

Poor Support called for a divide-and-conquer antipoverty strategy that combined a substantial increase in services and payments to the poor with different approaches to be fashioned for different subgroups (recall the "tagging is appropriate" welfare reform principle). Ellwood argued that with such a strategy in place, the nation might limit welfare payments to a period ranging from 18 to 36 months; adults still without jobs by the end of that period could be required to accept some form of public employment. Ellwood's time-limit proposal was based in part on his earlier research with a Harvard colleague, Mary Jo Bane, on the duration of spells of welfare receipt. That research indicated that a substantial share (in the original version almost half) of welfare cases close within two years of opening. If this result was correct, the implication was that more costly interventions could be avoided for many recipients by waiting for nature to take its course....

Work and Responsibility Act

As released, WRA built on the strategy established by FSA by increasing federal and state efforts to obtain child support from noncustodial parents, changing JOBS, continuing the process of eliminating the distinction between the regular (single-parent) and the unemployed-parent (two-parent) subprograms in AFDC, and developing national performance standards for agencies involved in delivering welfare services. The legislation went beyond FSA in developing a National Teen Pregnancy Prevention Initiative to "encourage responsible behavior." The act responded to the recommendations of the Welfare Simplification and Coordination Advisory Committee by proposing streamlining of eligibility procedures and standards across the AFDC and Food Stamp programs. State flexibility in welfare program design was to be increased to allow states greater latitude in setting program parameters without waivers. In particular, states were to be allowed to vary work incentives incorporated in payment computation and to eliminate welfare benefit increases for children conceived after their mothers began receiving assistance. Finally, new state demonstrations were proposed in such areas as payment procedures for the EITC [earned income tax credit], methods of job search assistance, and effects of state assumption of responsibility for ensuring that child support awards are paid on schedule. Thus while WRA increased state latitude in welfare program operation, it also took steps toward establishing an agenda for reform-oriented experimentation....

The welfare reform group recognized that the WORK innovation could be costly and could be difficult to implement on an adequate scale. Indeed, the lesson of experience, including that of Governor Reagan in California in the early 1970s, is that subsidized employment is difficult to do, and no state experiment with welfare work requirements has yet to attain the scale contemplated by WRA. But while certainly difficult to implement, a work assignment incorporated as a scheduled feature of JOBS case management had many attractive features. There is some evidence that work experience increases the chances that recipients will obtain unsubsidized employment. A work requirement is a way out of the problems posed by the design of financial incentives for work. A common work requirement provides more leeway for unifying the treatment of single- and two-parent families in AFDC; WRA offered states the option of eliminating the 100-hour employment restriction for two-parent families. Above all, a timed work requirement might assist in making the entire welfare-to-work process "time conscious." ...

Summary

WRA was a creditable effort at welfare reform. The problem is that there was little in it that would not have been there had the same task force produced draft legislation a year earlier. By delaying, the administration fueled expectation that something entirely different was in the wings, an expectation that WRA did not fulfill. By appearing to deliver its own initiative stillborn, the administration devalued it, thus opening the field for less thoughtfully constructed congressional and state alternatives. At least when viewed in terms of media attention, states have been responsible for far more action on the welfare reform front since 1992 than the federal government, and the administration's delay encouraged

Congress, governors, and, apparently, voters to fill the gap.

REPUBLICAN ALTERNATIVES

The major Republican congressional response to the Clinton administration's failure to deliver welfare reform was the Personal Responsibility Act (PRA). Wisconsin produced the boldest of the plans advanced by Republican governors.

Personal Responsibility Act

Originally championed by the new Speaker of the House, Representative Newt Gingrich of Georgia, PRA was a follow-up on the promise of welfare reform included in the Republican Contract with America introduced in August 1994 and was built on a reform scheme proposed in November 1993 by 160 House Republicans. As originally formulated, the plan tackled WRA and the underlying administration strategy for welfare reform virtually point by point. Everything was made tougher; the most important provisions involved the JOBS/WORK program, time limits, teen pregnancy, illegitimacy, program consolidation, federal and state financing, and aid to immigrants....

Legislative Changes

Many of the changes incorporated in the original PRA were modified during the first six months of the new Congress. The House of Representatives version of the law (H.R. 4) was passed in March 1995 and retained the "Personal Responsibility Act" title. The Senate Finance Committee passed a substitute bill, the Family Self-Sufficiency Act, later in the year....

Despite substantial conformity, important differences arose. The House legislation followed the original PRA in banning cash payments for children born to families already receiving assistance, to unwed mothers under 18 years of age, and to most noncitizens. The Senate legislation banned no children from assistance and let states determine whether aid was to be given to noncitizens. The House bill ended the JOBS program; the Senate bill kept JOBS, but in modified form. The House bill gave states the option of operating a simplified Food Stamp program using the same eligibility rules that are applied under TANF. In contrast, the Senate bill did not address the Food Stamp program. Both the House and Senate bills left Medicaid eligibility untouched. Indeed, eligibility for Medicaid would continue to be evaluated on the basis of the rules applied in the old AFDC program....

These differences were hardly insurmountable. But before they could be addressed, welfare reform was sidetracked by conflict between the White House and Congress over the federal budget. When Congress reconvened early in 1996, the outlook for welfare reform was clouded by the presidential campaign. In the meantime, the number of states involved in waiver-based welfare reform demonstrations continued to grow.

Wisconsin Works

The most ambitious of the state initiatives was produced in Wisconsin as a follow-up to the two-year time limit experiment described earlier. To conduct his Work Not Welfare experiment, Governor Tommy Thompson needed to obtain approval from the Wisconsin state legislature as well as from the federal government. The legislature approved the initiative but attached a provision calling for the state's social service agency to submit by 1995 "a proposal for welfare reform in this state" that would replace most public welfare programs by 1999. The proposal was to guarantee income support to needy persons who could not work, guarantee employment to those who could work but could not find jobs, and assure low-income persons "affordable child care" and "affordable health care."

The legislature's "end welfare" requirement was a boon to Governor Thompson. In the context of the national debate over welfare reform, the requirement allowed him to use state resources to develop and advertise a comprehensive reform scheme. The Hudson Institute, a conservative policy analysis organization, set up an office in Madison and organized foundation funding for technical support for a task force appointed to draft a plan. The proposal, called Wisconsin Works and nicknamed W-2, was completed in early spring of 1995. It was formally announced by Governor Thompson on August 3 of that year, following a Vermont meeting of the National Governors' Association. Enabling legislation was passed by the state legislature in March 1996.

Viewed from both state and national perspectives, W-2 is an extremely important development. It is the first fully articulated plan for what a state welfare system might look like in an era of block grants. For citizens concerned about the direction of public assistance policy under something like PRA, Wisconsin Works provides a picture of one direction that states might go should they be freed of the program restrictions previously contained in the Social Security Act.

W-2 is a strategy realized in a program. The strategy has six major features:

1. Virtually all cash assistance is linked to some form of employment.
2. The variety of situations and capabilities of persons seeking public assistance is addressed by tagging and case management.
3. The connection between benefits and dependence is reduced by decoupling cash assistance from access to health insurance and child care assistance.
4. State administrative control and incentives for efficiency are enhanced by allowing public and private agencies to compete for designation as local program operators.
5. The change in the orientation of public assistance as well as agency culture is dramatized by a shift in responsibility for public assistance from the state's social service agency to the employment service agency, the Department of Workforce Development.
6. The "end of welfare" is taken seriously: The state is committed to rapid and complete implementation, with all components in place by September 1997.

... In sum, W-2 is dramatic in ambition, scope, and detail. Once again, Governor Thompson challenged the Clinton administration, this time by demonstrating that a state could develop a comprehensive welfare reform package in far less time than had been required for the WRA. If implemented, W-2 would genuinely end welfare, as Wisconsin's legislature had required. Moreover, like most of the state's initiatives, W-2 involved considerable financial commitment, especially given the state's promise of universal means-tested access to child care and insurance for families with children.

The program appears to be a dramatic refutation of the arguments of some that states would respond to the fiscal incentives produced by a change to block grant funding with a "rush to the bottom." W-2 seems to be better characterized as a rise to the challenge.

Drama in scope and ambition notwithstanding, the W-2 announcement attracted little public attention outside the state, perhaps partly because the media had become inured to years of Wisconsin welfare reform hyperbole. Few appreciated the difference between W-2 and earlier programs. More important, however, was the shift of national attention to the struggle between Congress and the president over the budget. It began to appear that action on welfare reform would await another election. For Thompson, this outcome was galling. W-2 was not intended as just another waiver-based demonstration. Given the breadth of the proposal, something akin to the authorization contained in PRA was believed essential. By spring 1996 it began to appear that resolution would await the outcome of the coming presidential election.

President Clinton's Announcement and the End of the Impasse

However, the politics of welfare reform took a new turn the following May when President Clinton used his weekly radio address to claim credit for state welfare reform initiatives and to challenge Congress to act on welfare reform. "There are bipartisan welfare reform plans sitting in the House and Senate right now," he said, "that do what the American people agree welfare reform must do: They require welfare recipients to work; they limit the time people can stay on welfare; they toughen child support enforcement and they protect our children. So I say

to Congress: Send me a bill that honors these fundamental principles; I'll sign it right away. Let's get the job done."

The president congratulated Wisconsin for adding momentum to the "quiet revolution" in welfare reform with the W-2 proposal, which "has the makings of a solid, bold welfare reform plan." He then appeared to endorse the plan by pledging that his administration "would work with Wisconsin to make an effective transition to a new vision of welfare based on work." This endorsement was extraordinary given that the state had not even applied for waivers for W-2. Governor Thompson's staff scrambled to complete a waiver proposal, which the governor delivered personally to HHS.

This episode was a clear short-term victory for the president on the welfare reform issue. If Congress did not act, the president would respond to any Republican campaign challenge on welfare policy by claiming that it was Congress, and not he, that had prevented the accomplishment of welfare reform in 1996. Congress did indeed respond, and after reconciliation of House and Senate versions of reform legislation, the result was PRWORA (Public Law 104-193). Despite last-minute protests from various members of his administration and others, the president signed the bill in August.

PERSONAL RESPONSIBILITY AND WORK OPPORTUNITY RECONCILIATION ACT

PRWORA is the most substantial welfare reform legislation since establishment of the SSI program and revision and expansion of the Food Stamp program in the 1970s. The most significant change is the termination of entitlement by families to cash assistance provided under Title

IV-A of the Social Security Act (the authorizing legislation for AFDC). In place of the matching grant program, PRWORA creates block grants to cover TANF and related services. The new law restricts or eliminates provision of public assistance to most noncitizens, families that have received aid for more than five years, and children previously made eligible on certain criteria for SSI. The law contains major new policies aimed at reducing the rate of nonmarital births as well as substantial revisions in the Federal-State Child Support Enforcement Program, in the Food Stamp program, and in child nutrition programs.

The heart of PRWORA is replacement of AFDC, JOBS, and Emergency Assistance with a block grant for TANF. (The Emergency Assistance program provides matching funds for use by states to support families with children at immediate risk of destitution or homelessness.) Each state receives a fixed amount based on federal payments received for the three supplanted programs in fiscal year 1994, payments for fiscal year 1995, or the average for fiscal years 1992 to 1994, whichever is largest. Given that for most states caseloads have declined (see figure 1), the TANF block grant results in a net increase in federal funds over what would have been received under pre-PRWORA regulations. The TANF block grant is supplemented with a substantial increase in federal funding for child care. A contingency fund is established for support of states with exceptional unemployment rates, and states with either exceptional population growth rates or very low benefits are eligible for supplemental grants.

TANF funds are to be used to help needy families with children, assist parents in moving to self-support through work and marriage, prevent and reduce out-of-wedlock births, and "encourage the formation and maintenance of two-parent families." In general, how states are to do this is left open, but the law includes certain restrictions and performance requirements. States are required to sustain spending of state funds on the replaced programs plus child care at 75 percent of the spending done in fiscal year 1994. Eligibility for federally funded TANF is denied families with members who have received assistance for five years or more (states are allowed to exempt 20 percent of their caseloads from this requirement).

As in the original Clinton plan, adults receiving TANF assistance must "engage in work" after two years (or less at state option). The criteria for satisfying the work engagement requirement are left to states to define. However, in addition to the two-year work engagement requirement for individuals, the law follows PRA by requiring states to have a specific and increasing fraction of their entire caseload involved in certain work activities identified by the legislation. The required level of participation for single parents is 25 percent in 1997 and rises five percentage points a year to 50 percent in 2002. For adults in two-parent families, the required participation rate begins at 75 percent in 1997 and jumps to 90 percent in 1999. "Participation" initially means 20 hours per week for single parents; for parents with no children under six, the requirement rises to 30 hours by 2000. Adults in two-parent families must work 35 hours per week. States are allowed some variation in these standards, but the end result will still be a much higher level of activity required from recipients and more monitoring to enforce these requirements than under AFDC....

REFLECTIONS

Put another way, PRWORA has initiated change, but we are uncertain of the direction....

Seeing Consequences Will Be Difficult

... One possible consequence of the elimination of entitlement by TANF is that states will attempt to cut costs by making it more difficult to apply for aid. Wisconsin is already experimenting with a system, Self Sufficiency First, that requires persons seeking assistance to complete 60 hours of employment search before the state even begins processing their aid applications. Other states may practice more subtle means of dissuasion, and it is likely that some people in need will lose access to assistance altogether. This "entry effect" will never be captured by agency information systems because such systems cover only the status of persons approved for assistance. Under AFDC, persons meeting standards of need but denied access to assistance could and did seek legal aid. Careful attention needs to be paid to the way state systems come to accommodate, or dissuade, applicants.

Equity Is a Problem

Under AFDC, federal assistance was distributed to states on the basis of state expenditure effort, per capita income, and need—that is, the number of eligible families applying for assistance. While the details of the formula actually used may be difficult to justify, the principle seems sound. The lion's share of PRWORA funds will be distributed for the next five years on the basis of circumstances at the beginning of the decade. These circumstances were established in part by a recession that varied substantially across states in impact. In contrast, PRA proposed allocation of funds across states based on trends in population and numbers of poor households. It is likely that before long losers under the new system will demand redress.

Large-Scale Workfare Will Be Costly

As politically attractive as they may be in the abstract, welfare employment programs are costly to operate and difficult to manage. The reasons are clear: Even bad jobs require capital and some management (at minimum, rakes and straw bosses), and unlike "real" employment, welfare employment programs encourage high turnover. The skills required for management of effective workfare operation are quite different from those sought elsewhere in government, and they do not come cheaply. PRWORA requires an unprecedented level of participation in work and work-related activities, and the funds for meeting these standards come out of the same aggregate appropriation as basic benefits. The consequence may be expanded state costs, reduced benefits, or both....

The Bottom Still Looms

Regardless of motivation or dedication of governors, PRWORA creates substantial incentives for reduction in benefits. While the law includes some safeguards for maintenance of effort, the standard is set low (75 percent of 1994 expenditures if the state meets the work participation requirement) and the range of expenditure states are allowed to count as part of "effort" is broad. Moreover, states are permitted to set aside any amount of their TANF grants they like in a contingency fund to meet demand in the event of a recession or other development that increases need. For every state, the shift from AFDC to TANF at least doubles the cost to the state's general fund of financial assistance to the poor.

In the near term, the expansion of funds provided by caseload decline and the new block grant is likely to prevent any retreat on benefits. By the next budget cycle, however, the extent of reduction permitted under maintenance-of-effort requirements and the range of outlays that can be tallied to establish effort will be well understood. At this point, legislators will begin to appreciate the new terms of trade between public assistance and other state activities that PRWORA establishes. Likewise, the cost of meeting activity requirements will be better understood. Pressure will be felt to reduce welfare expenditures and shift the expenditure level that is sustained in the direction of supporting work programs. Spendable income for welfare recipients will, under this scenario, decline.

Earlier I argued that interstate variation in welfare benefits has in the past been reduced by incentives created by the matching grant formula. Those incentives are eliminated, or at least reduced, by PRWORA. Disparity in benefit levels is therefore likely to grow as some states drop benefits faster than others. This in turn may create incentives for high-benefit states to reduce outlays to discourage migration. It should be emphasized that these effects are hypothetical, but such predictions are not unwarranted. As evidence already cited indicates, states do respond to the incentives created by grant allocation procedures.

Again, the outcome of this process remains to be seen. But if CBO projections are accepted, PRWORA will result in only a 3 1/2 percent decline in federal outlays on public assistance between 1997 and 2003. Any decline in state outlays in excess of this amount will increase the federal share in social assistance, and such effects will be magnified if benefit reduction leads to greater costs for food stamps. The nearly inevitable outcome will be a greater federal fiscal role at the same time that federal administrative control is curtailed.

Cities Are Where Much Will Happen

For reasons rooted in the Constitution, negotiations over welfare reform have been almost exclusively a matter between states and Washington, DC. This emphasis on states obscures the likely concentration of effects of welfare reform in urban areas. A rough sense of this concentration can be gained from a recent study of public assistance receipt by the U.S. Bureau of the Census (1995). In 1991, 29 percent of the U.S. population lived in central cities of metropolitan areas. In contrast, 44 percent of recipients of AFDC, General Assistance (public assistance without federal contribution), and SSI did. PRWORA restrictions have their greatest effect on long-time recipients. The same study reported the geographic distribution of persons who reported receipt of public assistance for every month over the 1991–92 interval. *Half* of all persons reporting continuous receipt of AFDC lived in central cities. This allocation of population does not match the allocation of employment, so agencies charged with assisting people to find the employment required by TANF will have to reach beyond city and across county borders.

Many of the Poor Are Indeed Needy

It is easy to generate political support for abstractions like "eliminating fraud and abuse" or "illegal immigrants." But most polls indicate continuing public support for government assistance to people who really look needy—those who appear to make valiant efforts at self-support but, because of bad fortune or other circumstances, fail. Inevitably, the restrictions imposed by states because of PRWORA will produce and publicize tragic cases of deprivation because of government fiat. People who lose welfare after running up against the time limit, children abandoned, aliens claiming risk of death or worse at home—all will attract media attention, and all will be state responsibilities. PRWORA does not preclude aiding such folk; in some instances it just precludes using federal dollars to do so. To the extent that such cases, when given faces, reveal true need, local and state government will feel pressure to respond. . . .

Medicaid Is Still a Problem

Despite the importance of Medicaid to state budgets, welfare reform left the program largely untouched. Indeed, eligibility for Medicaid continues to be determined on the same basis as before. Congress thereby avoided a bruising battle with the health care industry, but it also left untouched one of the principal problems in the social assistance system.

Wisconsin Waits

The new law gives states the option of continuing operation of welfare demonstrations operated under federal waiver. Initial reports indicate that many will not do so, in part because of disinterest in sustaining evaluation programs based on random assignment and because some program features previously permitted only under waivers are allowable under new federal law. Ironically, the W-2 program still cannot be fully imple-

mented without waivers, for the proposal involves changes in Medicaid and food stamps, as well as changes in treatment of child support payments in benefit computation, that are not permitted under the new law. Despite the president's commitment to "work with Wisconsin to make an effective transition to a new vision of welfare based on work," the state's proposal has been rejected, and its offer to work with the federal government to develop a satisfactory evaluation scheme has been largely ignored. State budgeting for W-2 was in part based on claims established in prior years on federal savings generated by earlier innovations. It is now the federal position that such claims have been superseded by the TANF block grant. . . .

CONCLUSION

Here, then, is where we are. The nation has achieved interim relief for states for public assistance expenditures. This relief has been accomplished in substantial part by restricting access to welfare. The federal share of public assistance expenditures has been increased, while the federal role in managing the core of the program, now called TANF, has been reduced. The problem of developing and implementing a research agenda for studying program management and effects has yet to be addressed. The consequences of PRWORA are difficult to predict because they involve response to the program by both states and actual and potential assistance recipients. What is certain is that while the new legislation may have ended AFDC, it has most certainly not ended the struggle for welfare reform.

POSTSCRIPT

Has Wisconsin Ended Welfare As We Know It?

The public policy that is adopted to address the needs of those who have been left outside the economic mainstream will dramatically shape the world in the near future. Will the new work incentives and disincentives associated with staying on welfare create a whole new generation of middle-income families, or will they only succeed in creating a new generation of dropouts who will live in the dark shadows of society?

It must be remembered that we are dealing with a large number of lives. The latest statistics on poverty indicate that more than 36 million people suffered the effects of poverty in 1995. Although the poverty rate for white Americans was lower than any other racial group, the vast majority (67 percent) of poor people are white. What is even more startling is the fact that more than one in five American children live in poverty, and if we look at children in single-parent families, the rate soars well above 50 percent.

Consequently, whether the post-AFDC era is a boom or a bust has immediate implications for those who are least able to defend themselves—children who live in poverty. One place to start reading in this area is an essay by Daniel R. Meyer and Marian Cancian entitled "Economic Well-Being of Women and Children After AFDC," *La Follette Policy Report* (Winter 1997). Another policy analyst who warns of the dire prospects associated with the new welfare reform is Peter Edelman. Edelman has long been a vocal critic of the AFDC system, yet when President Clinton signed the new welfare bill Edelman resigned in protest from his position of assistant secretary for planning and evaluation at the Department of Health and Human Services. See his article "The Worst Thing Bill Clinton Has Done," *The Atlantic Monthly* (March 1997).

For the opposing viewpoint see Michael Tanner, Stephen Moore, and David Hartman, "The Work vs. Welfare Trade-off," *Cato Policy Analysis* (September 19, 1995). See also William A. Niskamen's article "Welfare and the Culture of Poverty," *Cato Journal* (Spring/Summer 1996). For a very strong indictment of antipoverty programs, read Walter E. Williams's "The Economics of Poverty," *Vision and Values* (January 1997).

Discussions of welfare reform are found in numerous places, from policy journals—see Gary Burtless and Kent Weaver, "Reinventing Welfare—Again," *The Brookings Review* (Winter 1997)—to articles in popular magazines, such as Adam Cohen's "The Great American Welfare Lab," *Time* (April 21, 1997).

On the Internet . . .

The European Union in the United States
This site of the European Union in the United States has everything from history to current status, as well as Web links and a search capability. *http://www.eurunion.org*

OECD Online
The Organization for Economic Cooperation and Development (OECD) resulted from the need to rebuild Europe after World War II, but it expanded to become truly international, with policies designed to expand world trade on a multilateral, nondiscriminatory basis. *http://www.oecd.org*

International Monetary Fund (IMF)
The home page of the International Monetary Fund links to information about its purpose and activities, news releases, and its publications, among other things. *http://www.imf.org*

International Trade Administration
The U.S. Department of Commerce's International Trade Administration is dedicated to helping U.S. businesses compete in the global marketplace. At this site it offers assistance through many Web links under such headings as Trade Statistics, Export Markets, Your Trade Rights, and Antidumping. *http://www.ita.doc.gov*

Social Science Information Gateway (SOSIG)
This project of the Economic and Social Research Council (ESRC) catalogs 22 subjects and lists more URL addresses from European and developing countries than many U.S. sources do. *http://sosig.esrc.bris.ac.uk*

World Bank
At this home page of the World Bank you can click on News, Development Topics, Regions and Countries, Partnerships, and more, as well as use its search feature. *http://www.worldbank.org*

PART 3

The World Around Us

For many years America held a position of dominance in international trade. That position has been changed by time, events, and the emergence of other economic powers in the world. Decisions that are made in the international arena will, with increasing frequency, influence our lives. In the global marketplace, trade relations are influenced by swings in the economies of trading partners. The environment is also a major concern for economists and other analysts today.

- Is Free Trade a Viable Option for the New Millennium?

- Does Free Trade Make the Poor, Poorer?

- Does Global Warming Require Immediate Government Action?

- Should Pollution Be Put to the Market Test?

- Has the North American Free Trade Agreement Been a Success?

ISSUE 14

Is Free Trade a Viable Option for the New Millennium?

YES: Robert J. Samuelson, from "Trade Free or Die," *The New Republic* (June 22, 1998)

NO: Patrick J. Buchanan, from "Toward One Nation, Indivisible: A Course of Action," *Chronicles* (July 1998)

ISSUE SUMMARY

YES: Columnist Robert J. Samuelson charges that critics of free trade ignore economics, which he feels is the one thing that "trade has going for it."

NO: Social critic and three-time presidential hopeful Patrick J. Buchanan argues that the purpose of international trade is to benefit American workers, farmers, businessmen, and manufacturers, not mankind in general.

The economic logic that supports international trade has changed little in the nearly 200 years since English economist David Ricardo (1772–1823) provided us with his basic insight that the patterns and gains of trade depend on relative factor prices. He argued that if there are differences in the "opportunity costs" of producing goods and services, trade will occur between countries; more important, all of the countries that engage in trade will benefit.

Although a large majority of economists accept the logic and policy conclusions of Ricardo's theory, the timeless debate rages on between "free traders" and those who ask for protection. The basic logic of international trade is indistinguishable from the basic logic of purely domestic trade. That is, both domestic and international trade must answer these fundamental economic questions, What to produce? How to produce it? and, For whom to produce? The distinction is that the international trade questions are posed in an international arena, one filled with producers and consumers who speak different languages, use different currencies, and are often suspicious of the actions and reactions of foreigners.

If markets work the way they are expected to work, free trade simply increases the size or the extent of a purely domestic market and therefore increases the advantages of specialization. Market participants should be able to buy and consume a greater variety of inexpensive goods and services after the establishment of free trade than they could before free trade. Why, then, do some people wish to close U.S. borders and deny Americans the benefits of free trade? The answer to this question is that these benefits do not come without cost.

There are winners and losers in the game of free trade. The most obvious winners are the consumers of the less-expensive imported goods. These consumers are able to buy the low-priced color television sets, automobiles, and steel that is made abroad. Other winners are the producers of the exported goods. All the factors in the export industry, as well as those in industries that supply the export industry, experience an increase in their market demand, which increases their income. In the United States, agriculture is one such export industry. As new foreign markets are opened, farmers' incomes increase, as do the incomes of those who supply the farmers with fertilizer, farm equipment, gasoline, and other basic inputs.

On the other side in the free-trade game are the losers. The obvious losers are those who own the factors of production that are employed in the import-competing industries. These factors include the land, labor, and capital that are devoted to the production of such items as U.S.-made television sets, automobiles, and steel. The less-expensive foreign imports displace the demand for these products. The domestic consumers of goods that are also exported to other countries lose as well. For example, as U.S. farmers sell more of their products abroad, less of this output is available domestically. As a result, the domestic prices of these farm products and other export goods and services rise.

The bottom line is that there is nothing "free" in a market system. Competition—whether it is domestic or foreign—creates winners and losers. Historically, Americans have sympathized with the losers when they suffer at the hands of foreign competitors. However, such sympathies have not seriously curtailed free trade.

In the following selections, Robert J. Samuelson is tempted to simply dismiss the protectionist arguments of Patrick J. Buchanan in the face of America's booming economy and trade deficits. Buchanan argues that the United States can no longer afford a free-trade policy in the new millennium. He maintains that America comes first and the rest of the world second: "What is good for the global economy is not automatically good for America."

YES

Robert J. Samuelson

TRADE FREE OR DIE

I.

In many ways, the timing of Pat Buchanan's plea for more protectionism could not be worse. The American economy is humming along, with unemployment around 5 percent since late 1996. If more than two decades of trade deficits have crippled us, the consequences are not immediately obvious. Not only is the economy of the United States now the strongest among advanced societies, but American companies still remain formidable, if not always dominant, competitors in many critical industries: computers and software; aerospace; biotechnology; communications and entertainment; banking and finance; business consulting; and medicine. The auto and steel industries—once given up for dead—have recovered from fierce foreign competition.

The coexistence of extraordinary prosperity and constant trade deficits is a paradox to be explained, but Buchanan ignores it. Reading him, you would not know that the United States is in a mighty boom. The temptation, then, is to dismiss his book as irrelevant. That is not a good idea. An all-but-announced Republican presidential candidate in 2000, Buchanan is a born-again protectionist, who sees his conversion as a harbinger of a broader shift among the public. "The Young Turks of the New Conservatism who would capture the Republican Party for Barry Goldwater in 1964 and Ronald Reagan in 1980 [were] free traders," he writes. "I know, because I was one of them." His hopes of a protectionist revival are not preposterous, regardless of the fate of his own candidacy. In a weakening economy, the message could play. Fears of an overseas job drain can be exploited; and working class Democrats (Reagan Democrats) can be wooed with promises of greater job security. A populist majority might one day rally to economic nationalism.

Until now, of course, protectionism has been a political flop. Every politician who has tried to ride it to the White House has failed: John Connally in 1980, Richard Gephardt in 1988, Ross Perot in 1992, Pat Buchanan in 1996. It's worth trying to understand why. A common theory is that protectionism does not have much of a constituency. It is good rhetoric, but in the end it does not attract many voters, because not many Americans would benefit from import restrictions, especially if they resulted in retaliation against American exports. The raw numbers seem to confirm this. In 1997, for example, imports equaled only 13 percent of the economy's output, or Gross Domestic Product, and this was nearly offset by exports, 12 percent of GDP. Such figures suggest that protectionism has only a tiny constituency.

Buchanan, by contrast, argues quite plausibly that trade politics must be seen in a broader context, and that the free-trade consensus that arose after World War II has been crumbling for decades. It rested on three pillars, he says, each of them now weakened. The first pillar was a general sense that American industry was invincible; but that confidence shattered in the late 1970s and early 1980s, when many venerable American companies (Ford, Caterpillar, U.S. Steel, Xerox, Intel) came under siege from foreign competition. The second pillar of the postwar period was the cold war: greater trade with our allies promoted their prosperity (it was said), and this inoculated them against communism. The end of the cold war obviously dispensed with this argument. And the third pillar was the once-common belief that protectionism (and the Smoot-Hawley tariff) had been a major cause of the Great Depression. But memories fade, and much modern scholarship discounts protectionism as a major cause of the Depression.

The correct implication is that protectionism could again find a large following. The present optimism of Americans masks a deep uneasiness about the global economy that, once today's boom ends (as it will), could reemerge. We face a collision between an instinctive nationalism and the relentless expansion of global markets. Just because protectionism is not a desirable response does not mean that every protectionist grievance is bogus. Many of its complaints are clearly true: burgeoning global trade and investment do erode national sovereignty and self-sufficiency; and they do threaten some industries and workers; and they do create divided loyalties for American companies between enhancing profits and preserving American jobs.

It would be unnatural if Americans did not worry about these developments. Moreover, the economy's exposure to global competition is greater than the raw trade statistics indicate. In 1997, for example, imports accounted for only about 13 percent of American car and truck sales. But the entire auto industry faces global competition, because imports could capture almost any individual sale; and foreign car firms now produce here. The same is true of many industries. Global competition doesn't yet affect a majority of workers, but its impact—real and psychological— extends beyond an isolated minority....

II.

One thing is certain: the case for free trade cannot honestly be made on the basis of heritage. The greatest virtue of Buchanan's book is to remind us that America has mostly been a protectionist nation.

The political culture is certainly receptive. The godfather of protectionism was Alexander Hamilton, whose "Report on Manufactures," written in 1791, urged a protective tariff to nurture industry. To Hamilton, American "wealth... independence and security" depended on "the prosperity" of manufacturing. "Every nation," he argued, "ought to endeavor to possess within itself all the essentials of national supply." The Tariff Act of 1789, which imposed duties of 5 percent on many imports, was the second law passed by Congress. Later tariffs went higher, and they stayed high for most of the nineteenth century. With the exception of slavery, they were the largest source of conflict between North and South.

The Tariff Act of 1828—the Tariff of Abominations—almost triggered secession. It imposed an average duty of 62 percent on 92 percent of the country's imports. The South Carolina legislature subsequently declared it and a revised tariff "null, void." A secessionist crisis was avoided in 1833 only because Congress agreed to reduce the tariff to 20 percent over ten years. In general, the South, a big exporter of cotton and a big importer of manufactured products, detested high tariffs. The North, with a larger manufacturing base, adored them.

* * *

One reason that tariffs stayed high was their role as the federal government's main source of revenue for most of the century. (The Civil War was the major exception.) But they were also kept high to protect industry. In the 1830s and 1840s, the Whig Party—headed by Henry Clay—urged national economic development through internal improvements (roads, harbors, bridges) and high tariffs. Lincoln, an early Whig, generally supported high tariffs.

Protectionism was often equated with patriotism. Listen to Justin Morrill, a Republican senator from Vermont who entered Congress as a Whig in 1855, and was among the most steadfast guardians of high tariffs until his death in 1898: "Free trade abjures patriotism and boasts of cosmopolitism. It regards the labor of our own people with no more favor than that of the barbarian on the Danube or the cooly on the Ganges." Buchanan enthuses over such flag-waving. He argues that high tariffs enabled America to become the world's great industrial power in the nineteenth century.

During the last half of the century, many individual tariff rates hovered around 50 percent, and the average tariff (on dutiable and non-dutiable items alike) was about 30 percent. They stayed high partly to repay the huge national debt run up during the Civil War. (The federal debt rose from $65 million in 1860 to $2.8 billion in 1866.) But there were other reasons for the persistence of the tariffs. They were blatant protectionism and fervent nationalism.

A historic reversal was accomplished by Cordell Hull, Roosevelt's secretary of state, who shepherded the Reciprocal Trade Agreements Act of 1934 through Congress. This law transferred much of Congress's power to set tariffs to the president, who could negotiate mutual tariff cuts with other countries. A former senator from Tennessee, Hull had long believed that trade fostered goodwill among nations. And the Depression produced a backlash against protectionism. The backlash continued after World War II. In the 1940s, the United States helped to create new global institutions to prevent the return of '30s protectionism and deflation. These included the International Monetary Fund, which would make short-term loans of foreign exchange, generally dollars, to countries with big trade deficits (the idea was to preempt competitive currency devaluations or protectionism); and the General

Agreement on Tariffs and Trade, which would negotiate and police tariff cuts and international trade rules.

Trade also quickly emerged as a central weapon against communism. The Japanese needed to trade to buy basic raw materials (food, fuel, minerals). "Japan cannot remain in the free world unless something is done to allow her to make a living," President Eisenhower said. Otherwise, "it is going to the Communists." For Europe, trade succeeded the Marshall Plan as a recovery strategy from war. In trade negotiations, American officials often made more concessions than they received. In 1954, the State Department proposed unilateral concessions on roughly half of all Japanese imports, from glassware to optical goods to cars. Hardly anyone—the textile, apparel, and shoe industries were major exceptions—felt threatened, because American industry and technology were so dominant.

* * *

In 1962, Congress passed John F. Kennedy's Trade Expansion Act, authorizing new trade talks, by huge margins (78–8 in the Senate and 299–125 in the House). As a 23-year-old editorial writer for the *St. Louis Globe-Democrat*, Buchanan was caught up in the fervor. Passage of the Trade Expansion Act, he wrote, was a "thumping administration triumph" that could "become the most potent cold war weapon in the free Western arsenal...." Although he thinks expanded trade was then justified, he says that Americans went overboard. Free trade is not just an idea, Buchanan argues; it is a false religion that "holds out the promise that if we follow the gospel of free trade, paradise can be created on earth." Buchanan contemptuously quotes the nineteenth-century French economist Frederic Bas-

tiat: "Free trade means harmony of interests and peace between nations.... We place this indirect and social effect a thousand times above the direct or purely economic effect."

On this, Buchanan is more clear-eyed than many free-trade enthusiasts. It is true that trade cemented America's cold war alliances, but this does not mean that trade can take us the next step— to universal peace and goodwill. What held the cold war alliance together was the cold war. It is dangerous to generalize from this experience; and a lot of history warns against viewing trade as a shield against war. Before World War I, Germany and Britain were major trading partners. Germany also traded heavily with Russia, Holland, and Belgium—and attacked them all.

Trade does not just bind countries together; it also arouses suspicions. In the 1980s, many Americans wrongly feared that the country would be taken over by the Japanese. Canadians feel constantly assaulted by American trade and culture, and so (to a lesser extent) do Europeans. Nationalism endures and endures; and although the tensions and conflicts rarely end in war, trade is not an automatic pacifier.

III.

What trade has going for it, of course, is economics. The most astonishing thing about Buchanan's book is that, although it is ostensibly about economics, it almost never engages in genuinely economic thinking. For Buchanan, the decision to expand or to restrict trade is mainly a political choice. Thus he ignores lower communications and transportation costs (container ships, transoceanic telephone cables, jets, satellites, and, now, the Internet) as driving forces; and as the cost of doing business across borders goes down, the demand to do business—including political pressures to permit it—goes up.

Neither Buchanan nor anyone else can repeal this relationship. Certainly countries can prevent trade by shutting themselves off from the world (as China did until the late 1970s), but it is harder and harder to do with surgical precision. With trade comes travel, and modern communications, and global finance. Controlling the process has proven arduous even for the countries (such as Japan) most determined to do so.

This is one reason why more and more countries have embraced the global economy across a broad range of industries and activities. The other reason is that the potential economic gains of doing so have become self-evident. Buchanan treats the process mainly as a zero-sum game: one country's gain is another country's loss. If this were true, there would not be much global trade and investment. When losers recognized their losses, they would withdraw. Trade would occur mainly as a consequence of sheer economic necessity—countries importing essential raw materials (fuel, food, minerals) or goods produced only in a few countries (commercial jets, for example); or as a consequence of coercion—the strong compelling the weak to trade on disadvantageous terms, an informal neocolonialism. Otherwise trade would wither.

What is true, of course, is that individual companies or individual workers can lose in trade. General Motors can lose to Toyota; Hitachi can lose to IBM. But what is bad for a company or an industry is not necessarily bad for a country. Moreover, domestic competition causes more job losses than trade. Consider, for example, the job losses counted by the consulting firm Challenger, Gray & Christmas. Between 1993 and 1997, it found almost 2.5 million job cuts by American companies. The top five industries were: aerospace and defense, 270,166; retailing, 256,834; telecommunications, 213,675; computers, 212,033; financial services (banking, brokerage houses), 166,672; and transportation (airlines, trucking companies), 136,008. None of these cuts involved global trade. The causes ranged from defense cutbacks (aerospace) to new technology (computers). But Buchanan wishes to leave the false impression that, but for trade, the economy would be far less turbulent and harsh.

* * *

Given Buchanan's ignorance of economics, it is no surprise that his history, too, is badly warped. To suggest that the vast industrialization of the late nineteenth century, and America's rise as the world's most powerful economy, owes a great deal to protectionism is absurd. In the last half of the nineteenth century, the American economy benefited from a virtuous circle. Railroads expanded dramatically. Between 1860 and 1900, the miles of track rose from roughly 30,000 to more than 200,000. Lower transportation costs expanded markets. In turn, this encouraged investment in new manufacturing technologies that lowered costs through economies of scale. Industrial output soared for all manner of consumer goods (clothes, shoes, furniture), for farm implements, for machinery. Larger markets and lower costs fostered new methods of retailing and wholesaling: the mail-order house Sears, Roebuck was founded in 1891.

None of this depended on protectionism. Some basic technologies (steelmaking, railroads) originated in Europe. And the United States also imported another vital ingredient of growth: people. In each of the century's last four decades, immigration averaged more than 5 percent of the nation's population. As for trade, it grew as the American economy grew. Between 1870 and 1890, both imports and exports almost doubled. The decisive limit on imports was the ability to export (as it is for most countries), not high tariffs.

Tariffs may have protected some American industries, but any effect on the overall economy is exaggerated. Suppose there were no tariffs; some companies might then have faced cheaper imports. To survive, American companies would have had to cut prices; and they could have done so by reducing wages. In this era, wages were what economists call "flexible": employers cut them when they thought that they must or they could. Between 1866 and 1880, annual wages for nonfarm workers actually declined 21 percent. But this did not mean lower living standards, because prices dropped even more. Over the same period, purchasing power for average workers rose 23 percent.

* * *

The point is that a country's capacity to achieve economic growth lies mainly in its own people, values, resources, and institutions. Trade supplements this in many ways. The simplest is comparative advantage, as it was classically conceived by David Ricardo. Countries specialize in what they do best, even if one country could produce everything more efficiently than another. Suppose the United States makes both shoes and supercomputers more efficiently than Spain. We need 100 workers to produce either one supercomputer or 1,000 pairs of shoes annually; and Spain needs 1,000 workers to make a supercomputer and 200 workers to make 1,000 pairs of shoes. Total production of computers and shoes will still be greatest if each country concentrates on its strength (shoes for Spain, computers for us) and trades with the other to satisfy its needs: America will have more supercomputers and shoes, and so will Spain.

Much trade of this type occurs. The United States imports shoes, toys, and sporting goods; it exports bulldozers, computers, and corn. Trade's greatest benefits, though, may transcend comparative advantage. Not everyone has to reinvent the wheel or the computer chip. Technologies, products, and management practices that have been developed abroad can be deployed at home. In theory, these gains can occur without a country opening itself to trade. Information can be stolen; products and processes can be imitated. In practice, however, it is much easier if a country is open.

For commercial or technological insight does not derive from a single dazzling flash. It consists in thousands upon thousands of small details. It encompasses how things are made, distributed, sold, financed, repaired, and replaced. The more isolated a country, the harder it is to come by all the details. Whatever its tariff rates, the United States in the nineteenth century was open in this critical sense. Its people traveled freely abroad; immigration was large; merchants were eager traders; and industrialists borrowed ideas from wherever they could.

These same processes also operated after World War II. All countries could (in theory) tap the same international reservoir of technologies, products, and management systems. Yet some countries did better than others, which was a reflection of their practices and policies. Despite mercantilist tendencies, Japan enthusiastically embraced trade; it systematically imported (via licensing agreements) foreign technology; and it routinely studied American management. The combination of high saving and proven investment opportunities propelled great economic growth, averaging about 10 percent a year in the 1960s. Countries that were more shut off (China, the former Soviet bloc, India) fared less well. And only when other Asian societies began imitating Japan did their economic growth accelerate.

* * *

This explains why poorer countries should now like trade. It has helped lift millions of people in Europe and Asia from abject poverty. But what's in it for us? Trade can help to erode a country's relative economic superiority, and for the United States it has contributed to such an erosion. As other countries advanced rapidly, our dominance of the early postwar decades was lost. But this history cannot be undone. To preserve our position, we would have needed to be ruthlessly protectionist in the 1950s and 1960s: a policy that deliberately aimed to restrain the economic progress of Europe and Japan. But this would have been unwise, and even Buchanan does not contend otherwise. To long for our superiority of the 1940s is an exercise in nostalgia. Still, what is not true, then or now, is that trade impoverishes us. It is not depressing our living standards. It is elevating them. Trade may enable poorer nations to catch up, or to grow faster

than we do; but this does not cause us to slow down. It is not a zero-sum game. We gain, too.

Competition is one way. Many countries now make and trade the same things, so comparative advantage doesn't really apply. Japan makes and trades cars, computer chips, and telephone switching centers; and so do the United States and Germany. The result is bigger markets that enable efficient producers to achieve greater economies of scale by spreading costs across more buyers. Prices to consumers drop. Boeing, Microsoft, and Caterpillar all have lower unit costs because they are selling to a world market. Domestic competition also intensifies. Imports compel domestic rivals to improve. Chevrolets and Chryslers are now better and more efficiently made because Americans can buy Toyotas and Hondas. In many industries—cars, copying machines, and machine tools, to name a few —American firms and workers have had to adapt to the best foreign practices and technologies.

* * *

What haunts free trade is the specter that all production will flow to low wage countries. Yet this does not happen, for two reasons. First, low-wage workers in poor countries are usually less productive than well-paid workers in rich countries. In 1995, Malaysian wages were almost 10 percent of American wages; but the productivity of Malaysian workers (output per hour worked) was also about 10 percent of American levels, according to Stephen Golub of Swarthmore College. Companies shift production abroad, Golub maintains, only when relative productivity exceeds relative wages. If Malaysians earn and produce 90 percent less, there is no advantage in moving to Malaysia.

Second, when developing countries export, they earn foreign exchange (mostly dollars) to import—and do so. The global market for pharmaceuticals and software could not exist without the global market for shoes and shirts. In practice, developing countries' trade with advanced countries is fairly balanced, whether in deficit or surplus, as [Table 1] shows. It gives developing countries' manufacturing trade with advanced countries as a share of their GDP. (The data is from Golub.) On economic grounds, then, the case against trade is puny. Gains dwarf losses. Still, the puzzle remains: If trade is good for us, why do we run massive trade deficits? We must (it seems) be doing something wrong if we regularly import more than we export. Well, we aren't. The explanation is that our trade accounts are incomplete. They omit a major American export which—if it were included in the reckoning—would bring our trade flows closer to balance. That American export is money.

The dollar serves as the world's major money: a means of exchange, a store of value. It is used to conduct trade and to make investments. In 1996, countries kept 59 percent of their official foreign exchange reserve in dollars; the next largest reserve currency was the German mark at 14 percent. Multinational companies keep accounts in dollars. So do wealthy individuals. In some countries, where people distrust the local money, dollars circulate as a parallel currency to conduct everyday business. Indeed, the Federal Reserve estimates that more paper dollars (the folding stuff) exist outside the United States than inside.

The United States provides the world a service, in the form of a fairly stable

Table 1

Trade With Advanced Countries 1995 Percent of GDP

	Exports	Imports	Balance
Brazil	1.7	3.1	−1.4
China	8.8	7.7	+1.1
India	3.8	3.3	+0.5
Indonesia	6.4	8.7	−2.2
Korea	12.3	13.9	−1.6
Mexico	19.3	16.8	+2.5

currency. To pay for this service, the world sends us imports. It is a good deal for us: every year Americans buy 1 or 2 percent more than we produce. This is the size of our current account deficit, a measure of trade and other current overseas flows (such as tourism and freight).

The concept here is the old idea of seigniorage: the profit that a government earns when it can produce money at a cost less than its face value. If a government can print a dollar for 5 cents, it reaps a 95 cent windfall when it spends that dollar. Similarly, the United States reaps a windfall when the world uses our money. The transfer occurs through the exchange rate; the world's demand for dollars holds the dollar's exchange rate high enough so that we do not balance our visible trade. (A high exchange rate makes imports cheaper and exports more expensive.) But for many reasons —intellectual laziness, theoretical messiness—most economists have not applied seigniorage to the world economy.

That is too bad. If they did, we would see that the trade debate's main symbol—the nagging trade deficit—does not symbolize what it is supposed to symbolize. It does not show that we are becoming "uncompetitive," or that we are "deindustrializing," or that we are "losing jobs" abroad. In any single year, shifts in the trade balance may reflect temporary factors. Stronger or weaker growth abroad will affect demand for our exports; stronger or weaker growth here will affect our demand for imports. Changes in technology or exchange rates may alter trade flows in particular industries and products. Yet the continuous trade deficits of the United States do not reflect any of these things. They reflect the world's demand for dollars. Perhaps that demand will someday abate (Europe's single currency, the euro, may provide an alternative global money); and if it does, the American trade account will swing closer to balance. For now, though, it is virtually condemned to deficit.

If we acknowledged this, much of the present trade debate would disappear, because the presumed goal of a "good" trade policy—a trade balance or a trade surplus—would be seen as unrealistic and probably undesirable. Instead, the debate over the economics of trade is simplistic and distorted. The supporters of free trade claim that it creates jobs; the opponents of free trade claim that it destroys jobs. Although both are true for individual workers and industries, they are usually not true for the economy as a whole. We could have "full employment" if we didn't trade at all; and in a workforce of nearly 140 million people, the number of net jobs affected by trade (jobs created by exports minus jobs lost to imports) is tiny. Trade's true advantage is that it raises living standards.

IV.

The trouble is that the trade debate should concern more than wages or jobs. Buchanan's political appeal lies in his unabashed nationalism, and he is correct that we do not trade for the benefit of the British or the Brazilians or the Chinese. Trade needs to be connected to larger national purposes, and free-traders have grown lax about making such a connection. They are too eager to reduce the debate to a technical dispute over economic gain and loss. Although Buchanan engages in the same exercise—and reaches the wrong conclusion—he is much more willing to cast trade in terms of advancing broader American interests, preserving our national identity, and maintaining our moral values. A lot of this patriotic chest-thumping is nothing more than rhetorical flourish. And yet Buchanan is actually onto something.

Since World War II, American trade policy has made two central assumptions. The first, inherited from the Depression, is that protectionism destabilizes the world economy and that free trade stabilizes it. The second is that free trade enhances American security interests. Both notions were once right, but times have changed. Matters are now more ambiguous. A big outbreak of protectionism would still harm the world economy. Too much economic activity depends on trade for it to be cut painlessly. Yet deepening economic ties among countries—"globalization"—may also create instability. As for trade and security, they were fused by the cold war. Our main trading partners were military allies, and they generally embraced democratic values. Now trade has spread to some countries that do not share our values and to some countries that one day might be adversaries (China and Russia, most obviously).

What has gradually disintegrated is the postwar convergence among economic, strategic, and moral interests. Global economics has raced well ahead of global politics, creating potentially dangerous instabilities that are only barely perceived and may not be easily subdued. Commercial interests may increasingly conflict with security interests or moral values. If we decide, for whatever reason, not to trade with India or China, other countries will probably fill the void. The possibility is hardly theoretical. After India's recent nuclear tests, the United States immediately imposed sanctions; but most other countries—Japan was an exception—did not. There are other examples, involving Iran, Libya, and Cuba. Commercial rivalries can undermine security alliances: If our "allies" aid our "adversaries," are they truly our allies? The very expansion of global commerce has also raised economic interdependence to a new level. Until now, the "world economy" has been viewed less as an organic whole than as the sum of its parts. It is the collective consequence of individual economies whose performance (though affected by trade) mainly reflects their own strengths and weaknesses. This may still be true, but it is less so. The growing connections among nations—through trade, financial markets, computer systems, people flows—may be creating an independent beast whose behavior affects everyone and is not easily controlled by anyone. Asia's economic crisis is surely testing the notion that growing "globalization" can boomerang. South Korea, Thailand, and Indonesia all borrowed too much abroad; Japanese, European, and American banks lent too much. Excesses went unchecked by either local or international governmental supervision. Economic growth in all these countries has now plunged. There are spillover effects, and this could portend future crises.

* * *

Protectionism's best case is that it might insulate us against potential global instability. We would sacrifice somewhat higher living standards for somewhat greater tranquility. But this is not what protectionists have in mind; and if it were, it would be hard—maybe impossible—to achieve.

Consider Buchanan's program. He would impose sliding tariffs on countries reflecting his likes and dislikes. Europe would be hit with a 15 percent tariff; Canada would be spared if it adopted our tariffs (otherwise foreign goods would pour into the United States via Canada). Aside from a 15 percent tariff, Japan would have to end its trade surplus or face tariffs that would do so. Poorer countries would face an "equalization" tariff to offset their lower wages (such tariffs could go to 90 or 95 percent).

The result, Buchanan says, would be "millions of high-paying manufacturing jobs for all our workers—immigrant and native-born, black and white, Hispanic and Asian—... and trade and budget surpluses as American workers find higher-paying jobs and contribute more to Social Security and Medicare, deficit reduction and tax reduction." Well, not exactly. If the program worked as planned, it would repatriate low-wage jobs making toys and textiles and eliminate high-wage jobs making planes and bulldozers. Overseas markets for American exports would shrink, because countries that could not sell to us could not buy from us. And it is extremely doubtful that Buchanan's program would work as planned. He ignores floating exchange rates: if we raise tariffs by 15 percent, other countries' currencies may fall by 15 percent, leaving import prices unchanged.

Moreover, anything like Buchanan's plan might also create so much uncertainty that it would depress global economic growth. Companies might not invest in the United States—to make toys or textiles—because they could not be sure that high tariffs would not be repealed or neutralized by exchange rates. Yet companies might not invest elsewhere, because they could not know whether the tariffs might work or, if they did not work, whether they might inspire higher tariffs. All countries would suffer from lower investment and growth.

* * *

The point is that global commerce has become so widespread that it cannot be wrenched apart, short of some calamity. It is increasingly hard to find major American companies (trucking firms, railroads, or electric utilities, perhaps) that do not have major overseas stakes, either through trade or investment. Coca-Cola sells 70 percent of its beverages outside North America; McDonald's has almost half its 23,000 outlets in foreign countries; Intel derives 56 percent of its revenues abroad. The quest for global markets is one of the economic hallmarks of our times. The recent announcement of the Chrysler/Daimler-Benz merger emphasizes the point. To the extent that people like Buchanan try to frustrate it, they will simply inspire more ingenious —and probably more inefficient—ways for companies and investors to try to evade new barriers.

... Here is the nub of the matter. The ultimate promise of ever-greater global commerce is a universal contentment based on a spreading addiction to material well-being. Prosperity has a tranquil-

izing effect. It dulls the dangers of undiluted nationalism. People increasingly lead the same lifestyles: drinking Coke, driving Toyotas, conversing on the Internet. All this numbs national differences and permits a growing overlay of international agencies and authorities needed to regulate the global economy. Countries see that they have a common stake in cooperation. There are disagreements and conflicts, to be sure, but they are small-time, and they substitute for larger human tragedies of war and poverty.

This is the underlying moral logic that justifies the commercialization of the world, though hardly anyone puts it quite so forthrightly. It is a seductive vision that can draw much inspiration from the experience of the last half century. Over this period, the world economy has been a spectacular success. It has helped power an enormous advance in human well-being. Free trade has triumphed to an extent that hardly anyone could have foreseen at the end of World War II.

In the end, however, the vision is almost certainly false. Just because people watch the same movies and eat at the same fast-food outlets does not mean that they have been homogenized. National identities are not so easily retired. For good and ill, ethnic and religious differences show a remarkable ability to survive the march of material progress. National affections and animosities endure; and combined with the terrible and unpredictable potential of modern technology, they preserve humankind's capacity for ordinary trouble and unimaginable tragedy.

The world is fusing economically more than it is fusing (or will ever fuse) politically. We have created a system that requires ever-greater amounts of global cooperation, because it generates new and unfamiliar forms of international conflicts. One day, perhaps, the irresistible force of world markets may meet the immovable object of nationalism. Protectionism and isolationism are not so much agendas as moods, and countries—including the United States—might react to domestic disruption and international disorder by blaming foreigners and trying to withdraw from a global system on which most nations now increasingly depend. Buchanan has inadvertently identified the dilemma, but he has done exactly nothing to resolve it.

NO

Patrick J. Buchanan

TOWARD ONE NATION, INDIVISIBLE:
A COURSE OF ACTION

It is time we looked at the world from a new perspective, one of enlightened nationalism. Clichés about a "new" global economy aside, there has always been an international economy—ever since Columbus stumbled onto the Western Hemisphere while seeking new trade routes to the East, in the hire of a nation-state, Spain. The Dutch East India Company was founded in 1602 to displace the Portuguese in the lucrative Far Eastern trade; and the Dutch West India Company, in 1621, to capture the American trade.

The American, economy, however, is more than simply a part of the international economy, and its purpose is not to benefit mankind but to benefit Americans first: our workers, farmers, businessmen, and manufacturers. What is good for the global economy is not automatically good for America, any more than what is good for our transnational elite is necessarily good for the United States.

A REVENUE TARIFF

America should declare to the world that the present global regime *must* be revised, that we no longer intend to make the world prosperous at the expense of our own country. A 15 percent revenue tariff on all imported manufactures and goods in competition with American-made goods would be a fitting way to declare our economic independence.

As part of the "Nixon Shock" of August 15, 1971—to jolt the world into understanding that the United States could no longer continue under the Bretton Woods agreement—a 10 percent tariff was imposed on Japan. Thus, we need not go back to the Tariff of 1816 to find a precedent for unilateral American action in defense of our economic security. Unlike Clinton's threat of a 100 percent tariff on Lexus cars, a 15 percent tariff would not destroy American businesses set up in good faith. The tariff could be imposed in stages: five percent immediately, five percent in six months, and the final five percent a year later, giving merchants 18 months to adjust. If Ronald Reagan could impose a 50 percent tariff to save Harley Davidson, surely we can

From Patrick J. Buchanan, "Toward One Nation, Indivisible: A Course of Action," *Chronicles*, vol. 22, no. 7 (July 1998). Adapted from Patrick J. Buchanan, *The Great Betrayal* (Little, Brown, 1998). Copyright © 1998 by PJB Enterprises, Inc. Reprinted by permission of Little, Brown & Company.

impose a 15 percent tariff to inaugurate a new industrial age in the United States.

The revenue tariff should be high enough to generate a powerful stream of revenue, but low enough not to destroy trade. With American merchandise imports now exceeding $700 billion a year, this 15 percent tariff would yield a cornucopia of revenue while giving American products a marginal new advantage in their home market. Every dollar in tariff revenue, in fact, could be used to cut taxes on income, savings, and investment.

Bismarck built the German nation by shifting taxation away from incomes and onto foreign goods. In a December 15, 1878, letter to the Reichstag, the chancellor spoke of a crisis in the German middle class, similar to our own, and proposed to emulate the Americans: "Reform of the taxation... must begin with the revision of the tariff on as broad a basis as possible so as to benefit this class of the community. *The more money that is raised from tariffs the greater can—and must—be the relief in direct taxes.*" (Emphasis added.) High tariffs, argued Bismarck, would also give Germany leverage in "fresh negotiations with foreign countries concerning new commercial treaties."

Bismarck was an apt pupil of the economic nationalists who made America the world's greatest industrial power. Under Bismarck's policy, Germany increased its share of world production from 8.5 percent in 1880 to 14.8 percent by 1913; in 1880, Germany and the United States together had less than a fourth of world output, but by 1913 the two countries had nearly half, while free-trade Britain's share was sliced from one-fourth to one-seventh. The great unacknowledged truth of the second half of the 19th century—and of the second half

of the 20th—is that the nations that followed the free trade dogma of the classical liberals lost ground to the nations that pursued the Hamiltonian policy of economic nationalism.

RECIPROCITY WITH THE EUROPEAN UNION [EU]

Europe would howl, but even under the old GATT [General Agreement on Tariffs and Trade] rules a nation running a chronic trade deficit may use tariffs to end the hemorrhaging. And our response should satisfy Europe. Believing in fairness, we accept full reciprocity: a 15 percent EU tariff on all manufactured goods made in the United States.

Lincoln called the cost of ocean transport "useless labor." Much of this useless labor can be done away with if European companies that wish to sell in America produce in America, and vice versa. Ford and GM have always built cars in Europe; Europeans forced them to. When American companies feared a protectionist Common Market, they created European subsidiaries to avoid being frozen out. Turnabout is fair play. Let BMW and Mercedes make their parts and assemble their cars here in the United States if they wish to sell here on equal terms. As for those who prefer the cachet of European-made goods, they ought not be denied the freedom to buy. But a 15 percent tariff does not amount to persecution of elites who call 55 percent inheritance taxes "progressive." That new BMW can be built in South Carolina as easily as in Bavaria.

Americans may face a social crisis, a racial crisis, a crime crisis. We do not face a crisis of consumer goods. There is nothing made anywhere that we cannot make here. America-Canada and the EU are huge and self-sufficient markets, with similar laws and regulations. Their standards of living and wage rates are comparable. A reciprocal trade agreement could strengthen and solidify both blocs.

But would reduced imports cost us our technological edge? History proves otherwise. The telegraph, electric light bulb, telephone, "horseless carriage," and airplane affected society as dramatically as the computer. Yet Americans invented and exploited them as no other nation, behind a tariff wall built by Justin Morrill, Bill McKinley, and "Pig Iron" Kelley.

With the American market alone almost as large as the European Union, we can support and sustain a diversity and level of production no other country can match. The small and medium-sized nations of Europe and Asia have no alternative but to create interdependencies. Germany is, after all, smaller than Oregon and Washington; the United Kingdom is smaller than Mississippi and Alabama; and Japan is smaller than Montana and less endowed with natural resources.

CANADA AND JAPAN

Should any country be exempt from the 15 percent tariff? Yes, Canada— if Canada adopts the same external tariffs. In NAFTA [North American Free Trade Agreement] Canada married her economy to ours, to the economic benefit of Ottawa. The United States today takes 80 percent of Canadian exports, and Canada's merchandise trade surplus with the United States in 1996 was $23 billion.

However, Canada would have to remain inside the U.S.-Canada free trade zone and accept American tariffs, or go outside. If Canada chose to depart, the 15 percent tariff on all manufactured goods would be applied to Canadian goods as well. With the United States far and away Canada's biggest customer, and with that surplus on the line, Canada would surely choose to remain inside an American free trade zone. But Canada would have to choose.

As the United States strengthens ties to Canada, we should put an early end to our huge, chronic trade deficits with Japan. The Japanese are a proud people. It is unseemly and destructive to be hectoring them endlessly to open their markets, buy our rice, remove non-tariff barriers, adopt free trade. Japan does not practice free trade for a simple reason: Japan does not believe in free trade. Japan puts its national interest in manufacturing and technology ahead of a free trade ideology that has America in its grip. Japan is different because it prefers to be different We should respect that. But while Japan's economic structure is no business of the United States, our trade deficits are our business. We should notify Japan that if an end to these trade deficits cannot be achieved through negotiation, it will be attained through unilateral U.S. action.

An horrendous imbalance in autos and auto parts is central to the American trade deficit with Japan. The United States should follow the Harley formula and impose a special tariff on imported Japanese autos and auto parts on top of the 15 percent revenue tariff. The Japan Tariff would enable the United States to recapture much of Japan's 30-percent share of the American auto market.

To avoid the tariffs, Japan could shift production of parts and the assembly of autos to the United States. These Japanese cars would be treated exactly like Fords or Chevrolets made in Michigan. Toyota, Nissan, BMW, and all foreign car makers would be welcome here, but to avoid tariffs they would have to produce here. The same would hold for GM, Chrysler, and Ford. Fords made overseas would face the same tariff as Mazdas made overseas. America would have the most competitive auto market on earth, but every company, foreign-owned or domestic, would play by the same rules, pay the same taxes, abide by the same laws, employ the same high-wage, high-quality North American labor. Jobs in the American auto industry would explode.

Japan is a great nation, and its people have wrought a great miracle. But the present unequal relationship cannot continue. Our sales to Japan in 1995, $65 billion, were one percent of our GDP; Japan's sales to us, $125 billion, were four percent of its GDP. With an economy twice as large as Japan's, we still spend six times as much on defense. We remit annually to Tokyo tens of billions of dollars in interest payments on the hundreds of billions of dollars of Treasury debt that Tokyo now holds as a result of having run up decades of trade surpluses at the expense of American workers. Historians will marvel that America let this happen.

Even the American Chamber of Commerce in Japan (ACCJ) is showing signs of despair. According to the ACCJ, only 13 of 45 U.S-Japan trade agreements since 1980 were successful in helping American businesses penetrate Japan's market. Ten were total failures. Said ACCJ President Bill Beagles:

> For many years, the American view was that a trade agreement with Japan spoke for itself.... However, the U.S. Government and American industry came to realize that this is not the case. An apparently successful negotiation may not

necessarily produce the expected market result.

This is unhealthy. As a First World nation, Japan has much in common with the United States. Our strategic interests are in harmony, and the possibility remains for a close relationship.

But it is not 1950 anymore. Reciprocity is required. If Japan can begin to harmonize her trade policies with ours, open her markets to our manufactures and agricultural products as we do for Japan's, there is no reason we cannot establish with Tokyo the same defense and trade relationship we have with Europe. There is no reason we cannot grow closer rather than drift farther apart.

OUR CHINA PROBLEM

China is fast becoming America's number one trade problem. In its drive for dominance in Asia, Beijing has exploited slave labor, consumed all the Western credit it could extort, stolen intellectual property, and strong-armed American companies like Boeing and McDonnell Douglas to manufacture in China as the price of a deal. "Forced technology transfers" are a routine demand in dealing with China. "When you invest in China," says one auto company executive, "China assumes it owns all of your intellectual property." The Manufacturing Policy Project puts the piracy rate of U.S. intellectual property in China at 98 percent: "Three days after Microsoft introduced Windows 95 in the United States for $89.95, copies were available throughout Asia for $4 or less."

Following the path to power laid out by Friedrich List, China treats the United States, the world's most advanced nation, like a colony, a source of raw materials and a dumping ground for manufactures. China sends us up to 40 percent of its exports—much of it high-tech manufactured goods—but buys less than two percent of our exports. While China runs a trade surplus in manufactures with the United States of more than $35 billion yearly, prominent among American exports to China are fertilizers, food residue and waste, ore slag and ash, wood pulp, animal and vegetable fats, meats, live animals, and cereals. The one high-tech export for which America runs a large trade surplus is aircraft; but once China masters the American technology it has extorted, Beijing will begin building its own planes. That is the way of economic nationalists.

From 1991 through 1996, China piled up $157 billion in surpluses trading with the United States. Its 1996 surplus of $40 billion was almost as large as the Pentagon procurement budget. In October 1996, China invested $11.8 billion of its surplus in U.S. bonds, making China the third-largest buyer of U.S. debt, after Japan and Britain. By September 1997, China had amassed more than $130 billion in foreign currency reserves, the world's largest hoard after Japan.

For a century Americans have been transfixed by the great "China market"; it was one of the reasons business groups urged McKinley to annex the Philippines. But the China market proved a mirage then, and it is a mirage now, a corporate illusion. If China vanished, the American economy would not feel a breeze. Our sales to China in 1996 ($11.9 billion) were one-fifth of one percent of our GDP. We sold more to Singapore. But China's sales to the United States—$52 billion worth of toys, textiles, shoes, bikes, computers,

etc., in 1996—were a crucial share of its entire economy and were the primary source of China's hard currency reserves.

The United States has the whip hand in this relationship, and it is time we used it. China is not only a trade problem, it is a national security problem. China is using the hard currency from its trade surpluses and international bank loans to buy submarines, destroyers, anti-ship missiles, and fighter aircraft from Russia, and to build long-range missiles to reach the West Coast of the United States. Yet we permit China to launch American satellites on Long March rockets, thus subsidizing the development of the Chinese strategic missile force.

America is taking a terrible risk feeding a regime whose character may be seen in its treatment of dissidents, Tibetans, Christians, and women pregnant in violation of China's barbaric one-child policy. While America should seek no confrontation with China, we should treat Beijing as the great power it has become.

We cannot practice true free trade with a nation that has no independent judiciary, where labor is conscripted, corruption is endemic, American goods face a 17 percent value-added tax and a 23 percent tariff, and many of whose corporations are government fronts. The United States should cancel China's Most Favored Nation status and negotiate a reciprocal trade agreement that recognizes our different societies and conflicting interests.

WHAT ABOUT MEXICO?

Mexico is another special case. We share a 2,000-mile border, ten million Americans trace their ancestry to Mexico, and our destinies are not separable. But NAFTA is not sustainable. NAFTA puts blue-collar workers from America into competition with Mexican workers who earn ten percent as much. American farm labor, paid a minimum wage near five dollars an hour, competes with Mexican farm labor paid 50 cents an hour. American employers now hang over the heads of their workers this constant threat: accept reduced pay, or we go to Mexico!

What makes the threat credible is that hundreds of companies have already done so. Under the *maquiladora program,* tax concessions are offered to American companies that place factories in Mexico to ship products back to the United States. New plants are opening at the rate of two a day. From San Diego to Brownsville, the Mexican side of the border is littered with signs of Fortune 500 corporations. Xerox, Zenith, Chrysler, GM, Ford, IBM, Rockwell, Samsonite, and GE have all opened plants south of the Rio Grande. By moving to Mexico, they evade American laws on child labor, worker safety, minimum wages, and health and pollution standards, as well as U.S. taxes; their products come back to undercut those made in factories that stayed in America and obeyed the laws of the United States.

The Japanese are also exploiting NAFTA. Matsushita, Hitachi, Sony, and Sanyo have assembly plants in Tijuana. Toshiba's plant is in Ciudad Juárez. Japanese and Korean companies are building auto plants. This Japanese investment in Mexico represents a shift of capital away from the United States. The CEO of the Japanese Chamber of Commerce in Mexico describes how it works: "Japanese investments reaching Mexico do not come directly from Japan. It is the United States [subsidiaries], the son, who is investing in Mexico, the grandson, of the main office."

President Clinton points with pride to the growth of American exports to Mexico. But prominent among those exports are parts for assembly into products for shipment back to the United States and capital equipment for factories being built in Mexico. Such "exports" destroy American jobs.

NAFTA must be renegotiated, or America's new Sun Belt will be south of the Rio Grande, and the consequences will be social and political as well as economic. Export the future of our working young, and those whose dreams have been destroyed will be heard from. America's merchandise trade deficit, an all-time record of $191 billion in 1996, is a cancer. Either we cut it out, or it will kill America. History teaches that when a nation's manufacturing sector has entered a period of relative decline, that nation will decline.

Our forefathers broke all ties with the mother country and risked their lives to achieve the economic independence we are piddling away. We need less of the gauzy spirit of globalism and more of the patriotic spirit of old George Meany:

> Practically every country in the world... has some type of restriction, some type of barrier, some type of subsidization for their own people, that gives their own manufacturers and workers an unfair advantage over the American worker.... When have we ever retaliated against the unfair barriers put up by these other countries which go back many, many years? And if we are to have a trade war, if that's the only answer, I imagine if we had an all-out trade war we would do quite well for one simple fact: We have the market. We have the greatest market in the world right in this country.

Amen. Let us emulate our greatest leaders and use our control of that national market to achieve our national aims. After the Revolution, the War of 1812, the Civil War, and World War I, tariff revenue helped erase America's deficits and pay off America's debt. The alternative is more years of receding wages and rising tempers among American workers until the social fabric is torn irreparably, the bonds of patriotism no longer hold, our vitality vanishes, and our economic divisions manifest themselves in class conflict between Industrial America and Third Wave America. We have nothing to lose by trying, except those policies that have put us on the slippery slope to national decline.

WHAT ABOUT THE WTO?

The World Trade Organization [WTO] was erected on ideas American patriots must reject. It subordinates everything to the demands of trade. It exercises a supranational authority in conflict with our forefathers' vision of an America forever sovereign and independent. Its dispute-resolution procedures shift to Geneva decisions that ought to be made in Washington: And if we refuse to abide by the WTO's edicts, America can be chastised and fined.

Run by nameless, faceless, foreign bureaucrats, the WTO is the embryonic trade ministry of a world government. There is no place for such an institution in a world where free nations negotiate their trade agreements in good faith and oversee the execution of those agreements themselves. The WTO is a monument to the one-world vision of Wilson and FDR. Our withdrawal—after the required six months' notice—would be an unmistakable signal that America

is back and that this nation is again the independent self-reliant republic which the Founding Fathers intended it to be.

KEEPING CAPITAL AT HOME

In a 1952 address to the University Club of Milwaukee, Ludwig von Mises declared that the "essence of Keynesianism is its complete failure to conceive the role that saving and capital accumulation play in the improvement of economic conditions." He admonished Americans to appreciate the role that capital had played in creating their unrivaled prosperity:

> The average standard of living is in this country higher than in any other country of the world, not because the American statesmen and politicians are superior to the foreign statesmen and politicians, but because the per-head quota of capital invested is in America higher than in other countries ...
>
> Do the American voters know that the unprecedented improvements in their standard of living that the last hundred years brought was the result of the steady rise in the per-head quota of capital invested? Do they realize that every measure leading to capital decumulation jeopardizes their prosperity?

Mises, a free trade libertarian, is toasting a century in which the United States was the most protectionist nation on earth. Hamilton was right: protectionism went hand-in-hand with record capital accumulation. A primary reason that America's growth rates have been anemic in recent decades, and our recoveries not as robust as they once were, is the $2 trillion in trade deficits this generation has run up. Too much of the seed corn of the American economy is now being exported all over the world. As Sir James Goldsmith warned:

> Today, capital is being transferred to the developing world in massively increasing amounts. In the period 1989–1992, the average capital transferred per year to emerging countries was 116 billion dollars. In 1993, the figure was 213 billion dollars and in 1994 it was an estimated 227 billion dollars. East Asia leads the field, with a rise in the annual rate of direct investment between 1984 and 1994 of 1100 percent.

How can the United States halt the hemorrhaging of capital? First, consider how America's capital goes abroad. There are several primary vehicles for the "decumulation" of American capital: imports ($2 trillion in trade deficits in 20 years); U.S. private bank loans; foreign investments by corporations, pension funds, etc.—foreign aid (perhaps $1 trillion in the Cold War) and IMF [International Monetary Fund], World Bank, and international bank loans; U.S. overseas defense expenditures; illicit trade (drugs); illicit wealth transfers to evade taxes. Each of these problems can be dealt with by strong action.

Imports. A 15 percent tariff on all products that compete with American-produced goods and a wage-equalization tariff on manufactures from low-wage countries would rapidly erase American merchandise trade deficits. Instead of capital going abroad to build plants for the assembly of goods to be sent back to the United States, capital would come home to expand our domestic industries and create American jobs. The deep tax cuts on investment and savings that the new customs revenue would finance would make America the most attractive investment site of all the industrial democracies.

Private bank loans. Although America cannot and ought not impose controls on the foreign loans or investment of America's big banks, all investment banks, mutual funds, and pension funds should be put on notice: the next time there is another default, another Mexico, another meltdown in Asia, those who made the profit take the loss. This is neither harsh nor punitive. Private banks and overseas investors must begin to realize that there is no global bankruptcy court to bail them out. Once they know their investments are no longer risk-free, the market will solve this problem.

Foreign investment and foreign lending. Again, the tariffs, which would wipe out the admission-free access that foreign countries now have to the American market, would have a chilling effect on the plans of transnational corporations to invest abroad or to move factories abroad. Comparative advantage would come home.

Foreign aid. Annual wealth transfers to foreign regimes like Egypt ($18 billion in cash reserves), Israel (a median income above $16,000), Greece, Turkey, Russia, and Pakistan make little sense. The Cold War is over; it is time for relics like foreign aid to be entombed. We cannot bribe nations to embrace free enterprise, and we ought not to pay nations not to fight one another. Far more serious is backdoor foreign aid, the tens of billions of dollars funneled yearly to foreign regimes through the IMF, World Bank, Asian Development Bank, etc. These relics of our "Marshall Plan mentality" have become global-socialist centers for the redistribution of American wealth. Why should American taxpayers guarantee loans to India or China, the leading beneficiaries of the World Bank? If these governments have worthwhile projects, let them finance the projects themselves, like we did when we were a developing nation. American-taxpayer guarantees for World Bank and IMF loans reward nations whose policies rarely merit such rewards.

Overseas defense expenditures. John Foster Dulles once said that a day was coming when the United States would have to conduct an "agonizing reappraisal" of commitments to defend nations that refused to bear their fair share of the cost of their own defense. With the Cold War over, that reappraisal is long overdue. NATO should not be expanded; new nations should not be added to the roster of those we are already committed to defending. And Europe should begin to bear the full economic cost of its own defense. While the United States retains a vital interest in preventing a hostile regime—that of a Hitler or Stalin —from overrunning Europe, that threat has never been more remote: England and France have nuclear deterrents; Germany is united and democratic; Russia is smaller than it was in the days of Peter the Great. No threat to any vital American interest remotely exists in Europe. It is time to bring American troops home and revise NATO so that America is no longer committed to go to war because some ancient border has been breached or because a forgotten trip wire has been activated in some forsaken corner of the old continent. The proper role of America in Europe is not to be a front-line fighting state but to be the "strategic reserve" of the West. America must restore to itself full constitutional freedom to decide when, where, and whether to involve itself in Europe's 21st-century wars.

The new relationship of America with Europe should be modeled on our *military* relationship with Israel. Where the Israelis provide the troops to maintain their own defense, the United States provides access to advanced weapons. Israel gives us no veto over what it does in its own interests, and we give Israel no ironclad guarantee that any war that Israel decides to fight will be our war as well.

In Asia, the great threat to stability and security is almost certain to come from China. But Beijing is already contained by geography: Islam to the west; a nuclear-armed Russia to the north; India and Vietnam to the south; Korea, Japan, and the American fleet to the east. Any Chinese military move would trigger an arms race across East Asia. Here, again, the United States should play the role of the arsenal of democracy and sell to the nations of Asia the modern weapons they need to resist intimidation or defend against Beijing's encroachments —while those nations provide the troops themselves. No more Koreas, no more Vietnams.

When the nations of Europe and Asia understand that they, not we, are primarily responsible for their security, they will cease acting like dependencies and begin acting like independent nations. It is past time for prosperous allies to begin paying the cost of their own defense. Defense of the West can thus begin to enhance, rather than drain, America's vitality.

Illicit drugs. Seventy to eighty percent of the marijuana and cocaine entering the United States, to destroy the soul of America's young, passes through

Mexico. To secure our southern border from this deadly traffic, we should cancel that provision of NAFTA which permits Mexican trucks on America's highways. Second, we should expand the U.S. Border Patrol. Third, we should lengthen the triple fence already built at San Diego, which has begun to cut back illegal immigration and complicate life for drug smugglers. Fourth, we should demand of Mexico greater cooperation in running down narcotics traffickers, and greater freedom and protection for American agents operating in Mexico. Finally, though the U.S. military does not belong in a policing role, American troops brought home from abroad should be moved to a southern border that is certain to be a crisis area in the 21st century.

Illicit wealth transfers to evade taxes. The scores of billions of dollars in tariff revenue should be used to eliminate taxes on savings, capital gains, and inheritances. With taxes on capital at zero in the United States, departed capital would come running home and new capital would come pouring in. Finally, the Republican Party should heed Mises' advice:

> No party platform is to be considered as satisfactory that does not contain the following point: As the prosperity of the nation and the height of wage rates depend on a continual increase in the capital invested in its plants, mines and farms, it is one of the foremost tasks of good government to remove all obstacles that hinder the accumulation and investment of new capital.

STRATEGIC INDEPENDENCE

At the end of World War II, the United States had a nearly autarkic in-

dustrial base; we produced everything needed for our national defense. That day is gone. In 1982, we began to run manufacturing trade deficits; by 1986, deficits in the trade of high-technology goods. American dependence on foreign sources for items critical to our advanced weapons systems has created a vulnerability unknown since doughboys had to use French artillery and tanks, British machine guns, and Allied planes —even though our own Wright brothers had invented the airplane. A decade ago, Admiral James Lyons, commander of the U.S. Pacific forces, warned, "All of the critical components of our modern weapons systems, which involve our F-16s and F/A 18s, our M-1 tanks, our military computers—and I could go on and on—come from East Asian industries.... Some day, we might view that with concern and rightly so." Lyons was echoed five years later by a former chairman of the Joint Chiefs of Staff, Admiral William Crowe, Jr.:

> The Gulf War was unique because America enjoyed the unanimous support of all its allies. Even so, cooperation was difficult.... The U.S. defense industrial base is already in danger of becoming too dependent upon foreign sources for strategic supplies. What if the next time we are called upon to respond, our allies decide it is in their best interest to sit it out?

Former Commerce official Erik R. Pages writes of the difficulties to which Crowe alluded:

> The Bush Administration was forced to intervene with foreign governments on over thirty occasions to guarantee delivery of critical military parts. As one high-level administration official commented, "If the foreign governments

were neutral or were not disposed to help us out, we could have run into some real problems. We were sweating bullets over it and the military was sweating bullets too."

Peacetime America may ignore such concerns; but it is a dangerous vulnerability when technology is vital to national power, crucial to military victory, and essential to saving the lives of Americans sent into combat. (We got a glimpse of what might happen during Vietnam, when Japan withheld the transfer of Sony TV cameras for missile guidance.) Foreigners today control the American companies responsible for the heat shield of the D-5 Trident missile and the flight controls of the B-2 bomber, the F-117 Stealth, and the F-22—the backbone of the 21st-century Air Force.

Overseas factories are far more vulnerable to espionage, labor problems, sabotage, political dictation, and attack by enemy or terrorist forces. There is no guarantee that American secrets are safe abroad. A clear and present danger exists when corporations with allegiance to no country gain virtual monopolies over items critical to American security. During World War II, Stalin's spies and our own homegrown traitors looted vital defense secrets, including those related to the atom bomb. Given this experience, for us to allow technology indispensable to our security to be kept outside the United States, vulnerable to theft or denial, is foolhardy. The time to end foreign military dependence is when new weapons systems are in the design stage. America should guarantee that no foreign dependency is built into any future generations of weapons. When it comes to technology vital to national defense, "Buy American" and "Made in the USA" are the rules that should apply.

The world is a dynamic place. No nation can ground its security in existing technological superiority. Superpowers that rest on their laurels invite the fate of the first global powers of the modern era: Holland and Spain. When former Treasury Secretary Richard Darman blurted, "Why do we want a semiconductor industry? We don't want some kind of industrial policy in this country. If our guys can't hack it, let 'em go," his was the smug voice of the elites of numerous nations that are no longer counted as great.

Unfortunately, President Clinton subscribes to the Darman view. His administration is outsourcing to foreign producers more components of American weapons systems than ever before. This penny-wise, pound-foolish policy strikes at the heart of American security and independence and ignores a truth taught by Adam Smith: "The great object of the political economy of every country is to increase the wealth and the power of that country."

POSTSCRIPT

Is Free Trade a Viable Option for the New Millennium?

Survey after survey confirms that the desirability of free trade is an issue on which a large majority of professional economists agree. Although economists are ardent supporters of free trade, they must grapple with the reality that the world David Ricardo modeled in 1807 is starkly different from the world we know as we enter the new millennium.

The concern that Ricardo could not predict is the present ability of capital and technology to cross national boundaries almost at will. This mobility of capital and technology suggests that a country's comparative advantages can radically change in a short period of time. Not so in Ricardo's world, where comparative advantages were stable and predictable. To illustrate comparative advantage, Ricardo spoke of the trade between England and Portugal in cloth and wine. In the nineteenth century it was highly unlikely that agrarian Portugal would seriously challenge the manufacturing base of England and equally unlikely that dreary English weather would ever produce a wine to compete with the vineyards of sun-drenched Portugal.

This kind of trade stability is found rarely in the modern world. Examples abound of comparative advantages won and lost overnight, as dollars and technology chase one another around the globe. Japan provides an interesting case study. Consider how quickly this country moved from dominance among Pacific Rim countries to fighting for its economic life as Korea, Malaysia, and their other Asian neighbors stole market after market from it.

The bottom line is clear: comparative advantage does lead to economic efficiency. But as with any market adjustment, there are serious dislocations, as less-efficient producers must make way for more-efficient producers. In the modern world this occurs quickly and sometimes unexpectedly. This does not mean that there is a shortage of advocates for free trade. Look at any textbook in economics; the case for free trade will be laid out clearly, forcefully, and without apologies. Alternatively, look to the conservative press, and it too will provide ample support for Samuelson's position. See *The National Review* (April 20, 1998) for three articles critical of Buchanan: "The Great Betrayed," by Robert Bartley; "Pat Answers," by Ramesk Ponnure; and "Nationalist Anthem," by John O'Sullivan.

We suggest that you examine Buchanan's book *The Great Betrayal: How American Sovereignty and Social Justice Are Being Sacrificed to the Gods of the Global Economy* (Little, Brown, 1998). You might also read Michael Find's "Marx, Smith or List?" *The Nation* (October 5, 1998) and John Gray's book *False Dawn: The Delusions of Global Capitalism* (New Press, 1999).

ISSUE 15

Does Free Trade Make the Poor, Poorer?

YES: William Greider, from "Global Warning: Curbing the Free Trade Free-fall," *The Nation* (January 13, 1997)

NO: Gary Burtless, from "Worsening American Income Inequality: Is World Trade to Blame?" *The Brookings Review* (Spring 1996)

ISSUE SUMMARY

YES: Columnist and social critic William Greider warns that blind acceptance and promotion of "free-market doctrine" must inevitably lead to deepening inequality and deterioration at home.

NO: Gary Burtless, a senior fellow at the Brookings Institution, concedes that the demand for and relative wages of less-skilled workers have plunged, but he maintains that this dramatic shift is not confined to the traded-goods sector.

Many people contend that the United States is in the midst of a radical redistribution of income. The rich are getting richer and the poor, poorer. This is indicated in the data, which measures the share of "real income" received by families ranked from lowest income to highest income and then separates the population into five equal groups, or "quintiles."

Income distribution patterns are markedly different before and after 1979. Prior to 1979 economic growth benefited all income groups. That is, whether you were poor (part of the first quintile), middle class (part of the second, third, or fourth quintile), or affluent (part of the fifth quintile), the average real income in your income group increased. True, some groups gained more than others over time, but, in the words of John F. Kennedy, "A rising tide raises all boats."

After 1979 this pattern changed. The tide of economic growth raised the yachts of the rich, just as it did in the pre-1979 period; but, apparently, the row-boats of those with meager or moderate means were washed into the "stagnant backwaters" of the economy. The real income, or purchasing power income, of the bottom 40 percent of all American households fell (the bottom 20 percent falling by 8.8 percent), while the real incomes of the top 40 percent rose (the real income of the top 5 percent rising by 45.5 percent). This represents a redistribution of income, but it is a redistribution from the poor to the rich. This is not an expected pattern in the "land of equal opportunity," where public policy has attempted to level the playing field for all rather than provide a few in society an unsurmountable lead in the race to the top of the mountain.

Much has been written about the underlying cause or causes of this radical shift in the distribution of income in the United States. (Note that the 1995 quintile shares reported in 1997 indicated a possible reversal of this pattern. For the first time since 1979, the most affluent households in the United States —the top 20 percent and the top 5 percent—experienced a very modest decline in their share of income. The share of all income received by the top 5 percent fell from 21.1 percent to 21.0 percent in the 1995 data compared to the 1994 data, while the top 20 percent share fell from 46.9 percent to 46.5 percent.) The disturbing pattern that characterizes the post-1979 period has been variously attributed to (1) the influx of unskilled immigrants—both documented and undocumented; (2) changes in age composition of the population—where 15-to-24-year-olds are a larger proportion of the potential workforce; (3) the marked rise in the percentage of the workforce with a college education, resulting in a wage gap when compared to those without advanced education; (4) the decline in the economic influence of the labor union movement; (5) the shift from an industrial-based economy to a service-based economy; (6) the rapidly rising skill levels required for employment in all sectors of the economy; (7) changing public policy—reducing the progressivity of federal taxes and curtailing the magnitude and extent of the "safety net"; (8) the growing presence of female-headed households; and (9) the globalization of the world economy.

It is the latter issue that is debated by William Greider and Gary Burtless in the following selections. Greider takes the position that the "freefall" in the incomes of middle-class Americans can be traced to the blind acceptance of free markets and free trade without the mediating influence of government. Burtless, on the other side, argues that there are many reasons for the "widening income gap" and that none of them are linked to liberalizing international trade.

YES

William Greider

GLOBAL WARNING: CURBING THE FREE-TRADE FREEFALL

The global system of finance and commerce is in a reckless footrace with history, plunging toward a dreadful reckoning with its own contradictions, pulling everyone along with it. Responsible experts and opinion leaders, of course, do not generally share my sense of alarm. Nor do most political authorities, who, in any case, seem thoroughly intimidated by economic events. Some important voices in business and finance do occasionally express similar anxieties, but multinational enterprise is preoccupied with its own imperatives, finance capital consumed by its own search for returns. Public opinion may be uneasy, even angry, but people generally are confused and rudderless.

The destructive pressures building up within the global system are leading toward an unbearable chaos that, even without a dramatic collapse, will likely provoke a harsh, reactionary politics that can shut down the system. This outcome is avoidable if nations will put aside theory and confront what is actually occurring, if they have the courage to impose remedial changes before it is too late.

If the positive energies of this revolutionary process are to be preserved, it has to be slowed down, not stopped, and redirected on a new course of development that is more moderate and progressive, that promises broader benefits to almost everyone. The economic problem requires governments to discard the hollow abstractions of financial accounting and begin rebuilding the tangible foundations for balanced prosperity, for work and wages, and for greater social equity—not only for older, wealthier nations but for the aspiring poor in the emerging "one world." It is far easier to describe some ways this might be achieved than to imagine that governing elites will act upon them.

The first priority is to reregulate finance capital. Governments will have to reimpose some of the control discarded during the last generation, both to stabilize financial markets and to make capital more responsive to the needs of producing economies. Measures like transaction taxes on foreign exchange would be a beginning. Such controls would take some of the profit out of currency trading and other speculative activities but would not inhibit long-term flows of capital for foreign investment and trade.

The popular belief that governments lack the power to control international finance is simply wrong: to disarm the exaggerated power and random follies of the global bond market, they can tighten terms for easy credit; in some arenas of credit, ceilings on interest rates can be reimposed; prohibitions on accepting transfers of offshore funds could shut down the banking centers where capital hides from securities laws and income taxes. Governments, in essence, must reclaim the ruling obligations of the nation-state from private markets.

The central economic problem of our present Industrial Revolution, not so different in nature from our previous one, is an excess of supply—the growing, permanent surpluses of goods, labor and productive capacity. The supply problem is the core of what drives destruction and instability: accumulation of redundant factories as new ones are simultaneously built in emerging markets, mass unemployment and declining wages, irregular mercantilist struggles for market entry and shares in the industrial base, market gluts that depress prices and profits, fierce contests that lead to cooperative cartels among competitors, and other consequences.

* * *

The shocking lesson of economic history —experience that now seems largely forgotten—is that vast human suffering and random destruction of productive capacities are unnecessary. From the crisis and turmoil of the early twentieth century, nations painfully discovered that there is nothing inevitable about these market forces or the social convulsions they sow if societies will act to counter them. A shared prosperity emerges, as Keynes taught, only when people throw off passivity and learn to take control of their fate.

Governments can counter the disorders and ameliorate losses mainly by stimulating consumption, creating more buyers for unsold goods—the rising market demand that activates idle factories and workers. The present regime is fundamentally pathological because it destroys consumer incomes while creating a growing surfeit of goods. Many different measures can push the global system in the opposite direction, but the underlying problem, bluntly stated, requires shifting returns from capital to labor, reversing the maldistribution of incomes generated by the marketplace under the rentier system.

Greater social equity is not only consistent with but required by a sound and expanding economy: When rising incomes are broadly distributed, it creates mass purchasing power—fueling a virtuous cycle of growth, savings and new investment. When incomes are narrowly distributed, as they are now, the economic system feeds upon itself, eroding its own energies for expansion, burying consumers and business, even governments, in impossible accumulations of debt. A relative few become fabulously wealthy, but a healthy economy is not sustained by manic investing. Nothing about modern technologies or the "information age" has altered these ancient fundamentals.

* * *

The genuine meaning of "one world" will be tested by how nations answer this question: Can the global system be turned toward a less destructive path without throwing poor people over the side? Older economies may be tempted to revert to insular, self-protective remedies, but this will destroy the promise of the globalizing revolution and could even produce its own implosion of commerce —balkanized struggles for markets that substitute political conflict for the economic disorders. The challenge of "one world" is to create the standards for a progressive system that everyone can trust, that does not leave anyone out.

The imperatives for a new world order can be boiled down to a series of mutually reinforcing propositions, each of which would help to redress the economic imbalances of supply and demand. They include the following ideas:

1. Tax capital instead of labor. Even a modest shift in tax structures can stimulate the creation of new jobs and wage incomes while it creates the mechanism for making investors and corporations more accountable for their behavior. The tax codes of most of the advanced industrial nations are tilted against work, focusing regressive payroll taxes on wage earners and their employers, thus raising the real cost for a company that expands its work force. By comparison, financial wealth is lightly taxed and, at least in the United States, is not subject to the property taxes that people pay on real-property assets like homes and businesses.

Reducing the tax barrier to employment can be done in a progressive manner that favors work for the less skilled —lower payroll tax rates on jobs at the lower end of the wage scale, higher taxes at the high end. That would provide a discreet incentive to multiply jobs for those who need them most—a cheaper and more effective approach than social

programs that try to help people after they are already poor or unemployed. The same principle could target the common practice, at least among U.S. companies, of escaping the social overhead of doing business by marginalizing workers in piecemeal jobs—the "temporary" or "contract" work that lacks decent wages or benefits. The supposed efficiency of these measures actually involves pushing the social costs—health care or income support for indigent retirees—onto others, mainly the general public.

Direct taxation of financial capital could also create a mechanism for rewarding the firms and investors who take responsibility for broader economic and social consequences while punishing the free riders. Globalizing corporations, which move jobs offshore and arbitrage tax concessions from different governments, ought to be treated less favorably than the enterprises that are conscientiously increasing their domestic employment. Capital investors, likewise, have a financial obligation to the commonweal that protects them.

A direct tax on wealth is not as radical as it may sound to Americans, since eleven other nations in the Organization for Economic Cooperation and Development, including Germany, already have modest versions. The principle is not different from ordinary property taxes or business-license taxes on merchants or professionals, since capital owners benefit from the public domain. For instance, Edward Wolff has proposed that the United States follow the model of Switzerland and adopt a system of modest, graduated rates that would start by exempting the first $100,000 of financial assets, tax the next $100,000 at a rate of only .05 percent and rise to a rate of 0.3 percent about $1 million. He calculates that such a system would have raised only $40 billion in 1994—a lot of money but hardly an onerous burden on the wealthy, nor a solution to the fiscal disorders.

A central purpose of taxing capital, however, is to establish the means for defining the responsibility of capital owners to each nation and its people. If capital wants to enjoy record returns from the global system, it must help pay for the economic and social wreckage it leaves behind. Once that principle is established, the tax code can begin to make distinctions among both corporations and investors, based upon their civic behavior.

"The emerging modern system gives a larger share of income and power to capital, yet the burdens of government and community have steadfastly been shifted to labor," as one financial economist explained to me. "At some point, we have to ask whether utterly free capital is a benefit to everyone. Free capital is certainly a benefit to the people who own the capital. But they couldn't exist if these governments did not exist to protect them. No one wants to locate the Chicago Board of Trade in Bangkok or Jakarta. They want to be in the United States or maybe five or six other countries, where their transactions and their wealth will be safe."

Similar logic could change the strategic calculations of multinational corporations as they disperse production, perhaps by making preferential distinctions in the tax code. If the national objective is to stimulate domestic employment, then capital or corporate stocks might get a reduction or even exemption from capital gains taxation if the corporate balance sheet confirms that the enterprise is increasing jobs by investing at home. Capital should be taxed at the full rate if

it is doing the opposite. The global dispersal of industry would not be stopped, but firms and shareholders would have to help pay for what they left behind.

This approach inevitably favors domestic companies over multinationals, but it also discards the fraudulent proposition that any tax break or subsidy to business automatically translates into a benefit for society at large. If that assumption was ever sound, it is clearly suspect in the era of globalizing corporations. Governments promoting the trading fortunes of multinationals have not yet answered the gut question: Who in the nation benefits from this process, owners or workers, capital or citizens?

2. Reform the terms of trade to insure more balanced flows of commerce, compelling exporting nations to become larger consumers of global production. The present system is propped up by the persistent trade deficits of wealthier nations, mainly the United States, a condition that cannot endure for much longer. Rhetorical promises notwithstanding, global agreements like the General Agreement on Tariffs and Trade (GATT) and the endless rounds of trade disputes have failed utterly to redress trade imbalances. Indeed, prospects are worsening as China and other major new industrial powers prepare to enter the world market. A fundamental principle, therefore, must be established: An industrial economy cannot expect to construct a vast oversupply of production for export while refusing to accept equivalent volumes of imports from others.

The system, in effect, has to provoke a meaningful showdown with the Japanese model of wealth accumulation—the mercantilist practices that exact zero-sum advantage at the expense of trading partners. Those economies that persist in accumulating huge trading surpluses should lose their cost-free access to foreign markets through emergency tariffs or other measures. On the other hand, nations that practice genuine reciprocity of buying and selling, including the aspiring poor nations, should be rewarded with preferences. In short, Japan and other Asian nations like China that follow Japan's strategic path would face an unsentimental choice: Either expand imports or expect to be stuck with excess productive capacity.

The objective of temporary trading barriers would not be to protect domestic industrial sectors but to force everyone to confront the underlying crisis of surpluses. Every trading nation, including poor nations hoping to become less poor, has a tangible stake in solving the supply problem because it poses a principal obstacle to adopting a pro-growth regime for the world. Under the current system, older economies may actually suffer from faster growth if their rising consumption simply generates a deluge of imports and larger trade deficits, while the foreign markets remain closed to their production. Until this zero-sum condition is corrected, the potential for greater growth will remain stymied. Emergency tariffs to correct a nation's financial disorders are an extreme measure, but not prohibited by GATT. If the United States threatened such measures, other nations might at last face up to the larger global problem of oversupply.

3. *Bring the bottom up—raising wages on the low end as rapidly as possible—by requiring trading nations to honor labor rights.* By defending human freedom, the trading system can establish that the collective right of workers to bid up their wages is sanctioned and protected. Morality aside, the economic objective is straightforward: Raising wages at the bottom enlarges the base of consumption for everyone's goods. Even in the best of circumstances, the downward pressures on high-wage labor markets will not abate soon, given the vast sea of available low-wage workers. But every gain in wage levels at the bottom, even a modest gain, translates into immediate economic benefit for the global system: more purchasing power.

At present, the system functions in reverse, eroding consumption by replacing high-wage labor with cheap labor. To be sure, the new industrial workers in Asia and Latin America have new wage incomes to spend, but overall the system experiences a net loss in the potential for mass consumption. The challenge, roughly speaking, is to create a global system that functions most energetically by pulling the bottom up instead of the top down. Many poorer nations are naturally hostile to the suggestion, fearing that they will lose the comparative advantage of cheap labor or political control over their work forces. But companies or nations that rely on repression and exploitation of the weak for trading advantage are not truly ready for membership in a "one world" economy. They should be penalized, even excluded.

The easiest way to accomplish this reform is to insert an enforceable "social clause" in the global trade agreements requiring all trading nations to honor long-established international rules for labor rights. As a practical matter, that is unlikely to happen at the level of GATT and the World Trade Organization, since both developing countries and multinational corporations are opposed to any labor reform.

The political opening lies in negotiating regional or nation-to-nation compacts that establish networks of social standards and extend trading preferences to those who honor them (the opportunity Bill Clinton failed to act upon when pushing NAFTA). Reciprocal trade agreements that link several rich nations with several poor nations could establish a working model that demonstrates the positive economic energies that flow from labor reform. As participants benefit on both ends, other nations, rich and poor, may see the wisdom of emulating the reform.

Nations are, of course, entitled to their sovereignty—the power to set domestic social standards free of foreigners' interference—but that does not require foreigners to buy their goods. Advanced economies need not meddle in other nation's domestic politics, since they can regulate the behavior of their own multinationals, both at home and abroad. If the national interest lies in bringing up wages worldwide, then governments may withdraw subsidies and tax preferences from companies that, like the U.S. electronics industry in Malaysia, actively seek to block labor rights of their foreign workers.

4. Forgive the debtors—that is, initiate a general write-off of bad debts accumulated by poorer nations. Extinguishing failed loans issued by international agencies such as the International Monetary Fund and the World Bank would free desperately poor economies, especially in Africa, to pursue more viable strategies for domestic development. The liquidation of debt obligations is fundamentally a stimulative economic measure since it frees cash for other pursuits, including active con-

sumption, and it is socially enlightened because it eases global poverty.

Writing off these debts is probably inevitable, in any case, since most of the loans can never be repaid. Right now, the interest costs simply bleed the poor nations further each year and often require new loans so they can keep up payments on old loans. Liquidation would free their meager cash flows for genuine development and at least the possibility that they may someday become significant consumers in the global system.

To accompany the debt forgiveness, however, the operating purposes of the international lending institutions must also be reformed. The I.M.F. and World Bank must develop greater respect for indigenous strategies for growth, promoting a more patient development of domestic economies instead of simply enforcing the financial imperatives of the global system. To cite the most obvious contradiction, these institutions routinely use their power to suppress wages and consumption in the developing countries when the advanced nations that finance their lending have an interest in achieving the opposite. If the lending institutions are unable to change direction, then sponsoring governments should withdraw funding and abolish them, writing off their loan portfolios in the process.

5. Reform the objectives of central banks so they will support a pro-growth regime instead of thwarting it. The purposes of monetary policy have to be returned to a more balanced and democratic perspective—an understanding that growth, employment and wages are crucial to a sound economy, no less important than the prerogative of stored wealth. So long as the Federal Reserve and the central banks of other nations stand in the way of more vigorous growth that might allow a reinflation of wages, the problem of weakening consumption and oversupply is sure to increase, accompanied by compounding debt burdens.

The policy choices embedded in the regulation of money and credit always involve difficult trade-offs between different risks—recession or inflation, idle capacity or overheated activity, failed debtors or financial speculation. But the consequences of these choices are not distributed evenly throughout society, especially when policy is always skewed toward the interests of wealth holders. Most of the leading central banks are ostensibly independent of politics, yet this does not prevent them from adhering faithfully to the narrow constituency of finance capital. Their prejudices are unlikely to change until the competing interests—labor, manufacturing and other sectors—organize counter-pressures demanding a more generous policy of economic growth. To make central banks yield, they should be reconstituted as open and accountable governing institutions.

Unfortunately, central banks are stuck in the past, still fighting the last war against inflation when the global system now faces the opposite danger—a massive deflation of prices, economic activity and debt. The trade-offs surrounding monetary policy have been profoundly altered by globalized finance and production. Yet central bankers continue to operate in the traditional manner, as if they were still regulating self-contained domestic economies. This anomaly leads them to err repeatedly on the downside—discouraging domestic economic activity and new investment in the name of stability—even as markets respond to global influences of supply and demand. If a new era of growth is to occur, new theoretical understandings must replace the traditional rules of central banking.

6. *Refocus national economic agendas on the priority of work and wages, rather than trade or multinational competitiveness, as the defining issue for domestic prosperity.* Obviously, these objectives are intertwined and interacting, but it makes a great difference as to which to put first. If advanced nations, especially the United States, concentrate on promoting employment and more equitable incomes, they can make a great contribution to the global system, in addition to domestic well-being, by boosting mass consumption. If governments continue to be preoccupied with globalization and promotion of the free-market doctrine, then they must inevitably accept the consequences of deepening inequality and deterioration at home.

The actions that governments could take will require new spending, but should focus less on government social aid programs and more on wage realities in private-sector labor markets. Many such measures are traditional forms of intervention: raising minimum wages, strengthening labor laws to encourage companies to share productivity gains with workers, restoring progressive taxation to redistribute income, curbing the luxurious corporate subsidies embedded in the tax code and government programs, underwriting major works projects like high-speed rail systems or urban housing rehabilitation.

If it is true that global pressures will drag down wages and employment for at least another generation, then the economic imperative for large-scale subsidized employment is inescapable. If people cannot find jobs that promise a living wage for families, then all the various social interventions that government undertakes will be futile. Instead, societies will accumulate another generation of dispossessed and alienated citizens.

The same essential question has to be asked of every public measure: Does it genuinely promise to enhance work and wages? In debating that question, people will discover that much of what government currently does is useless or even harmful to broadly shared prosperity. But the answers may also begin to bring the economic future into clearer focus, defining potential new pillars for domestic economic activity. Financial reform, for instance, might direct credit subsidies to sectors like housing or small-scale busi-

ness enterprises or a national child-care system—new business activity that becomes a significant employer while filling real needs. Every such step, of course, tends to distribute the economic returns more broadly through society and thus creates more buyers for the world's surplus production.

If people can get beyond passivity and insecurity, an era of economic experimentation lies ahead—ventures that explore new social and economic arrangements, projects that can be encouraged by government, not managed by it. Among rich and poor, people are already exploring ideas that may change their destiny, social invention that needs not wait upon market forces.

NO

Gary Burtless

WORSENING AMERICAN INCOME INEQUALITY: IS WORLD TRADE TO BLAME?

Since 1970 American incomes have become strikingly less equal. Living standards of poor and lower middle-class Americans have fallen while those of affluent Americans have continued to improve. And the trend toward inequality has not been confined to the United States. Nations throughout the industrialized world have seen income disparities rise since the late 1970s.

Many people blame rising income inequality on the growing importance of trade, especially trade with nations in the developing world, in the past quarter century. In *The Trap*, a bestseller in Western Europe, Sir James Goldsmith argues that free trade with low-wage countries has harmed and threatens to impoverish low-skilled and middle-class workers in the advanced industrial countries. A similar argument was used by Ross Perot and other U.S. opponents of the North American Free Trade Agreement, who warned that freer trade with Mexico would eliminate industrial jobs and reduce the wages of semi-skilled U.S. workers. More recently, Republican presidential aspirant Patrick Buchanan has called for an "equalization tax" on imports from third world countries to protect American workers against competition from Asian and Latin American workers who may be paid one-tenth the U.S. industrial wage. How well does the case against free trade stand up to the facts?

TRENDS IN U.S. INCOME INEQUALITY

There is no disputing the worsening trend in U.S. income inequality. Figure 1 documents the rate of change in income for Americans divided into five quintiles of the income distribution. Income changes are calculated after taking account of changes over time in the price level and changes in the size of families in different parts of the income distribution. (Average family size shrank after 1969, so it took less income to support families at the same standard of living.) The black bars represent income changes during 1969–79, the gray bars, changes between 1979 and 1993. During 1969–79, Americans in all quintiles made income gains, though people in the lowest income quintile made the smallest percentage gains. After 1979, incomes fell in each of the three bottom quintiles while continuing to grow in the top two. Compounded over the 24-year period, the differences in the rate of change in income imply dramatic movements in relative well-being. At the 5th percentile, income fell 34 percent; at the 95th percentile, it rose 43 percent. In 1969, income at the 95th percentile of adjusted personal income was a little less than 12 times income at the 5th percentile. By 1993, income at the 95th percentile was more than 25 times income at the 5th percentile.

Several developments lie behind the widening income gap, and most of them have little direct or indirect link to liberalized international trade. Significant gains in capital income during the decade of the 1980s, for example, caused unearned income to grow strongly in the top part of the income distribution. And at the same time, changes in the pattern of government transfers—with growing cash transfers going to the elderly, many of whom tend to be well up the income distribution, and shrinking cash transfers to the poor—reduced the effectiveness of those transfers in combating poverty. Changes in the structure of U.S. households also added to income inequality. Single-parent families are more likely to be poor than families that have two parents, and a much higher percentage of Americans now lives in single-parent families. Finally, the dramatic increase in paid employment among American women has tended to boost inequality since the late 1970s. In the 1950s and 1960s, families with a well-paid male earner were less likely than average to have a well-paid female earner. By 1993,

families with a highly paid male earner were *more* likely than average to have a highly paid female earner. These non-trade-related economic and demographic trends account for more than half the growth in overall U.S. income inequality since 1969.

EARNINGS INEQUALITY

Even if trade is not to blame for trends in unearned income or changes in the composition of American households, it could still be an important source of growing *wage* inequality. Figure 2, based on annual earnings reports in the Census Bureau's Current Population Survey, shows that between 1969 and 1993, earnings fell for men in the bottom 40 percent of the earnings distribution, remained unchanged for men in the middle quintile, and rose for men at the top. The disparate trends in wage earnings became more pronounced after 1979. Earnings fell sharply in low-wage groups, and wage disparities between well-paid and poorly paid men widened at an accelerated pace. Although overall wage trends have been much healthier for women (gray bars in Figure 2), women have also experienced widening earnings disparities, especially in recent years. After 1979 women in the top quintile saw their earnings climb more than 25 percent. For women at the bottom, annual earnings fell after 1979.

DOES TRADE HARM UNSKILLED U.S. WORKERS?

The argument that trade is to blame for U.S. earnings inequality rests on the assumption that trade hurts U.S. workers with skills similar to those of workers in developing countries. The intuition

Figure 1

Change in Adjusted Real Personal Income, by Quintile, 1969–93

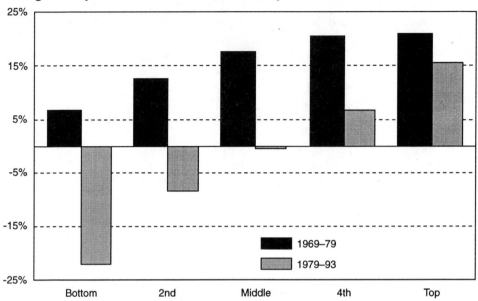

Note: Personal incomes are "adjusted" to reflect differences in family size. The top quintile extends only through the 97th percentile.

Source: Author's tabulations of the March 1970, 1980, and 1994 Current Population Survey files.

behind this view is straightforward: very poorly paid unskilled workers overseas take away job opportunities and drive down the wage of unskilled American workers.

It is easy to see in theory how surging exports from developing countries could harm less-skilled U.S. workers in the trade-affected industries. To counter the competition from cheap unskilled labor abroad, American employers must reduce the wages, or make less intensive use, of unskilled labor if they wish to remain in business. Presumably, some employers who continue to rely heavily on unskilled workers will go bankrupt, others will move production overseas, others will adopt new technologies that permit them to dismiss some unskilled work-

ers, and still others will specialize in new products where relative wages and factor prices favor production in the United States. No matter which alternative they choose, the demand for less-skilled workers in the traded-goods industries will fall. Shrinking demand will reduce the relative wage of less-skilled workers in comparison with highly skilled workers.

But if trade is the main factor behind the growing woes of unskilled workers in the traded-goods industries, then firms that do not produce internationally traded goods and services should take advantage of the shrinking wage of less-skilled workers by hiring more of them. If, instead, they also begin to pare back use of unskilled labor, it must be something other than (or in addition to)

Figure 2

Changes in Real Earnings, by Gender and Earnings Quintile, 1969–93

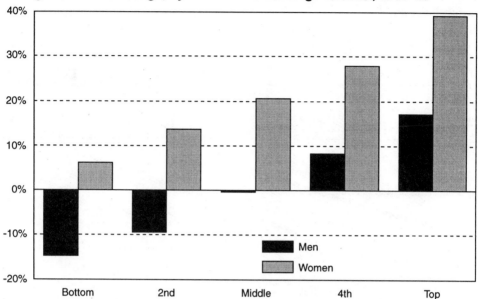

Note: Annual earnings of full-time, year-round wage and salary workers. Top quintile extends only through the 96th percentile for men and the 99th percentile for women.

Source: Author's tabulations of the March 1970, 1980, and 1993 Current Population Surveys.

trade that is lowering the demand for less-skilled workers.

Figure 3 helps show whether trade is behind the drop in relative demand for less-skilled labor. It compares wage inequality trends among male workers in two broad classes of U.S. industries— one (including manufacturing, mining, and agriculture) that is highly trade-affected and another (including construction, retail trade, personal services, and public administration) that is not trade-affected. (An excluded group of industries, including transportation, wholesale trade, finance, and insurance, falls in an intermediate category.) Earnings inequality is calculated as the ratio of annual earnings at the 90th percentile of the earnings distribution to earn-

ings at the 10th percentile. Male inequality is growing in both the most and the least trade-affected industries, and it is growing at the same rate— 47 percent between 1969 and 1993. Although wages are more equal among women in trade-affected industries than among women in the least-affected industries, wage inequality among women has grown faster in the nontrade industries since 1979—the very period in which U.S. trade problems and manufactured imports were concentrated. When the data for men and women are combined, the earnings ratio in the most trade-affected industries rose 29 percent between 1969 and 1993—exactly the same as the rise in inequality across all industries.

Figure 3

Ratio of Earnings of Male Workers at 90th Percentile to Earnings at 10th Percentile, 1969–93

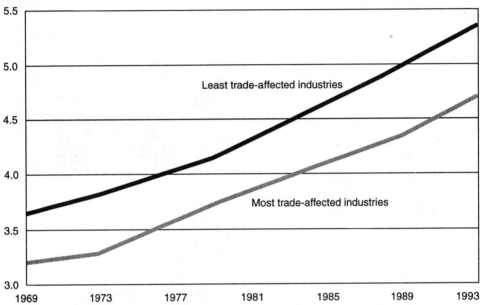

Note: Annual earnings of full-time, year-round wage and salary workers.
Source: Author's tabulations of selected Current Population Surveys.

The same pattern of relative earnings change is apparent in trends among workers with different levels of schooling. Educational pay premiums have risen since 1969 for every industry and for both sexes. But the premiums have not risen any faster in the industries most affected by trade than they have in other industries. For working men as a group, the premium for post-college education rose 36 percent between 1969 and 1993; for men in trade-affected industries, the premium rose 33 percent. And the gap in pay between high school dropouts and men with some college rose exactly as fast among men in trade-affected industries as it did among men as a whole. Women in the trade-affected industries had a somewhat larger rise in the post-college pay premium than women in other industries, but the difference is comparatively small.

Even though wage inequality and educational pay premiums moved in the same pattern across different industries, liberalized trade may still explain the pronounced shift toward greater inequality. In a competitive and efficient labor market, pay premiums for skill and education should eventually rise and fall together across industries, whatever the reason for the change in pay premiums.

But if the trade from newly industrializing countries in Asia and Latin America is placing special pressure on producers in trade-affected industries, we would expect these industries to shed low-wage workers *faster* than industries where com-

Figure 4

Percentage of Full-Time Equivalent Male Workers Without a High School Diploma, 1969–93

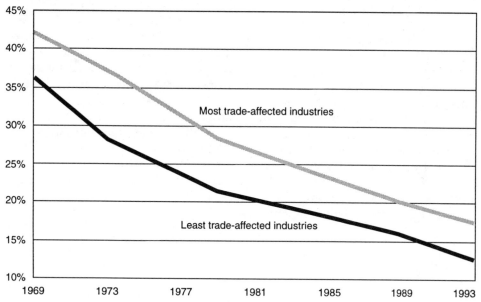

Source: Author's tabulations of selected Current Population Surveys.

petitive pressure comes exclusively from other domestic firms. To what extent was this the experience in the United States?

Between 1969 and 1993, trade-affected industries did indeed reduce the percentage of less educated workers on their payrolls (Figure 4). In 1969, 42 percent of male and 45 percent of female workers in trade-affected industries had no high school degree. By 1993, those figures had fallen to 18 percent for men, 17 percent for women. These trends certainly seem consistent with the view that liberal trade has deprived less-skilled workers of job opportunities in the traded-goods sector. But employment patterns in industries unaffected by trade moved in exactly the same direction. The percentage of male workers without a high school degree in the industries *least* affected by trade fell

from 36 percent in 1969 to 13 percent in 1993. If anything, industries unaffected by trade cut their use of low-skill workers even faster than trade-affected industries—a pattern that is extremely hard to square with the claim that foreign trade is the main factor behind soaring wage inequality.

BESET ON ALL SIDES

Over the past quarter century, the nation has seen a dramatic shift in the pattern of demand for workers with different levels of skill. Job opportunities for the less-skilled have shrunk, and relative wages for unskilled and semi-skilled workers have plunged. But these trends are not confined to the traded-goods sector. They are also apparent in industries, such as construction and retail trade, where international trade is a minor concern. International trade, it seems, has not been the decisive factor in the trend toward greater earnings inequality. Other developments have been at least as influential, if not more so.

Among economists, the leading explanation for increased wage inequality is changes in the technology of production. Such innovations as the personal computer or new forms of business organization have favored workers with greater skill and reduced the value of unskilled labor.

But other developments are also at work. Economic deregulation, new patterns of immigration into the United States, declining minimum wages, and the dwindling influence of labor unions have also contributed to the job woes of unskilled and semi-skilled workers. Liberal trade with the newly industrializing countries of the world has certainly played a part in worsening the job prospects of America's unskilled workers. But if we follow the advice of Ross Perot and Patrick Buchanan and erect a new wall of trade protection, we would do little to ease the plight of less-skilled workers. Too many other forces are conspiring to push their wages down.

POSTSCRIPT

Does Free Trade Make the Poor, Poorer?

Unless the current pattern of income redistribution is moderated, the United States will become a country of the "haves" and the "have nots." Many see the process as being well underway. The "haves" are becoming increasingly isolated in their exclusive communities, and the "have nots" are becoming increasingly concentrated in their deteriorating inner-city neighborhoods. The less movement that occurs between these two extremes, as the middle class disappears and the extremes are stretched farther and farther apart, the more distrust will grow and the more seeds of social unrest will be sown.

The cause of this perverse distribution of income is unclear. Greider would have us look to the pre-Reagan days, when the federal government was active in the American economy. For more on Greider's views, read his column that regularly appears in *Rolling Stone* or check out his books *One World, Ready or Not: The Manic Logic of Global Competition* (Simon & Schuster, 1997); *Who Will Tell the People: The Betrayed of American Democracy* (Simon & Schuster, 1992); and *How the Federal Reserve Runs the Country* (Simon & Schuster, 1992). Greider is not alone in his views. Colin Hines and Tim Lang, in their essay "The New Protectionism," *The Nation* (July 15 and 22, 1996), assert that "globalization unquestionably leads to lower wage economics." In "The Dark Side of Globalization," in the same issue of *The Nation*, Jerry Mandur asserts that "the only boats that will be lifted are those of the owners and managers of the process; the rest of us will be on the beach, facing a rising tide."

There is much written on the other side of this issue. Conservatives such as John O. McGinnis are horrified at the prospect of limited markets. See "Restraining Leviathan," *National Review* (March 11, 1996). For a more sophisticated reflection of Greider's thesis, refer to Norman S. Fieleke's "Is Global Competition Making the Poor Even Poorer?" *New England Economic Review* (November/December 1994). Finally, another strongly worded essay opposing government intervention is "Trade and Human Rights: The Case of China," by James A. Dorn, *Cato Journal* (Spring/Summer 1996).

ISSUE 16

Does Global Warming Require Immediate Government Action?

YES: Cynthia Pollock Shea, from "Protecting Life on Earth: Steps to Save the Ozone Layer," *Worldwatch Paper 87* (1988)

NO: Lester B. Lave, from "The Greenhouse Effect: What Government Actions Are Needed?" *Journal of Policy Analysis and Management* (vol. 7, no. 3, 1988)

ISSUE SUMMARY

YES: Cynthia Pollock Shea, a senior researcher with the Worldwatch Institute, argues that governments and industries should initiate a "crash program" designed to halt emissions of chemicals such as chlorofluorocarbons, which deplete the ozone, before irreparable damage is done to world agriculture, marine life, and human health.

NO: Professor of economics Lester B. Lave warns against drastic solutions that could themselves be harmful or, at a minimum, "costly if the greenhouse consequences are more benign than predicted."

The heat wave of the summer of 1988 was a memorable event. Electric bills skyrocketed as air conditioners ran day and night. Bright green lawns turned yellow-brown. Lakes, streams, and reservoirs fell to critically low levels; car washing was discouraged, lawn sprinkling was banned, and toilets were bricked. Citizens and policymakers alike were concerned that the world was entering the long-predicted and much-feared period of global warming associated with the greenhouse effect.

As summer turned to fall, then–presidential candidate George Bush promised voters that if he were elected, he would become the "environmental president." He would protect the environment from the advancing global warming—at least he would attempt to slow its progress. Once elected he joined other heads of state in a Paris environmental summit. This, in turn, led to the policy prescriptions that he introduced in a speech delivered at Georgetown University in early February 1990. Four broad policies were detailed in this speech:

1. *Increase the information base.* He proposed a sharp increase in U.S. expenditures on studies focused on "global climate change."
2. *Redirect and increase expenditures on basic energy research and development from $16.4 billion to $17.5 billion.* This represented a modest 6.4 percent

increase in the Department of Energy's budget and some redistribution of funds from civilian applied research and development programs to grants for basic research.

3. *A phaseout of most chlorofluorocarbons.* In line with a 1987 international agreement, the Montreal Protocol, President Bush proposed a 50 percent cut in the production of these powerful greenhouse gases that attack the ozone layer.

4. *A "plant-a-tree" program.* The Bush administration proposed planting a billion trees each year at a cost of $170 million annually.

The question is whether or not these presidential initiatives are appropriate in light of the costs and benefits of public action to slow or reverse the progress of global warming. Marginal analysis will help to determine how aggressive public policy should be in slowing the progress of global warming. Alternative policies will likely have increasing marginal costs and decreasing marginal benefits as more ambitious programs are employed. Two views of these costs and benefits are provided in the following essays. Cynthia Pollock Shea warns that if decisive action is not taken immediately to protect the ozone layer, we will face serious health hazards, reduced crop yields, decreased fish populations, and industrial damage. Lester B. Lave, on the other hand, argues that there is too much uncertainty to justify rushing forward with sweeping policy action. He preaches moderation.

Since the consequences of these policy decisions may be irreversible and not fully felt for many decades in the future, extreme care must be taken. Older generations may be totally immune from the consequences. It is the younger generations that will pay for any mistakes that are made now.

YES

Cynthia Pollock Shea

PROTECTING LIFE ON EARTH: STEPS TO SAVE THE OZONE LAYER

When British scientists reported in 1985 that a hole in the ozone layer had been occurring over Antarctica each spring since 1979, the news came as a complete surprise. Although the theory that a group of widely used chemicals called chlorofluorocarbons (CFCs) would someday erode upper atmospheric ozone had been advanced in the mid-1970s, none of the models had predicted that the thinning would first be evident over the South Pole—or that it would be so severe.

Ozone, the three-atom form of oxygen, is the only gas in the atmosphere that limits the amount of harmful solar ultraviolet radiation reaching the earth. Most of it is found at altitudes of between 12 and 25 kilometers. Chemical reactions triggered by sunlight constantly replenish ozone above the tropics, and global air circulation transports some of it to the poles.

By the Antarctic spring of 1987, the average ozone concentration over the South Pole was down 50 percent. Although the depletion was alarming, many thought that the thinning was seasonal and unique to Antarctica. But an international group of more than 100 experts reported in March 1988 that the ozone layer around the globe was eroding much faster than models had predicted. Between 1969 and 1986, the average concentration of ozone in the stratosphere had fallen by approximately 2 percent.

As ozone diminishes, the earth receives more ultraviolet radiation, which promotes skin cancers and cataracts and depresses the human immune system. As more ultraviolet radiation penetrates the atmosphere, it will worsen these health effects, reduce crop yields and fish populations, damage some materials such as plastics, and increase smog. Compounds containing chlorine and bromine, which are released from industrial processes and products, are now widely accepted as the primary culprits in ozone depletion. Most of the chlorine comes from CFCs; the bromine originates from halons used in fire extinguishers.

Spurred to action by the ozone hole, 35 countries have signed an international agreement—the Montreal Protocol—aimed at halving most CFC emissions by 1998 and freezing halon emissions by 1992. But the agreement is so riddled with loopholes that its objectives will not be met. Furthermore, scientific findings subsequent to the negotiations reveal that even if the treaty's goals were met, significant further deterioration of the ozone layer would still occur.

New evidence that a global warming may be under way strengthens the need to further control and phase out CFC and halon emissions. With their strong heat-absorbing properties, CFCs and halons are an important contributor to the greenhouse effect. Currently available control technologies and stricter standards governing equipment operation and maintenance could reduce CFC and halon emissions by some 90 percent. But effective government policies and industry practices to limit and ultimately phase out chlorine and bromine emissions have yet to be formulated. Just as the effects of ozone depletion and climate change will be felt worldwide, a lasting remedy to these problems must also be global.

THE OZONE DEPLETION PUZZLE

As a result of the efforts of many scientists, the pieces of the ozone depletion puzzle have gradually been falling into place. During the long, sunless Antarctic winter—from about March to August —air over the continent becomes isolated in a swirling polar vortex that causes temperatures to drop below -90 degrees Celsius. This is cold enough for the scarce water vapor in the dry upper atmosphere to freeze and form polar stratospheric clouds. Chemical reactions on the surface of the ice crystals convert chlorine from nonreactive forms such as hydrogen chloride and chlorine nitrate into molecules that are very sensitive to sunlight. Gaseous nitrogen oxides, ordinarily able to inactivate chlorine, are trans-

formed into frozen, and therefore nonreactive, nitric acid.

Spring sunlight releases the chlorine, starting a virulent ozone-destroying chain reaction that proceeds unimpeded for five or six weeks. Molecules of ozone are transformed into molecules of ordinary, two-atom oxygen. The chlorine emerges unscathed, ready to attack more ozone. Diminished ozone in the vortex means the atmosphere there absorbs less incoming solar radiation, thereby perpetuating lower temperatures and the vortex itself.

Paradoxically, the phenomenon of global warming encourages the process. Higher concentrations of greenhouse gases are thought to be responsible for an increase in the earth's surface temperature and a decrease in the temperature of the stratosphere. In addition, methane, one of the primary greenhouse gases, is a significant source of stratospheric water vapor. Colder temperatures and increased moisture both facilitate the formation of stratospheric clouds.

While many of the meteorological and chemical conditions conducive to ozone depletion are unique to Antarctica, ground-based research in Greenland in the winter of 1988 found elevated chlorine concentrations and depressed ozone levels over the Arctic as well. Although a strong vortex does not develop there and temperatures are not as low, polar stratospheric clouds do form.

The theories on how chlorine interacts on the surface of particles in polar stratospheric clouds are leading to worries that similar ozone-depleting reactions may occur around the globe. If chemicals such as sulfate aerosols from volcanoes and human-made sulfurs are capable of hosting the same catalytic reactions, global ozone depletion may accelerate even more rapidly than anticipated.

Consensus about the extent of ozone depletion and its causes strengthened with the release of the NASA Ozone Trends Panel report on March 15, 1988. Ozone losses were documented around the globe, not just at the poles. The blame was firmly placed on chlorofluorocarbons. The panel reported that between 30 and 64 degrees north latitude, where most of the world's people live, the total amount of ozone above any particular point had decreased by between 1.7 and 3 percent in the period from 1969 to 1986 (Table 1). The report further stated that while the problem was worst over Antarctica during the spring, "ozone appears to have decreased since 1979 by 5 percent or more at all latitudes south of 60 degrees south throughout the year." The hole alone covers approximately 10 percent of the Southern Hemisphere.

Within a matter of weeks the report's conclusions were widely accepted, and public debate on the issue began to build. Ozone depletion is occurring far more rapidly and in a different pattern than had been forecast. Projections of the amount and location of future ozone depletion are still highly uncertain. Although the fundamental mechanisms of ozone depletion are generally understood, the effect of cloud surface chemistry, the rate of various chemical reactions, and the specific chemical pathways are still in doubt. According to Sherwood Rowland, one of the first to sound a warning, policy decisions now and for at least another decade must be made without good quantitative guidelines of what the future holds.

Table 1

Global Decline in Atmospheric Ozone, 1969–1986*

Latitude	Year-round decrease (percent)	Winter decrease (percent)
53–64° N	−2.3	−6.2
40–53° N	−3.0	−4.7
30–40° N	−1.7	−2.3
19–30° N	−3.1	n.a.
0–19° N	−1.6	n.a.
0–19° S	−2.1	n.a.
19–29° S	−2.6	n.a.
29–39° S	−2.7	n.a.
39–53° S	−4.9	n.a.
53–60° S	−10.6	n.a.
60–90° S	−5.0 or more	n.a.

*Data for the area 30 to 64 degrees north of the equator are based on information gathered from satellites and ground stations from 1969 to 1986. Data for the area from 60 degrees south to the South Pole are based on information gathered from satellites and ground stations since 1979. All other information was compiled after November 1978 from satellite data alone.

Sources: U.S. National Aeronautics and Space Administration, Ozone Trends Panel; Cass Peterson, "Evidence of Ozone Depletion Found Over Big Urban Areas," *The Washington Post*, March 16, 1988.

EFFECTS OF ULTRAVIOLET RADIATION

At present, ozone absorbs much of the ultraviolet light that the sun emits in wavelengths harmful to humans, animals, and plants. The most biologically damaging wavelengths are within the 290- to 320-nanometer band, referred to as UV-B. But according to uncertain projections from computer models, erosion of the ozone shield could result in 5 to 20 percent more ultraviolet radiation reaching populated areas within the next 40 years—most of it in the UV-B band.

In light of the findings of the NASA Ozone Trends Panel, the U.S. Environmental Protection Agency (EPA) damage projections cited in this section are conservative. Although the EPA ranges are based on current control strategies, they assume ozone depletion levels of 1.2 to 6.2 percent. Yet all areas of the globe have already suffered depletion beyond this lower bound.

Globally, skin cancer incidence among Caucasians is already on the rise, and it is expected to increase alarmingly in the presence of more UV-B. Some 600,000 new cases of squamous and basal cell carcinoma—the two most common but rarely fatal skin cancer types—are reported each year in the United States alone. Worldwide, the number of cases is at least three times as high. Each 1 percent drop in ozone is projected to result in 4 to 6 percent more cases of these types of skin cancer. The EPA estimates that ozone depletion will lead to an additional 31,000 to 126,000 cases of melanoma—a more deadly form of skin cancer—among U.S. whites born before 2075, resulting in an additional 7,000 to 30,000 fatalities.

Under the same EPA scenarios, from 555,000 to 2.8 million Americans born before 2075 will suffer from cataracts of the eyes who would not have otherwise. Victims will also be stricken earlier in life, making treatment more difficult.

Medical researchers also fear that UV-B depresses the human immune system, lowering the body's resistance to attacking micro-organisms, making it less able to fight the development of tumors, and rendering it more prone to infectious diseases. In developing countries, particularly those near the equator that are exposed to higher UV-B levels, parasitic infections could become more common. The response may even decrease the effectiveness of some inoculation programs, such as those for diphtheria and tuberculosis.

Terrestrial and aquatic ecosystems are also affected. Screenings of more than 200 plant species, most of them crops, found that 70 percent were sensitive to UV-B. Increased exposure to radiation may decrease photosynthesis, water-use efficiency, yield, and leaf area. Soybeans, a versatile and protein-rich crop, are particularly susceptible. One researcher at the University of Maryland discovered that a simulated ozone loss of 25 percent reduced the yield of one important soybean species by as much as 25 percent. He also found that plant sensitivity to UV-B increased as the phosphorus level in the soil increased, indicating that heavily fertilized agricultural areas may be the most vulnerable.

Aquatic ecosystems may be the most threatened of all. Phytoplankton, the one-celled microscopic organisms that engage in photosynthesis while drifting on the ocean's surface, are the backbone of the marine food web. Because they require sunlight, they cannot escape incoming ultraviolet radiation and continue to thrive. Yet if they remain at the water's surface, studies show that a 25 percent reduction in ozone would decrease their productivity by about 35 percent. A significant destruction of phytoplankton and its subsequent decomposition could even raise carbon dioxide levels, speeding the warming of the atmosphere.

Zooplankton and the larvae of several important fish species will be doubly strained: Their sole food supply, phytoplankton, will be scarcer. For some shellfish species, a 10 percent decrease in ozone could result in up to an 18 percent increase in the number of abnormal larvae. Commercial fish populations already threatened by overharvesting may have more difficulty rebuilding due to effects of increased UV-B. Some species will undoubtedly be more vulnerable to increased ultraviolet radiation than others, and the changes are likely to be dramatic. Ultimately, entire ecosystems may become more unstable and less flexible.

Increased UV-B levels also affect synthetic materials, especially plastics, which become brittle. Studies conducted for the EPA estimated that without added chemical stabilizers, the cumulative damage to just one polymer, polyvinyl chloride, could reach $4,700 million by 2075 in the United States alone.

Ironically, as more ultraviolet radiation reaches the ground, the photochemical process that creates smog will accelerate, increasing ground-level ozone. Studies show that ground-level ozone retards crop and tree growth, limits visibility, and impairs lung functions. Urban air quality, already poor in most areas of the world, will worsen. In addition, stratospheric ozone decline is predicted to increase tropospheric amounts of hydrogen peroxide, an acid rain precursor.

Despite the many uncertainties regarding the amount of future ozone depletion, rising UV-B levels, and their biological effects, it is clear that the risks to aquatic and terrestrial ecosystems and to human health are enormous. The central conclusion of the EPA studies is that "the benefits of limiting future CFC/halon use far outweigh the increased costs these regulations would impose on the economy."

CHEMICAL WONDERS, ATMOSPHERIC VILLAINS

Chlorofluorocarbons are remarkable chemicals. They are neither toxic nor flammable at ground levels, as demonstrated by their discoverer, Thomas Midgley, Jr., in 1930, when he inhaled vapors from a beaker of clear liquid and then exhaled to extinguish a candle. A safe coolant that was inexpensive to produce was exactly what the refrigeration industry needed. E.I. du Pont de Nemours & Company marketed the compound under the trademark Freon. (In chemical shorthand, it is referred to as CFC-12). International production soared, rising from 545 tons in 1931 to 20,000 tons in 1945. Another use for the chemical, as a blowing agent in rigid insulation foams, was discovered in the late 1940s.

Over time, the versatility of the various CFCs seemed almost endless. CFC-11 and CFC-12 were first used as aerosol propellants during World War II in the fight against malaria. In the postwar economy, they were employed in aerosol products ranging from hairspray and deodorant to furniture polish. By the late 1950s, a combination of blowing agents CFC-11 and carbon dioxide was used to make softer furniture cushions, carpet padding, and automobile seats.

Many social and technological developments in recent decades were assisted by the availability of CFCs. Air conditioners made it possible to build and cool shopping malls, sports arenas, high-rise office buildings, and even automobiles. Artificial cooling brought comfort, business, and new residents to regions with warm climates. And healthier, more interesting diets are now available because food can be refrigerated in the production and distribution chain.

Even the computer revolution was aided by CFCs. As microchips and other components of electronic equipment became smaller and more sophisticated, the need to remove the smallest contami-

Table 2

Global CFC Use, by Category, 1985

Use	Share of total (percent)
Aerosols	25
Rigid-foam insulation	19
Solvents	19
Air conditioning	12
Refrigerants	8
Flexible foam	7
Other	10

Source: Daniel F. Kohler and others, *Projections of Consumption of Products Using Chlorofluorocarbons in Developing Countries*, Rand N-2458-EPA, 1987.

Table 3

Per Capita Use of CFC-11, CFC-12, and CFC-113, 1986 (Kilograms Per Capita)

	CFC-11	CFC-12	CFC-113	Total*
United States	.34	.58	.31	1.22
Europe	.47	.34	.12	.93
Japan	.23	.29	.43	.91

*Rows not completely additive due to trade.

Source: U.S. Environmental Protection Agency, *Regulatory Impact Analysis: Protection of Stratospheric Ozone*, 1987.

nants became critical. CFC-113 is used as a solvent to remove glue, grease, and soldering residues, leaving a clean, dry surface. CFC-113 is now the fastest growing member of the CFC family; worldwide production exceeds 160,000 tons per year.

An industry-sponsored group, the Alliance for Responsible CFC Policy, pegs the market value of CFCs produced in the United States at $750 million annually, the value of goods and services directly dependent on the chemicals at $28,000 million, and the end-use value of installed equipment and products at $135,000 million. Around the world, aerosols are still the largest user of CFCs, accounting for 25 percent of the total (Table 2). Rigid-foam and solvent applications, the fastest growing uses for CFCs, are tied for second place.

In 1987, global CFC production (excluding the People's Republic of China, the Soviet Union, and Eastern Europe) came close to 1 million tons. Combined production of CFC-11 and CFC-12 accounts for at least three-fourths of this total. Total per capita use of the three most common CFCs is highest in the United

States—at 1.22 kilograms—but Europe and Japan are not far behind (Table 3).

From 1931 through 1986, virtually all the CFC-11 and CFC-12 produced was sold to customers in the Northern Hemisphere. Since raw chemicals and products made with and containing CFCs were then exported, in part to developing countries, final usage was not quite as lopsided. Indeed, the Third World accounted for 16 percent of global CFC consumption in 1986 (Table 4). As populations, incomes, and the manufacturing base grow in developing countries, CFC use there is projected to rise.

Halons, which are used in fighting fires in both hand extinguishers and total-flooding systems for large enclosed areas, contain bromine, a more effective ozone destroyer than chlorine. Demand for halons, which were developed in the 1940s, quadrupled between 1973 and 1984 and is still growing at a rate of 15 percent annually.

Alarming though the latest ozone measurements are, they reflect only the responses to gases released through the early 1980s. Gases now rising through the lower atmosphere will take up to

Table 4

CFC Consumption by Region, 1986

Region	Share of total (percent)
United States	29
Other industrial countries*	41
Soviet Union, Eastern Europe	14
Other developing countries	14
People's Republic of China, India	2

*The European Community accounts for more than half, followed by Japan, Canada, Australia, and others.

Source: "The Ozone Treaty: A Triumph for All," *Update from State*, May/June 1988.

eight years to reach the stratosphere. And an additional 2 million tons of substances containing chlorine and bromine are still on the ground, trapped in insulation foams, appliances, and fire-fighting equipment.

Chlorine concentrations in the upper atmosphere have grown from 0.6 to 2.7 parts per thousand million in the past 25 years. Under even the most optimistic regulatory scenarios, they are expected to triple by 2075. Bromine concentrations are projected to grow considerably faster. Without a complete and rapid phaseout of CFC and halon production, the real losers will be future generations who inherit an impoverished environment.

REDUCING EMISSIONS

On September 16, 1987, after years of arduous and heated negotiation, the Montreal Protocol on Substances That Deplete the Ozone Layer was signed by 24 countries. Provisions of the agreement include a freeze on CFC production (at 1986 levels) by 1989, a 20 percent decrease

in production by 1993, and another 30 percent cut by 1998. Halon production is subject to a freeze based on 1986 levels starting in 1992....

The means to achieve these reductions are left to the discretion of individual nations. Most signatory countries are responding with production limits on chemical manufacturers. Although this approach complies with treaty guidelines, it effectively ensures that only those willing to pay high prices will be able to continue using CFCs. It also places the onus of curbing emissions on the myriad industrial users of the chemicals and on the consumers of products that incorporate them. Moving quickly to protect the ozone layer calls for a different approach —one that targets the largest sources of the most ozone-depleting chemicals.

When concern about the ozone layer first emerged in the 1970s, some industrial country governments responded. Since 56 percent of combined CFC-11 and CFC-12 production in 1974 was used in aerosols, spray cans were an obvious target. Under strong public pressure, Canada, Norway, Sweden, and the United States banned CFC propellants in at least 90 percent of their aerosol products. The change brought economic as well as environmental benefits. Hydrocarbons, the replacement propellant, are less expensive than CFCs and saved the U.S. economy $165 million in 1983 alone. The European Community adopted a different approach. In 1980, the member countries agreed not to increase their capacity to produce these two CFCs and called for a 30 percent reduction in their use in aerosol propellants by 1982 (based on 1976 consumption figures).

Despite rapid growth, CFC-113 emissions may be some of the easiest and most economical to control. The chemical is only used to clean the final product and is not incorporated in it. Thus emissions are virtually immediate; three-fourths result from vapor losses, the remainder from waste disposal. A U.S. ban on land disposal of chlorinated solvents that took effect in November 1986, consideration of similar regulations elsewhere, the high cost of incinerating CFC-113 (because it contains toxic fluorine), and accelerating concern about ozone depletion have all created strong incentives for solvent recovery and recycling.

Since CFC-113 costs about twice as much as other CFCs, investments in recovery and recycling pay off more quickly. Recycling of CFC-113 is now practiced on-site at many large computer companies. Smaller electronics firms, for which in-house recycling is not economical, can sell their used solvents to commercial recyclers or the distributors of some chemical manufacturers.

Capturing CFC emissions from flexible-foam manufacturing can also be accomplished fairly quickly but requires investment in new ventilation systems. New suction systems coupled with carbon adsorption technologies are able to recover from 40 to 90 percent of the CFCs released.

Another area that offers significant savings, at a low cost, is improved design, operating, and maintenance standards for refrigeration and air conditioning equipment. Codes of practice to govern equipment handling are being drawn up by many major trade associations. Key among the recommendations are to require worker training, to limit maintenance and repair work to authorized personnel, to install leak detection systems, and to use smaller refrigerant charges. Another recommendation, to prohibit venting of the refrigerant directly to the atmosphere, requires the use of recovery and recycling technologies.

Careful study of the automobile air conditioning market in the United States, the largest user of CFC-12 in the country, has found that 34 percent of emissions can be traced to leakage, 48 percent occur during recharge and repair servicing, and the remainder happen through accidents, disposal, and manufacturing, in that order. Equipment with better seals and hoses would reduce emissions and result in less need for system maintenance.

Over the longer term, phasing out the use and emissions of CFCs will require the development of chemical substitutes that do not harm the ozone layer. The challenge is to find alternatives that perform the same function for a reasonable cost, that do not require major equipment modifications, that are nontoxic to workers and consumers, and that are environmentally benign....

The time has come to ask if the functions performed by CFCs are really necessary and, if they are, whether they can be performed in new ways. If all known technical control measures were used, total CFC and halon emissions could be reduced by approximately 90 percent. Many of these control strategies are already cost-effective, and more will become so as regulations push up the price of ozone-depleting chemicals. The speed with which controls are introduced will determine the extent of ozone depletion in the years ahead and when healing of the ozone layer will begin.

BEYOND MONTREAL

An international treaty to halve the production of a chemical feared responsible for destroying an invisible shield is unprecedented. But unfortunately, for several reasons, the Montreal Protocol will not save the ozone layer.

First, many inducements were offered to enhance the treaty's appeal to prospective signatories—extended deadlines for developing and centrally planned economies, allowances to accommodate industry restructuring, and loose definitions of the products that can legitimately be traded internationally. The cumulative effect of these loopholes means that, even with widespread participation, the protocol's goal of halving worldwide CFC use by 1998 will not be met.

Second, recent scientific findings show that more ozone depletion has already occurred than treaty negotiators assumed would happen in 100 years. A recent EPA report concluded that by 2075, even with 100 percent global participation in the protocol, chlorine concentrations in the atmosphere would triple. The agreement will not arrest depletion, merely slow its acceleration.

Third, several chemicals not regulated under the treaty are major threats to the ozone layer. Methyl chloroform and carbon tetrachloride together contributed 13 percent of total ozone-depleting chemical emissions in 1985. As the use of controlled chemicals diminishes, the contribution of these two uncontrolled compounds will grow.

The recognition that global warming may have already begun strengthens the case for further and more rapid reductions in CFC emissions. CFCs currently account for 15 to 20 percent of the greenhouse effect and absorb wavelengths of infrared radiation that other greenhouse gases allow to escape. Indeed, one molecule of the most widely used CFCs is as effective in trapping heat as 15,000 molecules of carbon dioxide, the most abundant greenhouse gas. In light of these findings, logic suggests a virtual phaseout of CFC and halon emissions by all countries as soon as possible. Releases of other chlorine and bromine-containing compounds not currently covered under the treaty also need to be controlled and in some cases halted.

The timing of the phaseout is crucial. Analysts at EPA examined the effects of a 100 percent CFC phaseout by 1990 and a 95 percent phaseout by 1998. Peak chlorine concentrations would differ by 0.8 parts per thousand million, some one-third of current levels. And under the slower phasedown, atmospheric cleansing would be prolonged considerably: Chlorine levels would remain higher than the peak associated with the accelerated schedule for at least 50 years.

As noted, it is technically feasible to reduce CFC and halon emissions by at least 90 percent. Sweden is the first country to move beyond endorsing a theoretical phaseout. In June 1988 the parliament, after extensive discussions with industry, passed legislation that includes specific deadlines for banning the use of CFCs in new products. Consumption is to be halved by 1991 and virtually eliminated by 1995. Environmental agencies in Britain, the United States, and the Federal Republic of Germany have endorsed emissions reductions of at least 85 percent. Chemical producers in these three countries account for over half the global output of controlled substances.

Levying a tax on newly manufactured CFCs and other ozone-depleting substances is one way governments can cut emissions and accelerate the adoption of alternative chemicals and technologies. If the tax increased in step with mandatory production cutbacks, it would eliminate windfall profits for producers, encourage recovery and recycling processes, stimulate use of new chemicals, and provide a source of funding for new technologies and for needed research. Encouraging investments in recycling networks, incinerators for rigid foams, and collection systems for chemicals that would otherwise be discarded could substantially trim emissions from existing products, from servicing operations, and from new production runs. Research on new refrigeration, air conditioning, and insulation processes is worthy of government support. Unfortunately, international funding for developing such technologies totals less than $5 million.

As mentioned in the text of the Montreal Protocol, results of this research, as well as new technologies and processes, need to be shared with developing countries. Ozone depletion and climate warming are undeniably global in scope. Not sharing information on the most recent developments ensures that environmentally damaging and outdated equipment will continue to be used for years to come, further eroding the Third World technology base....

The scientific fundamentals of ozone depletion and climate change are known, and there is widespread agreement that both have already begun. Although current models of future change vary in their predictions, the evidence is clear enough to warrant an immediate response. Because valuable time was lost when governments and industries relaxed their regulatory and research efforts during the early 1980s, a crash program is now essential. Human health, food supplies, and the global climate all hinge on the support that can be garnered for putting an end to chlorine and bromine emissions.

NO

Lester B. Lave

THE GREENHOUSE EFFECT: WHAT GOVERNMENT ACTIONS ARE NEEDED?

Human beings are causing global-scale changes for the first time.... [A]rticles by Gordon MacDonald and Irving Mintzer document the "greenhouse" effect and give some indications of the environmental changes that will result. The possibility of such global changes rouses deep emotions in people: awe that humans have become so powerful, rage that we are tampering with the natural environment on a large scale, and fear that we might create an environment hostile to our progeny. Technologists tend to focus on the first emotion with the optimism that we can also find ways to head off or solve the problems. Environmentalists fix on the second, fearing that humans can only ruin nature. This article focuses on the third, asking what governmental or other social actions are possible and warranted. What should be done now and in the foreseeable future as a result of what is currently known about the atmospheric concentration of greenhouse gases, the resulting climate change, and the consequences for people?

WHY DOES THE GREENHOUSE EFFECT RECEIVE SO MUCH ATTENTION?

Scientists have been giving great attention to the greenhouse effect for more than a decade, despite the vast qualitative and quantitative uncertainties. The public joins scientists in the concern that current activities could create a much less hospitable planet in the future. Congress has also directed its concern to these issues. Congress generally regards programs whose impact is more than three to ten years in the future as hopelessly long term; it seems bizarre that greenhouse effects, which are a century or so into the future, have received major Congressional attention....

Greenhouse effects have the attributes of being (1) global (in the sense that all regions are affected), (2) long term (in the sense that near-term effects are undetectable and important effects on people and their well being are perhaps a century in the future), (3) ethical (in the sense that they involve the preferences and well being of people who have not been born yet, as

From Lester B. Lave, "The Greenhouse Effect: What Government Actions Are Needed?" *Journal of Policy Analysis and Management,* vol. 7, no. 3 (1988). Copyright © 1988 by John Wiley & Sons, Inc. Reprinted by permission. Notes omitted.

well as plants, animals, and the environment more generally), (4) potentially catastrophic (in the sense that large changes in the environment might result, as well as massive loss of human life and property), and (5) contentious (in the sense that coming to decisions, translating these into agreements, and enforcing agreements would be difficult due to important "spillover" or external effects, uncertainty, the incentives for individual nations to cheat, the difficulty of detecting cheating, and the difficulty of enforcing agreements even after cheating is detected). In addition, many of the likely public investments such as attempts to substitute for carbon dioxide producing activities would be expensive and disruptive. In other words, this set of issues exercises almost all of the tools of policy analysis and poses deep problems to decision analysts. Below, I point out some particularly attractive research areas, such as behavioral reactions, crucial to formulating policy regarding greenhouse gases.

Uncertainty. A dominant question in formulating greenhouse policy is: What is the uncertainty concerning current statements about emissions, atmospheric accumulation, resulting climate changes, and resulting effects on the managed and unmanaged biospheres? . . .

The Department of Energy has put major resources over the past decade into understanding the carbon cycle, the current sources and sinks of carbon in the environment and the mechanisms that handle increasing carbon emissions into the environment. It is safe to say that the carbon cycle is not understood well, with uncertainty regarding perhaps 20% of total sources and sinks of carbon entering the environment. Controversies surround the importance of deforestation,

the amount of carbon retained in the atmosphere, the amount being absorbed by the oceans, and the amount being taken up in plants.

The dynamics can be even more difficult to understand, because the oceans hold less carbon as they warm. Thus, there could be a destabilizing feedback of a warmer atmosphere leading to ocean warming, which induces release of carbon to the atmosphere. With the oceans becoming a net source rather than a sink, atmospheric concentrations would increase more rapidly, leading to rapidly increasing atmospheric temperatures, which induce ocean warming and carbon release. Is this scenario one that leads to disaster—or one where the ocean warming takes so long that fossil fuels are fully used and the increased carbon taken up by plants before the oceans warm enough to release appreciable carbon dioxide to the atmosphere? To what extent, and how quickly, would increased plant growth, due to a warmer climate, more rain, and higher atmospheric concentrations of carbon dioxide, absorb much more of the atmospheric carbon and slow or stop atmospheric warming?

The speed with which natural ecosystems can adapt to climate change is also a matter of concern. A large-scale climate change, comparable to a carbon dioxide doubling, has occurred over the last 18,000 years since the end of the last great ice age. While the temperature changes are comparable, the previous change occurred over 18,000 years while the change due to the greenhouse effect would occur over a century or so, perhaps one-hundred times faster. This rate of change could exceed the abilities of natural ecosystems to adapt. The amount of change is small, however, compared to what is currently experienced for the changes from day to night or season to season.

The issues related to carbon dioxide are much different from the issues related to other greenhouse gases. Neither of the two feedback mechanisms sketched above apply to CFC (chlorofluorucarbons) or methane. The Environmental Protection Agency estimates that about half of the atmospheric warming, after a century, would be attributed to gases other than carbon dioxide—an estimate that is markedly different from those of ten years ago. Much needs to be done to understand feedback mechanisms for the other greenhouse gases and to investigate possible interactions among the gases. For example, atmospheric warming is likely to increase the demand for air conditioning, which would lead to greater electricity use (resulting in increased carbon dioxide emissions) and to greater emissions of CFC from compressor leaks. The warming would also increase the demand for insulation, some of which would be foam insulation made with CFC, releasing much more of this gas to the atmosphere.

The current global circulation models are magnificent examples of technical virtuosity. The physical movements and energy fluxes of the atmosphere are described by partial differential equations that are too complicated to be solved explicitly. Thus the models depend upon expert judgment to decide what aspects of the problem should be treated explicitly within the model and how much attention each aspect should get. The current predictions of the consequences of doubling atmospheric carbon dioxide come mainly from models that treat the oceans as if little mixing occurred and there were no currents. The models also ignore many chemical reactions in the atmosphere.

Clearly, these models are "wrong" in the sense of being bad examples of reality. But the central question is whether failing to include these elements results in an error of 10% or whether the models could be wrong to the extent of predicting warming when these gases actually result in atmospheric cooling....

As shown below, exploring the consequences of this warming requires detailed predictions or assumptions for each area about climate, storm patterns, and the length of the growing season. These predictions are little more than educated guesses. For the modelers, this uncertainty is a stimulus to do better. For the policy analyst, the uncertainty must be treated explicitly in deciding what actions are warranted now and in the future.

Even vast uncertainty need not preclude taking preventive action. Uncertainty should induce caution and prevent decision makers from rushing into actions and commitments, however. For example, precipitous action would have led to forbidding military and 747 flights in the stratosphere in the early 1970s. Then, in the late 1970s, precipitous action might have led to building aircraft to fly in the stratosphere as much as possible. Finally, today aircraft flights in the stratosphere are regarded as irrelevant to stratospheric ozone levels.

It is prudent to be concerned about potentially disastrous effects and to be willing to take some actions now, even given the uncertainty. For example, American regulators insisted on building strong containment vessels around civilian nuclear reactors, even though they regarded the chance of a mishap that would require the containment vessel as remote. The USSR regulators did not insist on such safeguards, with quite different results between the problems at Three Mile Island and the tragedy at Chernobyl.

While there is major uncertainty, the policy conclusions about CFC emissions are different today from those about carbon dioxide emissions, as I discuss below.

Accounting for the uncertainty. The long-term effects of an increase in greenhouse gases are unknown and almost certainly unknowable. The physical changes, such as the gross increase in temperature for each latitude might be predicted, but it is unlikely that the dates of last frost and first freeze and detailed patterns of precipitation will be known for each growing area. Still more difficult to forecast is the adaptive behavior of individuals and governments. The accumulation of greenhouse gases could be enormously beneficial or catastrophic for humans. Or more likely, it would be beneficial at some times and places and catastrophic at others.

Preventive actions are akin to purchasing an insurance policy against potentially catastrophic greenhouse effects. Most people voluntarily purchase life insurance, even though the likelihood of dying in a particular year is very small. I suspect that people would be willing to pay a premium for a policy that would protect against an inhospitable Earth a century or so hence. But, the question is what type of insurance policy is most attractive and how much of a premium are people willing to pay.

Preventing all greenhouse effects is virtually impossible. If the climate changes and resultant human consequences are to be headed off, then heroic actions would be required immediately to reduce emissions of all the greenhouse gases throughout the world. For example, nuclear plants could be built to phase

out all coal-burning plants within several decades. The decision to do that would be enormously expensive and disruptive. Such a decision would have to be agreed to in every country and enormous resources would be required to implement it. I would not support such a decision for many reasons.

Short of such heroic measures, are there any actions that might be taken now, even though uncertainty dominates the predictions of effects? Prudence would dictate that we should take actions that might prove highly beneficial, even if they are unlikely to be needed, if their cost is small. Proscribing coal use is not an attractive insurance policy, but we should give serious consideration to limiting the growth rate of coal use. The world discovered after 1974 that there was not a one-to-one coupling of energy use and economic activity. Since then, the developed countries have experienced a considerable increase in economic activity while most countries use little or no more energy than in 1974. Reducing the emissions of other greenhouse gases would be less difficult and disruptive than large reductions in coal use. In particular, it is not difficult or expensive to switch to CFC substitutes that are less damaging and to stop using these chemicals as foaming agents for plastics and in consumer products.

Thus, one of the best ways to deal with uncertainty is to look for robust actions, actions that would be beneficial in the worst case, not harmful in other cases, and not very costly to take. Emphasizing energy conservation is perhaps the best example of a prudent policy. Conservation makes sense without any appeal to greenhouse effects, given the deaths and disease associated with mining, transport, and air pollution from coal. The greenhouse effects simply underline what is already an obvious conclusion, but not one that is being pursued vigorously. So much energy could be saved by adjusting fully to current market prices that sufficient conservation might be attained merely by encouraging this adjustment. In particular, large subsidies to energy use distort resource-allocation decisions significantly.

A second example of an inexpensive insurance policy is switching to less damaging CFCs and using less of them.

Another approach is to develop a strategy of reevaluation at fixed intervals or as new information becomes available. Instead of viewing the current decision as the only opportunity to worry about greenhouse issues, one can attempt to clarify which particular outcomes would cause greatest concern. Then one could revisit the issues periodically to see if uncertainty has been resolved or at least substantially diminished.

SOCIAL AND ECONOMIC CONSEQUENCES OF CLIMATE CHANGE

Announcement of an invention, such as a new drug, is generally greeted with public approval. Certainly there is recognition that innovations may bring undesired consequences, such as occurred with Thalidomide, and so premarket testing and technology assessment have been established and emphasized in many regulatory areas. An innovation seems to be defined in terms of the intent of the inventor to produce something that will make society better or at least to make him richer. On net, it is fair to say that such innovations are viewed positively, with the untoward consequences to be dealt with if they arise.

In contrast, an environmental change such as the greenhouse effect is viewed with horror. Such changes are generally not desired by anyone, but rather emerge as the unintended consequences of society's actions. Those who are horrified might admit that there are some changes that are likely to be beneficial, but they would still regard the overall effect as catastrophic. People tend to be more alarmed by large-scale, rapid environmental changes because the consequences would be important and uncontrollable.

Why are Americans such determined optimists about new technology and such determined pessimists about environmental changes? I suspect that much of the difference is explained by the good intent of the inventor versus the unintended nature of the environmental change. If so, this suggests that people have unwarranted faith in the good intentions of inventors, compared to the unintended changes from taking resources or using the environment as a garbage pail.

Deriving the social and economic consequences of climate change is more difficult than might appear. To be sure, if an area becomes so hot or dry that habitation is impossible, or if an area is under water, the consequences are evident. Thus, if sea level rose, the low-lying parts of Louisiana, Florida, Bangladesh, and the Netherlands would be drastically affected. The vast number of short-term effects are difficult to predict and evaluate. Furthermore, the long-term changes are likely to be less drastic (adjustment occurs to mitigate the difficulties, although this might take a long term for an ecosystem), and so the consequences will be even more difficult to infer.

In particular, a change in climate presents a challenge to farmers. If summers are hotter and drier in the corn belt, then a farmer growing corn in Illinois is going to experience crop failure more frequently, due both to droughts and to heat damage. As the climate changes, rare crop damage will give rise to occasional and then frequent damage. Will the Illinois farmer keep planting corn, surviving with the aid of ever-larger government subsidies? Or will he plant new crops that flourish under the hotter, drier climate?

Climate change also presents an opportunity. Sylvan Wittwer, a noted agronomist, observed that "... the present level of atmospheric carbon dioxide is suboptimal, and the oxygen level is supraoptimal, for photosynthesis and primary productivity in the great majority of plants." The increased atmospheric carbon dioxide concentrations would enhance growth and water-use efficiency, leading to more and faster growth. Charles Cooper remarks that a doubled atmospheric concentration of carbon dioxide "... is about as likely to increase global food, at least in the long run, as to decrease it. It is certain though, that some nations, regions, and people will gain and others will lose." A new climate regime with more precipitation and a longer growing season bodes well for agriculture—if we figure out what crops to plant and figure out generally how to tailor agriculture to the new climate regime, and how to deal with new pests.

The midcontinental drying, if it occurs, could mean the end of current agricultural practices in the midwest. This climate change might induce more irrigation, dry farming practices such as have been demonstrated in Israel, new cultivars, different crops, or even ceasing to cultivate this land. The increased rains might mean there was sufficient winter precipitation to provide water for summer irrigation; it would certainly mean that there was sufficient water elsewhere in the country to be transported to the midwest for irrigation. Large dams and canals might be required, but the technology for this is available. Certainly this water would be more expensive than that currently available, but there is no reason to be concerned about starvation or even large increases in food prices for the U.S. On net, food and fibers might be slightly more expensive or less expensive in the U.S. under the new climate, but the change is almost certain to be small compared to other economic changes.

For the U.S., there is no difficulty with finding the appropriate technology for breeding new crops that fit the climate, developing a less water-intensive agriculture, or for moving water for irrigation. The difficulty would be whether agronomists are given the right tasks, whether farmers give up their old crops and farming methods, and whether society can solve the myriad social problems associated with damming newly enlarged rivers and moving the water to where it is needed.

The "less managed" areas, including forests, grasslands, and marsh, might experience large changes and a system far from long-term equilibrium. These effects would be scarcely discernable in measured gross national product, but would be viewed as extremely important by many environmentalists.

Water projects and resources more generally might pose a greater problem. Large-scale water projects, such as dams and canals, are built to last for long periods. Once built, they are not easily changed. Thus, major climate change could lead to massive dams fed by tiny streams or dams completely inadequate for the rivers they are designed to control. Similarly, treaty obligations for the Colorado are inflexible and could pose major problems if there is less water flowing down the river. Similarly, the climate change would induce migration, both across areas in the U.S. and from other countries. The legal and illegal migration could pose major problems. Finally, Americans treasure certain natural resources, such as waterfalls. Climate change that stopped the flow at popular falls would be regarded seriously.

Commenting on energy modeling, Hans Landsberg wrote: "... all of us who have engaged in projecting into the more distant future take ourselves too seriously.... What is least considered is how many profound turns in the road one would have missed making 1980 projections in 1930! I am not contending that the emperor is naked, but we surely overdress him."

REPRISE: WHY SO MUCH CONCERN FOR THE GREENHOUSE EFFECT?

It is the symbolic nature of the issues that has drawn attention to the greenhouse effect. Anyone who thinks he can see 100 years into the future is mad. If humans have now acquired the power to influence the global environment, then it is likely that we will cause changes even larger than those discussed here within the next century or so. Both the greenhouse effect and other global changes could be predominantly beneficial or harmful to humans and various aspects of the environment, although they are likely to be beneficial in some times and places and detrimental in others. But a large element of the public debate is almost scandalized at the notion that the changes might be beneficial or made beneficial by individual actions and government policies.

The difficulty is public concern that global scale effects are now possible; we have had a "loss of innocence." In the past, if an individual ruined a plot of land, he could move on. If human actions caused major problems such as the erosion of the Dalmatian coast of Yugoslavia, there was always other inviting land. But, if the Earth is made inhospitable, there is no other inviting planet readily at hand.

I share this concern, but find it naive. Having acquired the power to influence the global environment, there is no way to relinquish it. No one intends to change the global environment by emitting greenhouse gases. Rather, the change is an inadvertent consequence of business as usual. The culprit is not a malevolent individual or rapacious company. Instead, it is the scope of human activities stemming from a large population, modern technology, and an unbelievable volume of economic activity. These culprits are not going to disappear, however much we might all wish that people did not have the ability to affect our basic environment. In this sense, the human race has lost its environmental innocence.

The symbolism is important because of the need to educate the public and government and gauge their reactions to this first global environmental issue. If people and governments show themselves to be concerned and willing to make sacrifices, the prospect for the future looks brighter. If instead, each individual and nation regards the effects as primarily due to others, and as someone else's problem, the increases in economic activity and advances in technology promise a future with major unintended changes in the Earth's environment.

Such changes could be dealt with by concerned global action to stop the stimulus and thus the response. Or they could be dealt with by individual and national actions to adapt to the consequences. However much I might wish for concerted action among countries, I do not believe this is likely to occur. There are too many disparate interests, too much to be gained by cheating, too much suspicion of the motives of others, and too little control over all the relevant actors. Thus, reluctantly, I conclude that mitigation through adaptation must be our focus.

For example, within the United States, federal environmental laws have been only a modest success in preventing environmental pollution. Ozone problems have worsened, ground water has become more polluted, and we seem no closer to dealing with radioactive and toxic wastes. When the scope of the problem becomes international, as with acid rain, there is little or no progress. Curtailing sulfur oxides emissions into the air necessarily involves promoting some interests while hurting others. Those who would be hurt are, not surprisingly, more skeptical about whether low levels of acid sulfate aerosols cause disease than those who believe that they would benefit. Getting agreement on action has proven essentially impossible for abating sulfur ox-

ides. It is hard to imagine that a debate among 140 nations on the greenhouse effect would lead to an agreement to adopt binding programs to abate emissions.

A multinational agreement on controlling CFC has been negotiated in 1987. This is an extremely encouraging, and surprising development. There are many obstacles to effective implementation, however, from ratification by each country to best faith efforts to abide by the sense of the agreement.

CONCLUSION

The greenhouse effect is the first of what are likely to be many long-term, global problems. Analysis is difficult because of the vast uncertainty about causes and effects, as well as of the consequences of the resulting climate change. The current uncertainties together with the costs of precipitous action imply that heroic actions to curtail the emissions of all greenhouse gases are not justified. Nonetheless, the current facts support a program of energy conservation, abatement, research, and periodic reconsideration that is far more activist than the current policy of the U.S. government.

I would like to thank Stephen Schneider and Jesse Ausubel for comments. This work was supported in part by the National Science Foundation (Grant No. SES-8715564).

POSTSCRIPT

Does Global Warming Require Immediate Government Action?

The harsh reality is that the environment is deteriorating. Very few, if any, physical scientists dispute this fact. What is disputed is the rate of decline in the global environment and whether or not citizens acting at the end of the twentieth century should try to alter this process. Do we have enough knowledge of the future to take dramatic steps today that will reshape the world of tomorrow? This is a hard question. If we answer incorrectly, our children and our children's children may curse us for our lack of resolve to solve environmental problems that were clear for all to see.

Shea and Lave agree that there is a clear and present danger associated with ozone-depleting chemicals, such as chlorofluorocarbons, which are also the gases that contribute to the greenhouse effect. What they disagree on is whether or not we know enough today to take immediate, decisive action. Do *you* know enough? If you do not, we suggest that you read further in this area. *It is your future that is being discussed here.*

A brief history of scientific concerns about the greenhouse effect, which stretches back to the late nineteenth century, is found in Jesse H. Ausubel, "Historical Note," in the National Research Council's *Changing Climate: Report of the Carbon Dioxide Assessment Committee* (National Academy Press, 1983). We should note that there are a number of other essays in *Changing Climate* that may be of interest to you. The Environmental Protection Agency (EPA) has published many studies you might want to examine. See, for example, the EPA's study entitled *The Potential Effects of Global Climate Change on the United States* (December 1989) and *Policy Options for Stabilizing Global Climate* (February 1989). An extensive analysis of the scientific, economic, and policy implications are also found in the *1990 Economic Report of the President.*

ISSUE 17

Should Pollution Be Put to the Market Test?

YES: Alan S. Blinder, from *Hard Heads, Soft Hearts: Tough-Minded Economics for a Just Society* (Addison-Wesley, 1987)

NO: David Moberg, from "Environment and Markets: A Critique of 'Free Market' Claims," *Dissent* (Fall 1991)

ISSUE SUMMARY

YES: Alan S. Blinder, a member of the Board of Governors of the Federal Reserve System, urges policymakers to use the energy of the market to solve America's environmental problems.

NO: Social critic David Moberg warns against giving businesses more flexibility and economic incentives, and he argues that clear public policy and direct government intervention will have the most positive effects on the environment.

Markets sometimes fail. That is, markets sometimes do not automatically yield optimum, economically efficient answers. This is because prices sometimes do not reflect the true social costs and benefits of consumption and production. The culprit here is the presence of externalities. Externalities are spillover effects that impact third parties who had no voice in the determination of an economic decision.

If, for example, my friend and coeditor Frank J. Bonello decided to "cut a few corners" to hold down the costs of his commercially produced banana cream pies, he might well create a *negative externality* for his neighbors. That is, if in the dark of night, Bonello slipped to the back of his property and dumped his banana skins, egg shells, and other waste products into the St. Joe River that borders his property, part of the cost of producing banana cream pies would be borne by those who live downstream from the Bonello residence. Since the full costs of production are not borne by Bonello, he can set a competitively attractive price and sell many more pies than his competitors, whom we assume must pay to have their waste products carted away.

If Bonello is not forced to internalize the negative externality associated with his production process, the price attached to his pies gives an improper market signal with regard to the true scarcity of resources. In brief, because Bonello's pies are cheaper than his competitors, demanders will flock to his doorstep to demand more and more of his pies, unknowingly causing him to dump more and more negative externalities on his neighbors downstream.

In this case, as in other cases of firms casting off negative externalities, the public sector may have to intervene and mandate that these externalities be internalized. This is not always an easy task, however. Two difficult questions must be answered: (1) Who caused the external effect? Was it only Bonello's banana cream pie production? and (2) Who bore the costs of the negative externality, and what are their losses? These questions require detective work. We must not only identify the source of the pollution, but we must also identify the people who have been negatively affected by its presence and determine their "rights" in this situation. Once this has been achieved, the difficult task of evaluating and measuring the negative effects must be undertaken.

Even if this can be successfully negotiated, one last set of questions remains: What alternative methods can be used to force firms to internalize their externalities, and which of these methods are socially acceptable and economically efficient? This is the subject of the debate that follows.

Alan S. Blinder warns against the limitations inherent in a market solution to the pollution problem; however, he still supports harnessing the power of the market in order to rid the world of the harmful effects of pollution. David Moberg, on the other hand, takes care to note that private market solutions can be effective. But he maintains that, many times, old-fashioned regulation can be even more effective.

YES
Alan S. Blinder

CLEANING UP THE ENVIRONMENT: SOMETIMES CHEAPER IS BETTER

We cannot give anyone the option of polluting for a fee.

—Senator Edmund Muskie
(in Congress, 1971)

In the 1960s, satirist Tom Lehrer wrote a hilarious song warning visitors to American cities not to drink the water or breathe the air. Now, after the passage of more than two decades and the expenditure of hundreds of billions of dollars, such warnings are less appropriate—at least on most days! Although the data base on which their estimates rest is shaky, the Environmental Protection Agency (EPA) estimates that the volume of particulate matter suspended in the air (things like smoke and dust particles) fell by half between 1973 and 1983. During the same decade, the volume of sulfur dioxide emissions declined 27 percent and lead emissions declined a stunning 77 percent. Estimated concentrations of other air pollutants also declined. Though we still have some way to go, there is good reason to believe that our air is cleaner and more healthful than it was in the early 1970s. While the evidence for improved average water quality is less clear (pardon the pun), there have at least been spectacular successes in certain rivers and lakes.

All this progress would seem to be cause for celebration. But economists are frowning—and not because they do not prize cleaner air and water, but rather because our current policies make environmental protection far too costly. America can achieve its present levels of air and water quality at far lower cost, economists insist. The nation is, in effect, shopping for cleaner air and water in a high-priced store when a discount house is just around the corner. Being natural cheapskates, economists find this extravagance disconcerting. Besides, if we shopped in the discount store, we would probably buy a higher-quality environment than we do now....

IS POLLUTION AN ECONOMIC PROBLEM?

... Nothing in this discussion ... implies that the appropriate level of environmental quality is a matter for the free market to determine. On the contrary, the market mechanism is ill suited to the task; if left to its own devices, it will certainly produce excessive environmental degradation. Why? Because users of clean air and water, unlike users of oil and steel, are not normally made to pay for the product.

Consider a power plant that uses coal, labor, and other inputs to produce electricity. It buys all these items on markets, paying market prices. But the plant also spews soot, sulfur dioxide, and a variety of other undesirables into the air. In a real sense, it "uses up" clean air—one of those economic goods which people enjoy—without paying a penny. Naturally, such a plant will be sparing in its use of coal and labor, for which it pays, but extravagant in its use of clean air, which is offered for free.

That, in a nutshell, is why the market fails to safeguard the environment. When items of great value, like clean air and water, are offered free of charge it is unsurprising that they are overused, leaving society with a dirtier and less healthful environment than it should have.

The analysis of why the market fails suggests the remedy that economists have advocated for decades: charge polluters for the value of the clean air or water they now take for free. That will succeed where the market fails because an appropriate fee or tax per unit of emissions will, in effect, put the right price tag on clean air and water—just as the market now puts the right price tag on oil and steel. Once our precious air and water resources are priced correctly, polluters will husband them as carefully as they now husband coal, labor, cement, and steel. Pollution will decline. The environment will become cleaner and more healthful. . . .

The Efficiency Argument

It is now time to explain why economists insist that emissions fees can clean up the environment at lower cost than mandatory quantitative controls. The secret is the market's unique ability to accommodate individual differences—in this case, differences among polluters.

Suppose society decides that emissions of sulfur dioxide must decline by 20 percent. One obvious approach is to mandate that every source of sulfur dioxide reduce its emissions by 20 percent. Another option is to levy a fee on discharges that is large enough to reduce emissions by 20 percent. The former is the way our current environmental regulations are often written. The latter is the economist's preferred approach. Both reduce pollution to the same level, but the fee system gets there more cheaply. Why? Because a system of fees assigns most of the job to firms that can reduce emissions easily and cheaply and little to firms that find it onerous and expensive to reduce their emissions.

Let me illustrate how this approach works with a real example. A study in St. Louis found that it cost only $4 for one paper-products factory to cut particulate emissions from its boiler by a ton, but it cost $600 to do the same job at a brewery. If the city fathers instructed both the paper plant and the brewery to cut emissions by the same amount, pollution abatement costs would be low at the paper factory but astronomical at the brewery. Imposing a uniform emissions tax is a more cost-conscious strategy. Suppose a $100/ton tax is announced. The paper company will see an opportunity to save $100 in taxes by spending $4 on cleanup, for a $96 net profit. Similarly, any other firm whose pollution-abatement costs are less than $100 per ton will find it profitable to cut emissions. But firms like the brewery, where pollution-abatement costs exceed $100 per ton, will prefer to continue polluting and paying the tax. Thus the profit motive will automatically assign the task of pollution abatement to the low-cost firms—something no regulators can do.

Mandatory proportional reductions have the seductive appearance of "fairness" and so are frequently adopted. But they provide no incentive to minimize the social costs of environmental clean-up. In fact, when the heavy political hand requires equal percentage reductions by every firm (or perhaps from every smokestack), it pretty much guarantees that the social clean-up will be far more costly than it need be. In the previous example, a one-ton reduction in annual emissions by both the paper factory and the brewery would cost $604 per year. But the same two-ton annual pollution abatement would cost only $8 if the paper factory did the whole job. Only by lucky accident will equiproportionate reductions in discharges be efficient.

Studies that I will cite later... suggest that market-oriented approaches to pollution control can reduce abatement costs by 90 percent in some cases. Why, economists ask, is it more virtuous to make pollution reduction hurt more? They have yet to hear a satisfactory answer and suspect there is none. On the contrary, virtue and efficiency are probably in harmony here. If cleaning up our air and water is made cheaper, it is reasonable to suppose that society will buy more clean-up. We can have a purer environment and pay less, too. The hardheaded economist's crass means may be the surest route to the soft-hearted environmentalist's lofty ends.

The Enforcement Argument

Some critics of emissions fees argue that a system of fees would be hard to enforce. In some cases, they are correct. We obviously cannot use effluent charges to reduce concentrations of the unsightly pollutant glop if engineers have yet to devise an effective and dependable devise for measuring how much glop firms are spewing out. If we think glop is harmful, but are unable to monitor it, our only alternative may be to require firms to switch to "cleaner" technologies. Similarly, emissions charges cannot be levied on pollutants that seep unseen —and unmeasured—into groundwater rather than spill out of a pipe.

In many cases, however, those who argue that emissions fees are harder to enforce than direct controls are deceiving themselves. If you cannot measure emissions, you cannot charge a fee, to be sure. But neither can you enforce mandatory standards; you can only delude yourself into thinking you are enforcing them. To a significant extent, that is precisely what the EPA does now. Federal antipollution regulations are poorly policed; the EPA often declares firms in compliance based on nothing more than the firms' self-reporting of their own behavior. When checks are made, noncompliance is frequently uncovered. If emissions can be measured accurately enough to enforce a system of quantitative controls, we need only take more frequent measurements to run a system of pollution fees.

Besides, either permits or taxes are much easier to administer than detailed regulations. Under a system of marketable permits, the government need only conduct periodic auctions. Under a system of emissions taxes, the enforcement mechanism is the relentless and anonymous tax collector who basically reads your meter like a gas or electric company. No fuss, no muss, no bother—and no need for a big bureaucracy. Just a bill. The only way to escape the pollution tax is to exploit the glaring loophole that the government deliberately provides: reduce your emissions.

Contrast this situation with the difficulties of enforcing the cumbersome command-and-control system we now operate. First, complicated statutes must be passed; and polluting industries will use their considerable political muscle in state legislatures and in Congress to fight for weaker laws. Next, the regulatory agencies must write detailed regulations defining precise standards and often prescribing the "best available technology" to use in reducing emissions. Here again industry will do battle, arguing for looser interpretations of the statutes and often turning the regulations to their own advantage. They are helped in this effort by the sheer magnitude of the information-processing task that the law foists upon the EPA and state agencies, a task that quickly outstrips the capacities of their small staffs.

Once detailed regulations are promulgated, the real problems begin. State and federal agencies with limited budgets must enforce these regulations on thousands, if not millions, of sources of pollution. The task is overwhelming. As one critic of the system put it, each polluter argues:

(1) he is in compliance with the regulation; (2) if not, it is because the regulation is unreasonable as a general rule; (3) if not, then the regulation is unreasonable in this specific case; (4) if not, then it is up to the regulatory agency to tell him how to comply; (5) if forced to take the steps recommended by the agency, he cannot be held responsible for the results; and (6) he needs more time....

Other Reasons to Favor Emissions Fees
Yet other factors argue for market-based approaches to pollution reduction.

One obvious point is that a system of mandatory standards, or one in which a particular technology is prescribed by law, gives a firm that is in compliance with the law no incentive to curtail its emissions any further. If the law says that the firm can emit up to 500 tons of glop per year, it has no reason to spend a penny to reduce its discharges to 499 tons. By contrast, a firm that must pay $100 per ton per year to emit glop can save money by reducing its annual discharges as long as its pollution-abatement costs are less than $100 per ton. The financial incentive to reduce pollution remains.

A second, and possibly very important, virtue of pollution fees is that they create incentives for firms to devise or purchase innovative ways to reduce emissions. Under a system of effluent fees, businesses gain if they can find cheaper ways to control emissions because their savings depend on their pollution abatement, not on how they achieve it. Current regulations, by contrast, often dictate the technology. Firms are expected to obey the regulators, not to search for creative ways to reduce pollution at lower cost.

For this and other reasons, our current system of regulations is unnecessarily adversarial. Businesses feel the government is out to harass them—and they act accordingly. Environmental protection agencies lock horns with industry in the courts. The whole enterprise takes on the atmosphere of a bullfight rather than that of a joint venture. A market-based approach, which made clear that the government wanted to minimize the costs it imposed on business, would naturally create a more cooperative spirit. That cannot be bad.

Finally, the appearance of fairness when regulations take the form of uniform percentage reductions in emissions, as they frequently do, is illusory. Suppose Clean Jeans, Inc. has already spent a considerable sum to reduce the amount of muck it spews into the Stench River. Dirty Jeans, Inc., just downriver, has not spent a cent and emits twice as much. Now a law is passed requiring every firm along the Stench to reduce its emissions by 50 percent. That has the appearance of equity but not the substance. For Dirty Jeans, the regulation may be a minor nuisance. To comply, it need only do what Clean Jeans is already doing voluntarily. But the edict may prove onerous to Clean Jeans, which has already exploited all the cheap ways to cut emissions. In this instance, not only is virtue not its own reward—it actually brings a penalty! Such anomalies cannot arise under a system of marketable pollution permits. Clean Jeans would always have to buy fewer permits than Dirty Jeans. . . .

OBJECTIONS TO "LICENSES TO POLLUTE"

Despite the many powerful arguments in favor of effluent taxes or marketable emissions permits, many people have an instinctively negative reaction to the whole idea. Some environmentalists, in particular, rebel at economists' advocacy of market-based approaches to pollution control—which they label "licenses to pollute," a term not meant to sound complimentary. Former Senator Muskie's dictum, quoted at the beginning of this chapter, is an example. The question is: Are the objections to "licenses to pollute" based on coherent arguments that should sway policy, or are they knee-jerk reactions best suited to T-shirts?* My own view is that there is little of the former and much of the latter. Let me explain.

Some of the invective heaped upon the idea of selling the privilege to pollute stems from an ideologically based distrust of markets. Someone who does not think the market a particularly desirable way to organize the production of automobiles, shirts, and soybeans is unlikely to trust the market to protect the environment. As one congressional staff aide put it: "The philosophical assumption that proponents of [emissions] charges make is that there is a free-market system that responds to ... relative costs.... I reject that assumption." This remarkably fatuous statement ignores mountains of evidence accumulated over centuries. Fortunately, it is a minority view in America. Were it the majority view, our economic problems would be too severe to leave much time for worry about pollution.

Some of the criticisms of pollution fees are based on ignorance of the arguments or elementary errors in logic. As mentioned earlier, few opponents of market-based approaches can even explain why economists insist that emissions fees will get the job done more cheaply.

One commonly heard objection is that a rich corporation confronted with a pollution tax will pay the tax rather than reduce its pollution. That belief shows an astonishing lack of respect for avarice. Sure, an obstinate but profitable company *could* pay the fees rather

*[Earlier in his book, Blinder warns his readers about simplistic answers to complex questions. He concludes that "if it fits on a T-shirt, it is almost certainly wrong."—Eds.]

than reduce emissions. But it would do that only if the marginal costs of pollution abatement exceed the fee. Otherwise, its obduracy reduces its profits. Most corporate executives faced with a pollution tax will improve their bottom lines by cutting their emissions, not by flouting the government's intent. To be sure, it is self-interest, not the public interest, that motivates the companies to clean up their acts. But that's exactly the idea behind pollution fees....

One final point should lay the moral issue to rest. Mandatory quantitative standards for emissions are also licenses to pollute—just licenses of a strange sort. They give away, with neither financial charge nor moral condemnation, the right to spew a specified amount of pollution into the air or water. Then they absolutely prohibit any further emissions. Why is such a license morally superior to a uniform tax penalty on all pollution? Why is a business virtuous if it emits 500 tons of glop per year but sinful if it emits 501? Economists make no claim to be arbiters of public morality. But I doubt that these questions have satisfactory answers.

The choice between direct controls and effluent fees, then, is not a moral issue. It is an efficiency issue. About that, economists know a thing or two.

Having made my pitch, I must confess that there are circumstances under which market-based solutions are inappropriate and quantitative standards are better. One obvious instance is the case of a deadly poison. If the socially desirable level of a toxin is zero, there is no point in imposing an emission fee. An outright ban makes more sense.

Another case is a sudden health emergency. When, for example, a summertime air inversion raises air pollution in Los Angeles or New York to hazardous levels, it makes perfect sense for the mayors of those cities to place legal limits on driving, on industrial discharges, or on both. There is simply no time to install a system of pollution permits.

A final obvious case is when no adequate monitoring device exists, as in the case of runoff from soil pollution. Then a system of emissions fees is out of the question. But so also is a system of direct quantitative controls on emissions. The only viable way to control such pollution may be to mandate that cleaner technologies be used.

But each of these is a minor, and well recognized, exception to an overwhelming presumption in the opposite direction. No sane person has ever proposed selling permits to spill arsenic into water supplies. None has suggested that the mayor of New York set the effluent tax on carbon monoxide anew after hearing the weather forecast each morning. And no one has insisted that we must meter what cannot be measured. Each of these objections is a debater's point, not a serious challenge to the basic case for market-oriented approaches to environmental protection....

RAYS OF HOPE: EMISSIONS TRADING AND BUBBLES

There are signs, however, that environmental policy may be changing for the better. The EPA seems to be drifting slowly, and not always surely, away from technology-driven direct controls toward more market-oriented approaches. But not because the agency has been convinced by the logic of economists' arguments. Rather, it was driven into a corner by the inexorable illogic of its own procedures. Necessity proved to be the midwife of common sense.

The story begins in the 1970s, when it became apparent that many regions of the country could not meet the air quality standards prescribed by the Clean Air Act. Under the law, the prospective penalty for violating of the standards was Draconian: no new sources of pollution would be permitted in these regions and existing sources would not be allowed to increase their emissions, implying a virtual halt to local economic growth. The EPA avoided the impending clash between the economy and the environment by creating its "emissions-offsets" program in 1976. Under the new rules, companies were allowed to create new sources of pollution in areas with substandard air quality as long as they reduced their pollution elsewhere by greater amounts. Thus was emissions trading born.

The next important step was invention of the "bubble" concept in 1979. Under this concept, all sources of pollution from a single plant or firm are imagined to be encased in a mythical bubble. The EPA then tells the company that it cares only about total emissions into the bubble. How these emissions are parceled out among the many sources of pollution under the bubble is no concern of the EPA. But it is vital to the firm, which can save money by cutting emissions in the least costly way. A striking example occurred in 1981 when a DuPont plant in New Jersey was ordered to reduce its emissions from 119 sources by 85 percent. Operating under a state bubble program, company engineers proposed instead that emissions from seven large stacks be reduced by 99 percent. The result? Pollution reduction exceeded the state's requirement by 2,300 tons per year

and DuPont saved $12 million in capital costs and $3 million per year in operating costs.

Partly because it was hampered by the courts, the bubble concept was little used at first. But bubbles have been growing rapidly since a crucial 1984 judicial decision. By October 1984, about seventy-five bubbles had been approved by the EPA and state authorities and hundreds more were under review or in various stages of development. The EPA estimated the cost savings from all these bubbles to be about $800 million per year. That may seem a small sum compared to the more than $70 billion we now spend on environmental protection. But remember that the whole program was still in the experimental stage, and these bubbles covered only a tiny fraction of the thousands of industrial plants in the United States.

The bubble program was made permanent only when EPA pronounced the experiment a success and issued final guidelines in November 1986. Economists greeted this announcement with joy. Environmentalist David Doniger... complained that, "The bubble concept is one of the most destructive impediments to the cleanup of unhealthy air." By now, many more bubbles have been approved or are in the works. Time will tell who was right.

The final step in the logical progression toward the economist's approach would be to make these "licenses to pollute" fully marketable so that firms best able to reduce emissions could sell their excess abatement to firms for which pollution abatement is too expensive. Little trading has taken place to date, though the EPA's November 1986 guidelines may encourage it. But at least one innovative state program is worth mentioning.

The state of Wisconsin found itself unable to achieve EPA-mandated levels of water quality along the polluted Fox and Wisconsin Rivers, even when it employed the prescribed technology. A team of engineers and economists then devised a sophisticated system of transferable discharge permits. Firms were issued an initial allocation of pollution permits (at no charge), based on historical levels of discharges. In total, these permits allow no more pollution than is consistent with EPA standards for water quality. But firms are allowed to trade pollution permits freely in the open market. Thus, in stark contrast to the standard regulatory approach, the Wisconsin system lets the firms along the river—not the regulators—decide how to reduce discharges. Little emissions trading has taken place to date because the entire scheme has been tied up in litigation. But one study estimated that pollution-control costs might eventually fall by as much as 80 percent compared to the alternative of ordering all firms along the river to reduce their discharges by a uniform percentage.

The state of Wisconsin thus came to the conclusion that economists have maintained all along: that applying a little economic horse sense makes it possible to clean up polluted rivers and reduce costs at the same time—a good bargain. That same bargain is available to the nation for the asking....

A HARD-HEADED, SOFT-HEARTED ENVIRONMENTAL POLICY

Economists who specialize in environmental policy must occasionally harbor self-doubts. They find themselves lined up almost unanimously in favor of market-based approaches to pollu-tion control with seemingly everyone else lined up on the other side. Are economists crazy or is everyone else wrong?

... I have argued the seemingly implausible proposition that environmental economists are right and everyone else really is wrong. I have tried to convey a sense of the frustration economists feel when they see obviously superior policies routinely spurned. By replacing our current command-and-control system with either marketable pollution permits or taxes on emissions, our environment can be made cleaner while the burden on industry is reduced. That is about as close to a free lunch as we are likely to encounter. And yet economists' recommendations are overwhelmed by an unholy alliance of ignorance, ideology, and self-interest.

This is a familiar story. The one novel aspect in the sphere of environmental policy is that the usual heavy hitter of this triumvirate—self-interest—is less powerful here than in many other contexts. To be sure, self-interested business lobbies oppose pollution fees. But, as I pointed out, they can be bought off by allowing some pollution free of charge. Doing so may outrage environmental purists, but it is precisely what we do now.

It is the possibility of finessing vested financial interests that holds out the hope that good environmental policy might one day drive out the bad. For we need only overcome ignorance and ideology, not avarice.

Ignorance is normally beaten by knowledge. Few Americans now realize that practical reforms of our environmental policies can reduce the national clean-up bill from more than $70 billion per year to less than $50 billion, and probably to much less. Even fewer understand the reasons why. If the case for market-based policies were better known, more and more people might ask the obvious question: Why is it better to pay more for something we can get for less? Environmental policy may be one area where William Blake's optimistic dictum —"Truth can never be told so as to be understood and not believed"—is germane.

Ideology is less easily rooted out, for it rarely succumbs to rational argument. Some environmentalists support the economist's case. Others understand it well and yet oppose it for what they perceive as moral reasons. I have argued at length that here, as elsewhere, thinking with the heart is less effective than thinking with the head; that the economist's case does not occupy the moral low ground; and that the environment is likely to be cleaner if we offer society clean-up at more reasonable cost. As more environmentalists come to realize that T-shirt slogans are retarding, not hastening, progress toward their goals, their objections may melt away.

The economist's approach to environmental protection is no panacea. It requires an investment in monitoring equipment that society has not yet made. It cannot work in cases where the sources of pollution are not readily identifiable, such as seepage into groundwater. And it will remain an imperfect antidote for environmental hazards until we know a great deal more than we do now about the diffusion of pollutants and the harm they cause.

But perfection is hardly the appropriate standard. As things stand now, our environmental policy may be a bigger mess than our environment. Market-based approaches that join the hard head of the accountant to the soft heart of the environmentalist offer the prospect of genuine improvement: more clean-up for less money. It is an offer society should not refuse.

NO

David Moberg

ENVIRONMENT AND MARKETS: A CRITIQUE OF "FREE MARKET" CLAIMS

The soot-darkened skies and fouled waters of Eastern Europe have given apologists for laissez-faire capitalism a new rallying cry: the "free market," far from being nature's enemy, is the environment's savior.

Some environmentalists have argued that there is no fundamental conflict between environmental responsibility and "free market" economics. Ecology, they contend, is ultimately sound, profitable business and environmental regulation must employ market forces if it is to succeed. They advocate giving business more flexibility and incentives, such as the right to buy and sell pollution rights, to increase efficiency and innovation so as to meet environmental goals.

Other environmentalists, however, continue to share a skepticism, with roots in both conservative and leftist traditions, about the compatibility of the market and the environment. This camp is also dissatisfied with the results of the first two decades of environmental regulation. Its advocates want a more aggressive democratic voice in what are usually private decisions. Ecological principles have become the basis for alternative models to capitalist markets, conflicting with or complementing the longstanding social class critiques. Ecologists have also opened another front criticizing not just the adequacy of market mechanisms but also market society in general and its exaltation of individual acquisitiveness and unbridled growth of commodity production.

All human societies have been shaped by interaction with nature, from the nomadism of hunters to the settled cultures of rich ecological niches, such as our own Northwest Coast or the slash-and-burn agriculture of tropical forests. Although earlier cultures undermined themselves by radically altering environments, stripping forests from the hills of Greece or raising the salinity of irrigated Mesopotamian soil, the worst depredation of the environment has come since the rise of capitalism. Now there is the prospect that human society has such an unsustainable relation with nature that both the future of humanity and the fate of thousands of other creatures is at stake.

From David Moberg, "Environment and Markets: A Critique of 'Free Market' Claims," *Dissent* (Fall 1991). Copyright © 1991 by David Moberg. Reprinted by permission.

But has capitalism itself been the cause of environmental damage or is the root problem industrial technologies or a growing population that consumes more and more goods?

Although the rapid growth of both population and global consumption magnifies every environmental impact, there are huge differences in environmental effects among nations, even the industrialized ones. The worst environmental insults are a result of modern industry, but not all industries degrade the environment equally. The nature of society, not just its size or technology, is largely responsible for the crisis in nature.

Obviously, the private market damages the natural environment because pollution is external to the balance sheets of private business. A factory owner doesn't pay to flush waste down the river or into the air; the costs are borne by nature as well as other people who share the environment. On the other hand, if a farmer preserves a marsh that cleans the stream's water, nourishes fish and wildlife, and prevents floods, he is paid nothing for those services. But if he sells it to be filled in for a shopping center, he will make money, and our accounting system evaluates this as economic growth, with no deductions for this loss of the wetland's natural functions. Likewise, nobody pays for the Amazon forest serving as "the lungs of the world" or preserving its diverse life forms for the future. So, the market doesn't adequately account for either negative or positive externalities.

If an ingenious entrepreneur devises a pollution-free production process that costs more than her competitor's, she will probably lose the market race: in most cases, nobody—except for a few generous souls—will pay the tab for her contribution to the common welfare. Now it is possible to level the playing field with taxes, fees, or penalties for the polluter, but it is difficult to assess the price of damage to the environment, especially if it is not a localized toxic spill but a global problem, like the greenhouse effect. Litigation over Exxon's Alaska oil spill or over compensation to the victims of Union Carbide's Bhopal disaster suggests the ethically and economically knotty problems.

WHO DETERMINES THE LOSSES?

There are similar problems if more direct environmental regulations are subjected to cost-benefit analysis: how much is a human life worth? Some economists argue that it's the person's likely future lifetime earnings. That makes an Indian peasant pretty expendable compared to a Connecticut executive. Such cost-benefit analyses illegitimately import values of the marketplace to answer questions that arise because of fundamental flaws in that same market system.

How much is a sea otter worth?, Business Week asked. Surveying people about how much the animals are worth to them or measuring lost income if sea otters disappeared may keep a few economists employed, but it does not answer the question. If only one respondent said it was of infinite value, that would throw off the survey. If you limit the response to how much a person would be willing to spend, the result would obviously be affected by how much money people have, a standard flaw of market preference analysis.

Nobody asks the sea otter how much otters are worth. But the presumption that human-kind's use of the world is the sole measure of its value is arrogant. Nor can anyone survey future generations on their valuations of nature. And trying to measure the environment in terms of clean-up costs makes the neat presumption, easy in economics but questionable in nature, that all processes are reversible.

So, correctly pricing the environmental effects of human activities is at best rough guesswork, an attempt to squeeze profound issues of value into a Procrustean bed of price. Ultimately, despite imported trappings of economic analysis, the decision is social: what does society value?

* * *

The market also fails to value adequately the depletion of nonrenewable resources. Again, future generations are largely ignored. How does the market allocate the right of a few generations in the twentieth and twenty-first centuries to use up most of the world's nonrenewable hydrocarbon resources? For a Brazilian gold miner or peasant, suffering in an economy burdened by huge external debts, short-term market rationality may dictate destroying the forest (just as the short-term rationality of the banks collecting their debts indirectly destroys the forest). But its resources of flora and fauna are lost, its land rendered useless. In different ways, then, the extreme inequities of income generated in the global market exhaust the planet —from the pressure of impoverished Third World masses on the land to the disproportionate consumption of nonrenewable resources and generation of waste in the richest countries....

Laissez-faire religion rests on the blind faith that maximizing profits will over time yield the most rational results. Yet even within a capitalist framework, far-sighted investment at the expense of current profits often makes sense. Critics

have charged, with compelling evidence, that the short-term preoccupations of American business have weakened the American economy. With regard to nature, myopic economic calculation is even more devastating. Given the scale and toxicity of human activity today, waiting for the market to signal a need for change may result in catastrophic, even irreversible damage, such as global warming or extinction of valuable species. There is a fundamental conflict, Daly and Cobb argue, between short-term profit maximization and the real needs and concrete resources of the whole community far into the future.

DEFERRING GRATIFICATION

Again, the calculations of the market are inadequate. Economists often discount a future sum of money, figuring its present value as the amount that, if put in the bank at current interest rates, would yield the future sum. For the same reasons that bedevil other efforts to price nature, such discounting fails to assess the future value of the environment. From a free-market perspective, it may be rational for the private owner to kill the goose that lays the golden egg—if it can be sold now for more than its discounted future value and the proceeds invested. But thereby, Daly and Cobb argue, "society has lost a perpetual stream of golden eggs."

When we consider how long certain toxic substances and especially radioactive wastes are likely to remain threats, the problem is compounded: we rob the inheritance of future generations and leave them with a poisonous debt. If future people could be consulted, they would never sign the one-sided contract now being written. We can conclude that for several different reasons the market doesn't accurately price goods so as to take account of their environmental consequences. It ignores negative and positive externalities, ill accounts for depletion of natural resources, inappropriately measures income and welfare, and fails to take responsibility for future generations' welfare.

* * *

Since the defense of the market usually rests in large part on its ability to allocate resources efficiently and provide accurate information through prices, this failure to incorporate the environment is not a trifling flaw.

Can it be corrected? Increasingly some environmentalists argue for "green taxes" that would adjust prices upward to include uncounted environmental costs. U.S. energy users don't pay directly for as much as $300 billion a year in subsidies and tax credits (at least $50 billion a year, mainly to fossil fuels and nuclear power), environmental degradation, damage to health, military expenditures (the Gulf War alone would have added approximately $25 a barrel to imported oil), or employment effects of energy policies, according to Harold M. Hubbard, a scientist at Resources for the Future. By other calculations, we should now be paying more than $100 a barrel for oil if all costs were included. But Hubbard acknowledges that "calculating the actual cost of energy is not a simple matter.... The answers that economists derive may depend as much on social values as they do on analytical solutions to well-defined problems."

If consumers had to pay directly for the full price of energy, several things would happen. First, there would be economic shock and an increase in inequality. In general, the proportion of income spent on energy declines as income increases, although the use of energy increases (at the lowest income levels a decline in car ownership modifies this trend). Then there would be attempts to cope, by cutting back some use (much use is not very discretionary), and then, more important, by increasing efficiency. Also, other energy alternatives would become more competitive. And there would obviously be public clamor to do something—from unleashing nuclear power to promoting solar energy.

U.S. experience after the OPEC price increases of the 1970s illustrates the mixed record on market response to higher energy prices. Because the economy was ill-prepared to absorb the shocks, much of the stagflation of the decade can be attributed to everybody's efforts to pass on the costs to someone else. But the U.S. economy, with some governmental encouragement, also became more energy efficient. In little more than a decade after the first OPEC price increase, the energy intensity of the U.S. economy—energy per unit of GNP—dropped by about one-fourth. Energy production, including new sources of oil, increased in response to higher prices—but far less than mainstream economists predicted.

Much of the efficiency gain was driven by government regulation as well as by market factors. But what's remarkable is how limited the response was, considering the potential. After all, even before the OPEC price hikes, Germany and Japan used roughly half as much energy per unit of GNP as the United States and afterward still made efficiency gains nearly as great or greater than the United States did. Further, using technologies that are commercially available now, the United States could reduce its electric energy consumption by 70 percent at less than the present cost of generating electricity, according to analyses by efficiency guru Amory Lovins's Rocky Mountain Institute. Although the U.S. auto industry, forced by federal standards as much as by prices, made dramatic efficiency gains, the auto industry is still far from realizing the potential of diesel or gasoline engines, not to mention more advanced power sources.

Still, raising the price to some estimated real price would be a clumsy, slow, inequitable way of bringing about needed changes. First, there is nothing intrinsically good—and a lot bad—about high energy prices. What society needs is an inexpensive way to get necessary work done without the externalized costs. The question is: how do we get there in the most socially desirable way?

WILL GOVERNMENT REGULATION WORK?

Direct government intervention is, despite market mania, often the best route. Japanese industries have become leaders in efficiency because "the government spurred their enthusiasm through a carefully coordinated, long-range program that continues even today," the *Wall Street Journal* recently reported. "One clear lesson to learn from Japan is that forcing core industries to become more energy-efficient is one thing that government *can* do well." Other industrialized countries are more energy efficient than the United States because of public investment in their public mass transit systems or because of explicit government strategies, such as Danish support of wind power.

Why hasn't the price of energy—even taking into account the decline

in real oil prices in the mid-eighties —spurred more response? Consumers often are ill-informed about alternatives and find it difficult to make lifetime energy cost assessments (cheap initial cost of a regular incandescent bulb is more persuasive than the argument that lifetime costs of an expensive compact fluorescent are lower, for example). Even many industries simply don't understand how energy efficiency can benefit them. They insist that they recover the entire cost of efficiency investments in a year or two, although they might plan on recovering other investments in five years. Sometimes consumers don't directly make decisions: developers or landlords may make choices based on their costs, leaving tenants with higher bills.

* * *

There are large-scale institutional obstacles to change as well. Automobile manufacturers are to some extent captives of tastes they have created, but like the rest of the auto-oil-highway complex, they have a huge stake in keeping changes incremental—only anticipation of direct governmental edicts on alternatives to gasoline engines is leading manufacturers to gear up for electric vehicles. And private companies are largely incapable of making the kinds of massive investments needed for expanded rail or mass transit.

There are countless other ways in which businesses and consumers would not respond rationally or quickly even to prices that fully reflect environmental costs. Especially in making a major transition, the market is sticky, chaotic, and inefficient. For example, many farmers would like to shift from a less chemically intensive regime, especially as they become aware that it is not only economically viable but much healthier. But making the transition can be too costly —for example, suffering severe losses for several years until alternative controls of pests and weeds begin to work well.

Or take the case of photovoltaic cells, clearly a much-needed technology of the near future. Even though deep-pockets energy corporations bought up solar cell firms in the seventies, U.S. companies have been abandoning the field, in some cases selling off to European firms. This highlights another limit to the market model of efficiency: there are significant cultural differences, especially regarding long-term investment, and differences in levels of government support for alternative energy policies. Both affect market responses.

REGULATION CAN HELP COMPETITION

Free-market enthusiasts insist that private businesses be allowed to innovate in response to market signals. But it is socially undesirable to treat the corporation as a black box, ignoring what goes on inside it and tinkering only with the price signals going in and then coping with what comes out. This is especially true in an era when large, multinational corporations dominate the global economy: their power, size, and internal governance distort idealized market responses to price signals.

Corporate policies vary significantly. At 3M Company, executives wisely instituted its "Pollution Prevention Pays" program and have saved $482 million since 1975, eliminated five hundred thousand tons of waste, and saved another $650 million through energy conservation. But what happens when a company compares polluting and nonpolluting alternatives and calculates that pollution does pay? Or take another example, representing a more familiar route in the eighties. Phillips Petroleum, under pressure of debt incurred in fighting off a hostile takeover, laid off experienced union workers and replaced them with ill-trained contract workers, took short-cuts on safety, and pushed production to the limit. The result was a major explosion in Pasadena, Texas, that killed twenty-six people and spread toxic materials throughout the environment.

Many businesses around the world have become more innovative and competitive as a result of strict environmental regulations. Both Germany and Japan have tougher standards than the United States and are growing faster. Some of the most strictly regulated U.S. industries, such as chemical, synthetics, and fabrics, have gained international competitiveness. Yet many businesses have chosen the path followed by a large segment of southern California's furniture industry: faced with tougher emissions standards, they fled to Mexico, where pollution laws are not enforced.

What makes one company prevent pollution while improving its ability to compete and another company endanger its employees and the surrounding community or flee abroad? Why does one business seize opportunities to become energy efficient and another respond to competitive pressures by shortchanging workers? How these distinct strategies emerge varies, but the general point is that when free marketeers talk about giving businesses flexibility and allowing the market to stimulate innovation, part of the flexibility and innovation will be socially good and part terrible. Why let private business make that momentous decision? Why should society wait until after the dirty deed is done to try to clean up the mess? . . .

NIGHTMARE OF CONSUMPTION

Despite our own problems of inequality of consumption, which tear at the social fabric of the United States, an overemphasis on commodity consumption is the industrialized world's environmental nightmare. In mass-consumption societies self-fulfillment is defined in terms of buying more things, which leads to a disproportionate use of the world's resources and contributes to waste crises, from localized conflicts over municipal dumps to global destruction of the ozone layer. Of course, if raw materials were more accurately priced and if corporations were responsible for what happened to the waste they produced, there could be more reusable or at least recyclable packaging and less waste, all without a loss of meaningful consumption.

Environmentalists have contended that we must recognize limits to growth, a most unpopular prospect for both liberals and conservatives. Technically, the limit to a sustainable economy is the amount of solar energy falling on the earth that can reasonably be captured, even though there are much stricter limits on supplies of nonrenewable resources. The specter of global warming or holes in the ozone layer suggests that we could reach the limit of our use of nonrenewable fuels faster than we actually exhaust the earth's resources. Certainly there is no way that the earth can support the spread of wealthy, industrialized nations' current extravagant consumption to the world's poor. Environmentalists are divided over what are the limits to the earth's capacity, but markets have no way of even considering the question: unending growth is both their assumption and goal.

The alternative does not have to be for the richer nations to take vows of poverty. Some of our problems come from relying on the dynamics of commodity production rather than considering what needs we have and how those can be best served. We want homes and offices that are comfortable and well-lighted. But electric utilities want to sell electricity. It would be better for everyone if they devoted their resources to promoting energy efficiency, but they will only do so, in most cases, if they are compensated for part of sales forgone through efficiency-reduced demand. Increasingly, public utility commissions are enforcing such policies, and municipally owned utilities have aggressively pursued this service-oriented alternative because they are not profit oriented.

Environmental concerns should be added to many other motivations—political, philosophical, religious—to challenge the model of "economic man" that market society helps to create. The highly individualistic, cost-minimizing, profit-seeking mentality of market society is not a result of "human nature" but a cultural construction that denies a place for many values and feelings that have appeared in most human societies. True, there are flaky manifestations of new-age spiritualism associated with the environmental movement, but the desire for a sense of human community and harmony with the world is widespread and authentic.

The logic of free-market economics creates untenable abstractions, as Daly and Cobb, following economic historian Karl Polanyi, emphasize. In the laissez-faire market vision, nature becomes land. Then land itself is left out of the calculation, with the assumption that it is interchangeable with humanly created capital. Life becomes labor, or abstract labor-power, and patrimony becomes capital. All values are reduced to prices. Time is not concrete history, incorporating natural biological processes, but rather an infinite series of equivalent seconds. Places with distinctive features disappear into an interchangeable abstract space. By contrast, ecology reminds us that we live in a concrete world, and that we often end up committing real, not just intellectual, violence upon nature, humanity, and history.

HOW DO WE DEAL WITH MARKETS?

So what do we do with markets? First, we must put them in their place, and that place is secondary to considerations of social values. The fundamental flaws in the market, from the environmental perspective alone, are enough to undo economists' claims for marketplace superiority. The market needs to be subordinated not only to nature but also to broader human values that form a limiting framework. That requires greater international cooperation. (This is already happening to a small extent with bans on whaling and the ivory trade and international agreements on reducing chlorofluorocarbons.) But ironically it also requires granting nations and communities power to enforce stronger standards to respond to their own local needs without having those undermined in the name of free trade.

Some environmentalists (including the Environmental Defense Fund and a group convened under senators Tim Wirth and the late John Heinz called Project 88) have argued that market-oriented regulations, such as tradable permits for discharges, will achieve environmental goals efficiently. The 1990 Clean Air Act revisions introduce such tradable permits, and the Chicago Board of Trade now plans a futures market in pollution permits. There are numerous objections: such trade *legitimates* pollution, it is likely to disadvantage the poor and powerless (especially if conducted on an international scale), regulatory regimes are already fairly flexible, and markets in such permits may be hard to establish and inefficient. The only evidence for efficiency so far comes from econometric studies already biased towards market solutions. Depending on the prices of permits or the level of taxes imposed, polluters could decide it was still cheaper to pollute.

Even more important, a focus on finding these market solutions diverts us from the main point. Nearly all these regulatory regimes represent attempts to control emissions, but as ecologist Barry Commoner argues in his book *Making Peace with the Planet*, regulatory efforts have at best slowed only slightly the rate of environmental deterioration. The real environmental successes have only come with outright bans of certain substances, such as lead in gasoline or paint. Instead of quibbling over how much toxic substance can be released, regulation should increasingly establish a standard of zero discharge. "The tax [on pollutants] can't work until you've done the wrong thing," Commoner says. "You can't have a market in pollutant rights until you have pollutants." The solution is prevention.

But prevention can't always be outright banning: for the foreseeable future, at least some hydrocarbons will be burned. In many cases, transitions to zero discharge may take time. During that period, using tradable permits or other market-oriented methods should be considered along with flexible regulation. But rather than a panacea, such devices represent an interesting gimmick of unproven value.

WHAT FORCES WILL WORK BEST?

There is increased interest in energy or carbon taxes to discourage fossil-fuel use and give better signals on the true costs of burning hydrocarbons, especially nonrenewable sources. Eliminating subsidies to dangerous or polluting sources, such as nuclear power, would also give more appropriate prices.

It's obvious that energy is mispriced and consequently misused, but relying on taxes to bring about a change through the market is likely to create great hardship for low-to-middle-income people and increase inequality. Ideally, a transition would not greatly increase energy bills but would increase energy prices steadily in tandem with changes to alternative, renewable energy sources, a different mix of technologies, and greater energy efficiency. If the government developed a strategy for transition to an essentially solar economy, then regular increases in energy taxes could be used for a variety of projects, including research. Federal, state, and local governments can have a tremendous impact: government purchases of solar cells or hydrogen- or electric-powered cars could speed the learning curve and cut prices quickly. Public investment would be needed to develop mass transit and railroads. A full-scale industrial extension service to promote energy efficiency and nonpolluting technologies could speed industrial transitions with less disruption. But

if energy taxes are going to work most effectively, it should not be simply through the indirect effect of higher prices but also through the investment of the new revenue in efficiency and alternatives.

*   *   *

Green consumerism and protest already have had some impact. McDonald's, responding to a campaign against its styrofoam clamshell, has switched packaging and is considering composting of its food wastes. Other businesses sense a good market, although many are as duplicitous as Mobil Chemical, whose representative said its "biodegradable" plastic trash bags "are not an answer to landfill crowding or littering.... Degradability is just a marketing tool.... We're talking out of both sides of our mouths because we want to sell bags." Green consumerism is an important phenomenon but is likely to remain marginal without other reinforcing measures.

There must first be clear public policy. A mixture of direct government actions (purchases, subsidies, prohibitions, research, and technical assistance) can be combined with changed market incentives (for example, taxes and markets in efficiency) in ways that complement each other. Public policy, however, should determine the direction.

The disastrous effects of centralized government control in the communist countries should remain a reminder that government is no guarantee of virtue. Clearly government in the United States and elsewhere has often been the captive of corporate interests. Environmental values, like other values, must be cultivated among the electorate if public policy is going to change. In the long run, altering the "economic man" outlook of market society will make environmental goals easier to attain.

Much of the progress toward environmental sanity in the United States has come as a result of grass-roots protest, environmental impact fights, and legal action over local issues. Often dismissed as NIMBYism—not-in-my-backyard—these movements are often concerned about other backyards as well. Even now the grass-roots protesters among environmentalists exert pressure on the bigger, established environmental groups that are entrapped in the rulemaking squabbles of federal legislation and tempted to form alliances with big corporations (at times having an influence, yet also subtly losing their independence).

Besides guaranteeing a free and full role for citizen protest, which big corporations especially want to eliminate, it is important that workers have broad powers to influence the safety and health of their work environment. Like the proverbial canaries in coal mines of the past, they are the first victims of pollution and toxicity. Giving them powers to protect themselves, with mandated worker health and safety committees in every workplace, protects everyone else.

Environmental values lead to a model of society that subordinates the market to nature, but environmentalists cannot claim nature as their model any more than the free marketeers can call their model "natural." No model of society is natural; all are historical, cultural creations. And nature itself has forever been altered by human culture.

A new model of society can aspire to respect nature and to make culture and nature as compatible as possible. The implications of the environmental critique go beyond traditional ecological issues. Many similar critiques of the market can be made on behalf of other cultural values. The market, for example, does not take into account the externalities of human poverty and inequality, economic dislocation, stunted work lives, and destruction of community. It gives the wrong price signals, the wrong information. In taming the market to protect nature, we should not forget the well-being of those most curious natural creatures—ourselves.

POSTSCRIPT

Should Pollution Be Put to the Market Test?

For the past 30 years a massive effort has been put forth in the United States to advance environmental protection by using laws and regulation. Efforts can be traced back to the 1970 National Environmental Policy Act (NEPA), the first modern environmental statute that required environmental impact statements on federal projects. That same year, Congress also passed the Clean Air Act, which replaced a weak environmental statute with enforceable, federal clean-air standards and timetables for industry to meet. Seven years later, the Clean Water Act (1977) was passed. This act established standards and permits, and it attempted to limit discharges in navigable waters and to protect wetlands from exploration.

At first, federal action was directed toward air- and water-pollution control; this was accomplished by issuing regulations and permits. The second set of initiatives focused on cleaning up hazardous waste dumps. This action was first authorized by the Resource Conservation and Recovery Act (RCRA) of 1976, which established a permit system for disposal sites and regulated underground storage tanks. Later initiatives in this area were authorized by the Comprehensive Environmental Response, Compensation, and Liability Act (CERCLA) of 1980. This act, known as Superfund, created a fund to finance the clean-up of hazardous waste sites.

What is significant is that, until recently, efforts to control, contain, and eliminate pollution and its effects have been accomplished largely by government regulation. Economists such as Blinder have argued for policies that capture and utilize the strength of the market. However, as Moberg argues, the opposition has been successful in warning public policy away from a free-market perspective that would allow "the private owner to kill the goose that lays the golden egg" and in the process deny society "a perpetual stream of golden eggs."

For a review of the legislation in the air pollution area, see Richard H. Schulze, "The 20-Year History of the Evolution of Air Pollution Control Legislation in the U.S.A.," *Atmospheric Environment* (March 1993). For a discussion of some of the ethical issues surrounding pollution permits, see Paul Steichmeier, "The Morality of Pollution Permits," *Environmental Ethics* (Summer 1993). And for other economic interpretations, see Dwight R. Lee, "An Economist's Perspective on Air Pollution," *Environmental Science and Technology* (October 1993) and Joe Alper, "Protecting the Environment With the Power of the Market," *Science* (June 25, 1993).

ISSUE 18

Has the North American Free Trade Agreement Been a Success?

YES: Joe Cobb, from "A Successful Agreement," *The World & I* (October 1997)

NO: Alan Tonelson, from "A Failed Approach," *The World & I* (October 1997)

ISSUE SUMMARY

YES: Joe Cobb, president of the Trade Policy Institute in Washington, D.C., asserts that the North American Free Trade Agreement (NAFTA) has been a success. He cites evidence that the average living standards of American workers have improved; that U.S. exports have increased; and that the average annual growth rates of the United States, Canada, and Mexico are greater than they otherwise would have been.

NO: Researcher Alan Tonelson negatively assesses NAFTA based on his contentions that the real winners were large U.S. multinational corporations, that median wages in the United States and Mexico have declined, and that the flows of illegal immigrants and drugs into the United States from Mexico are high.

The North American Free Trade Agreement (NAFTA) was signed into law in the fall of 1993. The passage of NAFTA was no simple matter. Although the basic agreement was negotiated by the Republican Bush administration, the Democratic Clinton administration faced the challenge of convincing Congress and the American people that NAFTA would work to the benefit of the United States as well as Mexico. In meeting this challenge President Bill Clinton did not hesitate to use a bit of drama to press the case for NAFTA. He gathered together former U.S. presidents George Bush, Ronald Reagan, Jimmy Carter, Gerald Ford, and Richard Nixon and had them speak out in support of NAFTA. The public debate probably reached its zenith with a face-to-face confrontation between Ross Perot, perhaps the most visible and most outspoken opponent of NAFTA, and Vice President Al Gore on the *Larry King Live* television show. The vote on NAFTA in the House of Representatives reflected the sharpness of the debate; it passed by only a slim margin.

In pressing the case for NAFTA, proponents in the United States raised two major points. The first point was economic: NAFTA would produce real economic benefits, including increased employment in the United States and increased productivity. The second point was political: NAFTA would support the political and economic reforms being made in Mexico and promote further progress in these two domains. These reforms had made Mexico a "better" neighbor; that is, Mexico had taken steps to become more like the United States, and NAFTA would support further change. Both of these two major points reinforced a third claim made on behalf of NAFTA: the improvements in economic and political conditions in Mexico might lead to a reduction in the flows of illegal immigrants and drugs into the United States. In fighting NAFTA, opponents in the United States countered both of these points. They argued that freer trade between the United States and Mexico would mean a loss of American jobs—Ross Perot's "giant sucking sound" was the transfer of work and jobs from the United States to Mexico. Opponents argued that the notion of passing NAFTA as a reward to the Mexican government was premature; the government had not done enough to improve economic and political conditions in Mexico.

Implementation of NAFTA began in 1994. But events in Mexico during 1994 and 1995 took an interesting series of twists. By December 1994 the Mexican economy faced a balance-of-payments crisis—and the peso began to depreciate. In order to prevent a collapse of the Mexican economy, President Clinton organized a $50 billion multilateral assistance effort that included $20 billion of U.S. credit. The Mexican government also took action, including making cuts in government spending and increases in interest rates. The net result of these events was a deep recession in the Mexican economy with a contraction of 7 percent during the first three quarters of 1995.

In assessing the impact of NAFTA, there are any number of different perspectives that can be employed. Should the focus be economic, political, or both? Should the evaluation concentrate on the benefits and costs to the United States, to Mexico, or both? Should Canada be added to the mix? How much of the economic and political history that follows NAFTA can be attributed to NAFTA, and how much can be attributed to other factors? When is the appropriate time for an evaluation?

Some of the difficulties of evaluation are captured in the following selections. Both were published four years after the passage of NAFTA and some three-and-one-half years after its implementation. Joe Cobb introduces a number of economic and political considerations to support his strong endorsement of NAFTA. Alan Tonelson also takes up economic and political arguments in presenting his equally strong rejection of NAFTA.

YES

Joe Cobb

A SUCCESSFUL AGREEMENT

During the heated debate about the North American Free Trade Agreement (NAFTA) in 1993, many claims and counterclaims were made about job losses.

Ross Perot coined the famous sound bite "a giant sucking sound" to describe American jobs going south. Now the evidence is in. Hundreds of thousands of U.S. jobs have *not* been destroyed, and the U.S. manufacturing base has *not* been weakened.

Instead, U.S. exports and employment levels have risen significantly as total trade among the NAFTA countries has increased, and the average living standards of American workers have improved. The general unemployment rate declined to 5.3 percent in 1996 from 6.8 percent in 1993.

In 1996, U.S. global trade (exports plus imports) totaled $1.765 trillion —over 23 percent of U.S. GDP [gross domestic product], compared with 10 percent in 1970. The Office of the U.S. Trade Representative (USTR) has estimated that by the year 2010, trade will represent about 36 percent of U.S. GDP. Today, more than 11 million U.S. jobs depend on exports, 1.5 million more than in 1992. Roughly a quarter of U.S. economic growth during the Clinton administration has been due to export expansion.

Total North American trade increased $127 billion during NAFTA's first three years, from $293 billion in 1993 to $420 billion in 1996, a gain of 43 percent. Canada and Mexico are already the top two U.S. trading partners, but if the post-NAFTA increase in trade with them had been with a single country, it would make that country the fourth-largest U.S. trading partner.

In 1996, U.S. exports to Canada and Mexico, at $190 billion, exceeded U.S. exports to any other area of the world, including the entire Pacific Rim or all of Europe. Mexico and Canada purchased $3 of every $10 in U.S. exports and supplied $3 of every $10 in U.S. imports in 1996.

While NAFTA involves both Canada and Mexico, the controversy in 1993 was whether adding Mexico would have bad effects for the American worker. But obviously, the economic growth from increased trade with Mexico has not hurt. U.S. exports to Mexico are up 37 percent from 1993, reaching a record $57 billion in 1996.

During NAFTA's first three years, 39 of the 50 states increased their exports to Mexico, and 44 states reported a growth in exports to Mexico during 1996, as the pace of U.S. exports to that country accelerated.

According to the U.S. Department of Commerce, U.S. exports to Mexico in the fourth quarter of 1996 were growing at an annualized rate of $64 billion. Moreover, U.S. market share in Mexico increased from 69 percent of total Mexican imports in 1993 to 76 percent in 1996.

Total two-way trade between the United States and Mexico was nearly $130 billion. During this period, U.S. exports to Canada also increased by $134 billion, or 33 percent. Total two-way trade between the United States and Canada was $290 billion in 1996.

A close look at the numbers shows there is a U.S. trade deficit with both Canada and Mexico, but the success of NAFTA once again proves there is nothing wrong with trade deficits, as economists have taught for over 200 years. The combined U.S. trade deficit with Canada and Mexico increased from $9 billion in 1992 to $39.9 billion in 1996. But since 1992, the U.S. economy has created 12 million new jobs (net). Manufacturing employment grew from 16.9 million jobs in 1992 to 18.3 million in 1993, an increase of 1.4 million net new jobs.

The U.S. Department of Labor lists more than 110,000 U.S. workers as certified for training assistance under NAFTA's Trade Adjustment Assistance Program, which indicates that Perot was not entirely wrong. Those Americans lost their jobs because of NAFTA. But the negative impact of NAFTA each week must have been very small if only 110,000 jobs is the total after three years.

Although 110,000 families were hit hard by NAFTA, the job-loss rate in the United States, as reported by the number of new unemployment insurance claims, is normally about 350,000 every week. Moreover, the U.S. economy currently creates more than 110,000 new jobs (net) in about two weeks. On the positive side of the employment issue, U.S. exports to NAFTA countries currently support 2.3 million U.S. jobs, according to the USTR.

A study by economist Richard Nadler, who reviewed U.S. standards of living before and after NAFTA was launched in 1994, found that the rate of increase in personal wealth has more than tripled since NAFTA was implemented.

His review measured the improvement in three ways: First, growth in disposable personal income, adjusted for inflation, averaged 1.89 percent annually in 1994–95, compared with 0.25 percent annually 1990–93. Second, personal consumption expenditures grew by an inflation-adjusted 1.76 percent annually during 1994–95, compared with 0.56 percent a year in 1990–93.

Finally, inflation-adjusted GDP per capita grew by 1.79 percent annually in 1994–95, compared with only 0.23 percent during 1990–93. Of course, there was a recession in 1990–91, which slowed down the economy in the pre-NAFTA period, but perhaps NAFTA has helped prevent a recession since then.

INVESTMENT BOOM

The major complaint against NAFTA by organized labor during the 1993 controversy over adopting the treaty was the fear that new investments would be made south of the border instead of in U.S. factories. There has indeed been an investment boom in Mexico, but the inflow has not seemed to have any depressing effect on the United States.

NAFTA has encouraged U.S. and foreign investors with apparel and footwear factories in Asia to relocate their production operations to Mexico. This diversion of investment from Asia to Mexico "saved the heavier end of clothing manufacture in the United States: the textile mills," according to Nadler.

NAFTA has been very good for the traditional southern textile states like North Carolina and Alabama, as well as for major U.S. agricultural states such as Montana, Nebraska, and North Dakota, whose politicians in Congress typically opposed it.

The investment boom in Mexico has been a major source of new demand for U.S. manufacturers of capital goods. The largest post-NAFTA gains in U.S. exports to Mexico have been in such high-technology manufacturing sectors as industrial machinery, transportation and electronic equipment, plastics and rubber, fabricated metal products, and chemicals.

A recent economic analysis published by the U.S. Federal Reserve Bank of Chicago concludes that NAFTA will lead to output gains for all three participant countries. The study concluded that, under NAFTA, the sustained annual growth rate of the three economies is permanently higher than it would be otherwise.

Mexico's GDP is predicted to rise by an added factor of 3.26 percent, U.S. GDP by 0.24 percent, and Canada's GDP by 0.11 percent. These gains are roughly twice as large as those predicted by previous forecasts of NAFTA's potential for accelerated growth in North American trade, output, and employment.

In general, bilateral Mexican-North American trade should increase about 20 percent as a result of NAFTA. This projected growth also means more U.S. jobs and a higher standard of living for American workers.

One of NAFTA's main purposes was to "lock in" the process of economic and political reform in Mexico, which started in the late 1980s. Mexico's membership in NAFTA, the World Trade Organization, the Asia-Pacific Economic Cooperation forum, and the Organization for Economic Cooperation and Development has created international commitments and linkages that politicians in Mexico cannot ignore.

Mexico's constitution was amended in 1996 to make the electoral process more transparent and independent of the government. These reforms had a dramatic effect on July 6, 1997, when opposition parties obtained a majority in Mexico's congressional elections for the first time. There can be no doubt that NAFTA is a major factor in Mexico's congressional elections for the first time. There can be no doubt that NAFTA is a major factor in Mexico's transformation toward a free-market democracy on the U.S.-Canadian model.

The proposals to expand NAFTA to include Chile and other countries of the Western Hemisphere are questioned by doubters, but the evidence is already clear. As a market for U.S. goods, the Western Hemisphere already is nearly twice as large as the European Union and nearly 50 percent larger than Asia. The Western Hemisphere accounted for 39 percent of U.S. goods exports in 1996 and was the only region in which the United States recorded a trade surplus in both 1995 and '96.

Moreover, while U.S. goods exports to the world generally increased 57 percent from 1990 to 1996, U.S. exports to Latin America and the Caribbean (excluding Mexico) increased by 110 percent during the same period. If current trends continue, Latin America alone will exceed Japan and western Europe combined as an export market for U.S. goods by the year 2010.

There should be no doubts about the success of NAFTA. Although only three years old, this international trade agreement has far exceeded the expectations of its advocates back in 1993. Even though three years may seem like too little time to reach any final judgments about NAFTA, it already is clear that critics of this agreement have been wrong on all counts.

NO

Alan Tonelson

A FAILED APPROACH

In 1992, Bill Clinton won the presidency in part by making a very quotable, trenchant point about George Bush's economic record. Everything that was supposed to be going up, he and Al Gore emphasized repeatedly, was going down. And everything that was supposed to be going down was going up.

Five years later, a similar point can be made about NAFTA, the North American Free Trade Agreement completed by the Clinton administration in late 1993. In fact, few public policy initiatives in recent memory have so mercilessly and consistently mocked their champions' predictions.

Today, NAFTA supporters want to extend the treaty's terms to the rest of the Western Hemisphere, starting with Chile.... [T]he administration is expected to submit to Congress its request for fast-track authority for these and a series of other major trade talks. But the cracked crystal ball of NAFTA lobbyists in and out of government should call into question not only their credentials as analysts but their entire approach to economic globalization.

NAFTA was advertised as nothing less than a godsend to the United States, Canada, and Mexico—a boon not only to broad-based prosperity throughout North America but for social progress and political stability in Mexico in particular.

By the entirely reasonable Clinton-Gore up-down standards, however, NAFTA's results have been positively perverse—except for the big U.S. multinational corporations that dominate North American trade flows.

The impact of NAFTA and NAFTA-style globalization has been especially damaging in the United States and Mexico, whose recent trade record will understandably be the focus of Congress' upcoming NAFTA expansion debate.

Since NAFTA's late-1993 signing, median wages in the United States and Mexico are down, as is employment in manufacturing, which generates an economy's highest-paying jobs on average.

The U.S. trade deficit with Mexico, on the other hand, is way up. So are flows of illegal drugs and immigrants from Mexico into the United States— even though NAFTA was supposed to make Mexico so prosperous that its people would be able to earn a decent living by staying home and out of

From Alan Tonelson, "A Failed Approach," *The World & I*, vol. 12, no. 10 (October 1997).

criminal activity. And despite NAFTA's ostensible national security dimension—preventing chaos on America's southern border—social and political instability in Mexico are way up, too, as is anti-Americanism.

NAFTA supporters point to two of their own rising indicators to score the agreement as a success: the simple post-NAFTA expansion of trade within North America and the continued healthy levels of U.S. exports to Mexico despite the peso collapse and subsequent Mexican depression.

Expanded trade, however, is at best a peculiar measure of economic policy success. In the first place, most of the U.S.-Mexico trade expansion has come in the form of rising U.S. imports from Mexico.

Rising imports, of course, can be a sign of national economic health, and bilateral trade deficits are not always bad or even important. But in America's current circumstances, the jump in imports from Mexico is adding significantly to a U.S. global deficit that sets new records every year. That deficit persists despite the vaunted competitive comeback of American industry during the 1990s, a historically weak dollar, and unimpressive recent relative growth rates.

Although macroeconomists have assured us that the gap would close, the Fed now judges the economy's overall growth rate is being cut by about a third. In fact, significantly reducing America's global trade deficit might actually enable the U.S. economy to grow fast enough to push up real wages for most Americans—something that hasn't happened on a sustained basis since 1973.

Just as important, expanded trade per se has no place as a major goal of U.S. foreign economic policy. It is simply a means to an end. The raison d'être of any economic policy is encouraging a healthy and sustained rise in living standards for the vast majority of Americans. Failure to meet this goal dwarfs any other economic achievements, whether low inflation, expanded productivity, rising stock markets, or even strong overall growth.

INTRA-COMPANY TRADE

As for the levels of U.S. exports to Mexico, a look beneath the surface reveals how misleading such aggregate figures can be. According to a UCLA study commissioned by the Clinton administration itself, post-NAFTA U.S.-Mexican trade has been driven "almost entirely" by the growth of intra-company trade.

Such exports, which represent a large (more than one-third) and growing share of overall goods exports, do more to destroy good jobs than to create them. The reasons can be complex, but the export argument is so central to the pro-NAFTA case that they are worth examining in some detail.

Traditional goods exports—which consist of sales of finished products from U.S. companies to unrelated customers abroad—boost American employment by expanding a company's customer base and thus require increased production and often more employees to meet the new demand. U.S. intra-company exports, for their part, consist of the shipments of parts and components of finished products from individual companies' U.S.-based factories to their overseas factories.

These foreign facilities perform further manufacturing or final assembly work. From the standpoint of creating high-paying manufacturing jobs for Americans, such exports are a growing problem, because in most cases the assembly or further manufacturing used to be done in this country.

Intra-company exports can still produce U.S. jobs in net if shipping some production abroad helps U.S. businesses increase final overseas sales or recapture markets at home—say, by enabling companies to customize their products to suit local tastes in new markets.

But much of the new U.S. manufacturing investment abroad is in countries like Mexico, whose people are generally too poor to buy what they make, and/or that are trying to export their way to national prosperity and thus artificially depress consumption. Moreover, the figures for U.S. industries like autos—where U.S. investment has been enormous—indicate that very little of what they produce in Mexico is exported outside North America.

Instead, much of the U.S. multinationals' foreign output gets sent right back to America for final sale. And since virtually no U.S. industries with big American payrolls have won back much domestic market share since NAFTA's signing, it's clear that intra-company trade amounts to America largely exporting to itself. This means that most of the new production in countries like Mexico is simply replacing production in the United States.

Exactly how much do U.S. multinationals produce abroad for eventual sale back to the United States? Only the companies and Washington know for sure. But the former want to keep this information secret—largely to avoid a public relations nightmare.

The latter simply swallows the corporate line about the need to protect trade secrets. In the case of Mexico, however, the scale of this ersatz exporting can be measured by looking at Mexican government figures. They tell us that, currently, 62 percent of all U.S. exports to Mexico are eventually reexported back to the United States—up from 40 percent before NAFTA.

When Vice President Gore debated Ross Perot in 1993 on the treaty's merits, he used booming new Mexican Wal-Marts as symbols for the huge new Mexican consumer market he claimed NAFTA would open for American companies and workers alike. A better symbol would be Mexican autoworkers performing sophisticated, highly productive manufacturing work that used to be done in America—at one-eighth the wage.

MEXICO'S CRISIS

NAFTA supporters offer a superficially convincing alibi for Mexico's ills, blaming them entirely on the peso crash, not the trade treaty. But they conveniently overlook the role played by NAFTA-style economic liberalization policies in triggering Mexico's crisis—principally, hooking Mexico on inflows of foreign capital that the country's corrupt leaders could sustain politically only by overvaluing their currency and artificially increasing the average Mexican's purchasing power. In addition, any U.S. administration failing to anticipate such an extraordinary event is obviously not competent to make Mexico policy to begin with.

The NAFTA lobby also insists that without the treaty, high-paying manufacturing jobs would continue to flee overseas—only they would wind up in East Asia, where manufacturers use far fewer U.S.-made inputs and therefore far fewer U.S. workers. They're right, but their point unwittingly indicts the broader globalization approach they favor.

In the world created by these policies:

- where the U.S. permits many of its biggest trading partners to shut out competitive American-made goods;
- where American companies therefore have little choice but to remain competitive by cutting costs through outsourcing to low-wage countries;
- and where the enormous U.S. market remains wide open to goods carrying American brand names but produced in countries where cheap and even child and slave labor is abundant, where unions are violently repressed, and where job safety and serious environmental-regulations protections are virtually unknown;

it is indeed better to use NAFTA to encourage production in Mexico rather than in China or Indonesia. Yet simply accepting these conditions ultimately condemns American workers and their foreign counterparts to a global race to the bottom in terms of wages and working conditions.

Replacing the failed NAFTA approach to North American trade alone will not turn globalization into a winner for workers at home and abroad. But with the fast-track debate looming this fall, it's the ideal place to start.

POSTSCRIPT

Has the North American Free Trade Agreement Been a Success?

Cobb begins his positive evaluation of NAFTA by stating that the NAFTA opponents' two major claims have been proven false: the U.S. manufacturing base remains strong, and hundreds of thousands of jobs have not been lost. Instead, for the overall U.S. economy, exports are up, employment has increased, total trade has expanded, and the average standard of living of American workers has increased. Cobb reports that during NAFTA's first three years the following has resulted: total North American trade increased by 43 percent, with 39 of the 50 states increasing their exports to Mexico; U.S. market share in Mexico increased from 69 percent to 76 percent; and U.S. exports to Canada increased by 33 percent. He accepts the U.S. Department of Labor's calculation of 110,000 American workers who qualified for training assistance under NAFTA but offsets this negative effect by stating that at current rates the United States creates more than this number of jobs every two weeks. He also states that U.S. exports to NAFTA countries support 2.3 million U.S. jobs. Furthermore, Cobb offers evidence to support his contention that living standards for American workers have improved, namely that "the rate of increase in personal wealth has more than tripled since NAFTA was implemented." With regard to investment, he agrees that NAFTA has created an investment boom in Mexico, but he argues that this has benefited the United States by increasing the demand for American-produced capital goods. As to political developments in Mexico, Cobb finds that NAFTA has produced positive outcomes in this domain as well.

Tonelson asserts, "Few public policy initiatives in recent memory have so mercilessly and consistently mocked their champions' predictions." He then offers empirical evidence to support his position: median wages in the United States and Mexico are down, as is employment in manufacturing; the U.S. trade deficit with Mexico is up; the flows of illegal immigrants and drugs from Mexico into the United States are up; and anti-Americanism and social and political instability in Mexico have risen. Tonelson also cites a Federal Reserve study that estimates that the trade deficit has cut the U.S. growth rate by about one-third. Citing a study done at the University of California, Los Angeles, that concludes that most of the increase in trade has been an increase in intracompany trade, Tonelson argues that the increase in intraindustry trade means that new Mexican production "is simply replacing production in the United States." Although he is willing to accept the argument that the loss of production to Mexico is better for the United States than the loss of production to the Far East, Tonelson believes that "simply accepting these conditions ultimately condemns American workers and their foreign counterparts to a global race to the bottom in terms of wages and working conditions."

For a taste of the debate before the passage of NAFTA, both pro and con, see *NAFTA: An Assessment*, rev. ed., by Gary Clyde Hufbauer and Jeffery J. Schott (Institute for International Economics, 1993); "Grasping the Benefits of NAFTA," by Peter Morici, *Current History* (February 1993); "The North American Free Trade Agreement," *Economic Report of the President 1993*; "The High Cost of NAFTA," by Timothy Koechlin and Mehrene Larudee, *Challenge* (September/October 1992); and "The NAFTA Illusion," by Jeff Faux, *Challenge* (July/August 1993). For more recent assessments of NAFTA, see "NAFTA's Positive Impact on the United States: A State-by-State Breakdown," by John P. Sweeney, *The Heritage Foundation FYI No. 160* (November 6, 1997); "NAFTA's Three-Year Report Card: An 'A' for North America's Economy," by John P. Sweeney, *The Heritage Foundation Backgrounder No. 1144* (May 16, 1997); and *NAFTA: Experience and Fast-Track Authority* by the Century Foundation (1997).

CONTRIBUTORS
TO THIS VOLUME

EDITORS

THOMAS R. SWARTZ was born in Philadelphia in 1937. He received his B.A. from LaSalle University in 1960, his M.A. from Ohio University in 1962, and his Ph.D. from Indiana University in 1965. He is currently a professor of economics at the University of Notre Dame in Indiana and a fellow of the Institute for Educational Initiatives. He and Frank J. Bonello have coauthored or coedited a number of works. In addition to *Taking Sides,* they have coedited *Alternative Directions in Economic Policy* (University of Notre Dame Press, 1978); *The Supply Side: Debating Current Economic Policies* (Dushkin Publishing Group, 1983); and *Urban Finance Under Siege* (M. E. Sharpe, 1993). He has also coedited or coauthored three other books. His most recent book is entitled *Working and Poor in Urban America.*

FRANK J. BONELLO was born in Detroit in 1939. He received his B.S. in 1961 and his M.A. in 1963, both from the University of Detroit, and his Ph.D. in 1968 from Michigan State University. He is currently an associate professor of economics and the Arts and Letters College Fellow at the University of Notre Dame in Indiana. He writes in the areas of monetary economics and economic education. *Taking Sides* is his seventh book. In addition to being coeditor on several publications with Thomas R. Swartz, he is the author of *The Formulation of Expected Interest Rates* (Michigan State University Press, 1969) and coauthor, with William I. Davisson, of *Computer-Assisted Instruction in Economic Education: A Case Study* (University of Notre Dame Press, 1976).

STAFF

Theodore Knight   List Manager
David Brackley   Senior Developmental Editor
Juliana Poggio   Developmental Editor
Rose Gleich   Administrative Assistant
Brenda S. Filley   Production Manager
Juliana Arbo   Typesetting Supervisor
Diane Barker   Proofreader
Lara Johnson   Design/Advertising Coordinator
Richard Tietjen   Publishing Systems Manager
Larry Killian   Copier Coordinator

AUTHORS

KATHARINE G. ABRAHAM is commissioner for Consumer Prices and Price Indexes at the Bureau of Labor Statistics, U.S. Department of Labor.

ROBERT ALMEDER is a professor of philosophy at Georgia State University and a member of the editorial board of the *Journal of Business Ethics.* He earned his Ph.D. in philosophy at the University of Pennsylvania, and he is the author of *Harmless Naturalism: The Limits of Science and the Nature of Philosophy* (Open Court, 1998).

ROBERT A. BAADE is a professor in the Department of Economics and Business at Lake Forest College in Illinois.

ROBERT M. BALL served as commissioner of Social Security between 1967 and 1973. He was also a member of the 1994–1996 Advisory Council on Social Security. He is the author of *Straight Talk About Social Security* (Twentieth Century Fund Press/Priority Press Publications, 1998).

ERIC BATES is investigative editor of *Southern Exposure* and a staff writer for *The Independent* in Durham, North Carolina. He is coeditor, with Bob Hall, of *Ruling the Roost: What's Bigger Than Tobacco, More Dangerous Than Mining, and Foul to Eat?* (Southern Exposure, 1989).

ALAN S. BLINDER is the Gordon S. Rentschler Memorial Professor of Economics at Princeton University. He is a former vice chairman of the Federal Reserve Board and a former member of President Bill Clinton's Council of Economic Advisers.

MICHAEL J. BOSKIN is a senior fellow at the Hoover Institution and the Tully M. Friedman Professor of Economics at Stanford University in Stanford, California. He is also an adjunct scholar at the American Enterprise Institute and a research associate at the National Bureau of Economic Research. He is the author or editor of over 100 articles and books, including *Some Thoughts on Improving Economic Statistics* (Hoover Institution Press, 1998).

PATRICK J. BUCHANAN sought the 1996 Republican nomination for the presidency, is frequently seen on television, and is the author of *The Great Betrayal: How American Sovereignty and Social Justice Are Being Sacrificed to the Gods of the Global Economy* (Little, Brown, 1998).

GARY BURTLESS is a senior fellow in the Brookings Institution's economic studies program. He is coeditor, with Barry Bosworth, of *Aging Societies: The Global Dimension* (Brookings Institution Press, 1998).

THOMAS V. CHEMA is a partner in the law firm of Arter and Hadden LLP. He was executive director of the Gateway Development Corporation of Greater Cleveland, a development agency. He earned his A.B. from the University of Notre Dame in 1968 and his J.D. from Harvard Law School in 1971.

JOE COBB is president of the Trade Policy Institute in Washington, D.C.

CHARLES CRAYPO is a professor of economics at Notre Dame University in Indiana. He is the author of *The Economics of Collective Bargaining: Case Studies in the Private Sector* (BNA Books, 1986) and coeditor, with Bruce Nissen, of *Grand Designs: The Impact of Corporate Strategies on Workers, Unions, and Communities* (Cornell University Press, 1993).

WILLIAM A. DARITY, JR., is the Cary C. Boshamer Professor of Economics at the University of North Carolina. He is coauthor, with Samuel L. Myers, Jr., of *Persistent Disparity: Race and Economic Inequality in the U.S. Since 1945* (Edward Elgar Publishing, 1998).

PAUL M. ELLWOOD, JR., is president and founder of the Jackson Hole Group, a prestigious study group that spawned many of today's policy ideas about health care economics, in Teton Village, Wyoming.

KATHLEEN FELDSTEIN is president of Economics Studies, Inc., a private consulting firm. She is on the boards of directors of Ionics, Inc., BankAmerica Corporation, Conrail Corporation, Digital Equipment Corporation, and the John Hancock Mutual Life Insurance Company. Her interests focus on fiscal and monetary policy and the impact of government policy on economic activity.

MARTIN FELDSTEIN is a professor of economics at Harvard University in Cambridge, Massachusetts, and a former chair of the Council of Economic Advisers. His many publications include his edited book *American Economic Policy in the 1980s* (University of Chicago Press, 1995) and *Empirical Foundations of Household Taxation,* coedited with James M. Poterba (University of Chicago Press, 1996).

MILTON FRIEDMAN is a senior research fellow at the Stanford University Hoover Institution on War, Revolution, and Peace. He received the 1976 Nobel Prize in economic science for his work in consumption analysis and monetary history and theory and for demonstrating stabilization policy complexity. He and his wife, who also writes on economic topics, are coauthors of several publications, including *Two Lucky People* (University of Chicago Press, 1998) and *Free to Choose: A Personal Statement* (Harcourt Brace, 1990).

JOHN S. GREENLEES is assistant commissioner for Consumer Prices and Price Indexes at the Bureau of Labor Statistics, U.S. Department of Labor.

WILLIAM GREIDER has been a reporter for more than 35 years for U.S. newspapers, magazines, and television. He is also a former assistant managing editor for national news at the *Washington Post,* where he worked for nearly 15 years as a national correspondent, editor, and columnist. He has served as on-air correspondent for six television documentaries for *Frontline,* the documentary film series of the Public Broadcasting System. In recent years, he has written a regular column on politics and national affairs for *Rolling Stone.* He is the author of *One World, Ready or Not: The Manic Logic of Global Capitalism* (Simon & Schuster, 1997).

JAMES J. HECKMAN is the Henry Schultz Distinguished Service Professor of Economics at the University of Chicago and a senior fellow of the American Bar Association. He is coeditor, with Burton Singer, of *Longitudinal Analysis of Labor Market Data* (Cambridge University Press, 1985).

ARTHUR L. KELLERMANN is a professor in the Departments of Internal Medicine, Preventive Medicine, and Biostatistics and Epidemiology at the University of Tennessee in Memphis, Tennessee.

LESTER B. LAVE is the James H. Higgins Professor of Economics at Carnegie Mellon University in Pittsburgh, Pennsylvania, with appointments in the Graduate School of Industrial Administration, the School of Urban and Public Affairs, and the Department of Engineering and Public Policy. He received a Ph.D. in economics from Harvard University, and he was a senior fellow of the Brookings Institution from 1978 to 1982. He is coeditor, with Arthur C. Upton, of *Toxic Chemicals, Health, and the Environment* (John Hopkins University Press, 1987).

GEORGE D. LUNDBERG is the editor in chief of Medscape <http://www.medscape.com>, a medical Web site for physicians, other health care professionals, and consumers. Before that, he served as editor of the *Journal of the Medical Association* for 17 years.

PATRICK L. MASON is an associate professor of economics at the University of Notre Dame in Notre Dame, Indiana, and an associate editor for the Southern Economic Association.

JOHN H. McARTHUR is a professor in the Harvard University Graduate School of Business Administration. A member of the Harvard Business School faculty since 1959, he served successively from 1973 as associate dean of the MBA program, associate dean for university affairs, and associate dean of the faculty, before assuming the post of dean from 1980–1995.

CHARLES W. McMILLION is president and chief economist of MBG Information Services in Washington, D.C., and a founder of the U.S. Congressional Economics Leadership Institute.

DANIEL J. MITCHELL is the McKenna Senior Fellow in Political Economy at the Heritage Foundation. He has also served as adviser on budgetary and tax matters to the Senate Finance Committee and as director of Tax and Budget Policy for Citizens for a Sound Economy. A regular contributor to such national publications as the *Wall Street Journal* and *Investor's Business Daily*, he is a frequent guest on radio and television and a popular speaker on the lecture circuit. He holds master's and bachelor's degrees in economics from the University of Georgia.

DAVID MOBERG is the senior editor of *In These Times.*

ADRIAN T. MOORE is director of economic studies at the Reason Public Policy Institute. He is also a policy analyst with Reason's Privatization Center and editor of the monthly newsletter *Privatization Watch* and the annual *Privatization Report*. He has written articles for *The American Enterprise, The Independent Review, Economic Affairs,* and *The Freeman,* and he is a regular contributor to *Correctional Building News.*

FRANCIS D. MOORE is in the Department of Surgery at Brigham and Women's Hospital and at Harvard Medical School in Boston, Massachusetts.

BRENT R. MOULTON is associate director for National Income, Expenditures, and Wealth Analysis at the Bureau of Economic Analysis, U.S. Department of Commerce.

DANIEL D. POLSBY is the Kirkland and Ellis Professor of Law at Northwestern University in Evanston, Illinois. He has also held academic positions at Cornell University, the University of

Michigan, and the University of Southern California. He has published many articles on a number of subjects related to law, including employment law, voting rights, broadcast regulation, and weapons policy.

ROBERT RECTOR is senior policy analyst for welfare and family issues at the Heritage Foundation in Washington, D.C., a public policy research and education institute whose programs are intended to apply a conservative philosophy to current policy questions. He is coauthor, with William F. Lauber, of *America's Failed 5.4 Trillion Dollar War on Poverty* (Heritage Foundation, 1995).

THOMAS RUSTICI is an instructor and head of undergraduate development at George Mason University in Fairfax, Virginia.

ROBERT J. SAMUELSON writes a column for *Newsweek* and the Washington Post Writers Group, and he is the author of *The Good Life and Its Discontents: The American Dream in the Age of Entitlement* (Vintage Books, 1997).

SYLVESTER J. SCHIEBER is vice president and director of Watson Wyatt Worldwide, an economic consulting company.

He was also a member of the 1994–1996 Advisory Council on Social Security.

CYNTHIA POLLOCK SHEA is a senior researcher at the Worldwatch Institute, a research organization with an interdisciplinary approach to global environmental problem solving. She is coauthor of the Worldwatch Institute's annual *State of the World* publication. Her principal interests include ozone depletion and energy and waste management technologies and policies.

ADAM D. THIERER is the Alex C. Walker Fellow in Economic Policy at the Heritage Foundation. He coauthored *Speaking Freely: The Public Interest in Unfettered Speech* (Media Institute, 1995).

ALAN TONELSON is a research fellow at the U.S. Business and Industrial Educational Foundation. He coauthored *The New North American Order: A Win-Win Strategy for U.S.-Mexico Trade* (University Press of America, 1991).

MICHAEL WISEMAN is a professor of urban and regional planning at the University of Wisconsin–Madison and a visiting scholar at the Russell Sage Foundation.

RICHARD WOLFFE is covering the Microsoft trial for the *Financial Times*.

INDEX